KARAKORAM
Hidden Treasures in the Northern Areas of Pakistan

EDITED BY STEFANO BIANCA

UMBERTO ALLEMANDI & C.
for

THE AGA KHAN TRUST FOR CULTURE

Preface

HIS EXCELLENCY PERVEZ MUSHARRAF, PRESIDENT OF PAKISTAN

Located at the meeting point between the spectacular mountain ranges of the Himalayas, the Karakorams and the Hindukush, the Northern Areas of Pakistan feature the densest assembly of awe-inspiring peaks and pride themselves on having ten of the highest mountains on earth. A visitor to the region cannot help but be overwhelmed by the stark and picturesque natural beauty of the area, and marvel at the determination of the hardy people who have dwelled for thousands of years in this rugged and remote country, seemingly beyond the scope of lesser mortals. The habitat of the Northern Areas also comprises a unique flora and fauna, the like of which are not to be found anywhere else in the world.

The Northern Areas of Pakistan therefore make a major contribution to the cultural diversity of world heritage. I am delighted that the Aga Khan Trust for Culture is publishing a book to pay tribute to the patrimony of this region and to present a range of conservation and rehabilitation projects that give a new and fascinating insight into the treasures of the Northern Areas.

Moreover, I would like to take this opportunity to express my appreciation for the measures that have been taken for the development of the Northern Areas through the collaborative efforts of many. I would also like to commend the significant contribution by the Aga Khan Development Network in community development, education, health, rural infrastructure, agriculture and associated fields. In recent years, they have complemented the Government of Pakistan's efforts for the promotion of education, development of communications, roads and power production, as well as the support of trade and tourism.

Through conservation, restoration and adaptive reuse of historic landmarks such as Baltit fort and Shigar fort, the Aga Khan Development Network has contributed in many ways to projecting the true image of Pakistan – not only to the citizens of Pakistan, but also to the international community. I assure them of our continued support.

May Allah the Almighty be with us in our endeavours.

Preface
HIS HIGHNESS THE AGA KHAN

This publication, prompted by the opening ceremony for the restored Shigar fort in May 2005, provides an introduction to the Northern Areas of Pakistan and to the projects implemented there by the Aga Khan Trust for Culture (AKTC) over the past twelve years. The event marks a significant moment in the ongoing cultural development efforts of the AKTC in the Northern Areas, as initiated with the restoration of Baltit fort in 1992. Ever since, the AKTC's activities have greatly expanded in scope, including restoration and adaptive reuse of other major landmark buildings, as well as ambitious rehabilitation programmes for historic villages in Hunza and Baltistan.

From the beginning it was clear to us that restoring monuments without improving living conditions in the historic settlements and giving new perspectives to their inhabitants would have been meaningless, or even counterproductive. Physical rehabilitation therefore went hand in hand with housing improvement, sanitation, local capacity building, the reviving of traditional arts and crafts, and creating new employment opportunities.

In a time of dramatic change, these projects demonstrate that renewal and modernisation can and must be achieved on the basis of a region's cultural heritage and that tradition and progress are not incompatible. Through their implementation, an extensive patrimony has been saved and made viable again. New income-generating activities that draw on existing natural and cultural assets have been developed with residents, and local communities were enabled to think more proactively about how to manage development pressures and how to protect essential natural resources for future generations. Meanwhile, the emerging cultural tourism along the ancient Silk Route presents the Northern Areas with an exciting new and diversified economic opportunity, which has to be mastered adequately.

The integrated character of this innovative cultural development endeavour has been underpinned and complemented by the work of other institutions of the Aga Khan Development Network (AKDN), such as the Aga Khan Rural Support Programme (AKRSP), which has a long record of supporting rural communities in the Northern Areas. When the AKDN institutions first began working in northern Pakistan more than twenty years ago, it was one of the poorest areas on earth.

Since that time, nearly four thousand village-based organisations in such fields as women's initiatives, water use and savings and credit have been established. The quality of life of 1.3 million people living in the rural environment — which in many ways was representative of the majority of the population of Asia and Africa — has been dramatically improved. Per capita income has increased by three hundred per cent, savings have soared, infant and maternal mortality rates have declined by more than eighty per cent, and there have been marked improvements in male and female education, overall life expectancy, primary health, housing and sanitation, and cultural awareness. Continued close cooperation with the Government of Pakistan has enabled these efforts to bear fruit, with the result that now the Northern Areas count among the most progressive provinces in Pakistan in terms of the increased well being of rural populations.

What has been achieved in the Northern Areas contains many lessons and can serve as a model for other mountain regions in Central Asia. With the end of conflict and the introduction of reforms in Tajikistan and Afghanistan, challenging new opportunities have arisen, which the AKDN is pursuing through an area development approach. In various regions and sites in Afghanistan, for example, projects include the rehabilitation of important components of the Old City of Kabul, such as the Timur Shah mausoleum and Bagh-e Babur gardens, as well as a variety of social programmes including rural development initiatives and micro-credit schemes. The integrated development approach also applies to the establishment of the University of Central Asia, which has campuses in the mountainous areas of Tajikistan, Kazakhstan and the Kyrgyz Republic.

It is my hope that the political divisions between the isolated mountain regions of Central Asia, all of which are quite recent, can be transcended in the coming years, that the sources of their shared regional heritage can be revived through new channels of mutual exchange and that societies which have been deprived of access to international know-how can develop their own versions of progress and modernity — in harmony with their traditions of the past and carefully drawing on their precious natural and cultural resources. One of the world's most fascinating areas bridging East and West will thus find a new way to prosperity and reclaim its historically rooted cultural identity.

Contents

Introduction: Reclaiming the Cultural Heritage of the Northern Areas as Part of an Integrated Development Process

STEFANO BIANCA, DIRECTOR, HISTORIC CITIES SUPPORT PROGRAMME

Hunza and Baltistan, two high valleys located at an altitude of over two thousand metres in the upper catchment area of the River Indus and deep within the Karakoram mountain range, abound with spectacular treasures of nature: eight-thousand-metre-high mountain peaks such as the Rakaposhi and K2, endless glaciers, rare flora and fauna, as well as carefully terraced agricultural fields and ingenious irrigation techniques which demonstrate how man can make the best use of nature under harsh living conditions. While overall the mountain desert prevails, selected spots have almost miraculously taken on the character of lush oases and cultivated garden-orchards, as the result of centuries of human effort.

Since time immemorial, human beings have attempted to deal with the indomitable nature of the area, seeking mercy from omnipresent spiritual forces, venerating divine manifestations in a sacred landscape and leaving mysterious marks of their own existence and aspirations – enigmas carved into rocks and boulders which modern scientists are trying to interpret. Later, the cultural power-houses of the wider region – such as the Greco-Buddhist centres of Gandhara and Taxila, the cities of Iran and Transoxania, the dominions of Kashmir, Khotan and Tibet – found ways of communicating and intermingling across the high mountain ranges that stood between them. Animism, Hinduism, Buddhism and various branches of Islam left their successive imprints in the area, often influencing each other. The heritage of the higher Indus and the Hunza valleys preserves many material and non-material traces of this cultural exchange, still entrenched in local building techniques, customs, religious beliefs and oral traditions. In Hunza, for instance, tales about Alexander the Great and his troops – some of whom supposedly remained in the valleys after returning from their Indian adventure – are still part of the 'living history' transmitted by the village elders.

Unlikely as it may appear to modern-time observers, glaciers and precarious more than five-thousand-metre-high passages between the mountain peaks did not deter holy men and spiritual leaders from spreading their message to areas 'on the other side', nor did they prevent whole ethnic groups from important migratory movements – whether of a peaceful or aggressive nature. Neither did the confusing variety of languages discourage people of Indo-Aryan, Iranian, Turcoman, Chinese or Tibetan origins from engaging in cultural and commercial exchanges which eventually expanded into the intercontinental framework of the Silk Routes connecting China with Central and South Asia, and from there with the world of Islam and medieval Europe, both centred around the Mediterranean.

The unique blend of nature's pristine splendour and the wealth of archaic cultural traditions in the Northern Areas aroused the curiosity of early Western travellers, explorers and scientists – an interest which developed in parallel with the growing appetite of the colonial empires, to whom the geopolitical importance

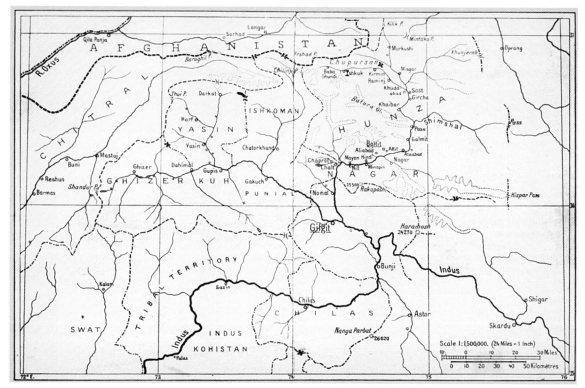

Fig. 1. Map of the Gilgit area (D. Lorimer, 1930s), with the Hunza valley north of Gilgit and Baltistan (upper Indus valley) east of Gilgit, in the right lower corner.

of the area had not escaped. In the late nineteenth century, Hunza thus became an important arena of the 'Great Game' – the power struggle between Russia, China and the British Empire.

More recently, the easy availability of worldwide communication tools and travel facilities has transfigured the once arduous central section of the old Silk Route into a tourist attraction. Modern *homo faber*, taking for granted the mixed blessings of a hitherto unimaginable technological development, is tempted to access and to consume natural and cultural resources at high speed, and often without much consideration being given to the conditions which have enabled the continuous growth of such treasures. It was not until the late 1970s, however, that the Northern Areas of Pakistan became more widely accessible through the construction of the Karakoram Highway between Islamabad and Kashgar. Within just a few years, the new road exposed the local inhabitants to the full impact of modern Western civilisation – which itself has undergone tremendous changes since the first industrial revolution in the early nineteenth century.

Today's situation, then, is characterised by the inevitable clash between, on the one hand, an age-old, inward-looking mountain society (whose feudal traditions lasted until 1974) and, on the other hand, modern civilisation with the combined impact of its secular governance systems, industrial products, capitalist economy and powerful, omnipresent communication tools. Whenever endangered local traditions are exposed to a new (and often disruptive) type of development, fundamental questions arise, such as: How can the shock resulting from the sudden, compressed impact of modern civilisation be absorbed without destroying intrinsic traditional values and achievements? How can the dynamic forces of 'progress' be tamed, adapted

Fig. 2. View of Burzil pass looking south, with post runner's shelter in the far centre (D. Lorimer, 1924).

Fig. 3. The Nager valley at Sikanderabad, looking east (D. Lorimer, 1935).

Fig. 4. Hattu Pir near Astor (D. Lorimer, 1935).

Fig. 5. Old track cut into the mountain near Hattu Pir (D. Lorimer, 1935).

and integrated into local customs and living traditions? How can the existing cultural resources and social assets of local communities, rather than being ignored or suppressed, be enhanced to become driving factors of a controlled and fruitful evolution?

The present book has been conceived in response to such questions and deals with them at various levels. Since any intervention must be based on intimate knowledge of the given historic, geographic and cultural context, as well as awareness of precious values and assets, Part I offers seven articles by distinguished scholars which give an insight into the current status of research about the Northern Areas. These contributions are by no means intended to be exhaustive and have no encyclopaedic ambition; rather, they mean to provide, in an almost kaleidoscopic manner, valuable background information from various angles by leading specialists in the domains of history, geography, ethnography, social development, art and architecture. While representing different disciplines, nations and cultural traditions, all writers have in common their knowledge of, and love for, the area, acquired during long field missions. Their articles will also guide the reader towards the rich scientific literature on the subject, as featured in the footnotes and the bibliography at the end of the book.

Part II complements these introductions through a description of a series of actual interventions in the fields of planning, environmental protection, restoration (and adaptive reuse) of historic buildings, rehabilitation of traditional villages, improvement of living conditions, enterprise development and local capacity building. The corresponding projects have all been carried out over the past twelve years by the Aga Khan Trust for Culture (AKTC) through its Historic Cities Support Programme (HCSP). The projects and activities presented do not claim to have definitive answers to the fundamental questions raised above, nor are they based on any specific ideological premises. Nevertheless, they are conscious of the given conditions and respectful of the values at stake. They try to respond in pragmatic manner to perceived needs and opportunities that emerge from a continued dialogue with local communities. In that sense, they act as interesting pilot projects, the long-term benefits of which will have to be carefully monitored.

Indeed, any intervention in such circumstances is experimental by nature, insofar as it is without precedent. Strategies and procedures have to evolve on the basis of continuous feedback from the field, because they apply to an environment which is in full transition, moving rapidly from an ancient rural way of life towards more urban living conditions. Moreover, no such intervention can rely on a 'static' framework of given parameters, since the reference points are constantly changing as part of ongoing worldwide development trends.

The underlying changes in social and cultural paradigms may not always be explicit, but constitute important factors in ongoing development trends. Many of the traditional social conventions which used to hold the community together in the past have been weakened over the last few decades. Meanwhile, modern governance tools of a much more abstract nature tend to be substituted for them, but find it hard to be absorbed and internalised by local communities and are hence not fully effective. Accordingly, current planning, development and rehabilitation efforts have had to operate in a sort of ambiguous institutional vacuum. Arising problems have, however, been overcome by drawing on the cooperation, goodwill and insight of the community and its representatives, and this has added a distinctive social quality to the process and its results.

In such a situation of transition and uncertainty, cultural heritage has a particular role to play, since it can inspire the self-confidence, social coherence and emotional stability needed to achieve cultural continuity. This, however, presupposes that local communities are put into a position to view their tradition with new eyes. Instead of taking it for granted, they need to assess it actively in order to retain by conscious choice what is of value – which may also involve an initial detachment. Occasionally, they may need to strip inherited traditions of old, obsolete and even oppressive connotations in order to reclaim their deeper meaning and to reactivate vital energies from within. Outsiders can often help in this process of reclaiming cultural identity, precisely because they are detached enough to discern and appreciate values which those still immersed in old practices may tend to overlook when suddenly confronted with radically new lifestyles and attitudes.

To help release consciousness about the deeper values of a local society's own tradition thus appears to be a matter of dialogue; but an abstract, theoretical discourse will hardly be effective, particularly when it comes to the crucial interaction between people and their built environment. Tangible projects are needed, which visualise and demonstrate how certain aspects of a contemporary lifestyle can be reconciled with – and incorporated into – traditional patterns of life. While strict conservation principles may apply to unique landmark buildings, the traditional historic fabric must be allowed to evolve and to assimilate modern facilities, such as electricity and sanitation.

Fig. 6. River crossing over Gilgit river at Sumal (D. Lorimer, 1935).

Fig. 7. The high plateau of Altit village with the fort on the edge of the cliff, seen from the west (D. Lorimer, 1935).

Fig. 8. The cliff of Altit fort above the Hunza river and the village on the high plateau beneath it, seen from the east (D. Lorimer, 1935).

To become productive and socially acceptable, conservation must therefore be made an integral part of development and vice versa. This deceptively simple statement is at the very heart of the philosophy of the Aga Khan Trust for Culture and its Historic Cities Support Programme and has guided its various interventions in many Islamic countries from 1992 onwards. In this context, the restoration of Baltit fort as a renewed symbol of cultural identity and civic pride served as the springboard for a new type of integrated cultural development project. The restoration effort not only brought employment to the area but also helped justify, revive and adapt ingenious traditional building techniques which are now being replicated by people in the rehabilitation of their own houses. The next logical step was to save the old village of Baltit, beneath the fort, from being abandoned in favour of scattered modern construction in the precious terraced fields around the village. Moving the cattle out from the houses, paving the streets and providing proper sanitation to each house was a negotiated rehabilitation effort which engaged local residents collectively in terms of both thinking and using their own hands. Eventually, the project became a living demonstration of the fact that old cultural traditions and modern technical resources need not be incompatible.

These endeavours, in turn, have motivated the local community, assisted by professionals from the AKTC's local subsidiary, the Aga Khan Cultural Service-Pakistan (AKCS-P), to reflect about wider strategic development issues — such as extension of existing settlements, locating roads and public facilities, preserving precious agricultural land and the use of unique cultural and natural assets as a basis for sustainable economic development. As a result, a number of land-use plans were drawn up and discussed with the participation of local communities; arising conflicts were brought out and resolved; and the need for conscious anticipatory control mechanisms to be handled by the respective constituencies themselves was put forward. Through this very dialogue, it has been possible to nurture new institutions such as the Karimabad Town Management Society and the Karakoram Area Development Organisation, later followed by the Shigar Town Management Society and the Baltistan Cultural Foundation. The active participation and follow-up provided by these community-based institutions has been and remains essential to the success of the various projects.

Over the past decades, the economy of the Northern Areas has moved from a precarious agricultural subsistence system to increasingly cash-dependent modes of exchange, with a rapidly growing, tourism-driven service sector as a major source of income. Although subject to great fluctuations, adventure tourism has become the main motor of economic and physical development in the Northern Areas. Mountaineering expeditions, Far-Eastern visitors flocking to enjoy the apricot blossom and a growing share of culturally interested 'Silk Route' tourists have resulted in increasing numbers of visitors (which, however, can drop dramatically in the case of political or religious unrest in the area) and in mushrooming hotel construction in Hunza.

As shown by the fate of cultural sites all over the world, tourism can be an ambiguous agent. On the one hand it can unlock an important socio-economic development potential; on the other hand, if not appropriately managed, it can lead to the progressive devastation of the natural and cultural values which first attracted it and can thus destroy the very assets it is supposed to capitalise on. Given the relatively pristine character and the fragile balance of the environmental systems in the Northern Areas, a special, ecologically oriented and culturally compatible type of tourism needs to be promoted, which respects, appreciates and takes care of existing resources.

The AKTC and its subsidiary AKCS-P are aware of this task and aim to contribute to it in a variety of ways: first, strategic land-use planning assistance is provided to local Town Management Societies; second, an inventory of important landscapes, sites, clusters and single buildings is being drawn up, covering most regions of the Northern Areas; third, special circuits for visitors interested in cultural heritage, in treasures of nature or in traditional crafts are being devised, in conjunction with the nurturing of skilled artists and craftsmen and the promotion of their products; fourth, a number of very special sites have been identified and designed to accommodate quality tourism – individual visitors or small groups – and to enable them to interact sensitively with authentic landscapes, buildings and local communities.

Of paramount importance in this context is the completed restoration of Shigar fort/palace, which is being celebrated by the publication of the present book. Finding appropriate and viable adaptive reuses for the decaying empty shells of the old forts and palaces in Hunza and Baltistan was a

Figs. 9, 10. The last stretch of the steep pathway leading to Baltit fort and passing under a 'hanging' mosque, from above and from below (D. Lorimer, 1935).

major challenge for the AKTC. Individual, custom-tailored solutions were and are to be found for all of them in dialogue with the owners, the regional *raja* families, who are no longer in a position to maintain them. A variety of reuses has been earmarked for each case, considering the building's physical state, historic importance and potential for soft transformation, and also keeping in mind the possible development benefits to be derived by the respective local communities. Solutions range from pure consolidation and conservation (Altit fort) via conservation-cum-museum exhibitions and cultural activities (Baltit fort) to partial adaptive reuse as a very special 'historic' guesthouse (Shigar palace). The rehabilitation of Shigar fort, further described in this book, will hopefully play a pioneering role in attracting a new type of culturally responsive leisure tourism and therefore open new perspectives for the Northern Areas.

Without going into any more detail in this introductory note, it is worth mentioning that the various implemented projects presented in this book have set in motion a self-propelled rehabilitation process, which will gain momentum with every further step. Staff training and education of local communities through the very implementation process has been a major factor of success – and can be seen as an important non-material contribution to the development of the Northern Areas.

Crucial to our endeavours has been the continued support of a great number of institutions and individuals who have been involved over the past years. In particular, I would like to thank our partner agencies who have – both conceptually and financially – supported this innovative cultural development endeavour. NORAD (the Norwegian development agency) contributed significantly to the village rehabilitation projects in Karimabad and Ganish. It also co-financed the restoration of Baltit fort and Shigar fort and took the initiative of setting up a donor coalition for Baltistan. The Japanese Embassy in Islamabad has generously contributed to the rehabilitation programme in Altit and several historic settlements in Baltistan through its Grass-Roots Assistance Programme. The SDC (the Swiss development agency) was instrumental in launching handicraft development projects in both Hunza and Baltistan and in nurturing the growth of corresponding local institutions. Financial contributions from the Getty Grant Program towards the conservation of Baltit fort are gratefully acknowledged. Finally, cooperation with the International Union for the Conservation of Nature under the sponsorship of NORAD has resulted in an innovative linkage between natural and cultural heritage inventories.

While direct community involvement was essential for the successful implementation of the various projects described in this brochure, support from local government agencies was equally important. Their relevance will increase in the future, particularly regarding legal back-up to the decisions of the Town Management Societies and public-sector investments in infrastructure, schools and hospitals. In this respect, a fruitful cooperation with successive Chief Secretaries of the Northern Areas and the Public Works Department has already been in place over the past years. Without their continued cooperation and support, many of the presented programme achievements would have been impossible.

The visual material (particularly the precious, previously unpublished architectural documentation) is owed to the year-long efforts of the AKCS-P field team and represents only a fraction of the material that is now becoming available. Contemporary photographs taken by the AKCS-P team for the book have been complemented by fascinating historic photographs from the David L. R. Lorimer collection, made in the 1920s and 1930s and conserved in the School of Oriental and African Studies (SOAS), University of Lon-

Figs. 11-13. Samples of architectural heritage in Hunza. Above, a small neighbourhood mosque in Baltit; below left, a mosque and watchtower (*shikari*) in the village of Thol (Nager valley); below right, the carved timber frame of a door at Altit fort tower (all D. Lorimer, 1935).

don, which kindly authorised their use in this context. Including Lorimer's pictures was not done for nostalgic purposes, but simply for their unique documentary value and the possibility for comparing existing conditions at a sixty- to seventy-year interval.

Our sincere thanks go to all the above-mentioned institutions and organisations, as well as to the large number of dedicated individuals – Pakistani and international professionals – who over the years have greatly contributed to the success of the presented projects. May their joint efforts continue to bear fruits in terms of a harmonious and culturally sensitive development of this large treasure-house hidden in the Karakoram range.

1. Pre-Islamic Heritage in the Northern Areas of Pakistan

HARALD HAUPTMANN

The 2400-kilometre-long mountain range composed of the Hindukush and the Karakorams in the north and the Himalayas in the east forms a seemingly impenetrable barrier separating the Indian subcontinent from the highlands of Central Asia and China. Yet the history of this part of the world, supported by archaeological finds, proves that throughout hundreds and thousands of years important cultural movements were able to overcome this obstacle. Such was the case for the Greco-Hellenistic influences of the empire formed by Alexander the Great which reached as far as the higher Indus valleys; and such was the case for the expansion of Buddhism from the Indian subcontinent to China, which proceeded along similar routes from south to north across the mountains. Another stream of cultural influences penetrated the mountain ranges from west to east, that is, from Iran and Transoxania through the highlands of Central Asia into the Indian subcontinent. Finally, the trade along the ancient Silk Route created an inverse, equally important stream, leading from China to the Middle East and to the Indian subcontinent, although since the sixteenth century an increasing international sea trade was to reduce the importance of this connection.

All these movements were based on routes established by the highly ramified Indus river system, which had cut several gateways into the high mountain ranges and allowed migrations and invasions, as well as trade and cultural exchange, to happen along its valleys (fig. 14). The lower routes along the valleys of Ghizer, Gilgit, Hunza, Shigar, Shyjok and Astor were complemented by passes leading across the interposed 'Bam-î Dunya (the 'roof of the world') – such as the Baroghil (3804 m), Khora Burt (4630 m) and Darkot (4575 m).[1] Gilgit, the 'gate to India', served as the main hub interconnecting the north-south routes from China to the Punjab with the west-east routes between Iran and Kashmir and Ladakh, via Chitral. The new Karakoram Highway (KKH), opened in 1978, more or less follows one of the main old north-south connections along part of the Indus and Hunza rivers. It has made this mountain area much more accessible to travellers and researchers than it used to be in previous centuries.

EARLY PILGRIM ACCOUNTS

A reconstruction of the early history of this region is rendered more difficult by the lack of indigenous historical traditions based on written documents. Chinese sources dating from the Han dynasty (Western Han from 206 BC to AD 9 and Eastern Han from AD 25 to 220) for the first time refer to historical developments in Central Asia which also affected the region today called the Northern Areas. Later Chinese sources relating to the period of the Chinese-Tibetan conflicts during the seventh and eighth century AD present more details concerning the local principalities in the south-west of the mountain ranges bordering the Tarim basin and also speak about the dangerous paths leading through these mountains.

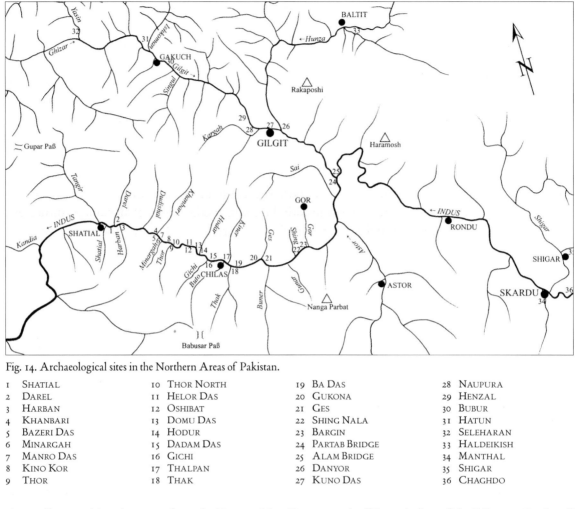

Fig. 14. Archaeological sites in the Northern Areas of Pakistan.

1	SHATIAL	10	THOR NORTH	19	BA DAS	28	NAUPURA
2	DAREL	11	HELOR DAS	20	GUKONA	29	HENZAL
3	HARBAN	12	OSHIBAT	21	GES	30	BUBUR
4	KHANBARI	13	DOMU DAS	22	SHING NALA	31	HATUN
5	BAZERI DAS	14	HODUR	23	BARGIN	32	SELEHARAN
6	MINARGAH	15	DADAM DAS	24	PARTAB BRIDGE	33	HALDEIKISH
7	MANRO DAS	16	GICHI	25	ALAM BRIDGE	34	MANTHAL
8	KINO KOR	17	THALPAN	26	DANYOR	35	SHIGAR
9	THOR	18	THAK	27	KUNO DAS	36	CHAGHDO

According to a historic source from the Eastern Han Dynasty – the "Description of the Western Regions" from the Han Shu accounts[2] covering the period between AD 25 and 221 – a southern branch of the ancient Silk Road led from Guma (Pishan) in the Tarim basin (west of the famous trade centre Khotan) through the south-western mountain chain of the Hindukush and Karakoram to Nandou and to a kingdom called Jibin (Chi-pin). Jibin has been identified with the region of Kapisha-Peshawar and Nandou with the plain of Gilgit.[3] The most terrifying and extremely arduous path at the end of this route has also been described in later Chinese accounts as *xiandu*, the 'suspended crossing' or 'hanging passages'. Albert Herrmann tried to identify this track as the Kilik or Mintaka pass at the present Chinese border and the Hunza valley.[4] But most scholars localise these routes in the narrow and often adventurous pathways cut into the slopes of the Upper Indus gorges.

Itineraries written by three famous Chinese pilgrims who travelled in the Karakoram region refer to these gorges as the most difficult part of their journey. Fa Hsien (Faxian), after crossing the 'Snow Mountain', came to a small kingdom he calls T'o-lieh (Ta-li-lo) in about AD 400. This Buddhist place of pilgrimage was famous for its twenty-four-metre-high statue of the Bodhisattva Maitreya, made of carved and gilded timber. T'o-lieh has usually been identified with a side valley of the Indus called Darel, but this name seems more likely to refer to the whole Diamar district with its political and religious centre at Chilas and Thalpan.[5] From here, the first known Chinese traveller to the area went to the kingdom of Udyana, or Swat, after he had passed the dangerous 'route of the hanging chain' in the deep gorges of the Indus of nowadays Indus-Kohistan. The same 'southern route' was taken by another Chinese pilgrim called Songyun, sent as an envoy by the empress of the Great Wei dynasty in AD 518 during a period when the Upper Indus region was under the supremacy of the Hephthalite kings. His official mission in Udyana (U-chang) in the Swat valley and in Gandhara was "to obtain Buddhist books in the west". In his accounts, he presents a vague description of the political situation in the Northern Areas, mentioning the land of Po-lulai, or Little Palūr, usually located around Gilgit.[6]

ROCK CARVINGS AND INSCRIPTIONS AS A SOURCE FOR HISTORIC RESEARCH

Besides these pilgrims' accounts and Chinese historical records, another group of documents turned out to be a major source for the historical development in the Northern Areas. These are the rock carvings located along the old routes between Central Asia and the Lower Indus plains across the Karakoram range – some of them coinciding with the new KKH. Here we find one of the greatest collections in the world of ancient images and inscriptions carved into the rock, unique in their diversity. They are incised into the rocky slopes and boulders of the Indus gorge, starting from Shatial in Indus-Kohistan up to Gilgit, Ishkoman and Hunza, and extending as far as Baltistan, Ladakh and Western Tibet. A high concentration of rock carvings exists on a stretch about a hundred kilometres wide between the Indus gorges west of Shatial and the Raikot bridge (fig. 14). Here, especially in the widened basin of Chilas-Thalpan with its hot and desert-like sandy environment, the typical dark brown varnish-like coat covering the surface of the rocks could easily be engraved with stone instruments or metal chisels. Smaller clusters of petroglyphs, but not of such elaborate execution, also occur in the side valleys of the Indus and higher mountain basins, along the old pathways. The so-called 'Sacred Rocks' of Haldeikish in the Hunza valley (pl. 5), with their carvings showing ibexes, hunting scenes, and inscriptions in Kharoṣṭhī, Brāhmī, Sogdian, Bactrian, Tibetan and Chinese represent one of the most important epigraphical monuments in the western Himalayas.[7] Altogether more than fifty thousand rock carvings and six thousand inscriptions have been recorded and the number is increasing every year as a result of further exploration.

Although the two reliefs of a standing Buddha at Naupura in the Kargah valley (near Gilgit) and of a sitting Buddha on another rock at Manthal (near the Satpara lake at Skardu) have been known to the scientific world since 1880 and 1844 respectively,[8] the rock art galleries along the Upper Indus were neglected by archaeological research for nearly another century. As early as 1884, the Hungarian traveller Karl Eugen von Ujfalvy had published rock carvings and inscriptions from Baltistan and mentioned similar representations from Gilgit, and even Chitral.[9] The first scientific study of rock carvings and inscriptions in this mountain range goes back to the name of the German tibetologist August Hermann Francke, who, from 1902, published his first archaeological studies about Ladakh and Baltistan, pointing also to Buddhist representations in Chilas.[10] Ghulam Mohammad was the first to publish Buddhist rock carvings in the region of Gilgit and in Chilas itself, in his book of 1905 *Festivals and Folklore of Gilgit*.[11] The discovery of the famous *Gilgit Manuscripts*, found by M. S. Kaul Shastri in one of the *stupas* of the Buddhist monastery at Naupura near Gilgit in 1931,[12] unveiled the high standard of Buddhist spirituality in this mountainous region and helped to establish a list of rulers of a local dynasty, the Palola Ṣāhis of the kingdom of Bolōr from the late sixth to the beginning of the eighth century AD. Another scientific study of rock carvings and

Fig. 15. Prehistoric carvings.
From top to bottom, Dadam Das:
Caprine; Chilas III: Caprine;
Dadam Das: Blue Sheep.

inscriptions is owed to Sir M. Aurel Stein, whose observations of 1942 were published posthumously.[13]

But the impulse of more systematic research and documentation was given by Karl Jettmar,[14] who had joined the 1955 and 1956 expeditions of Adolf Friedrich of the University of Mainz dedicated to ethnological explorations in the valleys of the Hindukush and Karakoram. In 1973, as he was travelling again along the old Karakoram track and saw the big concentration of petroglyphs in different styles downstream of Chilas at the mouth of Minargah in the Indus valley, he realised the significance of the clusters of rock carvings in tribal areas, at that time mostly inaccessible. The decision to start systematic research had to wait until the opening of the new Karakoram Highway. In 1980 he founded the Pak-German Study Group together with Ahmed Hasan Dani, the Nestor of Pakistan Archaeology. Since 1984, the project is incorporated as a research unit in the Heidelberg Academy for Humanities and Sciences, with the aim of processing previously collected material, supplementing it by further expeditions, and publishing the rock carving sites successively and systematically in the context of an emerging cultural and political historic condition of the area.[15] Indeed, these inscriptions and petroglyphs are far more than accidental graffiti or a 'visitors' book' made by foreign invaders, merchants and pilgrims. They provide information about cultural variety, the transformations of climate, flora and fauna, as well as the changes of religion, from pre-Islamic time back to prehistory and even to the epi-palaeolithic period, that is, the ninth/eighth millennium BC.

The dating of the petroglyphs is made possible by stylistic comparisons and superimpositions, by analysing the engraving technique and, last but not least, by assessing different stages of the patina. During the Buddhist period, some carvings are accompanied by inscriptions in Kharoṣṭhī, Brāhmī, Bactrian and Sogdian, presenting another source of historical information. There are some isolated inscriptions in Chinese, but also in Tibetan, and even one in Hebrew. Many different themes, topics, and styles can be identified in these carvings, where the range of the region's history is reflected. More than eight different main stages in stylistic development can be distinguished, as summarised in the following paragraphs.

PREHISTORY: HUNTERS AND GATHERERS
The most ancient group of rock carvings with a varnish-like patina, which is identical to that of the rock thus allowing attribution to an earlier prehistoric age, includes above all pictures of animals and hunting scenes (fig. 15, pl. 5). These engravings constitute only about five per cent of the entire material. In the drawings 'on the contour' performed in a so-called sub-naturalistic style, hunting animals like ibexes are most frequent, followed by markhor, blue sheep, red deer and wild cattle. Predators are stylised as in other provinces of rock art in Central Asia and the Near East, which can be dated to the ninth or eighth millennium, that is, the epi-palaeolithic or Neolithic period.[16] During this period after the retreat of the glaciers, and especially between the sixth and third millennia BC, this region had a denser vegetation, due to

a more balanced and humid climate. This favourable environment with a rich variety of wild animals attracted groups of hunter-gatherers. With the beginning of the Bronze Age, in the third millennium BC, the landscape gradually transformed into the present Artemisia steppe, as a result of a much drier climate and lower precipitation.

The compact representation of the body with its belt-like division is characteristic of this early group, which also has parallels in the early rock art of the Near East, Caucasus and Central Asia. The animals executed in a more abstract 'bi-triangular style' are depicted individually

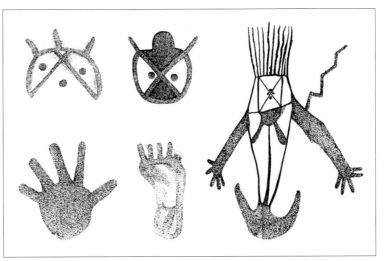

Fig. 16. Carvings of the Bronze Age. Chilas IV and Ziyarat: masks of shamans; Dadam Das: hand; Oshibat: foot; Ziyarat: masked figure with crown, representing a demon, deity or shaman.

side by side, not arranged into group scenes. The representation of a male figure with raised arms standing in front of an animal is rare and occurs only in a few examples. Surprisingly, there are pictures of humped cattle, common in the lowlands. In rare cases, there are also representations of birds.

A conclusive interpretation of the concentrations of petroglyphs as being sites for religious or ceremonial functions is still not possible, since there have been no other archaeological finds (such as stone artefacts) which could be connected with these carvings. Nevertheless, one could conjecture that some of the galleries may have served as ceremonial centres of communities or tribes. Pictures of animals, as in the late Palaeolithic cave paintings of Western Europe, are mostly related to magic practices of hunters attempting to cast a spell on the hunted animal and to secure its preservation – a ritual which could also apply to some of the Karakoram carvings. There are rare representations of the hunter himself, sometimes equipped with a simple bow. More frequent prints of hands and feet may symbolise the presence of man, by representing his personal mark (fig. 16, below).

NORTH AND CENTRAL ASIAN INFLUENCE IN THE BRONZE AGE
The second group of carvings includes mask-like representations which have a direct link to similar motifs in rock carvings from the Early Bronze Age belonging to the Siberian Okunev culture in the Charkassian-Minusinsk basin or the Altai, and attributed by radio-carbon dating to the end of the third millennium BC.[17] These masks or mascoids show a face diagonally subdivided into four segments[18] (fig. 16, above); dots indicate eyes and vertical lines on the head may represent hair, horns or even rays. It could be speculated that the meaning of these images was related to shamanistic rituals, since in later periods hunters seem to wear masks, probably to deceive the game. Even today in the Karakoram, the guise of a fox, made of cloth, is used in hunting the chakor.[19] According to local legend, the birds made a contract with the fox, so that once a year on a certain day he was permitted to chase one of them. Thereafter, the birds need not fear the fox, and the hunter disguised as a fox would therefore have easy play.

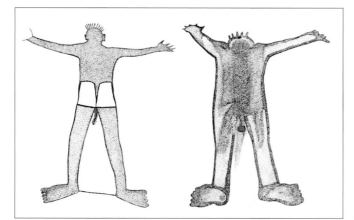
Fig. 17. Carvings of the Bronze Age. Chilas VI: giant;
Dadam Das: giant.

Another significant feature of this Bronze Age group are about fifty representations of a so-called 'giant' or 'giant deva' – male anthropomorphic figures with extended arms (fig. 17), which represent a particularly impressive motif in rock art.[20] Most of them are depicted in human life size at prominent places, like the giants in Khanbari on a rock high above the torrent of the Indus (pl. 3). Sometimes, these figures occur in the neighbourhood of imprints of human hands and feet, or combined with pictures of snakes, but never with other figures or symbols. Similar giants were found at fifteen sites along the Upper Indus, even as far as Ladakh, where two representations are known at Samrah. Some of these naked male figures are more than two metres high. Details of the face are never depicted, the heads sometimes show raised hair strings, or the indication of ears. In this type of representation, the faces are apparently related to the mentioned anthropomorphic masks characteristic of the Okunev culture in the third millennium BC. The giants of the Indus have been connected with similar representations in China, Mongolia and Siberia. Such images of 'masked big men' are engraved and painted on tomb slabs in the cemetery from Karakol in the High Altai, dating to the early second millennium BC.[21] The question still remains, as to what they are supposed to represent. Perhaps they portray ancestors or local deities which held an important place in the rituals of these cattle-breeding nomads of the Bronze Age. Or, they may represent shamans who acquired supernatural power to transfer the soul of a high-ranking dead person into the realm of spirits or ghosts. In one figure at Chilas VI, later additions of breasts seem to change these obviously terrifying figures into more harmless female beings.[22] These shamanistic concepts are apparently derived from Central Asian or South Siberian prototypes and may indicate a movement of northern population groups into the Indus valley.

NORTHERN NOMADS IN THE UPPER INDUS VALLEY

During the second millennium BC, the history of the mountain areas still remains in relative darkness. Some light is being shed on this period by new archaeological discoveries, as well as significant motifs in rock art. From sites such as Daeen (in the Ishkoman valley) an early group of megalithic circles, similar to grave enclosures from the Late Bronze Age in the Transhimalaya, have emerged, which are clearly of earlier origin than the Iron Age 'megaliths' in Kashmir or in South India. Representations of a chariot as at Thor-North suggest the infiltration of a new life style introduced by a chiefdom of horse-breeders.[23]

The third chronologically and stylistically defined group in rock art is characterised by the representation of animals which, because of their slightly abstract features, belongs to the Eurasian 'Animal Style'. They mark the presence of 'northern nomads' descendent from the Central Asian steppes. Assyrian sources report several nomadic invasions into the Near East by the Gimmirai-Cimmerians between the reign of Sargon II (721-705 BC) and Assurbanipal (669-662 BC). They were followed by a second wave of nomadic invaders, the Scythians, who crossed the Caucasus and threatened the political scenery of the Near East, as far as Egypt, for nearly a century.

The Median great king Kyaxares was able to bring the Scythian menace to a sudden end in 616 BC and to expel these rider nomads from his realm into the northern steppes. In Persian sources the name Śaka is also used for Scythians and may designate eastern nomadic groups known from the later Chinese records Han Shu where they are called Sai-wang. A first wave of Iranian speaking nomads is indicated by carvings of animals like deer or ibexes which seem to be 'standing on tip-toes'.[24] Such images found along the Upper Indus and up to Ladakh are frequent during the Early Iron Age (the Maiemir phase)[25] in eastern Kazakhstan and in the Altai, as can be seen in the so-called stag-stones of the Sayan-Altai type, or in ornamental metalwork dating back to the ninth/eighth century BC. For instance, a mirror from the Altai presents stags in this typical pose of 'toe dance', as seen in a bronze from Ujgarak, near the river Syr-Darja. Other carvings showing stags and ibexes of elaborate design and high artistic quality represent heraldic symbols (pl. 4), which can be connected with the nomadic art of the early Scytho-Śaka nomads, who also crossed the mountains along the Indus via Ladakh.

Among the petroglyphs from Chilas, there is an ibex chased by a cat-like predator – perhaps a snow leopard with its typical long bushy tail. Below the scene there is a curled animal without legs, resembling a caterpillar.[26] Other images of ibexes or cat-like animals with their legs ending in ring-shaped paws, have prototypes in bronzes in the Pamir or Ordos. Like the ibex, the wild sheep is a typical motif in the art of the eastern steppes, while the stag seems to be more representative of the western art of the Scythians. This symbolic animal, whose heraldic use has been claimed for tribal identity, was also found at Obo Uzu near Thalpan (fig. 18).[27] Similarly, it appears in bronze plaques from the Tagar II culture (Šurovka), as seen in the famous stag from Kostromskaya in the Kuban, or in a quiver plate from the Tšilik valley in Eastern Kazakhstan.

Characteristic S-volutes as ornamental infills to the body are seen in a group of carvings in Ladakh and at Rutok in western Tibet, which seem to reflect symbolic signs found on bronzes from the early western Zhou period in China, that is, dating from the eleventh to the ninth century BC.[28] From severely plundered grave-yards in the Northern Areas, a number of bronze plaques depicting ibexes, stags and horses show the same abstract rendering of the body as in the carvings.[29] These images of animals have their direct counterparts in the early nomadic art of Central Asia, Siberia and the Wolga region.

Fig. 18. Carvings of the 'Eurasian animal style'. Iron Age. Thalpan: ibex; Thalpan-Obo Uzu: stag.

Fig. 19. Gold ring of Pattan with details of individual pieces (Indus-Kohistan). Archaeological Museum, Peshawar.

Relations with northern groups like the Śaka is revealed by a lucky find from Pattan in Indus-Kohistan (fig. 19). It consists of a golden hollow bangle and a large, solid golden ring, which is said to have been cut into fifty-seven pieces by the local finders.[30] Together, these objects weigh over sixteen kilograms. In a broad carved frieze on the ring, well-modelled stylised animals such as camels, rams, tigers, deer, boar, rabbits, standing horses with bridle and pommel, as well as eagles, are depicted – a complete Asian zoo. Characteristic for the representation of human beings are the artificially elongated sculls of the men from the steppes. This custom is known from the Hsiung-nu, the Huns. The costumes and the use of a *goryt* are also obvious 'Scythian' elements. Judging by its shape, as well as the interlaced patterns of the animal-relief, the Pattan ring may perhaps be an import from the plains of the steppe, but could also be a product of local goldsmiths. A similar example is known from the famous Siberian collection of Peter the Great. Yet another ring of gold of the same type has been recently discovered in the Siberian *kurgan* (hill-type tomb or tumulus) of Aržan II dating to the seventh century BC. Therefore the proposed dating in the first century BC, the period of Śaka king Maues of Taxila, should be revised.

IRANIAN INFLUENCE

As a result of the expansion of the Achaemenid empire under the great king Kyros II (559-529 BC) beyond the borders of Media and Persis into the west of India, that is, the provinces of Ga(n)dara (or Gandhara) and Hinduš (or Sind), Iranian influence extended as far as the Upper Indus valley. Here, stylistic influences may have been introduced by merchants along the known trade routes rather than by military activities. A group of isolated incisions shows a new style in the garment and armament of depicted warriors and in the drawing of animals (fig. 20). These petroglyphs are characterised by linear contours, as shown in examples from Thor North, Kino Kor Das and in the 'altar rock' at Thalpan. There, ibexes, stags, horses or fabulous animals are depicted in the typical 'Knielauf'-position (with bent knees), a characteristic motif known from Achaemenid art.[31] To the same cultural influence belongs a scene with a warrior dressed with broad belt, fringed skirt and leggings, the so-called 'anaxurides', slaughtering a goat (fig. 20, right).[32] This Persian-type costume recalls similar representations on the reliefs along the stairway of the *apadana* at Persepolis, or on the gold plaques of the Oxus treasure.

Only a few elements in the rock carvings enable us to draw conclusions about the historical situation in the Northern Areas during the last centuries BC. During the campaign of the Macedonian king Alexander the Great from Bactria to the Indus, he nearly entered the mountain region when he captured the stronghold of Aornos above the river before he reached Taxila in 326 BC. The 'birdless rock' (Arrian IV.30.4) has been identified as mount Una in the bend of the Indus near Thakot, in Indus-Kohistan. But Alexander's short reign and the following era of Hellenism inaugurated by the Seleucid kingdoms in Central Asia did not affect the remote world in the Upper Indus. During this period, the Mauryan empire arose in the Indian subcontinent and extended its predominance up to the Indus valleys. Aśoka, one of the outstanding emperors of this dynasty (approximately 268 to 232 BC), who held the regency at Taxila before he was enthroned, successfully promoted the spread of the new doctrine of Buddhism from the subcontinent to Central Asia. His famous edicts written in Kharoṣṭhī are engraved on the granite rocks of Mansehra situated on the ancient route leading from Taxila to Chilas and Gilgit through the Kaghan valley and across the Babusar pass.[33]

With the decline of Greco-Bactrian supremacy, the emerging Parthian empire seems to have influenced the Upper Indus region as well. A much greater impact on this area was due to the intrusion of the Iranian

Fig. 20. Iranian influence. Thalpan: horse with bent knee; Kino Kor Das: mythical creature;
Thalpan: a man with a sword slaughtering a goat.

speaking Śaka from the Central Asian steppes. As a result of tribal migrations, they were compelled by the nomadic Yüeh-Chih to move to Bactria where they terminated the supremacy of the Greco-Bactrians in 130 BC. Since the beginning of the first century BC, they were forced to recede further westwards into the Indus plains. Maues (Moga), the first powerful king of the Śaka (around 80-70 BC), was able to extend his power over Swat and Taxila into the Punjab. His reign preceded the major Indo-Scythian dynasty of Azes that ruled a territory covering the Punjab and the Indus plains (50 BC-AD 30). The reign of the Śaka kings was succeeded by a short-lived Indo-Parthian kingdom ruled by Gondophares and his successors that reached from Seistan to Sind and Punjab. Until now there is only scanty and controversial evidence concerning the possible existence of local principalities controlled by Śaka rulers in the mountain valleys.

THE EARLY BUDDHIST PERIOD IN THE UPPER INDUS REGION

The next stylistic group of rock carvings represents the first climax in the region's history, combined with the rise of Buddhism and the first use of inscriptions.[34] The early Buddhist period, after the turn of the millennium until the third century AD, falls into the period of the formation of the empire of Kuṣāṇa. At its climax it covered a territory from Samarkand and Bactria to the Ganges and Sind. From his new capital Puruṣapura (Peshawar) emperor Kaniṣka, the most powerful ruler of this dynasty, was also able to incorporate Kashmir with the Upper Indus under his reign. The precise dates for the era of the Great Kuṣāṇa, from its commencement in AD 78 (the beginning of the Śaka period) or more likely from around AD 134/142 until its collapse in AD 278, are still being disputed. There is also no agreement about the end of the later Kuṣāṇa caused by the Sasanian emperor Shapur II (AD 310-379). Sites like Alam bridge (near Gilgit), Shatial, Chilas and the sacred rocks of Haldeikish in Hunza present inscriptions in Kharoṣṭhī.[35] This script (derived from Aramaic, the official script of the Persian state chancelleries) was introduced either by the Persians or during the Maurya dynasty (320-185 BC) under Candragupta or Aśoka and was used for official documents mainly in the middle-Indian language Gāndhārī at the court of the Greco-Indian and Indo-Scythian kings (third-fourth century AD).

The rock carvings from the early Buddhist period, which, in spite of their simplicity are of high artistic quality, were never found in clusters. Carvings from Chilas II contain many representations of *stupas* of an

Fig. 21. Early Buddhist period.
Pilgrims with incense burner worshipping a *stupa*.

early type, resembling the famous three *stupas* from Sanchi or Amaravati of the Satavahanas period. In one of them, the 'canonic' characteristics of a *stupa* are clearly articulated:[36] a stairway (*sopāna*) leads to a platform (*medhī*); the dome (*aṇḍa*) for the preservation of the reliquary is surmounted by a *harmikā* (a square platform and a triple parasol) (fig. 21). In front of the *stupa* stands an adoring monk with a raised incense burner, and on top of it is a person with a belted dress, carrying a jug and a flag. A tree symbol and a votive *stupa* complete the scene. The inscription in Kharoṣṭhī, which has been dated 50 BC to AD 50, says "this carving is made by Buddharakṣita" (a protégé of Buddha).[37] Attaching the picture of a *stupa* on a rock was apparently considered a good deed to substitute for a built votive *stupa*. This pious gesture is the explanation for the great number of carved *stupas* in the Upper Indus valley, sometimes accompanied by the engraved devotional formula beginning with *devadharmo yaṃ* "this is a pious donation of..." or the short dedication *namo buddhāya* "veneration to Buddha". However, at Chilas II names of Hindu deities such as Kṛṣṇa and Balarāma[38] have also been inscribed.

Monks and missionaries from the Punjab, travelling through the Khanga valley, Swat, and across Kashmir via the Astor or Gilgit route, are said to have introduced Buddhism to the northern regions, which later became famous for their numerous sacred places. Images of elephants and Indian humped cattle, carved next to the earlier *stupas*, may be explained by visitors from the south. These Buddhist travellers and merchants visited the bazaars at Gilgit, Chilas and Shatial, as well as the sanctuaries in Naupura, Thalpan and even in Thor, Gichi or Shing Nala. The inscriptions along the routes obviously quote their names but never provide any clue as to the goods of the interregional trade. Salt must have been one of the main products imported from the salt range in central Punjab into the mountain region. In exchange, the inhabitants of the Upper Indus could offer gold washed from the river sands, but also other minerals and precious stones, gems, furs, leather, articles of wood and woollen fabrics.

THE CLIMAX OF BUDDHISM IN THE NORTHERN AREAS

During the so-called 'Golden Age of Buddhism' from the fifth to the eighth century AD, the region around Chilas with its unique concentrations of carvings clearly represents a political as well as an important sacred centre[39] (figs. 22-24). The clustering of carvings around an old ferry crossing marks the importance of this passage to the northern bank of the Indus. Thalpan, at the meeting point of routes leading from Hodur to Gor and through the Kiner Gah to Gilgit, was the place of a Buddhist sanctuary and perhaps also of a monastery. The above-mentioned Chinese pilgrims' travelogues marvel at a huge wooden Maitreya statue at Ta-li-lo, which may also be the one referred to by Al-Bīrūnī in his account about the famous 'idol' in the Shamil land or Shamilan belonging to the Upper Indus valley.[40]

The history of the Northern Areas between the fifth and the eighth century AD is determined by the existence of two kingdoms:[41] in the east, the powerful state of 'Great Palūr' (equivalent to the later Bolōr from

30

Fig. 22. Climax of Buddhism. Chilas-Jayachand: from left to right, scene with sitting Bodhisattva Avalokiteśvara, Buddha Śākyamuni, votive *stupa*, Buddha Vipaśyin, the adoring donor Siṅhoṭa, and standing Bodhisattva Maitreya.

Tibetan annals) occupied the area of Baltistan including Astor; in the west, the other important principality was 'Little Palūr' (according to later Tibetan sources called Bruźa), covering the area of Gilgit, including the tributary valley up to Yasin. Because of its strategic position at the gateway to India this region also played a key role in the Chinese-Tibetan power struggle during the seventh and eighth centuries.

Since the end of the fifth century until the beginning of the eighth century the political scenery is dominated by the dynasty of the Palola Ṣāhis.[42] Out of their centre of power in Great Palūr, they gained control over Little Palūr, and through there became connected to the domain of the Hephthalites who reigned in the region of Chitral. Their history is mainly based on the famous *Gilgit Manuscripts*, and on the epigraphic evidence from a series of so-called Gilgit bronzes with their dedications. Names of kings occur in rock inscriptions from Danyor[43] and Hatun,[44] including mention of a local ruler. Rock inscriptions from the Gilgit and Diamar districts complete these sources. To date, about eight kings and nine queens representing this dynasty are known.

So far, it is impossible to draw the border lines of the area controlled by the kingdom of the Palola Ṣāhis. Judging from the inscriptions, their dominion reached from Little Palūr as far as the northern bank of the Upper Indus, where they came in direct contact with the third power in the Northern Areas, the Daradas or Dardana. They were the ruling lords of the Indus valley, dominating a stretch from Shatial to Chilas (with the bridgehead Thalpan) and as far as the gorges beyond Nanga Parbat. Chilas served as their most powerful outpost and had the task of controlling the important trading and interregional communication network in the Upper Indus valley.

Narrative records of the T'ang Shu and Tibetan annals refer to the struggle between the Chinese and the Tibetans.[45] Between AD 720 and 745 Tibetan armies invaded Bolōr (Great Palūr), thus terminating the supremacy of the Palola Ṣāhis in Baltistan. From there they even dared thrust into Bruźa (Little Palūr) and went as far as the Oxus region where the Arabs had confronted the Chinese. To regain Chinese suprem-

Fig. 23. Climax of Buddhism. Left, Thalpan: central scene of the Ṛṣipañcaka ('worst evil') Jātaka with ascetic sitting on a rock under a tree with five animals: caprine, pigeon, raven, snake, wild boar. Right, Chilas-Jayachand: tiger (*vyāghrī*) Jātaka. Lying Bodhisattva offering his blood to a tigress which is too weak to feed her cubs. From above a rocky slope prince Mahāsatva with his brothers Mahādeva and Mahāpranāda and a tree nymph are watching the scene.

acy in Little Palūr, general Kao Hsien-Chi's army traversed the Pamir route and the Karakorams, apparently via the Darkot pass,[46] and invaded the Yasin valley in AD 722 and again in AD 737. After the defeat of the Tibetans, the Little Palūr kingdom seems to have survived in a state of loyalty to the Chinese Tang dynasty. For the subsequent centuries there are no documents from Chinese or Tibetan sources which throw light on the medieval history in the Northern Areas. Al-Bīrūnī, the Ḥudūd al-'Ālam and the Śaka itinerary provide scanty information about this region. Until the intrusion of Islam into Baltistan in the fifteenth century, the mountain region between the Hindukush and the western Himalayas was to remain a dark corner of the Indian subcontinent.

During this period, Kharoṣṭhī (written from right to left) is followed by Brāhmī, the second Indian scripture (written from left to right). More than eighty per cent of all inscriptions are written in different forms of Brāhmī, ranging from the late Kuṣāṇa to the early Gupta type of the fourth century AD. A few inscriptions, like those at Hatun in the Ishkoman valley are made in the less known Śāradā and Proto-Śāradā developed from Brāhmī.

All the wealth, elegance and expressive quality of Buddhist art becomes visible in the carvings around Chilas-Thalpan, with their elaborate representations of *stupas*, Buddhas and complex *jātakas*, or scenes from Buddha's life (figs. 22-24; pl. 6). These masterly chiselled pictures exhibit different styles or influences from India, east Turkestan or Gandhara. The devotional depiction of the *stupa* now became the predominant motif in rock art. In contrast to earlier pictorial schemes, these *stupa* engravings were now characterised by a different style and significant architectural elements (fig. 22).[47] Above the elevated and stepped platform (*medhī*) and sometimes decorated dome (*aṇḍa*) the row of umbrellas (*chattrāvali*) is presented in an exaggerated manner, crowned by banners and bells. A striking fact is that most of the large-size depictions of sacred buildings in Chilas-Thalpan are sponsored by only two people called Kuberavāhana and Siṅhoṭa.[48]

From Thalpan I, one of the most elaborate representations of a sitting Buddha is preserved, featuring Buddha's first sermon at Sarnath near Benares.[49] Gautama Buddha, a descendent of a noble family, was born as prince Siddhartha in about 563 BC in the village of Lumbini in the neighbourhood of Kapilavatthu in Nepal. At the age of twenty-nine he left his family to choose a vagrant life as a mendicant ascetic. After acceding to supreme knowledge, which he obtained while meditating under a pipal (or *bodhi*) tree, the tree of enlightenment, he decided to preach wisdom to mankind. Sitting in the famous deer park he enunciated the four noble truths: sorrow, the cause of sorrow, the removal of sorrow, and the way leading to the removal of sorrow. He showed the paths to secure deliverance from this sorrow and suffering to his first followers by bringing the 'wheel of doctrine to turn'.

Some of the most exceptional images of Buddhas and Bodhisattvas (in incarnations as Maitreya, Mañjuśrī and Avalokiteśvara) seem to be rooted in acts of veneration by Kuberavāhana – a fact not only proved by the inscription but also by the same style of carving. This group also comprises the famous scenes from the earlier life of Buddha, such as the *jātakas* of Ṛṣipañcaka, 'great evil' (fig. 23, left), and king Śibi in Thalpan, the *vyāghri* or tiger *jātaka* in Chilas (fig. 23, right), and the temptation of Buddha through the daughters Tanhā, Aratī and Rāga of the demon king Māra in Thalpan[50] – which enables us to date this significant group of carvings within at least a generation during the sixth century. Small-scale *stupas* of delicate miniature-like execution with deep incised inscriptions are donations on behalf of two other worshippers named Vicitradeva and Varuṇeśvara.[51] Further research may provide more information about the precise dating of these various carvings, and perhaps also about the social background of the sponsors.

A fine carving from Chilas I displays representations of Bodhisattva Maitreya with the three-pointed crown (fig. 24), the future Buddha and protector of the new doctrine, and of Avalokiteśvara, the embodiment of mercy and wisdom, who is called upon by humans in distress. The Bodhisattva is a being on the way to enlightenment who has renounced the attainment of Nirvana, the sole aim of Buddhism. Near the saintly beings a *stupa* and a 'vase of plenty' (*pūrṇaghaṭa*) is depicted. The inscrip-

Fig. 24. Climax of Buddhism. Thalpan: sitting Buddha Śākyamuni with standing Bodhisattva Vajrapāni behind.

Fig. 25. Sogdian and other influences. Above, fire-altars. Below left, Thalpan: bust of the god Śiva. Below right, Dadam Das: standing Śiva (?) with trident (triśūla).

Fig. 26. Thalpan: saddled horse in amble, with headgear, Sassanian-Sogdian style.

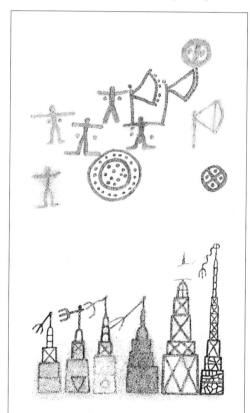

Fig. 27. Battle-Axe people. Hodur: above, scene with humans, axes and disc symbols; below, group of tower-like *stupas*.

tion in Brāhmī are dedications by the pious worshippers Siṅhoṭa and Gamanaśūra.[52] Another famous carving from Thalpan shows Buddha under the tree of enlightenment, sitting on a lotus flower. The inscription in Brāhmī mentions the patron, who has donated this dedication, represented by the adorant and the *stupa*.[53]

SOGDIAN MERCHANTS

During the reign of Buddhism, other religious traditions coexisted with it in the Upper Indus valleys, demonstrating the ethnic diversity of this region. Until now, eight engravings of fire-altars show the existence of the Iranian religion of Zoroaster, which was introduced by Sogdian merchants during the Kuṣāṇa period (fig. 25, above).[54] The majority of these symbols was found at Shatial, which served as an emporium where traders from Central Asia are also represented with numerous inscriptions. As early as the third century Sogdian merchants from Samarkand first entered the Upper Indus after organising the trans-Asiatic trade along the Silk Road from China to Syria. Extraordinarily elegant drawings of noble horses at Thalpan with head harness and saddle, apparently ambling, may also indicate their influence in this region (fig. 26).[55] Similar pictures in mural paintings at Pendžikent from the seventh/eighth century (as well as in Ajanta and Alchi) seem to represent a status symbol of an aristocratic society in Central Asia and in the Middle East. But the horses could also be interpreted as symbols of local deities. A series of heraldic symbols, the so-called *tamgas* known from different periods in Central Asia and characteristic for the Sogdians, give further evidence of their presence (fig. 25, above, centre).[56] This emblem may testify the membership of the merchant to a certain clan or ethnic group. A portrait of Śiva at Thalpan and another divine image from Dadam Das (fig. 25, below) indicate the worship of Hindu gods, as attested for the Kuṣāṇa period with the cult of Śiva and Parvati.[57]

Besides the rich epigraphic material in Brāhmī, which mostly dates from the fifth to the eighth centuries AD, there are also inscriptions in Sogdian, documenting the presence of this important ethnic group. They comprise more than six hundred inscriptions in Middle Iranian, about a dozen in Bactrian and Middle Persian, but the majority are in Sogdian.[58] These inscriptions with typical Central Asian names reveal their eminent role in the international relations within the inter-Asian network of the Silk Road. The westernmost site of Shatial at the Upper Indus seems to have functioned as a trade centre for Sogdians coming from the north via the valleys of Tangir or Darel. From here, these foreign merchants were not allowed to enter further into the Indus valley and to reach Kashmir or

Fig. 28. Chaghdo (Baltistan): rock painting showing the veneration of *stupas*. Redbrown and ochre paint on white wash.

the lowlands of Gandhara via Chilas. The occurrence of other foreign names in these inscriptions indicates the presence of Hephthalites, that is, Huns, since many noble families were of this origin.

Far-reaching international connections are indicated by a series of Chinese inscriptions, engraved by merchants, pilgrims and envoys, as documented at Haldeikish in Hunza. A sole inscription in Hebrew at Gichi (Campsite) was also made by a merchant. Tibetan inscriptions were frequent in Ladakh, but some have also been recorded at the Buddhist mountain sanctuary of Shigar in Baltistan, as well as at Gilgit river, indicating Tibetan occupation during the eighth century AD.

BATTLE-AXE PEOPLE

The latest important group of petroglyphs reflects a completely new ethnic element along the Indus, which occurred during and after the ninth to the tenth century in sites around Chilas, Hodur and also in Hunza (fig. 27).[59] During this period, carvings representing a primitive form of *stupa* are still common, whereas the canonic representations of the *stupa* with the *aṇḍa*, which contains the relics of Buddha, are seldom. The *stupas* display a more tower-like contour, whose sacral character is indicated only by banners or tridents. These mostly abstract depictions of the ancient *stupa*, also called '*stupa*-derivates', are sometimes careless in execution and show no inscriptions of their donors. This radical change in style obviously indicates that Buddhism had lost its prominent position and may also reflect the altered political and ethnic context during this period. Works of continued Buddhist character are supplemented with or even damaged by rougher schematic carvings. Battle scenes with horsemen and warriors carved in simple lines clearly demonstrate

Fig. 29. Buddha relief from Manthal (Satpara) near Skardu (9th century AD).

the troubled situation in the valley. The main images are a variety of battle axes and disc wheels, to be interpreted as sun symbols. Battle axes with an upward curved serrated blade are sometimes carved over representations of *stupas*, thus displaying the destruction of these Buddhist buildings. Since there are also battle scenes showing foreign warriors fighting with Buddhists, the carvings seem to indicate an anti-Buddhist movement of a new population, which at the beginning was illiterate. These non-believers seem to represent local tribes who lived in the upper part of the Indus valley and in the higher mountainous regions. They infiltrated the valleys and basins and transformed the cultural patterns of the whole region.

THE RENAISSANCE OF BUDDHISM IN GILGIT AND BALTISTAN

During the ninth and tenth centuries AD, Buddhism seems to have revived in some parts of the Upper Indus valley and around Gilgit, as becomes evident from the latest group of *stupa* carvings. The famous Buddha reliefs from Naupura near Gilgit and Manthal (Satpara) near Skardu (fig. 29) represent the late phase of the 'Golden Era of Buddhism' between the eighth and tenth centuries.[60] The carving of a standing Buddha on the rock of Saling near Khaplu and the fine relief of a Bodhisattva in Parkuta belong to a group of Buddhist monuments including the Buddha images around Kargil (Baltistan).[61] The renaissance of the old religion is strongly indicated by the carved monolith found at Bubur in Punyal and an extraordinary fresco from Baltistan – a newly discovered painting from Chaghdo, near the village of Nor east of Skardu (fig. 28).[62] The fresco demonstrates the veneration in which *stupas* were held: three *stupas* of Tibetan style are shown on terraces, and the colourful scene consists of mostly seated worshipers, arranged in two separate groups of apparently noble persons, and of saddled horses. The motifs depicted refer to the 'seven precious possessions' of the Cakravartin: queen, minister, general, jewel, wheel, horse and elephant. The elegant pictures are reminiscent in style of the paintings at the monastery of Alchi in Ladakh, dating from the twelfth or thirteenth century.

Stupas at Naupura and Henzal near Gilgit, and at Thol, first reported by Aurel Stein in 1907,[63] are architectural remnants of this period. In 1992, it was possible to identify a visible monument high above Jutial at Gilgit, known as 'Minar of Taj Moghal', as a remaining Buddhist building. According to local legend, Taj Moghal was a king of Badakshan, who had defeated Tor Khan, the ruler of Gilgit.

EPILOGUE: ARCHAEOLOGY IN THE NORTHERN AREAS
One of the main aims of future research is the more detailed investigation of the rich archaeological and historical heritage in the Northern Areas. More than half of about sixty sites with rock carvings between Shatial and the Raikot bridge have already been surveyed. Yet a better understanding of the historical and cultural background of these monuments also needs to become a subject of current scientific projects. Along the ancient routes in the valleys, many ruins of settlements, smaller forts and sanctuaries still have to be identified. The important Buddhist hill-site at Shigar in Baltistan, with a monastery and a large number of *stupas*, is waiting for more intensive research. The dramatic dimension of recent plundering which occurred in many still unexplored cultural and historical monuments in the Northern Areas has become obvious from archaeological objects originating from illegally excavated and destroyed ancient cemeteries. Even most of the monumental stone grave circles at Seleharan (Yasin) or Barandas in Ishkoman, northwest of Gilgit, are threatened by this new development. Thanks to the activities of the Aga Khan Cultural Service-Pakistan (AKCS-P), some of the beautiful mosques and *raja* palaces in Hunza and Baltistan have been carefully restored. Yet, in this region, where different cultures and empires have been meeting over several millennia, there has been no scientific excavation at all since 1938. The documentation and systematic publication of the rock art galleries in the Upper Indus region in northern Pakistan and Ladakh can therefore only be a first, although important, step to illuminate the long history of this mountain region.

The drawings of figures 2-7, 9-14 by E. Ochsenfeld, figures 1 and 8 by M. Bemmann. Photographs from archive "Heidelberg Academy of Humanities and Sciences, Rock Carvings and Inscriptions along the Karakorum Highway".

[1] The first description of the pass routes through the mountain ranges was presented by Hermann and Robert von Schlagintweit in 1856 and 1857. In the Bibliography see: Schlagintweit 1875; Rizvi 1999; Heichel 2003.
[2] In the Bibliography see: Hill 2003. See also Tsuchiya 1999, p. 353; Jettmar 2002, p. 174.
[3] In the Bibliography see: Tsuchiya 1999, pp. 353, 354.
[4] In the Bibliography see: Herrmann 1935, map 16.
[5] This identification with Darel as "an exact transcription of the name" T'o-lieh goes back to Cunningham 1871, p. 82. In the Bibliography see also Stein 1921, p. 6; Jettmar 1980, pp. 9-11. According to Dani 1983, pp. 3-4 and 1995, p. 15, Talilo would more easily correspond to "the whole of the Chilas zone".

[6] In the Bibliography see: Jettmar 1980, p. 10; Jettmar 2002, pp. 118-119; Dani 1995, pp. 15-18 and map 3; Dani 2001, pp. 144-145.
[7] In the Bibliography see: Dani 1985. A final publication is in preparation in MANP.
[8] In the Bibliography see: for the Naupura Buddha: Biddulph 1880, pp. 108-112 with fig. on pp. 108-109; for the Satpara Buddha: Vigne 1844, vol. II, p. 261; Duncan 1906, pp. 270-279 with frontispiece, also describes the ancient dam of Satpara lake with its double sluice-gate to regulate the outlet of the 'Sadpor' rivulet. The upper gate was originally decorated with two small Buddha figures.
[9] In the Bibliography see: Ujfalvy 1884, pp. 247, 248, 269, figs. XVIII-XIX.
[10] In the Bibliography see: Francke 1902 and 1903.
[11] In the Bibliography see: Ghulam Muhammad 1907, p. 110 published from Chilas a sketch of a still visible *stupa* on stone 39: MANP 6, p. 58, no. 39:1.

[12] In the Bibliography see: Shastri 1939; Jettmar 2002, pp. 157-173; Von Hinüber 1979.

[13] In the Bibliography see: Stein 1944, p. 19, pl. IVa published the carvings of a *stupa*, three Bodhisattvas, and five Brāhmī inscriptions which were destroyed during the highway construction before 1978. See MANP 6, pp. 98-10, no. 84.

[14] In the Bibliography see: Jettmar 1980b; Jettmar-Thewalt 1987.

[15] In the Bibliography see: Hauptmann 1996; Bandini-Bemmann-Hauptmann 1997. Final publications in the series H. Hauptmann (ed.), *Materials for the Archaeology of the Northern Regions of Pakistan* (Mainz) (MANP) and *Antiquities of Northern Pakistan. Reports and Studies* (ANP). See also Nasim Khan 2000a.

[16] In the Bibliography see: Jettmar-Thewalt 1987, p. 12; Bandini-Bemmann-Hauptmann 1997, pp. 36, 52-53, nos. 8-10; MANP 5, pp. 25-26.

[17] In the Bibliography see: Nikolaj-Leont'ev-Kapel'ko 2002; Novočenov 2002, p. 44, figs. 9. 11, 1-11.

[18] In the Bibliography see: Francfort-Klodzinski-Mascle 1990, p. 8, fig. 5; Bandini-Bemmann-Hauptmann 1997, pp. 52-53, nos. 1-3.

[19] In the Bibliography see: Bandini-Bemmann-Hauptmann 1997, pp. 48-49, fig. 4.

[20] In the Bibliography see: Dani 1983, p. 24, pl. 11; Bandini-Bemmann-Hauptmann 1997, pp. 36-37, fig. 1 and pp. 52-53 no. 6; especially MANP 5 (2005) pp. 14-20, pls. 7-8, nos. 78:1, 81:2; 85:1; 95:1.

[21] In the Bibliography see: Kubarev 1988, p. 60, fig. 44 and p. 62, fig. 46.

[22] In the Bibliography see: Dani 1983, p. 24, pl. 11; Jettmar-Thewalt 1985, p. 24, pl. 22.

[23] In the Bibliography see: Jettmar-Thewalt 1987, p. 13.

[24] In the Bibliography see: Jettmar 1991, p. 5, fig. 4, pl. 4; Bandini-Bemmann-Hauptmann 1997, pp. 54-55, no. 2.

[25] In the Bibliography see: Francfort-Klodzinski-Mascle 1990, pp. 13-16.

[26] In the Bibliography see: Jettmar-Thewalt 1987, pp. 13-14, pl. 6; Jettmar 1991, pl. 4; MANP 6, no. 69:1-3.

[27] In the Bibliography see: Bandini-Bemmann-Hauptmann 1997, pp. 54-55, no. 1; MANP 6, no. 30:379.

[28] In the Bibliography see: Francfort-Klodzinski-Mascle 1990, p. 18, figs. 20-23.

[29] In the Bibliography see: Dani 2001, pp. 432-438 pl. 55, 3.4 and pl. 56, 3 (from Tangir valley). See the bronze plaque from Kandia valley: Jettmar-Thewalt 1987, pl. 7; Jettmar 1991, p. 6, pl. 3.

[30] In the Bibliography see: Jettmar 1991, pp. 11-17, figs. 16-22; Jettmar 2002, p. 100, figs. 26, 1-14.

[31] In the Bibliography see: Jettmar-Thewalt 1987, pp. 13-14, pl. 4; Bandini-Bemmann-Hauptmann 1997, pp. 38-39, fig. 1.2 and pp. 54-55, nos. 7-9; MANP 6, nos. 30:60, 73, 115, 116, 190, especially no. 226.

[32] In the Bibliography see: Jettmar-Thewalt 1987, p. 13, pl. 5; Bandini-Bemmann-Hauptmann 1997, pp. 38-39, figs. 1, 3 and pp. 54-55, nos. 10, 12.

[33] In the Bibliography see: Fussman 1993.

[34] In the Bibliography see: Jettmar-Thewalt 1987, pp. 15-17; Bandini-Bemmann-Hauptmann 1997, pp. 32-33, 40-44.

[35] In the Bibliography see: Fussman 1993.

[36] In the Bibliography see: Dani 1983, pp. 106-116, nos. 82, 84, 86, 87, 90; Jettmar-Thewalt 1987, pp. 15-17, pls. 9-11; Bandini-Bemmann-Hauptmann 1997, pp. 40-41, nos. 1-3, 60-61.

[37] In the Bibliography see: Fussman 1989, p. 14 nos. 6,1 and p. 21, no. 12,1.

[38] In the Bibliography see: Dani 1983, p. 106, no. 80 and p. 114, no. 89; Fussman 1989, pp. 10-11, nos. 3,2.3; Jettmar-Thewalt 1987, p. 16, pl. 12 doubt the occurence of the names of the goddess Hārītī and of several kings in the inscriptions around Chilas as proposed by Dani. For the reading of the names Kṛṣṇa and Balarāma see Fussman 1989, pp. 4-6.

[39] In the Bibliography see: Jettmar-Thewalt 1987, pp. 18-20; Bandini-Bemmann-Hauptmann 1997, pp. 33, 42-44.

[40] In the Bibliography see: Jettmar 2002, p. 154.

[41] In the Bibliography see: Jettmar 2002, pp. 116-156.

[42] In the Bibliography see: Von Hinüber 2004.

[43] In the Bibliography see: Von Hinüber 1989, p. 64.

[44] In the Bibliography see: Von Hinüber 1993, pp. 4-19; 2004, p. 65.

[45] In the Bibliography see: Beckwith 1987, p. 30; Jettmar 2002, pp. 122-125.

[46] In the Bibliography see: Beckwith 1987, pp. 30, 132-133; Jettmar 2002, p. 127; Tsuchiya 1998, pp. 54-55.

[47] In the Bibliography see: Bandini-Bemmann-Hauptmann 1997, pp. 60-61, no. 5. MANP 6, pls. 71-73.

[48] In the Bibliography see: Von Hinüber 1989, pp. 78, 86-87, inscription nos. 70, 71a, 72a, 73, 74, 81-85; MANP 6, nos. 30:4, 5, 27, 28; 37:4; 38:2 (Kuberavāhana); nos. 4:1; 6:5; 20:2, 15 (Siṅhoṭa).

[49] In the Bibliography see: Jettmar-Thewalt 1987, p. 20, pl. 14.

[50] In the Bibliography see: for *R̥sipañcaka jātaka*: MANP 6, pp. 121-122, nos. 30:D, 30:X; for *Śibi jātaka*: Dani 1983, p. 150-154, no. 115; for *Vyāghrī* (tiger) *jātaka*: Dani 1983, p. 170, no. 125; Jettmar-Thewalt 1987, p. 19; Bandini-Bemmann-Hauptmann 1997, p. 44, no. 3; MANP 6, pp. 43-44, nos. 30.a, 30.b; for Māra's daughters: Dani 1983, p. 142, no. 106; Jettmar-Thewalt 1987, p. 20; MANP 7, p. 211, no. 195:428-430.

[51] In the Bibliography see: Von Hinüber 1989, p. 87, nos. 50-52; MANP 6, nos. 30:177, 184, 244, 57:2.

[52] In the Bibliography see: Jettmar-Thewalt 1987, p. 20, pl. 16.

[53] In the Bibliography see: Dani 1983, pp. 146-148, no. 111; Jettmar-Thewalt 1987, p. 20, pl. 13.

[54] In the Bibliography see: Bandini-Bemmann-Hauptmann 1997, pp. 64-65, no. 7; MANP 2, pp. 34-35; MANP 5, p. 37, pl. 25, no. 37:12.

[55] In the Bibliography see: Dani 1983, p. 223, nos. 194, 195;

Jettmar-Thewalt 1987, p. 24, pl. 21; Bandini-Bemmann-Hauptmann 1997, pp. 56-57, no. 7; MANP 6, p. 154, no. 30:240.

[56] In the Bibliography see: Jettmar-Thewalt 1987, p. 23; Bandini-Bemmann-Hauptmann 1997, pp. 58-59, nos. 4-9. See also the image of a man in a Sogdian cloak, p. 43, no. 1.

[57] In the Bibliography see: Bandini-Bemmann-Hauptmann 1997, p. 62, no. 12; MANP 5, pp. 20-22, no. 1:12.

[58] In the Bibliography see: Sims-Williams 1992; Sogdian inscriptions in Shatial: MANP 2, pp. 57, 62-72.

[59] In the Bibliography see: Dani 1983, pp. 185-204; Jettmar-Thewalt 1987, pp. 25-27, pl. 24; Bandini-Bemmann-Hauptmann 1997, pp. 46-47; Jettmar 2002, pp. 106-109.

[60] See footnote 12. In the Bibliography see: Dani 1995, p. 82; Dani 2001, pp. 33, 153, pls.14-15; Klimburg-Salter 1982, p. 21, fig. 4; Jettmar 2002, pp. 131-132.

[61] In the Bibliography see: for Saling: Klimburg-Salter 1982, fig. 2; for Parkuta (Mehdi Abad): the relief was documented by the Pak-German Study Group in 1998.

[62] In the Bibliography see: for Bubur: Dani 2001, p. 168, pl. 17 proposes a date in the eighth century; Jettmar 2002, p. 106, figs. 27, 1-3; for Chaghdo: the painting was discovered by Nazir Ahmad Khan in 1994 (Nazir Khan 1998; see also Nasim Khan 2000b) and copied by the Pak-German Study Group in 1996. Original documentation by S. Hauptmann-Hamza, drawing for publication by E. Ochsenfeld.

[63] In the Bibliography see: Stein 1907, p. 20, fig. 4; Jettmar 2002, p. 132.

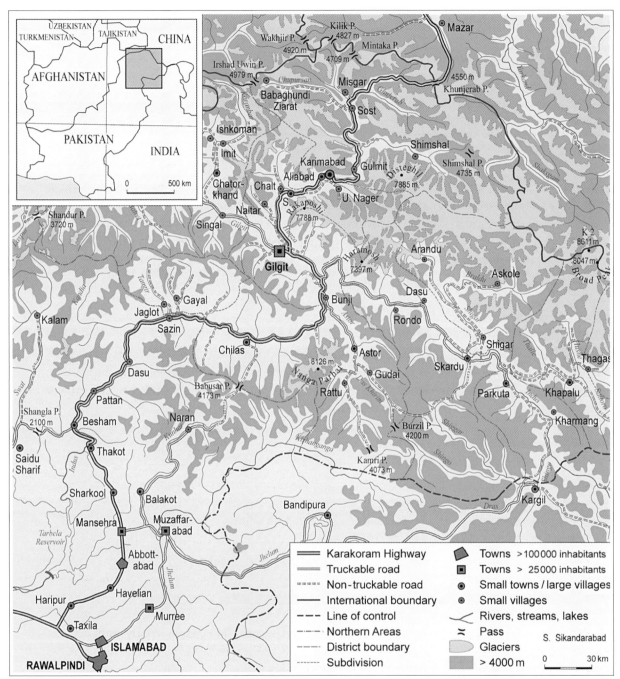

Fig. 30. Overview map of the Northern Areas of Pakistan. The Hunza valley extends south-north from Gilgit to Sost.
Baltistan is focused on the higher Indus plain between Skardu and Khapalu (Khaplu), south-east of Gilgit.

2. The Karakoram Landscape and the Recent History of the Northern Areas

HERMANN KREUTZMANN

The specific environmental conditions of the inner Asian mountain arc and its location in the arid belt framing inner mountain basins, plateaux and valley bottoms as desert-like structures are responsible for the typical landscape of the Northern Areas of Pakistan. The steep and deeply incised valleys linking the 'water towers of mankind' (as the glaciated regions are frequently referred to) with the low-lying plains of the Punjab on the southern side contrast with the smooth and gradual descent from the high passes such as the Khunjerab pass (4550 m) towards the Takla Makan desert (Tarim basin) of China's Xinjiang province or towards the Pamirian plateau. Consequently, we find a highly differentiated landscape composed of narrow and steep valley locations, wider basins with flat valley bottoms, pleistocene terraces and scree slopes linked to a dendritic tributary river network. Separated high pastures and forests are to be found elevated above these deserts and steppes. The enigma of this extreme ecological variation has confronted researchers for many decades and posed questions about the challenges faced by early settlers sustaining their livelihoods under harsh environmental conditions. Some explanations are given below.

ENVIRONMENTAL PROPERTIES AND ECOLOGICAL PARAMETERS
The Karakoram mountains (71°-79° E, 35°-36° N) petrographically and orographically form one major component of the Himalayan arc separating South and Central Asia. Traditionally, two toponyms have been attributed to this range in the Turkic language: Karakoram and Muztagh. The first derives from the expression for black gravel or black rock, while the latter refers to snowy mountains. Although it might seem to be a contradiction in perception, both terms reflect vital features of the geomorphology and glaciology which, on the one hand, offer weathered gravel and dark debris on steep slopes and pleistocene terraces in the valley bottoms and on the other hand are characterised in the upper zones by the most extensive ice cover outside the polar regions giving a rather luminous appearance in contrast.

With an average area of twenty-eight per cent glaciation and regional maxima up to forty-eight per cent (for example the Siachen glacier region) these snowy mountains differ significantly in ice coverage from the neighbouring Himalayas (eight to twelve per cent). The whole range of five hundred kilometres in length is only transected by river gorges at two points: the Shyok river in the east and the Hunza river in the west cut through the main ridge thus creating the canyon-like valleys with bordering flat river terraces and outwash fans/scree slopes. The deeply incised main rivers are difficult to tap for irrigation purposes as the elevation between water level and settlement terraces sometimes spans a vertical distance of more than one hundred metres. Traditionally, other solutions for the provision of irrigation water were found, such as the predominant utilisation of water from tributary rivers.

The Hunza valley has some of the steepest slopes on earth, leaving limited space for cultivation. Between the Hunza river at Altit (2100 m) and the Ultar I peak (7390 m) the average inclination of the slope is about sixty per cent. In Baltistan it is less and valley bottoms are in general wider. The alluvial sediments in the valley bottom at Shigar (2400 m) are responsible for the flatness as well as the remote mountain peaks of approximately 6300 metres altitude located twenty-five kilometres away, resulting in less steep slopes than in the Hunza valley.

The valleys represent a typical subtropical steppic high mountain environment with altitudinal zonation of vegetational cover. The classification of vegetational belts begins at the valley bottom with desert conditions. Next comes artemisia steppe, where most permanent settlements are located. Following the slope gradient upwards, one comes to humid-temperate stretches, where coniferous woods occur locally at northern exposures. Above this is found the zone of high pastures; an important economic resource composed of valuable meadows reaching upwards to the zone of perennial snow and ice.

Climatically the Karakoram mountains form a barrier between the monsoon dominated lowlands of the Indian subcontinent and the arid belt of Central Asia with its huge desert basins of the Tarim and Ferghana. The Karakoram valleys are thus affected by a monsoonal climatic regime as well as by westerly depressions forming a transition zone. In the vertical dimension, extreme differences of precipitation conditions have been recorded between arid, desert-like valley bottoms and the humid nival zone, thus separating potential settlement regions from those where sufficient humidity is available.[1] The total annual precipitation in the Hunza valley at Karimabad is as low as 145 millimetres on average; in Skardu it is around 210 millimetres and consequently ranges well below minimal requirements for rain-fed (barani) cultivation. On the other hand, measurements of ablation and related calculations suggest maximum precipitation at five thousand metres altitude of approximately two thousand millimetres.

The significant difference in gradient explains the desert conditions in the villages and the enormous glaciation in the upper elevations, the typical environmental feature of the Northern Areas of Pakistan with high rising peaks such as K2 (8611 m), Hidden Peak (8068 m), Broad Peak (8047 m), Gasherbrum II (8035 m), Nanga Parbat (8126 m), Rakaposhi (7788 m) and Disteghil Sar (7885 m) towering above the arid valleys.

Seasonal average temperatures vary by an amplitude of 25 °C, with maxima in July/August and minima in January. In a glaciated region like the Karakoram, these variations determine and activate the volume of available meltwater for irrigation in the valley bottoms. During summers, the Hunza river offers fifty-two times more water than during winters, the extremes of run-off in the Shigar river varied in 1986 by a factor of 87.[2] These extremes apply in a similar manner for the Gilgit, Upper Indus and Shyok, all of which derive their major discharge from glacier melt. The period of seasonal meltwater release relates to the climatic conditions and determines in connection with the altitudinal location of settlements the length of the cultivation period for crops in these irrigation oases.

The average duration of annual growing cycles ranges from 307 days for Gilgit (1450 ml), 260 days for Karimabad (2300 m), 250 days for Shigar (2400 m) to 195 days only for Misgar (3102 m). Relief, availability of meltwater and flat land, as well as a sufficiently long vegetation period in different locations (al-

Fig. 31. The Hunza valley at Gojal with the Tupodan peaks in the background.

Fig. 32. The Ultar high pasture above Karimabad, overtowered by *Bubulino Tin*, the pin-needle mountain.

titude, aspect), form the parameters for the possibility of establishing sustainable irrigation oases in the Karakoram. The storage capacity of the mighty ice towers is tapped and meltwaters are deviated towards irrigated fields in locations which compose ecological and agro-technological niches with favourable conditions for crop farming. Thus the irrigated oases of the Karakoram are located on river terraces, outwash fans and scree slopes in the arid low-lying valley bottoms. They allow a maximum utilisation of the limited vegetation period where the provision of sufficient meltwater from side valleys is safeguarded through a highly sophisticated network of irrigation channels. Overall these cultivated areas cover less than one per cent of the Karakoram mountains, at the same time forming the focal points for human settlements and livelihoods.

Interrelated to intensively farmed irrigated oases are seasonal pastures incorporated into the system of combined mountain agriculture to be found as the dominant agro-pastoral strategy in the Northern Areas of Pakistan.[3] Combined mountain agriculture has the advantage of simultaneous fodder production in the permanent homesteads for herds which are grazed in the high-lying pastures during the summers. The limiting factor here is the provision of up to nine month's feed which has to be produced on private or common property village lands. The pastures are located in higher elevations where environmental conditions support the natural growth of shrubs and grass in the artemisia steppe and above. The extensively utilised pastures cover about half the area of northern Pakistan and can only be used during three to four months in the summer. The example of the Hindukush-Karakoram-Himalaya region shows not only that herd sizes can be increased by incorporating high pastures into the domestic economy, but at the same time the quality of natural grazing in the high pastures has been estimated as double to quadruple that in the lower zones of the arid mountain valleys. Consequently, the traditional settlement and agricultural production system utilise the salient features of the given environment which is at substantial risk due to a set of environmental hazards linked to the steepness of slopes, high relief energy, erosion processes and glacial movement.

For the last 170 years more than a hundred damaging events have occurred in the Hunza valley, recorded in archival sources, oral traditions, travelogues, reports, interviews and observations.[4] The movement of glaciers has been the single most important factor of destructive forces accounting for nearly half of all recorded events. Glacial movements cause direct destruction when glacier advances lead to the covering of cultivated lands, irrigation systems and roads. More serious effects are generated from lake formations in the river valleys due to glacier advances and the forming of natural dams. Severe hazards occur when these glacier dams break and the water stored in the temporary reservoirs is released in huge floods. Ranked in second position are snow and ice avalanches, which are as influential as the combined phenomena of mudflows and rockslides. Weather related action from wind and thunderstorms has been of minor importance here. All these events have affected habitations, cultivated areas, roads and bridges to varying degrees. Earthquake-triggered mass movements have not been as damaging in the northern and central Karakoram valleys as compared to the Hindukush where most epicentres are located. The threat of destruction is mainly linked to glacier action and snow avalanches and, to a lesser degree, to mudslides and rock falls. The range of all these events is limited to comparatively small locations, while only glacier-related disasters have exerted supra-local effects.

Fig. 33. Precarious suspension bridge across the Hunza river, linking a remote village with the KKH.

Fig. 34. Rockfalls, landslides and avalanches are a permanent danger for the KKH road track cut into the mountain slope.

Taking the Hunza valley as an example of an area of high risk and occurrence of natural hazards it can be observed that there have only been four events which led to the complete abandonment of settlement sites during the nineteenth and twentieth centuries. The 1830 mudflow and glacier advances in the Chupursan valley were the most dramatic events since a whole tributary valley of the Hunza river had to be renounced for permanent settlement in consequence. All the villages were destroyed and covered under a thick layer of fluvial deposits. Only in the 1920s did systematic resettlement start again, continuing today. Less than two decades later, in 1858, the severe rock fall at Sarat and the damming of the Hunza river caused the flooding of all villages from Sarat to Pasu. In addition to the loss of village lands due to the undercutting of terraces, the newly-established village of Sarat was abandoned and only resettled after 1931.

During the same period a small settlement, Sholemal (or Abdullah Khan Dasht), on the southern bank of the Pasu glacier had to be abandoned due to glacier retreat which resulted in dried-out channel heads cutting off the meltwater supply to the hamlet. It had never been resettled until the Aga Khan Rural Support Programme (AKRSP) recently undertook trials to bring irrigation water back to the valuable land. Further down the valley the village of Matum Das (meaning 'black desert') was abandoned in 1893 after a mudflow destroyed the irrigation channel and the settlement of people from Jaglot and Jutal. Re-named as Pratabsinghpura, and nowadays called Rahimabad, in 1905 the recultivation of Matum Das was begun by Hunza settlers, who managed to establish a new irrigation network and a prosperous village.

Considering the potential long-term risk of habitations in the Hindukush-Karakoram, the examples from the Hunza valley might explain the persistence of settlements despite a growing population and the expansion of villages. The cases from the Hunza valley represent a functional approach in view of site selection and persistence of habitations. The remaining data suggest that nearly all villages have been affected in different degrees by natural hazards resulting in loss of cultivated lands and destruction of irrigation and communication networks. Thus the resource potential of existing villages has been diminished by catastrophic events, which did not, though, destroy nuclei settlements that adapted different strategies to cope with the losses. Harsh environmental conditions have not stopped people from settling, cultivating and expanding the inhabited area and village lands from generation to generation. Who are the people who developed these coping strategies in such a harsh environment?

LINGUISTIC DIVERSITY LINKED TO IMMIGRATION AND SETTLEMENT
From a village survey[5] of the languages in the mountain belt of northern Pakistan, some striking patterns immediately emerge within the surveyed region: the western and central part is dominated by Indic languages; in the centre we find two valleys where the only dialects of the isolated Burushaski language are spoken, while the eastern part is dominated by the Sino-Tibetan Balti language. Speakers from the Altaic and Iranian language groups are to be found in the northern border areas with Afghanistan and Xinjiang (China). More than twenty-five different languages belonging to the four above-mentioned groups have been recorded in the Eastern Hindukush and Karakoram. The corresponding, even more complex,

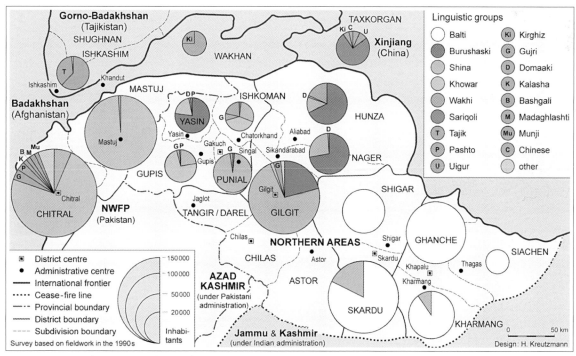

Fig. 35. Linguistic diversity in northern Pakistan.

spatial distribution patterns are still somewhat mysterious, but in an initial step some linkages between the origin and migration history of members of different language groups can be established. Basically four groups need distinction:

Autochthonous languages in compact settlement areas
The isolated language of Burushaski, confined to this mountain region, belongs to this category. No link to any other language group has been established so far. Karl Jettmar summarised the "...evidence suggesting that this other group [the Burusho] goes back to an antecedent stratum of immigrants or even the original inhabitants".[6] In his opinion it is most probable that the two Burushaski-speaking valleys of today – Hunza and Yasin – were once connected via the Gilgit valley and that Shina has superseded and replaced Burushaski there. In this category of autochthonous languages a similar role can be attributed to the Nuristani idioms which are mainly to be found in a compact area of diffusion in the Eastern Hindukush. Likewise Balti has to be added as the dominant language of Baltistan which, together with Purik and Ladakhi, forms the westernmost exponent of an archaic dialect of Tibetan. Traces suggesting an expansion, contraction or displacement of the distribution areas of these language groups have been presented from toponymic incongruencies and from narratives describing migration processes.

Indic languages of early migrants
Scattered information is available about the initial immigration of Prakrit speakers. Evidence is based on oral traditions and linguistic analysis. Most probably immigration started about a millennium ago and resulted in a process of occupying the lower parts of the valleys by the ancestors of the present-day Khowar, Maiyã and Shina speakers. Gilgit and Chitral became their political centres from which further settlements spread into the side valleys. Along with these migrants, Domaaki speakers arrived in the mountain belt and became prominent as the professional groups of musicians and blacksmiths. As professionals providing services they settled with Shina and Burushaski speaking groups.

Later immigrants and refugees from Eastern Iranian and Altaic language groups
During the last two centuries, scattered groups of refugees and migrants settled in various valleys of the Hindukush-Karakoram. In general, they were allocated cultivable land at the upper limit of settlements and have been instrumental in the expansion of the *ecumene* by converting pastures into cropped land. From Badakhshan speakers of Iranian idioms such as Munji, Madaghlashti and Wakhi, Turk refugees from the northern fringes, such as Uigur and Kirghiz, who found a temporary or permanent abode in those valleys must also be mentioned.

Immigration of Gujur nomads from the Indus basin
Following the transformation of vast areas in the Punjab into canal colonies the grazing grounds of Gujur nomads were reduced. As a consequence of these developments, which commenced in the second half of the nineteenth century on a big scale, Gujur nomads migrated to the mountain rim in search of pastures. This process of lowland-highland migration continues today. Some Gujur settled in Chitral and the Northern Areas.

The classification of established language groups in the Eastern Hindukush and Karakoram distinguishes autochthonous settlers and extra-mountainous/extra-territorial immigrants. In addition two more groups should be mentioned which have been important for recent migration processes:

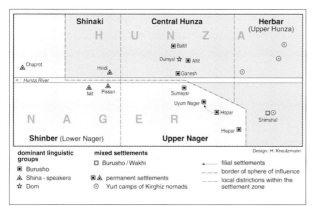

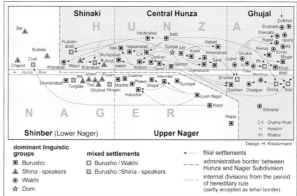

Fig. 36. Settlement patterns in the Hunza valley in the early 19th century.

Fig. 37. Settlement expansion until the mid-20th century.

Intra-montane migration

In search of cultivable land and grazing grounds a significant migration within the mountain belt took place during the twentieth century and is continuing. New settlements were established in previously unoccupied territory either on barren terraces through irrigation or by converting temporary pasture settlements into permanent villages. Shina and Burushaski speakers from the Hunza valley migrated down river. Nowadays irrigation colonies are to be found in the vicinity of Gilgit town and as far away as Punial, Ishkoman and Yasin. A comparatively recent development is the migration of households to the commercial and administrative centres of Chitral and the Northern Areas in search of non-agrarian employment.

Temporary population exchange between lowlands and highlands

The quota of down-country languages such as Urdu, Punjabi and Pashto becomes statistically significant only in the few urban centres of northern Pakistan. There the percentage of households stating one of those languages as their mother tongues during the last census can rise to nine per cent of the resident population, while in the average of the rural areas it is only one per cent.[7] Most of these temporary immigrants are either officers and bureaucrats on duty or entrepreneurs in the bazaars. In the other direction an increasing number of montane out-migrants seeks education, employment and business opportunities in the urban centres of down-country Pakistan. Taking into account the seasonal or temporary character of these migrations the unique and persistent position of this linguistic region is underlined.

Qualitative classification has shown the range of different language groups and their dominant areas of distribution as a result of settlement history. A quantitative analysis of the survey data supports the statement of regional linguistic centres of gravity. Balti is the dominating language in all subdivisions in the Skardu and Ghanche districts. More than a quarter million mother-tongue speakers have been identified during the survey. Thus this Tibetan language outnumbers Shina, the dominant idiom of the Gilgit and Ghizer districts. More than 150,000 inhabitants returned Shina while in the Gilgit district, including Hunza and Nager, Burushaski comes second. In Ghizer Yasin-Burushaski speakers (Werchikwar) trail the number of Khowar speakers, a fact which underlines the function of this region as an intermediate zone between Chitral and Gilgit. Over long periods Ghizer was under Chitrali rule and revenue schemes, resulting in the presence of members of the hereditary leadership and of settlers from Chitral. Four out of five persons in Chitral are Khowar speakers. In neighbouring Wakhan Woluswali (Badakhshan, Afghanistan), three quarters of the population speak Wakhi while across the Amu Darya boundary in Rajon Ishkashim (Gorno-Badakhshan, Tajikistan) nearly two thirds belong to the same language group. In the contiguous Taxkorgan county (Xinjiang, China) Sariqoli dominates Wakhi. Both languages are related and belong to the Eastern Iranian branch. Wakhi settlement regions are to be found in the upper parts of the Hunza, Ishkoman and Yarkhun valleys. Next follows Gujri with local importance in the Gilgit subdivision and Ghizer. Smaller groups of Domáaki, Uigur, Kohistani and Pashto speakers, each of less than two thousand persons, reside in the Gilgit and Ghizer districts.[8] Differentiated spatial patterns need an investigation on a large scale. Thus the development of settlement and society in line with linguistic variegation is presented in greater detail in a case study from the Hunza valley.

PRINCIPALITIES OF THE KARAKORAM: LEADERSHIP AND SOCIAL STRUCTURE

The development of settlements in the Karakoram valleys and the outline of irrigated oases are strongly linked to certain power structures, which reflect the initiative for amelioration of barren lands, domination of social groups and strength to levy taxes from comparatively poor mountain farmers. Irrespective of prevailing ecological conditions we find two distinguished sets of traditional social organisation in the rural societies of the Karakoram. In view of their structural origin and participatory hierarchies they have been termed principalities and republics.[9] The basic distinction refers to semi-autonomous and independent principalities with hereditary rule or imposed/acquired external rule in the northern Karakoram valleys such as Gupis, Yasin, Ishkoman, Punial, Gilgit, Hunza, Nager, Astor, Skardu and Khaplu. Local *mir*, *raja* or *tham* dominated peasant farmers of differentiated social standing and executed control, levied taxes and requested forced labour services from rural households.

In contrast, the republics look back on a different historical experience of conquest. Following the Yusufzai Pashtun immigration and dominance in Swat and Indus Kohistan (since the fourteenth century) so-called acephalous or segmentary societies or republics have emerged in the mountainous interface between integrated lowlands and remote highlands, in this case the southern valleys such as Chilas, Tangir, Darel, Gor, Kandia and so on. These societies are traditionally based on an egalitarian social structure to which all landowners belong. Members of the landed class are entitled to be part of all decision-making processes dealing with distribution of land, construction and maintenance of irrigation channels and so on. Hereditary rule of a single family or dynasty is unknown in these areas. Every member of the in-group possesses equal rights. Counselling is done in the Pashtun-style *jirga*, a local assembly basing its decisions on overall consent. In addition to the landed class there exists a subordinated group of landless people which functions as labourers on the fields and as shepherds. Those immigrant people are excluded from decision-making processes and other forms of participation.[10]

In this respect Hunza is a well-understood representative of the principality type. Traditionally Hunza was under the rule of a *tham* who traced his background to the *ayasho* (coming from heaven), meaning coming from outside, that is from Gilgit, and not necessarily being part of the dominant autochthonous ethno-linguistic group of Burusho. Under their rule Hunza was segregated in seven sections (*maqsòo*). The Lower Hunza valley (Shinaki) formed one section, Central Hunza consisted of four *maqsòo* (Altit, Baltit, Ganish and the *thuaán khanánts*), while the upper valley (Gojal) was divided in two sections. This spatial pattern did not reflect the social standing in any respect. Self-esteem of the different ethno-linguistic groups was interpreted from these sections and contributed to competition and alienation. Burusho frequently per-

2.

3.

4.

5.

6.

Previous page
1. View of the Nager valley with Deran peak in the background.

2. Villagers building a mountain track
connecting the Karakoram Highway with Shimshal,
in Upper Hunza.

3. Carvings of two giant figures at Khanbari
(Bronze Age).

4. Carvings of animals in the Iranian style
at Kino Kor Das (Iron Age).

5. Local girls trained by the AKCS-P
documenting petroglyphs from the 'Sacred Rocks'
of Haldeikish (Hunza).

6. Carving at Thalpan, showing a *stupa*
with Brahmi inscription and Buddha enthroned
on a lotus flower under the tree of enlightenment
(6th-7th century AD).

7-9. High alpine landscapes.
Above, Rush glacier and Rush lake.
Below, a high pasture above Karimabad,
with the Lady Finger peak in the background.

7.

8.

9.

11.

10. View of the elevated plateau of Altit village, with the fort in the centre, the Hunza valley below it and the Nager valley in the background (see also pl. 15).

11. Irrigated and cultivated agricultural terraces reclaimed from rocky platforms (Hunza valley).

12. Drying apricots on the rooftops over old Altit village.

12.

13.

13. The fortified village of Ganish below Karimabad.

14. Many old settlements in Hunza
are built on steep terraced slopes (Karimabad).

15. The huge cliffs descending from Altit fort
(below the clouds) into the Hunza river.

14.

16. The park-like apricot orchard belonging to Altit fort.

17. Harvesting millet, to be dried and stored for the winter months.

18. A girl on the rooftop of a house spreading out grains to be dried.

16.

17.

18.

19.

19. The 'bowl' of Karimabad with cascades of agricultural terraces beneath the village and Baltit fort.

20. The old village of Ganish, encircled by a loop of the Karakoram Highway.

22.

23.

21. Looking from Altit fort toward the Ultar range
and the cliffs above the village plateau
(see pl. 10 for opposite view).

22. Agricultural terraces in Karimabad during the apricot blossom.

23. An isolated farmhouse benefiting from direct irrigation
by the river.

24. Water from the glaciers to replenish the irrigation channels
further down.

24.

25.

26.

27.

28.

25. Interior of a traditional Hunza house
(courtesy National Geographic Society).

26. Mama Zaibo in Karimabad (see p. 92).

27. Stone walls are an integral part
of the agricultural landscape (Karimabad).

28. Traditional settlement structure
with terraced houses below Baltit fort.

29.

30.

29. Freshly harvested fields above the Indus river,
between Hunza and Baltistan.

30. A side valley of the Shyok river,
near Tagas, Baltistan.

31. Desert-like silt and sand deposits
on the upper Indus riverbanks, near Skardu.

32.

32. Shigar village and the fort seen from above.
In the background, the Shigar oasis
and the silty plain of the upper Indus,
the spine of Baltistan.

33. Typical village landscape in the Shigar oasis,
with irrigation channels flowing through
the densely planted settlement.

33.

Fig. 38. Baltit fort – the seat of the *mirs* of Hunza – towering above the historic settlement of Baltit (now Karimabad).

Fig. 39. The steep landscape above the village of Altit, with the fort cliff standing above the Hunza river and the KKH.

ceive themselves as the warrior group, while Wakhi and Shina speakers are regarded as nourishers of the society who provide the dearly-needed basic food items for Central Hunza and the ruling elite.

This attribution was reflected in the tax system at the beginning of the twentieth century when the two sections of Gojal were made to pay in kind four fifths of all grain and livestock taxes in Hunza, while only one fifth of the population lived there.[11] On average, the inhabitants of Gojal were taxed ten times higher than those in Central Hunza. The taxes levied in Gojal and Shinaki significantly surpassed the amount the *tham* gained from his own lands, cultivated under forced labour schemes (*rajaki*), and from his herds in pasture grounds. The example shows the degree of differentiation prevalent in the societal layers of the Hunza community. Overall, the social position of Burusho was esteemed higher than that of Wakhi and Shina speakers, let alone Dom artisans. But in contrast to the general pattern we find high positions in all ethno-linguistic groups. The advisor to the ruler and chief executive of certain tasks (*wazir*), as well as other functionaries (*uyónko*), belong to the Burusho but in the same group Burusho load-carriers and gold-washers can also be found. A sophisticated system of weaving a fabric of loyal supporters of a comparatively weak ruler characterised the society prior to colonial interference. Loyalty was created across social boundaries through foster relationships (*uúsam*) between the ruling elite and ordinary farming households of all groups.

After the British takeover in Gilgit and Hunza, the colonial administration took an instrumental role in appointing and backing hereditary and/or invested rulers. Political agents in Gilgit observed the developments in the respective valleys and interfered in local politics to such an extent that they allocated subsidies and posts to loyal supporters. Thus they created and fostered a ruling elite, backed by their military supremacy and administrative skills. Mir M. Nazim Khan (1892-1938) of Hunza was such an appointee, who utilised British backing for extracting huge amounts of taxes for the upkeep of his court, for the implementation of major irrigation schemes and infrastructure assets, as well as for enabling Hunza people to cultivate barren lands outside Hunza, for example in the vicinity of Gilgit.

The ruler's power was not limited to levying dues and extracting forced labour from the people; he was also the patron who initiated the agricultural year by ploughing the first furrow and releasing irrigation water to fertile soils. During the growing cycle, he was consulted as the only local authority when rainfall was scarce, or springs and glaciers did not release sufficient water. He was attributed with the power of rain-making. At harvest time, he lead the rituals connected to the festive calendar. The winter season saw the *tham* and his entourage engaged in hunting in Gojal, feasting upon the plentiful food and meat resources of the local farming households who provided huge quantities of firewood, while the Shinaki delivered wines (*mel*) and spirits (*arak*). In many respects, the local elite composed of the *tham*, *wazir* and other office-bearers (*uyónko*) represented a societal microcosm in which different instances of jurisdiction were possible and the *tham* was the final decision maker in his court, regularly held in Baltit fort. Telephone connections to all villages in Hunza were established early in the twentieth century and enabled the *tham* to keep close control and surveillance on all movements and developments within his principality. In consequence the settlement structure of the Hunza valley is strongly connected to control mechanisms and social structure, as well as to the imaginative and innovative visions of rulers and farmers.

SETTLEMENT HISTORY
The Hunza valley, comprising the two formerly independent principalities of Hunza and Nager, has experienced a different pattern of population dynamics than other valleys. Basically the number of inhabitants doubled during the fifty years between 1931 and 1981 and has further increased since. The impact of this population growth has found its spatial expression in the expansion of settlements within the valley and the establishment of extra-territorial migrant colonies outside the former principalities. The settlement process in Hunza has been reconstructed for the last two hundred years.[12] For reasons of structural change this epochal growth cycle might be divided into four different phases:

Period of nuclear villages (pre-1800)
Of all villages in Central Hunza existing today, the oldest seem to be the three original *khan* (fortified villages) of Ganish, Altit and Baltit, as well as the artisans' settlement of Dumyal or Berishal. The Dom have served as musicians and blacksmiths to the Burusho farming communities of the three 'original' villages in the main irrigation oasis of Central Hunza.[13] Until today the remnants of the old nuclei suggested a close relationship between site selection and defence purposes while safeguarding access to water supply and agricultural lands at the same time. Hindi constituted the only *khan* in the lower region of Shinaki where Shina speakers have been living. The upper part of the Hunza valley was dominated by Kirghiz nomads, who seasonally utilised the high pastures there. The system of fortified villages and their structural elements were quite common all over the Hindukush-Karakoram region, giving protection in times of threat from outside intruders.

*Pre-colonial phase of oases expansion
and internal colonisation (1800-1891)*

The first quarter of the nineteenth century experienced the establishment of a number of filial settlements in Central Hunza linked to population growth and the innovative expansion of the irrigation network under Tham Silum Khan III. At the same time this ruler extended the sphere of Hunza dominance northwards, expelled Kirghiz nomads from Gojal and allowed immigrating Wakhi settlers to found villages within the Burusho *cordon sanitaire*. The northern passes were controlled from the *khan* of Misgar and Khudabad, while in the south Maiun formed an important defence line towards Gilgit. All new

Fig. 40. The terraced slopes between Baltit fort and Altit fort (in the background) irrigated by water channels running down from the nearby glaciers.

villages of this period were designed as compact settlements with fortifications in the traditional *khan* style. Along the routes a system of obstacles and barriers (*darband*) had been introduced to control the movements of inhabitants and travellers between the settlement areas of different sections (*maqsòo*) of Hunza. The number of villages increased from five to twenty-five during this period of internal colonisation.

Settlement concentration processes under colonial supremacy (1892-1947)

Hunza neither resembled a remote microcosm nor the main arena of the so-called 'Great Game' when Russia and Great Britain tried to expand their spheres of influence into the Karakoram valleys.[14] Initially the Hunza *tham* tried to take advantage of both contenders. In the end Hunza lost its independence and became a part of British India, retaining certain degrees of autonomy. The shape of Hunza changed when international boundaries were demarcated as a result of the 'Great Game'. Boundaries between British India and China were negotiated and defined, territory claimed by the *tham* became unavailable and was lost until today.

The short but effective 'Hunza Campaign'[15] of 1891 had a lasting influence on the settlement patterns. The structural element of *khan* disappeared and a process of populating unfortified hamlets (*girám*) within the village lands started, thus reducing the distance between habitations and fields. In connection with the construction of new irrigation channels the colonisation process of barren lands was extended into the peripheral regions of Shinaki and Gojal. A number of new villages was founded especially during the forty-six-year-long reign of Mir M. Nazim Khan (1892-1938). He and his *wazirs* were the prominent figures during the second phase of internal colonisation. The expansion led to a compact network of contiguous major oases in Central Hunza and to the improvement of cultivable tracts according to available technology. From the beginning of the twentieth century a dialogue, sometimes a dispute, developed between the *mir* of Hunza and the British colonial administration in Gilgit about the carrying capacity of the Karakoram valleys. The *mir* demanded barren land within the Gilgit agency for cultivation and the establishment of irrigation oases. Both actors could profit from such schemes and consequently different resettlement projects for Hunza farmers resulted: in 1908 the first lands were allocated in Matum Das (Rahimabad); the second scheme followed in 1912; the channel project of Oshikandas provided Hunza farmers with 312 acres of land and the Bagroti landowners with 1188 acres in 1938-1939; from 1940 onwards different irrigation schemes in Danyor attracted more migrants. Besides the founding of those irrigation colonies individual farmers acquired agricultural lands in the vicinity of Gilgit town.[16] This emigration process has continued until today although nowadays the pull of Gilgit as a workplace for non-agrarian occupations supersedes the attraction of improvement projects.

Village growth and response to improved communication systems (from 1947 to the present)
Since the independence of Pakistan and the improvement of communication lines towards the Indus basin, the dominant factors alleviating population growth in the Hunza valley have been the expansion of existing villages, emigration to Gilgit and extra-montane migration down country. Basically the process of founding new independent villages has been stopped; exceptions occurred during the rule of the last *mir* of Hunza, Jamal Khan (1945-1974): Sarteez (1950), Imamabad and Jamalabad (1960) in Gojal. All villages have experienced an increase in households and a concentration process of settlements. The extension of jeep roads to Hunza and Nager since 1957 and the opening of the Karakoram Highway (KKH) in 1978 supported a reorientation of site selection for commercial and administrative buildings in the villages towards access roads where small bazaars have been developed. Valuable agricultural lands were converted to commercial sites for the construction of physical infrastructures. New building materials brought in from distant bazaars allowed for cheaper construction of housing.[17] As a general observation settlement concentration is governed by the network of communication lines for motorised transport.

Fig. 41. New settlement patterns, service activities and types of construction prompted by improved road accessibility: the modern section of the historic village of Ganish, on the new KKH during apricot blossom season (see also pl. 20).

Improved accessibility has not only supported the transport of goods but also enhanced the mobility of people. Rural-urban migration towards Gilgit town has led to the resettlement of a substantial number of households there. In contrast to extra-montane migrants, who temporarily leave their rural villages in search for wage-labour in the industrialised south, settlers in Gilgit have separated themselves from their inherited land property and have become permanent citizens of Gilgit town. Nevertheless, economic links within the community are strong and have led to an extension of commercial undertakings from Gilgit into the Hunza valley in recent years. The KKH supports commuting between village and town. Thus an actual evaluation of the settlement process in the Hunza valley has to be discussed in line with the overall population growth in the Northern Areas and in Pakistan.

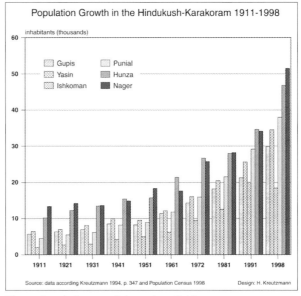

Fig. 42. Population growth in northern Pakistan.

POPULATION GROWTH IN THE HINDUKUSH-KARAKORAM

Comparing the population growth of the high mountain belt of Pakistan with the rest of the country, calculations prove that both sub-regions have registered overall population increases during the twentieth century and that the average annual growth rate is higher in the lowlands than in the mountain regions. Analysing the data on a regional level in a historical perspective and calculating area population densities and growth rates, a differentiated demographic pattern emerges. The first half of the twentieth century registered moderate growth rates of population in the mountain belt (0.67% per year) while since 1951 significantly higher annual rates (2.30%) have been recorded. In the early phase developments in the Hunza subdivision reflected a higher growth rate (1.11%) than average but a lower one (1.93%) since 1951. Regional differentiation presents low rates in the western (Chitral) and eastern (Baltistan) wings while the centre (Gilgit and Ghizer) grows much faster. The latest census data from 1998 support the hypothesis that substantial growth rates are recorded in the valleys of northern Pakistan, while at the same time out-migration continues to be a significant behavioural pattern to increase household incomes and to diversify income resources at a higher level of expertise. The construction of the KKH and improved accessibility have played a dominant role in changing livelihoods.

THE KARAKORAM HIGHWAY AND ITS SOCIO-ECONOMIC IMPACT

The first link for 'modern' traffic between northern Pakistan and down-country Pakistan was established from the railhead in Havelian (North-West Frontier Province) via the Kaghan valley in 1949. The selected route followed a colonial mule track supporting the British administration and garrisons in the Gilgit agency.[18] It was only after independence that the first jeep reached Gilgit – a cul-de-sac of its own – before the track was extended towards Hunza in 1957. The jeep-worthy road across Babusar pass (4173 m) remained open for three months in the summer only; during the rest of the year air links transported valuable supplies at high cost.[19]

After the inception of Pakistan's first Village Aid Five-Year Plan in 1956, development efforts based on public funds reached the mountains and were made available in the Gilgit agency. A participatory approach facilitated the construction of suspension bridges to span the Hunza river near Danyor and the Gilgit river at Sher Qila. Villagers provided three quarters of the cost, all the unskilled labour and cut all the wood for bridge construction from communal forests.[20] At this early stage of development, the Central Government covered seventy-five per cent of all non-recurring expenditure and fifty per cent of recurring expenditure,[21] trying a holistic approach by introducing new wheat varieties, new ploughs, different fruit varieties, improved livestock (pedigree bulls, merino rams and so on), silkworm production and new weaving looms for local tweeds. Out of the annual Village Aid Programme's budget of Rs. 300,000 (approximately US $ 65,000 at that time), two thirds were spent on transport alone. A lack of accessibility meant high costs for the allocation of goods from the lowlands to the places of need in the mountains. Consequently, the remaining budget for development projects was substantially reduced. Not surprisingly, the transport charges for one *maund* (one *maund* equals 37.32 kg) of goods from Rawalpindi to Gilgit amounted to the multiple of its value.

Fig. 43. The recent construction of the Aliabad irrigation channel which links the Hassanabad glacier with the fertile oasis of Central Hunza. The same rock-blowing and retaining wall construction techniques are used for building road tracks.

In order to reduce transportation costs of basic goods an Indus valley road from Swat was proposed and in 1959 construction began. As a result of the Pak-China Border Treaty of 1963 bilateral, cooperative efforts led to what has been termed the Pak-China Friendship or Karakoram Highway (KKH). By 1975 the KKH was accessible to trucks and since 1978 regular traffic has plied between Rawalpindi and Gilgit. In addition to trans-montane exchange of goods, the Highway brings subsidised foodgrains from down-country Pakistan into the region. It is the lifeline for the ever-growing food deficit of northern Pakistan. Cereals, fresh meat (imported as live animals for slaughter in the bazaars) and cooking oil account for more than three quarters of all imports from the lowlands. The per capita dependence on supplies through this artery is highest for Gilgit district and significantly lower in Chitral and Baltistan. Chitral is seasonally cut off from external supplies until the tunnel under the Lowari pass might be completed. Baltistan has been linked to the Karakoram Highway through an asphalted road which now enables year-long traffic communication and a rapid change of market prices for basic commodities. The Baltistan road did not exist as such in previous times when Baltistan was oriented towards Srinagar. In 1963, a first road link to Gilgit was established across the Deosai plateau, two years later through the Indus valley. The road was extended and asphalted in the mid-1980s. In addition to its ubiquitous military importance, huge quantities of food are brought into the region to supply army personnel, tourists and growing numbers of local farming and trading households.

Prior to discussing the economic gains and losses from the KKH, some of the ensuing socio-cultural changes need to be mentioned. We have to acknowledge the fact that the KKH did not just open up a new world of communication and exchange, but that this artery amplified existing exchange relations which had a major impact on local societies and behavioural patterns as well. The availability of an improved traffic infrastructure coincided with imposed social change. Between 1972 and 1974 Pakistan's prime minister Zulfiqar Ali Bhutto abolished the autonomy of local rulers. Mir Jamal Khan was the last Hunza *tham* who survived his demise only for another two years. The close watch and control executed by the hereditary ruler lost its strength, more opportunities and personal liberties for local enterprising people emerged.

With the apparent power vacuum, new administrative structures came into effect. Local bodies and integrated rural development projects replaced the infrastructural functions of previous rulers; village organisations and community self-help groups emerged. The KKH enabled more people to out-migrate from the remote mountain valleys in search of jobs and education. Both endeavours became successful and changed the social structure significantly. Education and economic entrepreneurship mixed up the previous social layers originating from the traditional elite structure. Former influential groups lost their traditional dominance, since control over mobility and migration could no longer be executed. The new elite was grouped around economic success, which is strongly linked to trade, tourism and professionalism. Consequently, today we are confronted with a hybrid system of old and new, of tradition and modernity, of inherited and acquired respect. The developments connected to the opening of the KKH have left their mark on all societies in the Northern Areas of Pakistan and posed a challenge to planning regional development by state authorities and government institutions. Incorporation of the formerly remote mountain valleys into the mainstream of Pakistan's economy and society has been their task ever since.

As early as 1972, M. Abdullah's Government Report advocated a regular supply of basic food items to northern Pakistan from the grain chambers of lowland Punjab. The proposed concept favoured an exchange of a different range of cash crops from the mountain valleys with surplus staple foods from the plains, with transport subsidised from public funds. In Abdullah's opinion self-sufficiency in grain production could not be achieved in the mountain valleys. For example, the highly subsidised and competitive price for wheat flour (*ata*) could not be met by local producers. Consequently, the proportion of food produced locally is steadily decreasing. In some villages of the Hunza valley local production of *ata* nowadays is less than one third of the household's annual consumption. Similar trends are observed in other regions of the Northern Areas. The dependency on down-country supplies for other consumer goods is even higher. For the first time in history there are no periods of starvation and famine now for such disasters have been prevented by subsidies and crisis management from the Federal Government and the World Food Programme.

Robert Chambers's observation that research and development projects follow networks of roads[22] has been supported by the extension of major development projects to this region in the aftermath of the KKH construction. The Government of Pakistan and non-governmental organisations with international funding have established a number of rural development and community service projects with substantial impact on the physical infrastructure, local trading, education and health services. Their efforts have also focussed on the extension and improvement of existing agricultural resources. By applying economics of different scales of production they aim to increase productivity through the cultivation of valuable niche

Fig. 44. The rapidly developing Karimabad bazaar with shops and small hotels – a focal point for tourists.

products, such as seed potatoes, vegetable seeds and special varieties of fruit. The exchange of goods between lowlands and highlands is the driving force behind this concept.

In periods of crisis, these development models based on long-distance trading relations for cereals and other staples are vulnerable. This potential scenario must be kept in mind. Road closure due to natural or man-made hazards could provoke dire results. In the case of the Karakoram Highway, engineer corps maintain the road and most natural hazards – especially in spring and during the monsoon season – are managed in such a way that the affected stretches can be reopened after a short while, although repair costs are high for providing this year-long service. Providing such a high standard for transportation is a singular achievement in such difficult terrain. Less control can be exercised over highway robbers and/or politically motivated activists who threaten the safety of travel along this single lifeline, exploiting its single status to execute pressure. These unstable conditions also affect other spheres of global and inter-regional exchange, such as tourism and trade.

The initial construction of the KKH as an artery between the lowlands and the Karakoram led to a secondary road network of link roads. In the Hunza valley more than ninety-five per cent of all households are connected with a jeep-worthy or truck-worthy road by now. In the side valleys, such as the Gilgit, Ishkoman, Yasin and Astor, and Baltistan, the same density is aimed at. New suspension bridges were constructed with bilateral aid. The majority of link roads has been financed by public funds and regional development plans; some have come into existence as a productive physical infrastructure programme of the AKRSP. Especially in remote areas with only a few scattered settlements, this development agency has taken the role of a planning institution for accessibility and market connections. Road construction has become the second most important activity of this rural development programme only to be surpassed by the construction of irrigation channels. The emphasis on the construction of tertiary roads by private sector development organisations such as the AKRSP has continued up to today, while the government maintains the KKH and the Skardu highway, and constructs secondary roads.[23] The major arteries in the urban and semi-urban centres of Gilgit, Karimabad, Skardu and Chitral belong to that category. The change in government and recent changes in world politics have convinced the President of Pakistan, Pervez Musharraf, to implement major projects in road construction: asphalt roads connecting Ghizer and Chitral districts via Shandur pass (3700 m) and the route across Babusar pass (4100 m) linking the KKH at Chilas with Kaghan and Hazara. The improvement of accessibility was a major driving force for the establishment of tourism in the Northern Areas of Pakistan as a local source of income generation.

TOURISM IN NORTHERN PAKISTAN – OPPORTUNITIES AND CONSTRAINTS
Sustainable development in general and sustainable tourism in particular are concepts for future generations who should be enabled to make an adequate living in a specific setting. In the Northern Areas of Paki-

stan we are confronted with a mountainous environment of a unique and extraordinary quality. In the age of globalisation, however, it is a fact that even the remotest region on earth does not remain unaffected by movements of the world markets. Obviously, international tourism is the best proof of this thesis as people leave their home country and continent in order to visit remote mountain regions in search of something different. In the Northern Areas, the incentives to enjoy views of magnificent peaks, go trekking and be exposed to an exotic mountain culture are overwhelming.

What are the chances of sustainable tourism in northern Pakistan? The potential advantages of tourism have been abundantly highlighted and include job provision in off-farm employment, additional incomes from the service sector, reduction of out-migration, increase of the overall income of a location and/or region, catalyst effects in favour of secondary and tertiary beneficiaries from the tourism industry and diversification of economic activities. In general, tourism can act as an agent of change and, to some extent, as an incentive for protecting cultural heritage and natural landscapes if properly controlled. On first sight there seem to be only advantages.

Better scrutiny, however, tells us that there are three phases with different risks and benefits. During the initial phase, tourism development indeed generates additional revenues and off-farm income opportunities which are rarely matched by cash crops or other niche productions. Overall, this is the most profitable phase. In a second step major investments are undertaken: physical infrastructures such as hotels, restaurants and souvenir shops are built and opened. Great expectations are connected with these innovative and challenging actions. All investments are based on household and lineage savings and/or loans from banks and national, regional or community-based finance corporations. In a third phase, saturation point is reached.

Fig. 45. On top of the Khunjerab pass (4550 m) linking Pakistan with China.

Fig. 46. A member of the old gold-washer community searching for the fine gold dust found in alluvial deposits.

Increasing numbers of entrepreneurs try to participate in the market, the supply outgrows the demand and benefits from the huge investments dwindle. Previously unexpected environmental and social follow-up costs enter the accounts. If during this phase a major crisis occurs, disaster threatens a broad layer of society, which loses out on income and investments.

The scenario described here is derived from the recent Hunza experience. The early entrepreneurs fared best and remained ahead of their competitors if they invested modestly. Tourism became a valuable sector of economic activities in which representatives from all layers of society participated and invested. At one point, both the son of the last *mir* and the high-school peon became hotel owners. Everybody who could afford to invest a substantial sum of money tried to get a share in the tourism business. Nevertheless, the social structure of tourism reflects more than any other economic activity the traditional social structure of Hunza. The biggest hotels of Karimabad belong to the sons of the last *mir* and *wazir*. The traditional elite, either from the ruling families (*gushpur*) or from the *wazirkuts*, is significantly over-represented in the group of government employees and private tourism entrepreneurs, hotel owners and guides. They successfully manage to take advantage of their early contacts with foreign visitors, their language and hospitality skills, as well as their social ranking. No other group of people has been so well organised in maintaining strong loyalty and keeping a personal share in the tourism business by excluding others. On the other hand, all investors have taken a great risk in such a vulnerable enterprise, paid substantially high prices and faced losses.

When the hotel boom took off in Hunza, the demand had already slowed down and competition with other global destinations was growing. While visitor numbers stagnated and the average duration of stay shrank, the investment in new constructions continued on borrowed money. Different crises – either home-made in Pakistan or outside the country with effect on the country – have occurred since the mid-1990s, with intervals becoming shorter. But nothing had an effect like that of 9/11 (9 September 2003) when from one day to the next the best tourism season in seven years dramatically collapsed. Even an increase in domestic tourism does not compensate for this loss as profit margins become smaller. Tourism operators had to close offices, tourist guides were laid off, demand for services and local products became almost non-existent, loans were defaulted and bankruptcy of tourism entrepreneurs was lying in wait. People who had earnt a substantial income from tourism, went back to their roots and practiced mountain agriculture again, the only insurance they possess unless drawing a pension from a previous engagement in government jobs.

How did the federal administration cope with these developments? The reduction of peak royalties by fifty per cent through the government has not attracted more international expeditions so far. The experience of 9/11 has dramatically shown how vulnerable the tourism sector in northern Pakistan is and how little prognostic value can be attributed to the promises of sustainable tourism. At present, a slight recovery can be observed. The celebration of the fiftieth anniversary of the first ascent of K2 by Ardito Desio initiated further modest growth. To sustain a renaissance of tourism as a major source of income favourable and peaceful conditions are required.

From this discussion it follows that tourism might remain a major source of income for the Northern Areas in the future. Yet it should be one and not the only source of revenue to be promoted in this specific setting. Over-reliance on this source is not advisable, as too many parameters are beyond the control of local entrepreneurs. In this regard sustainability means developing safe sectors such as mountaineering, trekking and individual tourism for different segments, with a particular emphasis on ecological and cultural interests.

[1] For a detailed discussion of the ecological potential of the Northern Areas please refer to Hermann Kreutzmann (ed.), *Sharing Water. Irrigation and Water Management in the Hindukush - Karakoram - Himalaya*, Oxford University Press, Karachi-Oxford 2000.

[2] Detailed information on the Shigar valley is based on the data presented in the dissertation of Matthias Schmidt, *Boden-und Wasserrecht in Shigar, Baltistan. Autochthone Institutionen der Ressourcennutzung im zentralen Karakorum*, Bonn 2004; and his article "Interdependencies and Reciprocity of Private and Common Property Resources in the Central Karakorum", in *Erdkunde* 58 (4) 2004.

[3] The utilisation of pastures, varying livelihood strategies and its importance has been covered in Eckart Ehlers and Hermann Kreutzmann (eds.), *High Mountain Pastoralism in Northern Pakistan*, Franz Steiner-Verlag, Stuttgart 2000.

[4] The results of disaster-related research in the North-Western Karakoram have been published by Edward Derbyshire, Monique Fort and Lewis Owen, "Geomorphological Hazards Along the Karakoram Highway: Khunjerab Pass to the Gilgit River, Northernmost Pakistan", in: *Erdkunde* 55 (1), pp. 49-71, 2001; Hermann Kreutzmann, "Habitat Conditions and Settlement Processes in the Hindukush-Karakoram", in *Petermanns Geographische Mitteilungen* 138 (6), pp. 337-356, 1994, from which the data presented here are derived.

[5] The findings of the linguistic survey have been published in Hermann Kreutzmann, "Sprachenvielfalt und regionale Differenzierung von Glaubensgemeinschaften im Hindukusch-Karakorum. Die Rolle von Minderheiten im Konfliktfeld Nordpakistans", in *Erdkunde* 49 (1), pp. 106-121, 1995.

[6] The quote is taken from Karl Jettmar, "Bolor - a Contribution to the Political and Ethnic Geography of North Pakistan", in *Zentralasiatische Studien* 11, p. 429, 1977. See also Karl Jettmar, "Northern Areas - an Ethnographic Sketch", in Ahmad Hasan Dani, *History of Northern Areas of Pakistan*. Historical Studies (Pakistan) Series: 5, Islamabad 1989, pp. 59-88.

[7] Data provided by the Government of Pakistan, "1998 District Census Report of Gilgit", Islamabad 2000, p. 26.

[8] For detailed maps and survey data see Hermann Kreutzmann 1995.

[9] John Staley introduced these two clusters from his observations and earlier literature; see John Staley, "Economy and Society in the High Mountains of Northern Pakistan", in *Modern Asian Studies* 1969, 3, pp. 225-243. For further references and recent studies see Zahid Javed Janjua, "Tradition and Change in the Darel and Tangir Valleys", in I. Stellrecht (ed.), *Karakorum-Hindukush-Himalaya: Dynamics of Change*, Cologne 1998, pp. 415-427.

[10] In her dissertation Elizabeth Staley observed distinguishing features between these two societal settings. The cultural landscape of the republics was devoid of any orchards, a trait which has been related to the land rotation system of *wesh*. Agricultural tasks are predominantly executed by indebted wage-labourers from outside, who are tolerated as employees. Intensity of crop farming has been low and cultivable land abounds. In comparison with the principalities, the agricultural resources of the republics are abundant and under-utilised. There landowners work their smallholdings (on average less than one hectare per household) themselves and are engaged in intensive exploitation of available resources. The upper limits of certain crops are significantly higher in the principalities than in the republics. Natural forests have been depleted to a high degree. Scarce water resources are optimised in a highly sophisticated system of water management by ascribing qualified priorities to different crops, orchards and meadows; see E. Staley, *Arid Mountain Agriculture in Northern West Pakistan*, Lahore 1966.

[11] For further elaborations on the social structures in Hunza detailed information is provided in Hermann Kreutzmann, *Hunza - Ländliche Entwicklung im Karakorum*, Dietrich Reimer Verlag, Berlin 1989, pp. 166-179, and Hermann Kreutzmann, *Ethnizität im Entwicklungsprozeß. Die Wakhi in Hochasien*, Dietrich Reimer Verlag, Berlin 1996, pp. 282-289.

[12] The sources of information include oral traditions about the extension of irrigation networks and the establishment of filial settlements, colonial reports and records, as well as travelogues (for details see Hermann Kreutzmann 1989, pp. 48-59. The systematic recording of genealogical affiliations of founders of new settlements and village histories have supported the reconstruction of the expansion process.

[13] In 1981 Dumyal was renamed Mominabad (see Anna

Schmid, "Minority Strategies to Water Access: The Dom in Hunza, Northern Areas of Pakistan", in H. Kreutzmann (ed.) *Sharing Water. Irrigation and Water Management in the Hindukush - Karakoram - Himalay*, Karachi-Oxford 2000, pp. 116-131), in 1983 Baltit became Karimabad and Hindi was renamed Nasirabad.

[14] For an evaluation of the historical developments and its effects on Hunza's exchange relations see Hermann Kreutzmann, "The Karakoram Highway. The Impact of Road Construction on Mountain Societies", in *Modern Asian Studies* 1991, 25 (4), pp. 711-736; Hermann Kreutzmann, "Challenge and Response in the Karakoram. Socio-Economic Transformation in Hunza, Northern Areas, Pakistan", in *Mountain Research and Development* 1993, 13 (1), pp. 19-39; and Hermann Kreutzmann, "The Chitral Triangle: Rise and Decline of Trans-Montane Central Asian Trade, 1895-1935", in *Asien-Afrika-Lateinamerika* 1998, 26 (3), pp. 289-327.

[15] Contemporary accounts of the Hunza Campaign have been given by E. F. Knight, *Where Three Empires Meet*, London 1895 (reprint: Lahore 1986); Nazim Khan, *The Autobiography of Sir Mohomed Nazim Khan, K.C.I.E. Mir of Hunza*, Karimabad 1936, (mimeographed).

[16] IOL/P&S/12/3288: "Administration Report for the Gilgit Agency for the Years 1938, 1939"; Kreutzmann (1989, p. 183). The irrigation scheme of Harathingdas (nowadays Jalalabad) by farmers from Teisot and Bilchar was completed in June 1939

(IOL/P&S/12/3285: Gilgit Agency Diary June 1939). The villages with migrants from Hunza and Nager include: Nomal, Naltar, Gujur Das (Sultanabad), Jutal, Gwachi and Diding Das (Muhammadabad). At the junction of the Ishkoman and Gilgit river Hunza settlers have cultivated the colony of Golodas; in Ishkoman some settled in Bar Jangal.

[17] The costs for a selection of building materials such as cement, corrugated iron sheets and wooden beams from the Indus valley have undercut purchasing and construction costs with locally available and treated products such as dressed stone and timber from fruit trees.

[18] Before 1935 the Gilgit agency was supplied with goods via Burzil pass (4200 m) from Srinagar. After the lease of Gilgit to British India the Babusar route was expanded and improved by military engineers and contractors for the summer caravans. Both routes were closed in winter due to heavy snowfall.

[19] Air traffic between the Punjab and Gilgit was introduced as early as 1927.

[20] L. P. Clark, "Progress in the Gilgit Agency", in *Eastern World* 1960, 14, p. 22.

[21] Clark 1960 cit., p. 21.

[22] Robert Chambers, *Rural Development. Putting the Last First*, London, Lagos, New York 1983, p. 13.

[23] World Bank, *The Next Ascent. An Evaluation of the Aga Khan Rural Support Program, Pakistan*, Washington 2002, p. 29.

3. Changing Development Patterns in the Mountain Areas

ABDUL MALIK AND IZHAR ALI HUNZAI

This case study presents an example of village-based participatory rural development initiated by the Aga Khan Rural Support Programme (AKRSP) in 1982 in the extreme northern parts of Pakistan, which later became the precursor for a Rural Support Programme (RSP) movement in Pakistan and elsewhere. Initially started in the five districts of the Northern Areas and in the Chitral district of the North West Frontier Province of Pakistan, this participatory rural development model has now been widely replicated across Pakistan and in many countries in Africa and Central Asia. The experiences of the AKRSP and that of its replicas share important common elements both in terms of the approach and the ultimate impact upon the communities.

The present article, however, focuses on the AKRSP and looks at its experiences as a key rural development agency in remote and mountainous northern Pakistan. Most of its information is based on the proceedings of an international workshop organised by the AKRSP in December 2003 to celebrate its twenty years of experience in rural development in the Northern Areas and Chitral (NAC). About ten different thematic papers were produced to capture the lessons in rural development, and this article has greatly benefited from those papers. In addition, a recent study titled *Scaling up RSPs in Pakistan* was used as another important source, particularly with regard to conceptual models and impact on poverty and livelihoods.

CHALLENGE AND RESPONSE

The six districts of northernmost Pakistan that constitute the Programme Area of the AKRSP are located in the middle of the four highest mountain ranges in the world at the juncture of China, Afghanistan and Kashmir. Spread over an area of 87,298 square kilometres, the Northern Areas and Chitral provide home to an ethnically diverse population of about 1.2 million. Three decades ago, the area was among the poorest and geographically isolated parts of Pakistan. Most people were relying on subsistence agriculture for a living, and in most cases production was inadequate to fulfil the minimum consumption needs. The problem was further exacerbated by a chronic deficit of basic social, physical and market infrastructure. Key events in the 1970s and early 1980s, such as the abolition of princely states and the construction of the Karakoram Highway, as well as growing government attention to the region (due to its proximity to critical points like Siachen and the Indian border) were, however, offering hopes for progressive change and improvement.

The launch of the AKRSP by the Aga Khan Foundation in 1982 was another landmark event in the history of the Northern Areas and Chitral. Starting its operation initially in one district, Gilgit, the AKRSP was able to expand quite rapidly to cover almost all of the five districts in the Northern Areas as well as the Chitral district in the North West Frontier Province, eventually working with a population of about one million people. The primary aim of this programme was to improve the living standards of the people in the Northern Areas and Chitral. The AKRSP started its work with the intention of acting as a catalyst for rural development by organising and mobilising local communities – working with them to identify development opportunities and enabling the provision of services needed to tackle the specific problems of high mountain regions.

In doing so, the AKRSP focused its attention on three constraints: first, lack of organisation and organisational skills; second, lack of technical know-how; and third, dearth of capital. The assumption behind concentrating on these three elements was that once they are organised and resourced with financial skills and capital, people could take on larger development challenges by making an effective use of their resources and opportunities. Based on this premise, all households, including the poorest ones, were encouraged to come together to form village organisations, including organisations that gave voice to women, and identify projects that would benefit everyone. Members were encouraged to save money and to build their capacity in skills ranging from credit and accounts management to pest control for crops.[1]

Fig. 47. Women's Organisation orchard in Yasin, Ghizer region.

Fig. 48. Women's Organisation orchard in Passu, Upper Hunza.

Thus faith in the ability and willingness of people to improve their lot is the cornerstone of the conceptual model of the AKRSP. What poor communities need is a catalyst that can unlock their true potential by motivating them to organise themselves into community-based organisations which can then serve as a platform for planning and managing the development in a participatory manner. This model was based on ideas and practices learned from more than a century of experience, beginning from the cooperative movement in nineteenth-century Germany and continuing on through the work done in Comilla, then East Pakistan and now Bangladesh, in the 1950s and 1960s.[2]

Based on twenty years of experience, the role of the AKRSP can be categorised into three broad categories: first, the AKRSP has mobilised and organised communities to generate more effective demand for better public goods and services, targeted at both the household and village levels. Second, it has fostered linkages between organised communities and service providers (government, private sector, or others) for the supply of services. Third, it has directly supplied services where there was a dearth of supply or the supply lacked quality.[3]

Fig. 49. Agricultural development in Sost, Upper Hunza.

THE INTERVENTIONS AND THEIR IMPACT

The AKRSP did not go to the communities with a blueprint of activities to be carried out. The interventions were, however, broadly defined by the AKRSP's overall focus on organising people, improving their skills and building the capital base. The activities carried out under these three broad categories were, in fact, evolved in response to the needs and strengths of the communities, as a true reflection of participatory development. Not surprisingly, the greatest demand was for infrastructure development; for example, irrigation channels and roads, and skill-building in farm management – a logical choice made by the communities in view of their dependence on agriculture and their geographic isolation.

The portfolio of activities, therefore, grew and evolved over time in response to the changing needs of the communities that they articulated through their village-based institutions called Village Organisations (VO) and Women's Organisations (WO). In broader terms, the programme components of the AKRSP comprised social organisation, women's development, natural resource management, physical infrastructure development, human resource development, enterprise promotion and micro-finance. Table 1 gives a brief quantitative summary of achievements over the last twenty years.

TABLE 1. ACTIVITIES SUMMARY	NORTHERN AREAS AND CHITRAL
1. Total number of community organisations formed (nos.)	4,147
2. % of households covered	78%
3. Community members trained in various skills (nos.)*	24,230
4. Total number of infrastructure projects completed (nos.)	2,512
5. Forest trees supplied (million)	25.0
6. Fruit trees planted in partnership with AKRSP (million)	3.92
7. Improved seeds of cereal, fodder and vegetable (kg)	926,643
8. Improved breeds of livestock (nos.)	6,410
9. Poultry birds supplied (nos.)	724,716
8. Entrepreneurial and vocational trainings (nos.)	7,192
9. Total savings with VOs/WOs (US $ million)	7.7
10. Total amount of lending to the communities (US $ million)	30.4

* Around 80% of this training was related to the management of natural resources
Source: AKRSP Records

Table 2 depicts the economic picture of the Northern Areas and Chitral for the period 1991-2001. It shows that incomes were less than one third of the national average in 1991, rising to more than half of the national average in 2001. While national economic growth slowed considerably in the 1990s, the Northern Areas and Chitral economy experienced impressive growth in per capita income of eighty-four per cent from 1991 to 2001.

TABLE 2. TRENDS IN INCOME PER CAPITA (US $)			
	Pakistan	Northern Areas and Chitral	NAC as percentage of Pakistan
1991	424	131	31
1994	440	176	40
1997	487	232	48
2001	415	241	58

Source: Government of Pakistan, Federal Bureau of Statistics; AKRSP, Farm Household Income and Expenditure Surveys.

This economic growth has had a direct impact on poverty as well. Table 3 shows that while poverty showed a rising trend in the national economy, it dropped dramatically in the Northern Areas and Chitral from about two thirds to about one third of the population from 1991 to 2001.

TABLE 3. TRENDS IN POVERTY (HEAD COUNT INDEX %)		
	Pakistan	Northern Areas and Chitral
1991	26.1	67
1994	28.7	54
1997	29.8	45
2001	32.1	34

Source: Government of Pakistan, Planning Commission; Malik and Wood (2003)

Notwithstanding the usual problems with attribution, the available evidence is strong enough to suggest that the AKRSP's contribution to economic development in the Northern Areas and Chitral has been substantial. For instance, the incomes of village-organisation member households were found to be fifteen to twenty per cent higher than those of non-members. This difference increased with the number of members per household and the length of their membership. The economic rate of return on the AKRSP investments also points towards the substantial benefits generated by the AKRSP. Using conservative assumptions, the calculated economic rate of return for the AKRSP's investment falls in the range of sixteen to twenty-four per cent – well above the usual experience in similar programmes.[4]

The AKRSP's experience of tackling poverty contains many lessons. The first and foremost lesson is specific to the remote and geographically isolated and land-locked mountainous terrains that often form spatial poverty traps – such as the Northern Areas and Chitral. Experience shows that such areas can and do benefit from non-targeted mainstream rural development interventions (aimed at improving physical infrastructure, agricultural extension services and so on), particularly during the initial phases of intervention. This is true because in such conditions the majority often falls in the poverty bracket due to physical, human and natural resource limitations; hence, there is little need for targeting.[5] In the Northern Areas and Chitral, relatively equal distribution of key natural resources (for example, land) has been instrumental in making the non-targeted approach work for the majority.

Fig. 50. Building a link road to the KKH at Bargo Bala, Gilgit province.

Having advocated the efficacy of a non-targeted approach, it is also important to mention here that some level of targeting is essential to keep the relevance of the rural development programme for those who have no capacity to take advantage of such interventions. Such groups often fall into the category of chronically poor, excluded groups. They need to be distinguished from others and should be addressed through a combination of productive and social protection measures.[6]

The second lesson pertains to the connection between poverty and vulnerability. In such areas, vulnerability remains an important challenge even for graduating households, owing to the fragility of the geographic environment, greater dependence on meagre natural resources, heavy dependence on limited human resources, and volatility of the off-farm sector. Special attention to inherent risks – posed by limited diversification of income sources and by limited integration with mainstream markets for goods and services – is therefore a prerequisite. In this context, safety nets and continued mainstream packages remain important areas of intervention.[7]

The third but crucial lesson regards the integration of such remote areas with the mainstream markets. The AKRSP's experience shows that the effect of rural development interventions is best felt when there is higher macroeconomic growth and when the communities are better linked to mainstream markets. This was demonstrated by the growth performance of incomes in northern Pakistan – higher in the first half of the 1990s and much lower in the second half, following broad national trends.[8] Similarly, better integration with the national markets and improved public policies (for example greater investment by government) clearly increased the effectiveness of the AKRSP's interventions. Chitral and Gilgit showed differential gains owing to differential access and public investment in those two districts of the Northern Areas and Chitral.[9]

Through organising communities into village-based institutions, the AKRSP has undoubtedly created a vibrant mechanism at the grass-roots level that has the ability to deliver development services in an effective and accountable manner by forging partnerships with various service providers including the state, private and citizen sector. At the same time, well aware and mobilised communities are now in a better position to articulate their voice in order to obtain better services from the state and other providers, and to consume those services in an efficient manner. There are many examples showing how the organised communities of the Northern Areas and Chitral have forged partnerships with other players to access social services in the health and education sector, thus synergising the interventions of the AKRSP with those offered by other agencies.

Seen in the light of the AKRSP's experience, social mobilisation models aimed at promoting collective action seem to prove more effective when: first, such models are embedded in the local institutional history; second, such models foster institutions that follow local preferences and needs, instead of relying on fixed and blueprint approaches; third, these institutions are infused with democratic norms, renewed with new organisational knowledge and backed by broad-based public support.[10]

The process of organising communities into village institutions has generated an interesting debate in the AKRSP – the issue being that collective action is increasingly threatened by the forces of individualisation and the changing socio-economic needs of people. As a result, while some old institutions are losing their relevance, a diverse set of new institutions has emerged, largely influenced by the urge of the AKRSP to cope with new challenges.[11] Thus, there is a need to define social organisation as the 'ability to act collectively when need arises', rather than looking at it as a 'permanent and fixed' arrangement.

The formation of separate institutions for women (the WOs) was probably the most significant step towards encouraging women to play a role in the public sphere. On the surface, this initiative may appear to support segregation of women instead of mainstreaming them. In reality, however, it proved to be a strategic step towards allowing women to discuss their problems and take on village level challenges in the socio-culturally sensitive context of the Northern Areas and Chitral.[12] These institutions provided a unique platform for rural women of the Northern Areas and Chitral to access various development services, significant among them was the opportunity to save their money with formal systems. In a context where women have had very little control over resources, for example land and household properties, the WO savings proved to be a unique tool for empowerment.[13]

Despite the AKRSP's continuous efforts and achievements quoted above, women in the Northern Areas and Chitral still lag behind men in terms of attaining their goals on the education, health and employment front. Similarly, their role in the public sphere (particularly at the political front) is still marginal. According to the AKRSP's experience, the problems that slow down the pace of integration are lack of a clear understanding of gender concepts, lack of frequent dialogue between the staff and quarters of certain stakeholders (for example religious groups) who resist a greater role of women, and excessive focus on gender sensitisation instead of devising tangible programmes.[14]

The promotion of equality gender rights and interests in culturally sensitive areas like the Northern Areas and Chitral, therefore, requires efforts to clarify gender concepts among all stakeholders, investment in programmes that directly improve the conditions and position of women (for example employment generation), and frequent dialogue with the religious and cultural opinion leaders.[15]

COMMUNITY MANAGEMENT OF INFRASTRUCTURE AND NATURAL RESOURCES

The AKRSP became involved in community infrastructure development not because it was a part of some preconceived package but because communities identified the physical infrastructure – particularly irrigation channels and roads – as their prime development priority. This is not surprising given the heavy dependence of people on agriculture and their lack of mobility due to lack of feeder roads and bridges. In response to this huge demand, the AKRSP invested in physical infrastructure but always looked at infrastructure grants as investment in the social organisation – with the belief that it provided an incentive to the communities to form village organisations. Interestingly, it was the infrastructure projects that had the greatest impact on rural livelihoods, through enhancing the value of their productive agricultural assets and through increasing the mobility of goods and services to and from villages.[16]

Experience shows that infrastructure projects implemented through community institutions are much better maintained and are cost effective.[17] Furthermore, operational insights suggest that the impact of community infrastructure improvements, apart from being very visible, can spark a whole range of processes and financial innovations at each stage of the project cycle that provide a sound basis for promoting ownership, transparency and accountability in community infrastructure. One key innovation was the introduction of a three-stage dialogue process ('Diagnostic Survey') for participatory project identification, preparation and appraisal. Similarly, charging each community with full responsibility for project maintenance was another procedural innovation that helped in creating a better sense of ownership and sustainability in community infrastructure.[18]

Fig. 51. Irrigation channel near Sost.

Repeated evaluation studies have confirmed the substantial benefits created by the AKRSP's interventions in agriculture, livestock and forestry. In aggregate terms, the Natural Resources Management component of the AKRSP was able to generate economic rates of return around twenty-five per cent. This success was made possible through creating synergies with other programme components of the AKRSP, for example infrastructure development and social organisation as well as with the interventions of other private and public-sector players. One such synergy can be traced in the interplay between infrastructure and management of natural resources. By

Fig. 52. Irrigation channel and agricultural development at Hanuchal, Gilgit province.

Fig. 53. Irrigation channel in the Chitral region.

Fig. 54. Irrigation channel in Nomal, Gilgit region.

constructing irrigation channels in partnership with the AKRSP, communities were able to increase the stock of land and irrigation water, thus increasing the production and productivity in agriculture. In addition, the pressure on natural resources such as wildlife and alpine forests was substantially reduced.[19] Similarly, construction of link roads and bridges resulted in a better integration of farms with markets through facilitating the mobility of farm produce and inputs to and from villages.[20]

Another important synergy was established between the AKRSP's social organisation pattern and the management of common properties. In certain cases, communities have formed effective institutions for the management of common property, thus applying conservation principles for their own benefit. The AKRSP has learnt that natural resources, particularly those shared by many villages, are better managed through the formation of grass-roots institutions that forge effective linkages with the relevant partners. One such example is the Khunjerab Valley Organisation (KVO) – a cluster of VOs fostered by the AKRSP – that is involved in the conservation of Khunjerab National Park in partnership with the government forest department and the International Union for the Conservation of Nature.[21]

ENTERPRISE PROMOTION AND MICRO-FINANCE

Increased production of agricultural goods coupled with increasing integration of the Northern Areas and Chitral to local and national markets motivated the AKRSP to introduce collective marketing models. However, the experience of cooperative marketing has shown mixed results, with many of the collective marketing institutions falling out of the market over time. In retrospect, the debate on what really works in collective marketing essentially comes down to the importance of business acumen, a better understanding of the market and the ability to match supply and demand in terms of both product quantity and quality. Only those who possessed the right ingredients of the factors quoted above were able to survive and benefit from this approach.[22]

A second set of interventions carried out by the AKRSP under its enterprise promotion theme included support to individuals and groups of entrepreneurs in setting up their business. Again, this experience showed mixed results. Businesses that were based on a true comparative advantage survived, while others suffered.[23] Another AKRSP experiment was to set up its own enterprises in key sub-sectors such as seed production, wool processing and apricot processing, taking into account that non-governmental organisations often found themselves at a crossroads, due to divergent values with regard to possible conflicts between equitable development and individual business profits.[24] One conclusion that came out of the AKRSP experience in providing direct services to individual enterprises and in setting up fully owned businesses was that these two approaches carried a high risk of distorting the market and offered limited outreach. Based on these lessons, the AKRSP is now limiting its role to being a facilitator only.

A major boost to enterprise promotion was provided by the AKRSP's micro-finance scheme, which has been unique in many ways. It started out with a savings programme for VO and WO members as an integral part of its conceptual model (organisation, skills and capital). This collective saving served as collateral for accessing bulk credit from the AKRSP credit programme and later it provided the basis for initiating an internal lending programme by the village and women's organisations themselves.

Fig. 55. Livestock and breed improvement in Haramosh, Gilgit region.

One of the problems of the AKRSP's micro-finance programme was lack of attention to issues of sustainability during the initial years. Since micro-finance was developed in response to the needs of the communities (as opposed to introducing a preconceived system), the issue of sustainability was somewhat ignored during the early years. It was only after 1996, when the AKRSP started levying market rates, that their financial sustainability became a key objective. Greater pressure to attain self-sustainability eventually led the AKRSP to experiment with products, which were not entirely consonant with its social and economic development objectives.[25]

The AKRSP's micro-finance programme has had a substantial impact on the social organisation of local communities. The use of collective savings as collateral for group lending to VOs and WOs, proved, however, very damaging in those cases where individual loan defaults were covered by the collective savings – an unfair burden borne by the savers who were not borrowing. Similarly, the inherent conflict between the dual objectives of VO micro-finance, that is, savers wanting higher returns and borrowers wanting lower interest rates, was a source of discord. Meanwhile, the overall positive effects on collective community development are evident. The WO saving programme, in particular, proved to be a cementing force for organising female society, since it motivated women to meet regularly.

SUSTAINABILITY AND PROJECT REPLICATION

The very premise of forming village-based institutions was to develop a self-propelling development mechanism at grass-roots level. Community-managed infrastructure projects, sustainable internal lending programmes practiced by VOs and WOs, and financially viable agricultural input stores run by groups of AKRSP-trained master trainers are some examples of ensuring sustainability through village institutions. Yet the greater challenge ahead lies in continuing the institutional support to these village groups, that is, developing their capacities to address emerging challenges posed by the increasing socio-economic differentiation of the Northern Areas and Chitral. The AKRSP as a support institution continues to depend on donor funds for this value added intermediation. Great care is, however, being taken by the AKRSP to develop financially sustainable institutions that offer greater cost recovery prospects. The formation of the first micro-finance bank by the AKRSP in 2002 is one such example of making the development services sustainable.

Through demonstrating the effectiveness of the participatory rural development model in the Northern Areas and Chitral, the AKRSP has influenced the thinking of government, donors and local communities, and thus enabled them to replicate its participatory model in other parts of Pakistan as well as outside Pakistan. So far, nine RSPs have been formed in different parts of Pakistan and most of these RSPs are backed by the government both financially and politically. Similarly, there are several rural development programmes initiated by the Aga Khan Development Network outside Pakistan, including those in Africa, Central Asia and the Gulf region. As a result of the success shown by the AKRSP, the concept of 'community-driven development', once unknown, now appears in all significant national and provincial development policies and projects. Rural Support Programmes have also had significant influence on poverty reduction strategies, on approaches to local governance and on the adoption of micro-finance and community-owned infrastructure as mainstream development strategies.

Fig. 56. A woman entrepreneur in Baltistan.

[1] Aga Khan Foundation (AKF): Aga Khan Rural Support Programme: Pakistan Project Brief, n.d.

[2] Stephen F. Rasmussen et al, *Scaling Up RSPs: Pakistan Case* (paper presented at a conference in Shanghai 25-27 May 2004), RSPN and World Bank 2004.

[3] See note 2.

[4] OED (Operations Evaluation Department): *The Next Ascent: An Evaluation of the Aga Khan Rural Support Programme. Pakistan*, World Bank, Washington DC 2002.

[5] Abdul Malik and Mujtaba Piracha, *Poverty Trends and Issues in Northern Areas* (Paper in Progress), findings presented at the Chronic Poverty Conference, University of Manchester, UK 2003.

[6] Geof Wood and Abdul Malik, *Poverty and Livelihoods*, AKRSP, Islamabad, Pakistan 2003.

[7] See note 6.

[8] Safdar Parvez and Stephen F. Rasmussen, *Sustaining Mountain Economies: Sustainable Livelihoods and Poverty Evaluation*, AKRSP 2002.

[9] See note 5.

[10] Geof Wood with Sofia Shakil, *Collective Action: From Outside to Inside*, AKRSP, Islamabad, Pakistan 2003.

[11] See note 10.

[12] Aalya Gloekler and Janet Seeley, *Gender and AKRSP - Mainstreamed or Sidelined?*, AKRSP, Islamabad, Pakistan 2003.

[13] AKRSP, *The Strategy for Institutional Development* (Draft), AKRSP, Gilgit 2004.

[14] See note 12.

[15] See note 12.

[16] Abdul Malik et al, *Community Infrastructure*, AKRSP, Islamabad, Pakistan 2003.

[17] See notes 2 and 16.

[18] See note 16.

[19] Aljoscha M. Gloekler, *Natural Resource Management*, AKRSP, Islamabad, Pakistan 2003.

[20] See note 16.

[21] See note 19.

[22] Fatimah Afzal, *Enterprise Development*, AKRSP, Islamabad, Pakistan 2003.

[23] See note 22.

[24] Fatimah Afzal and Abdul Malik, *North South Seeds* (Draft), AKF, Geneva 2004.

[25] Maliha H. Hussein and Stefan Plateau, *Microfinance*, AKRSP, Islambad, Pakistan 2003.

4. Hunza in Transition: Now and Then... and Then Again

JULIE FLOWERDAY

Emile Durkheim, a significant social theorist of the last century, observed that in the process of a society informing itself of its environment, it produces environment as an image of itself.[1] That is all well and good, but what happens when a society's image of the environment shifts so much that the earlier and later versions are irreconcilable? Such was the case I faced in Central Hunza during my dissertation research (1993-1995). The objective of this anthropological investigation was to explore the relationship between changing landscape and shifting knowledge.

For this purpose, I used photographs of landscape and cultural activities from the 1930s to visually interpret cultural changes which occurred in the following sixty years, up to the 1990s. The late Colonel David Lorimer, a former British colonial political agent, took plenty of photographs during his linguistic re-

Fig. 57. Baltit fort and fields (D. Lorimer, 1934-1935).　　Fig. 58. Baltit fort and bazaar (J. Flowerday, 1999).

Fig. 59. Baltit fort and village (D. Lorimer, 1934-1935). Fig. 60. Baltit fort and Karimabad village (J. Flowerday, 1999).

search in the area in the mid 1930s. Based on his work, I later produced an exhibition called *Hunza in Treble Vision: 1930s and 1990s* (2000-2001). Old photographs taken by Lorimer were displayed alongside new photographs I took at the same sites in the 1990s. A set of two contrasting photographs – presented as single and double vision, respectively, highlighted the diminished importance of early sites. I affixed a third photograph to each pair, to document changes in culture, and arranged these sets, which I called 'treble vision', thematically, to draw attention to shifts in socio-political power, economy, environment and the rise of the nation-state.

In the discussion below, which builds upon this earlier work, I will focus in greater detail on residents' understanding of the earlier and later times. There were marked disparities between people, most especially by age. My investigation of the relationship between changing landscape and shifting knowledge throws light on a process of cultural change internalised in reconstructing the 'self'. The notion of 'self' was not an arbitrary creation, but dependent on changing conditions of which it was a part.

Consider the two visions as two periods. Lorimer's photographs of landscape and cultural activities from the 1930s stand in stark contrast to corresponding images from the twenty-first century. Lorimer's 1930s photographs captured a perspective of Hunza from the colonial period (1892-1947) at a time when local hereditary rule and its subsistence economy still bore semblance to life before the arrival of British rule – minus, of course, organised activities of defence and offence. He made 238 glass lantern-slides and a catalogue from photographs he took during fifteen month's residence in Central Hunza (1934-1935) as a civilian scholar. The slides and catalogue read like an intelligence report – accounting for landscape, local rule, architecture, economy, crafts, daily activities and festival celebrations.

This extraordinary resource resulted from equally unusual circumstances. In the 1930s Lorimer was among a privileged few non-local persons with access to Hunza. As a former political agent of the British Indian Army stationed at the Gilgit agency (1920-1924) which oversaw Hunza, he had clearance from British officials to reside in Hunza as a civilian for the purpose of research. Based on his first-hand knowledge of the local community from political agent annual visits, he also had approval from the ruler to reside there. Indeed, his return to Hunza was not surprising. As a political agent, he used much of his free time, hobby-fashion, documenting Burushaski, an unwritten language used by Gilgit Scouts (militiamen) from Hunza, which, to the puzzle of linguists, was unrelated to a complex of great languages converging in this part of Central Asia.

By the time Lorimer returned to Hunza as a civilian scholar he had a three-volume study of *The Burushaski Language* in press (1935, 1935, 1938) and the support of a Leverhulme Fel-

Fig. 61. Tham Mir Mohammad Nazim Khan (D. Lorimer, 1934-1935).

lowship to advance his study of Burushaski by documenting its use in everyday life. Lorimer's lantern-slides paralleled this linguistic research but, regrettably, he died (1962) before publishing his written results. The slides and catalogue were among the few items he completed.

In Lorimer's visual account, colonial presence appeared in the background in the shape of bridges and in the construction of the Imperial road from Srinagar. The foreground highlighted people's daily lives and portrayed Hunza as an isolate – much like its language. It was a pre-industrial society dependent on subsistence agriculture locked away in a maze of mountains, unknown to the rest of mankind until the arrival of the British. In Lorimer's view the people of Hunza were heroes not for their accomplishment of great feats but for their endurance in living under extreme conditions of mountain desert.

Photographs I made in the 1990s paralleled Lorimer's work by updating his record of landscape, rule, architecture, economy, crafts, daily activities and festival celebrations. In the 1990s, Hunza existed as a political subdivision of the Gilgit district, one of five districts in the Northern Areas under the protectorship of Pakistan – a burgeoning industrial nation-state.

Following the construction of the Karakoram Highway, landscape was cut through by roads carrying lorries loaded with goods from China and seasonal produce from Hunza, by local, public and private vans

Fig. 62. Baltit polo ground
(D. Lorimer, 1934-1935).

Fig. 63. Polo played at an international
tourism conference (J. Flowerday, 1999).

transporting commuters and resident travellers here and there, and by coach loads of tourists (especially before the events of 11 September 2003). Electric lines and satellite dishes occurred above eye level, while pipes carrying water traced concealed subterranean paths. Architecture revealed a range of external influences, bearing materials unknown and unavailable in the earlier period. Every village had at least one bazaar area, schools, clinics and institutional structures established by the state of Pakistan, as well as non-governmental development projects. In the 1990s, these were common features.

The two periods were not only incomparable, but those living in the first half of the nineteenth century could not have predicted what their society would look like and how people would think seventy years later. And residents living in the twenty-first century could not abbreviate their present condition to the earlier time... though they knew at some level that the two periods were interconnected.

Bear in mind the two contrasting images of the environment. The first belonged to the early decades of the twentieth century. At that time political rule was an inheritable right fixed in a genealogy longer than England's House of Windsor. Those most successful in leading the traditions of that Hunza society were men with social positions vested in landed tenure. From rulers to commoners, all depended on agriculture, tree cultivation and herding. People ate what they produced, which concurrently internalised activities of faith, practices of marriage and daily routine. These practices intimately attached them to a common political centre and economy. Life was reproduction. The environment was an active image of the recreation of land, people, animals and spirits that assured the future of it all.

By contrast, the second image belonged to the twenty-first century. There were no official heritable rulers. Public administrators were locally elected officials or civil servants appointed by the state of Pakistan. Landed resources that formerly provided the primary source of sustenance gave way to cash crops, which, like other pursuits, generated capital to support a bazaar economy. Fields could not produce the goods a bazaar could bear. Life under these new conditions was united with service institutions — like banks, schools, hospitals and government offices — and linked to technologically determined communication systems of elec-

Fig. 64. Ploughing (D. Lorimer, 1934-1935).

Fig. 65. Tractor (J. Flowerday, 1995).

Fig. 66. Broshal historic water reservoir.

Fig. 67. Broshal new water reservoir.

tricity, piped water, computers, satellite dishes and thoroughfares. Tourism was the strongest industry. Occupations varied considerably, as did people's individual prospects.

In the space between these two images – the one based on Lorimer's 1930s photographs and the other on my efforts in the 1990s – a daily diminishing number of people lived through the disparity... that is, those who *knew the difference*. They were elders who helped metamorphose one society into the other. Most, however, were no longer influential in the social scheme of things. Leaders of the rising society were younger and groomed through their experience; they had a different perception of environment. Landscape changed. Cultural practices shifted. As earlier images fragmented, hopes arose for a future that was unlike the past.

This situation encouraged me to consider Durkheim's perspective in a new way. The time lapse of sixty/ seventy years was invaluable for probing people's altering images in a changing environment. Understanding how this happened was not Durkheim's primary concern, but he provided an important observation about newness. He observed that the mind could not create a new idea out of nothing. Should we discover an entirely new being without analogue in the rest of the world, it would be impossible for the mind to grasp; it could only be represented in terms of something else that the mind already knew.[2]

Though newness, by virtue of being new, appears to us as different, it is integral to what is known. The beauty of this notion is that it makes sense of people's different images over time and provides a way of

Fig. 68. Mama Zaibo.

Fig. 69. Bibi and granddaughter.

Fig. 70. Mr Noor.

seeing how it works. Two constructions with examples are offered to demonstrate this thesis:

Construction one

The first construction – *then and now* – is a difference that is relative to the speaker. The difference is not age alone. Old and young speak from experience and correspondingly contemplate the environment of the twenty-first century from self-knowledge. The real difference is the variable conditions that inform their knowledge and reflect self-identity. Whereas details of narratives given by older people bore distinguishing characteristics of earlier conditions internalised in their self-identity, such details were absent in younger people's accounts. Younger people did not know themselves through a hereditary autocrat and they had no interest in titles that had no power and, thus, no effect on their lives. They spoke of their grandparents' time from a position of *opus operandi*, thus situating their identity in a state system of recent conditions.

Consider Mama Zaibo's comments during one of our interview sessions. Now in her seventies, she sensed the strangeness of her own recollections. She was looking through an album I made from 175 of Lorimer's photographs of Hunza from 1934-1935. I was listening to her recital of 'commonplace' descriptions – the bygone local ruler-ship, the spiritual animation of the land, the communion of economic and personal activities – when she paused and reflected: "Only people who have experienced such things can trust such things as true. Otherwise, such things sound very strange".

Mama Zaibo was not referring to extraordinary events, to such things as inexplicable musical refrains from mountain desert. Nor was she thinking about strange creatures of great or small proportions living in boulders, or others that came to eat the dead. Mama Zaibo was referring to the ordinary events of her own life. The photographs opened a tangle of thoughts that were no longer irrefutable on the landscape of the twenty-first century or that were incontestable in her mind.

In daze-like attention her eyes lifted from an image of a *serai*-like structure (an enclosure that housed pack animals and people) photographed by Lorimer and she began speaking of her first experience of buying something from a bazaar. She was just a young girl, possibly seven or eight years old when she was sent almost five miles to buy salt for her household. "I was sent to Mr Ayub and Mr Dawar's shop to buy salt with one heavy rupee. I got ten *seers* (nearly 10 kg) of salt for only one rupee; and I brought it home. This salt lasted for more than two years."[3]

Fig. 71. Children (D. Lorimer, 1934-1935).

Fig. 72. Children imitating a political event (J. Flowerday, 1999).

Details of her narrative make it accountable to the conditions of which she was a part. It could not belong to any other time than when the brothers – Mr Ayub and Mr Dawar – had their shop, which *then* was one of a few places selling goods brought in from outside the local settlements of Hunza and Nagir. Where else could Mama Zaibo look than in vacant space? Residents dismantled the brothers' shop almost forty years ago, building in its place a garage. No trace of their shop was left; and in the 1990s, elaborate markets were commonplace in every village.

Mama Zaibo's narrative was further distinguished by a silver rupee and by salt. The silver rupee, issued by the British Indian Government, fell into disuse after Partition (1947). Current transactions were carried out in currency issued by the Government of Pakistan. Though coined rupees existed in the 1990s, none were silver or large and none of the old coins were presently in popular circulation.

Commercial salt likewise was unique. In Mama Zaibo's youth, when women and girls had some free time they might walk five or more miles to known locations where they collected salty tasting earth. They carried basket-loads home on their backs, which they siphoned with water through a *chutkus* (a specially constructed basket) to use for cooking. Rulers and noble families enjoyed rock salt brought from distant valleys; otherwise salt was rare and none was iodised. Indeed, commercial salt was generally not available to the public until the 1950s, an event concurrent with the construction of the first jeep-worthy road from the large trade-town of Gilgit, sixty-five miles away. Even then it took three days to cover the distance.

Mama Zaibo's grandchildren, by contrast, knew only commercial salt, which they purchased locally at their convenience in small half-kilo packets. Trade and the growth of bazaars made salt mundane and ordinary. It was a common condiment of cooking, a favoured complement to milk tea and among other things a cure for common health ailments. At the turn of the twenty-first century medical opinion suggested that a consequence of the surfeit of salt was high blood pressure and related health problems. The rising position was not getting salt, but rather knowing how to reduce its intake.

Without knowing this background, Mama Zaibo's narrative appeared senseless to those who did not know the earlier time when salt was rare – incongruent images that made her self-conscious. Not everyone knew,

Fig. 73. Serai-Bazaar (D. Lorimer, 1934-1935).

and generally younger people did not care to know, the difference of when there was a single bazaar, when people used silver rupees, or, indeed, when salt was not processed and iodised.

The following short vignette, which also concerns salt, demonstrates one reaction by younger people. It was a cold wintry afternoon as we huddled around the embers of a fire earlier stoked for tea. Mr Niat Shah, a man in his mid-thirties, our host, looked through the album of Lorimer's photographs. As he turned the page to a photograph of a basket sitting at the door of a house, I asked, "What is a *chutkus*?" He hesitated, then replied: "In olden times we used the *chutkus* for *baru* (buckwheat) uh... no. It was used for making breads. We used that one for *baur*, (the container that held bread-making equipment)." He paused and then added: "Also shepherds used the *chutkus*. The *chutkus* is that pot used for storing milk. That is called the *chutkus*." When another man in the group told him the *chutkus* was used for making salt, he replied: "Then, I don't know how to make salt from the *chutkus*. I never saw it used in my time."[4]

At the turn of the twenty-first century, information about the *chutkus* was fragmented, displaced by the occurrence of commercial salt. The growth of bazaars and suppliers, concurrent with new generations of people, made salt ordinary. Young people born under recent conditions assumed that salt was available and incorporated that expectation in their normal identity of life in Hunza.

The difference of *now and then and then again* was relative – but critically anchored by those social conditions to which *newness* belonged. Mama Zaibo could trace the change in her lifetime; Niat Shah could not. Accordingly, newness, by virtue of being new, appeared as different though it was integral to what was known. Though this supports Durkheim's observation, it also points out that knowledge was discrete – not universal. That is, not everyone knew salt in a single way. Knowledge passed discretely through generations of people born into altering conditions over time. Mama Zaibo's generation interconnected a time of the past – when people used water collected from salty tasting earth – with the present circumstance of buying prepackaged iodised salt from a local shop.

Construction two
The second construction, which I offer with respect to changing perceptions of environment, concerns people's ways of manifesting the discreteness of knowledge. Furthermore, it implicates this process in social power. The focus is recognising *the other*. As noted above, few of those who were young in the 1930s were currently leaders in the society of the twenty-first century. Rather those born under altered conditions of economy and political order were the rising leaders – seers and broadcasters – of change. *Otherness* took a twist in this setting.

Fig. 74. Woman and girls embroidering (D. Lorimer, 1934-1935).

Fig. 75. Craft shop
(J. Flowerday, 1999).

Inside the social scheme of the 1930s *otherness* was played out between rulers, an elite body of supporters, the ordinary folk and a small group of bondsmen. Narratives given in response to Lorimer's photographs by older people commonly depicted the *other* as members of these social groups in reference to their own social position. The labyrinth of details given by them intertwined landscape with their self-identity.

In contrast, some younger people used social demarcations from the earlier social scheme in another way. One comment I heard several times was: "Ha! They were the elites, but now they are ordinary, just like the rest of us!" Younger people shared no comparable status with the old economy or system of rule. Theirs was a market economy run by private and public administrators. The elite were no longer men of landed tenure. Current public leaders were businessmen and state bureaucrats.

So, how was this difference played out? In the following interview situation Bibi, an older resident in her seventies, myself and two male companions in their twenties were sitting together in a courtyard whose outside door opened to a public path. The door was ajar and Bibi sat comfortably cracking peach kernels with a three-year-old granddaughter sitting in her lap – glancing from time to time at the album of Lorimer's photographs. She was saying: "When we work from the hands, work hard, then we can get some property and some other things..." [At that moment some girls walked by, looked in at this lady cracking peach kernels and started to laugh, saying:] "Look! Look! She is cracking peach kernels!" [They walked away laughing and Bibi became agitated, then annoyed, and retorted:] "You are laughing at me but this is honest work [respectable] work. You don't know!" [You don't know any better; you are ignorant!].

A companion who had accompanied me for translation explained: "The young girls now prefer to buy oil in the bazaar even if their mothers press pure oil from the peach or apricot kernels." How different this was from the earlier period when peach and apricot kernels were treasured for so many diverse purposes. This oil was valued for massaging an aching body, treating a cold or sick stomach, caring for hair and skin cosmetically, accenting food dishes and, when used in a specially constructed lamp, for lighting a house.

A little later when I purposefully drew Bibi's attention to the *chutkus*, she turned to my companion and scolded: "Don't ask this question. [She was referring to me and continued:] She's really having a laugh at us." When my companion told her that I had asked about this device from others, Bibi quipped: "If she asked before, then what's the difference? (That is, what is the difference between the other people and me?) They're saying something different or I'm saying something different. If she's asked before, why is she asking me? It's the same process."[5] What lay behind Bibi's reaction was sensing a social divide. Though she sat in the sanctuary of her own residence, outsiders [here young resident girls and a foreign woman researcher] challenged her inner worth and intelligence.

She was not the only elder to sense distancing from younger people; and the young girls who laughed at Bibi were also not alone. Sometimes older members of the population referred collectively to young people as the Dalda generation, the generation who knew how to spend rupees (Pakistani currency), to get what they wanted but had no clue how to create anything with their own hands. The young people, according to some elders, were impractical and knew nothing. "They think oil comes from a can! They don't know hard work and they don't know how things work."

In contrast, some young people similarly stereotyped older people as in the following story. The story goes: "Once there was a bride sitting next to the Shiri Dako [the ceremonial pillar in the traditional house]. She was shy. A neighbour came to offer her congratulations and brought with him some flour as a gift. The bride extended her arms, palms up, to receive the flour. When, however, she tried to accept the flour properly, she could not. She had stretched her arms either side of the pillar and so her hands and the flour were separated from her body by that pillar."

"This was a problem. [My companions began to laugh.] So the senior man in the family called for a wise man. After some time he came. Then this wise man deliberated. Then after some more time he ordered two men to go to the roof of the house and another two men to dig the pillar out of the floor of the house [some more laughter]. After some hours the pillar was lifted and the bride got her flour. [And, now everyone was laughing and making comments such as,] How silly the old people are. They can't think clearly to work out simple solutions."

The joke was found throughout Pakistan. Dalda oil, too, was a product of Pakistan. Strikingly, both the old and young used metaphors from the larger State society of which they were a part, simultaneously demonstrating the contemporariness of old to young as well as the disparity between them.

Otherness was contemporary and expressed in changed social power. Elders no longer spoke with authority from conditions that created their other identity. They had no recourse to a *tham* (heritable ruler). And men of status with positions of power were not farmers. Rather, rising power was situated with younger people in a scheme based on different knowledge connected with global market patterns and a nation-state.

Thus, Durkheim provided an insight when he observed that a society projects an image of its environment as an image of itself, and he also opened a discussion of how images change. In the two constructions offered above, knowledge was held discretely. Not everyone had the same knowledge – a distinction most especially evidenced by age and self-identity. As conditions of economy and political power took *new* form, the way people understood themselves also shifted. It did so through the ever-recurring appearance of young people who accepted as normal to their time what older people saw as newness. Thus people born at different times were carriers of the altering environment. They made newness normal, as part of themselves and their social identity.

This discussion captures only a small piece of a larger biological process in which older generations die out and younger people rise to redefine and transmit their knowledge of environment. Yet the nexus where altered knowledge begins is

Fig. 76. Aliabad KKH (J. Flowerday, 1999).

also critical. It would be a mistake on my part to leave the reader with the notion that older members of the population were filled with dissolution. Without sacrifices and efforts made by them to encourage their children and grandchildren to succeed in the expanding economy, the contrast of *Now and Then* might be another version of *Then Again...* Many young people knew this and several elders voiced this circumstance in the following excerpts from recent interviews.

"In the old time we led a very poor life. In this time we are thankful to God for all our Blessings. Now all my children are doing jobs [working for money.]" (Api Zeebon of Ganish, 2004).

"By the grace of God now we have clean water, the streets are renovated due to cooperation with the Aga Khan Culrtural Sevices Pakistan. We are extremely thankful to the AKCSP or else we would still be living with our animals." (Dado Yaqub of Ganish, 2004)

"At that time there was great poverty. We only had resources from our house, nothing came from outside. (We depended only on what we made ourselves.) Now poverty is finished. We are eating and drinking well. We are living comfortably. That earlier time was not good. At this time it is nice. Now everything comes (is available to us). At that time, things were not good. That time was one of poverty, but now, by the grace of God, it is a good time." (Dado Amir Hayat, Mominabad, 2004)

[1] Emile Durkheim, *The Elementary Forms of Religious Life.* New York: Free Press 1995 (1915, 1965).
[2] See note 1.
[3] Julie Flowerday, Dissertation: *A Construction of Cultural His-* tory from *Visual Records for the Burusho of Hunza, Pakistan*, University of North Carolina, Chapel Hill 1998, p. 184.
[4] See note 3.
[5] See note 3.

5. Vernacular Architecture and Construction Techniques in the Karakoram

RICHARD HUGHES

The Karakoram mountains contain a most remarkable number and variety of historic buildings of monumental and domestic scale. Their survival up to the present shows how well they have served their inhabitants; it is proof of excellent material qualities, of superb construction detailing, of regular maintenance and of minimal external pressures for change. Since the opening up of the region by the Karakoram Highway (KKH), this important architectural heritage has become readily accessible for tourists and for specialist research. Meanwhile, this very event and the ensuing recent development trends also constitute a considerable threat to the survival of the Northern Areas cultural heritage.

The historic buildings of Hunza included many magnificent old strongholds, now represented by the surviving Baltit and Altit forts and the fortified village of Ganish. These forts bear testimony to the times of the historic Silk Routes from China to northern India and Europe (which provided the local principalities with rich raiding opportunities), while in the late nineteenth century, the local kingdoms became involved in the 'Great Game', the political and military 'tournament of shadows' between the British and Russian Empires. There are still good-quality structural remains of other traditional forts and palaces found to the south and west in Gilgit, Gupis and Yasin. Further east, intact structures are to be found, for example at Rondu, Skardu, Shigar, Kiris and Khaplu. In former times there were many other forts – at least seven in Hunza before the British military campaign at the end of the nineteenth century. Once demolished, these structures completely disappeared, including underground archaeological features.

On a smaller building scale, historic villages are still intact, mostly including 'core' cluster housing with associated animal byres, stores, simple shops and mosques and other religious buildings. Historic mosques and tombs of saints (*astanas*) are found throughout the Karakoram landscape and are spectacular pieces of architecture. Up in the remoter side and high altitude valleys and summer pastures, individual farms and small clusters of houses tend to cling to the most precarious mountainsides.

All these traditional buildings are characterised by the use of building materials found at hand, that is rubble and dressed stone, soil (as 'adobe' blocks or '*pisé*' rammed earth) and timber (softwoods today but mostly deciduous hardwoods in the past). These materials were used in the most simple of ways for ordinary buildings. Important buildings involved itinerant craftsmen proudly showing off high-quality structural engineering skills and carving. The older monuments, probably dating back more than a thousand years, illustrate indigenous features and also cultural influences derived from the west (typically from Afghanistan but from as far as western Turkey) and the south-east (Ladakh and Kashmir). Within the region, the use of 'cator and cribbage' construction techniques has reached its zenith, presenting us with wonderful testimonies of elaborate timber building techniques.

Fig. 77. Baltit fort and village from the front, in the 1930s (courtesy Royal Geographic Society).

Fig. 78. Baltit fort from the rear, towering above the ravine of the Ultar *nullah* (courtesy Royal Geographic Society).

Today, traditional buildings and settlements in the main valleys are rapidly being replaced and upgraded – much construction work being done in the self-help mode or by governmental and non-governmental organisations in the field of health, education and agriculture. The first signs of change go back to the 1950s with the early construction works of the Public Works Department. This was then followed by some initial development schemes sponsored by the Ismaili communities and dramatically increased with the later activities of the Aga Khan Development Network programmes.

Many of these recent building activities have resulted in new architectural styles and structural technologies related to those found around Rawalpindi, for example. The more sophisticated buildings, including schools and hotels, are now characterised by concrete frames of columns and beams with infilled panels. New ordinary houses are typically built with concrete block load-bearing walls. New roofs are made of corrugated galvanised sheet steel. These new self-built structures commonly show poor architectural and engineering designs, as well as crude craftsmanship, since little construction practice is being transferred from previous vernacular craft skills. At the same time, the historic houses and monuments are becoming rare 'antiquities' and are threatened by decay. Therefore, efforts to understand, revive and adapt traditional building techniques are needed, both for new construction and for restoration purposes.

Hence, this article aims to throw some light on the vernacular construction techniques of the region and on the morphology of its most prominent historic structures – the forts and palaces. Beyond this historic approach, however, it is important to analyse the strengths and weaknesses of traditional building techniques in terms of engineering principles, use of materials, siting, reaction to large stresses, risk of natural hazards, and so on, in order to evaluate how traditional techniques can best be used and adapted under contemporary conditions. This is the underlying theme of the second, more technical part of this article, which is complemented by considerations on the restoration of historic buildings in chapter 9 of this book.

Fig. 79. Altit fort on the high cliff commanding the Hunza river and the old village on the high plateau beneath the fort (see also pl. 40).

ORIGINS AND STRUCTURAL CHARACTERISTICS OF TRADITIONAL BUILDINGS

There are few surviving historic buildings more than about five hundred years old, though it is the case that materials, such as wood and stone, have been reused from older ones, providing a continuity of construction tradition. Houses were not built for longevity. Though they may stand on the footprint of older houses, and indeed look old, most are relatively recent. Forts and other defensive structures tend to have been removed – as part of feudal power struggles – and then from the late nineteenth century, obliterated to reduce the local capabilities to resist control of the British colonial administration. The forts surviving the purge became palaces of the *mirs* and *rajas*, masking the older and rougher innards built by the robber chiefs who had been raiding the transcontinental silk routes. As such buildings required near constant repair they were easily abandoned or replaced: Baltit fort was saved *in extremis* before it fell down, but Nager fort collapsed.

Most surviving historic buildings are therefore mosques and *astanas*, these retaining most of the as-built and sacrosanct architectural arrangements and the more elaborate ornamentation. So, while we know from oral and written history that settlement of the mountains goes back to pre-Islamic times, there is little architectural evidence to support this, with minimal ability to appreciate early tribal differences of building styles and engineering practices. Carbon 14 dating of the Altit fort *shikari* (tower) timbers proves an origin slightly more than one thousand years ago and the first phase of development of Baltit fort dates back about 750 years. Otherwise, there is some evidence of Buddhist courtyard cell structures, for example at a monastery site at Shigar probably dating to the late first century BC.

101

It is therefore impossible, so far, to describe the origins and any continuity and development of building styles. However, for a few distinctive structural engineering features it is possible to see them in a wider historical context suggestive of copying ideas, for example transposed as a result of trading, of tribal or family migration, or being mimicked by paid itinerant or captured craftsmen.

As simple houses follow simple building techniques, there is no need to suggest a prototype or origin of the structural system from elsewhere. The complex roof structure resting on four timber posts placed around the central *ha* (the core of the room) creates a semi-dome effect supported off the main beams and provides a central smoke vent. It is a logical approach when using small-sized timbers and desiring a higher central head room. It is also a roofing technique known from classical antiquity, for example around the eastern Greek Mediterranean, in Persia and in Buddhist periods of India and Sri Lanka. As a ubiquitous prototype, it allowed many spatial and functional variations according to social needs and tribal traditions.

In the surviving historic monuments, timber 'cators' (horizontal timber straps found in wall faces) have a long tradition possibly derived from central Anatolia some nine thousand years ago. This is a technique that has been researched in the earthquake-prone landscapes of the Middle East and North Africa. Based on quality of design and construction it reaches its functional best in Macedonia and in the Karakoram. 'Cribbage' columns (vertical timber box frames found typically at wall corners) are most sophisticated in the Karakoram but this may relate to the availability of wood. For the Karakoram, a Ladakh origin is indicated, based on structures found in Baltistan where decorative motifs on sixteenth- and seventeenth-century mosques and *astanas* have a Buddhist affiliation and therefore could have originated more than two thousand years ago.

The prerequisite for siting houses and settlements in the Karakoram region has always been the avoidance of dynamic land-modifying geomorphological processes. No doubt in the early days this happened by trial and error, this theory being supported by the number of disappeared settlements in Yasin valley, for example. These have been identified from old maps and were located on outwash fans and unstable scree slopes. More recent settlements took into account observations accumulated by many generations of inhabitants, especially farmers highly sensitive to every mood of their land. The historical settlements generally tended to avoid floodplains and actively eroding cliff edges. Less predictable were hazardous locations resulting from snow and rock avalanches, landslides, mudflows and glacier surges. Such building locations were neither better nor worse in terms of resisting strong earthquakes, which, fortunately, do not very often reach a damaging magnitude in this region.

Choice sites were those with an element of natural defence, good microclimatic aspects, a fair supply of water and with nearby soil slopes able to be improved for farming. Given the mountainous topography there is nearly always a local supply of easily-won building materials. However, sophisticated engineering was commonly required to import water supplies via irrigation channels. Many of these are seen today as spectacular winding threads across the mountain faces and have become an integral part of the highly important historic landscape. Often houses sought a large boulder against which the walls could be set (a 'mother-stone' or anchor) – perhaps continuing a shepherd tradition of penning animals. Forts often took advantage of up-standing rock outcrops and cliff edges.

Figs. 80-85. Traditional house construction (all by D. Lorimer, 1935).
Top left, the *wazir's* house located in the highest section of Baltit village, just beneath the fort.
Top right, a small lane and adjacent houses on the steep slope of the old Baltit village.
Centre and below left, stages of traditional house construction with rubble stone and timber beams.
Below right, the central roof opening of the *ha* resulting from an overlay of three narrowing, diagonally superimposed layers of beams (compare with fig. 97).

Overall, the present distribution of settlements indicates that the safest locations have been settled for the longest time, with historic buildings proving the stability of the respective places. Meanwhile, new settlements are now tending to move onto land where there is increased vulnerability to natural hazards.

In respect of traditional housing, a number of common characteristics can be discussed: they are mostly single storey to avoid wall deformation due to slender wall construction. Houses tend to hug the ground, thus limiting exposure to the freezing winter winds. They are larger where flat space is available and small when built in clusters or on steep manmade terraces or natural rock slopes. Generally, house size does not totally depend on material availability – structural materials are plentiful, even if hard to win. Stone was used when possible and otherwise replaced by soil. Roofs are mostly flat and are provided with a compacted soil cover. This allows for simple beam systems and offers the possibility to use the roof terrace for summer outdoor living. There

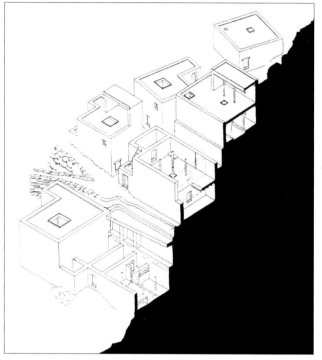

Fig. 86. Axonometric section of the terraced village slope below Baltit fort, with tiers of stepped housing clusters (see also fig. 272).

are exceptions to this, where former colonial buildings have gently pitched soil roofs. In some valleys south of Gilgit pitched roofs, typically built with timber planks, reduce snow accumulation and create a large cavity above the ceiling, providing thermal insulation and a safe storage space. On very steep slopes, houses are often terraced and follow the contour lines, so that the stepped roofscape results in cascading verandas. Up in the mountain pastures, the summer houses are quite different to those in the valleys, no more than loosely clustered single-space round huts composed of low loose rubble walls with thatched conical roofs. Farm animals are kept in low-walled corrals.

The traditional stone walls of domestic rural Karakoram structures are generally weak: this is because they have shallow foundations (without spread footings) so are highly susceptible to differential movements and cracking. Most walls are built with stone rubble of variable quality found locally and placed rather haphazardly in point to point contact. Between the stones thick irregular mortar mud is then placed or thrown to fill the gaps and increase structural stability. Often large stones are used for the inside and outside wall faces. They are internally adjusted and wedged in place to establish a vertical face. Frequently stones change size in vertical direction: as the wall approaches shoulder height, the stones get smaller because they are manually lifted. The internal core of the wall is progressively infilled with small loose rubble, stone chips discarded from knapping and leftover mortar. In domestic buildings 'through-stones' and long 'quoins' are rarely used.

In the following paragraphs, a much more detailed analysis of the most prominent traditional fort and palace structures in the Northern Areas is given, while the discussion of equally important religious buildings, such as mosques, *khanqahs* and *astanas* is left to the authors of chapters 6 and 7 of this book. However, much of the construction techniques and structural issues presented in this section, also applies to the monumental religious buildings.

A TYPOLOGY OF FORTS

Forts and palaces are the largest and most spectacular type of monument found in the region. All surviving forts, as well as the sites of disappeared ones, have been visited during the conservation campaigns for Baltit and Shigar forts and thus it is possible to construct a typological development model, taking account of their style, age, location and function (based on excellent contemporary accounts) but excluding architectural details and ornamentation.

Type 1

This building is the 'fortified' tower-house, with the *shikari* tower of Altit fort and Baltit fort Phase 1 being good historic examples. Typically, this type comprises a free-standing tower of three or more floors with an enlarged top shooting gallery and with one or more attached single-storey basic living rooms. Baltit was once a single tower-house but was quickly extended into three such units. These were then interlinked to become a cluster complex able to be changed into a large-sized fort. The fortified family house was common throughout the western Karakoram and indeed the classic form is still to be seen in the Indus valley south of Gilgit, down to Besham. New but traditionally designed tower-houses are found in Tangir and modernised versions are now springing up in roadside development areas around Chilas. As the Altit *shikari* tower is scientifically dated to be more than one thousand years old, this fortification type has a long history and provides us with evidence of the oldest surviving buildings in the Karakoram (fig. 88). The distribution of these forts is suggestive of a high degree of autonomy. In Hunza many tower-houses existed and seem to have formed networks of watchtowers – originally perhaps of private character, but then as part of an overall defensive system for the valley, run from the control hub at Baltit. Only a few of them have survived in Karimabad and Ganish (pls. 13, 118).

Fig. 87. Hypothetic reconstruction of various stages of the development of Baltit fort, from a single to multiple watchtowers, and eventually (after the collapse of the upper parts of the towers) to the consolidated predecessor of the present fort shown in fig. 89, pl. 34.

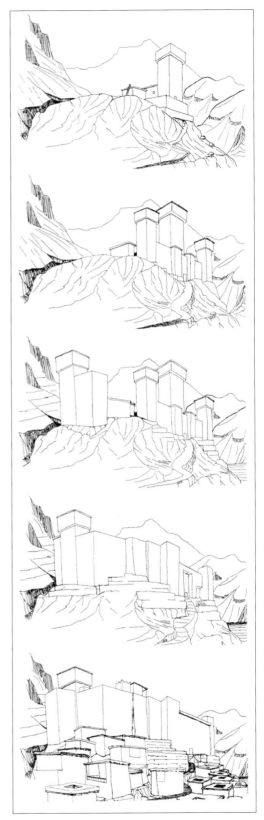

Fig. 88. The main tower of Altit fort,
representative of the 'Type 1' stage of fort construction.

Fig. 89. Today's condition of Baltit fort (after restoration),
composed of various layers of rooms wrapped around the initial
tower structures, representative of 'Type 3' fort construction.

Type 2

As seen at Baltit, the small-scale tower-house gave rise to the more substantial fort with greater military
capability – supporting a feudal lord with his private army and entourage and controlling stores, water supply, routes and associated servant houses and villages. In the Indus and Hunza valleys these forts appear to
be of two types. Type 2 is the pure purpose-built fort, typically a square structure with four corner *shikari*
towers. Classic examples are the fort on the roadside of Besham, the great Swat fort and, further to the west,
Gupis fort and Chitral fort (the one withstanding the famous 1895 siege, but then replaced by a 'colonial'
and imitation 'Moghul' structure.) An untypical example is buried within the early phases of Baltit fort
and another is the core structure of Gilgit fort. This type of fort builds upon examples found to the west,
for instance in Afghanistan. Gilgit and Hunza appear to be the eastern limits of its distribution.

Type 3

Another type of the local, larger fort results from complex phased expansions of a smaller edifice – such
as found within Baltit, Altit, Nilt, Nager and Astor forts – each one being irregularly formed in response
to the topography and varying functional demands, thus showing a unique shape and internal arrangement.
Baltit, with its constricted footprint, develops upward and is wrapped around with further and precariously

Figs. 90, 91. Left, the fortified palace of Kharmang (from De Filippi, 1924, p. 36) and, right, the fortified palace of Rondu, representative of 'Type 5' forts/palaces.

founded layers of rooms – each phase marked by an added external shell. The last episode here is the present whitewashed wall overlooking Karimabad.

Type 4
The clustering of old and disparate housing elements also gave rise to the 'fortified village'. Here, the settlement consisted in tightly packed houses, mosques and stables that became encapsulated within a defensive wall. Usually the defences were completed with *shikari* watchtowers. Ganish is a fine surviving example where the buildings are mostly stone and rather haphazardly distributed within the cluster. Only one of seven towers survives at the main village entrance (pl. 118). South of Gilgit, Gor and Harban villages are tight clusters of wooden structures regularly planned with a set of external towers and connected houses facing inwards. Baltit village once also had a defensive wall and a ring of watchtowers. The line of the wall can be traced and one tower fully survives. The old mill above the Berber channel is the remnant of what must have been a five- or six-storey *shikari*, with massive walls and possibly the tallest in Hunza.

Type 5
Another more mansion-like type of fortification was developed in Baltistan, as a typical residence of the local *rajas*. Here the building is square or rectangular, two or three storeys high with a rectangular grid of rooms and with the top floor having a central courtyard with surrounding veranda. Such structures are not more than three hundred years old. Excellent examples are found at Rondu, Skardu, Kiris and Khaplu.

Rondu fort (fig. 91) was rebuilt a hundred years ago with reused materials and in the same form. It is about twenty-five by twenty metres and is mostly two storeys high, with surviving elements of a third one. Half the top floor is ruinous, with walls and roof missing. The external walls are of cator and cribbage timber technique. Ground-floor walls have stone infill with adobe in the first floor walls. Externally it is rendered, except on the wooden elements where render is detached or was not applied. The first floor is reached by passing through a ground-floor room (now an open area) and then up a right twist spiral wooden stair – not of a real defensive capability and perhaps reflecting the fort's relatively recent construction date. The first floor rooms are set around a two-storey canopied courtyard measuring about 6 x 4.5 metres with a 1.5-metre-wide veranda.

Kiris is a single phase building comprising two floors set on a base platform. The building sits at a high point with houses to east, north and west. There are cliffs immediately to the south with fields beyond the settlement. The platform is of large stones and boulders un-rendered with occasional small openings on the east and south sides for animal waste removal. The superstructure cator walls are more than one metre thick. Wall filling is all of adobe blocks; they were last rendered eight years ago and have added chopped straw while the walls are finished with a fine slip and then mud paint. There is just one way in via a raised entrance platform and the staircase has a right-angle bend to the left through the wall, suggestive of a defensive design. Lower rooms now used for animals and storage were once winter quarters. The living space today is on the first floor where there are twenty rooms set around the courtyard.

These forts may have developed out of the more complex Kashmiri fortified house, for which there is one surviving example – Shigar palace. The original structure was built partially off a massive boulder in a square and with an architecturally sophisticated rectangular arrangement of rooms. It was then radically extended and built up to its present form. At Khaplu, the palace is a unique five-storey tower with a full-height central light well and with an arrangement of three concentric rows of rooms around it – the most important being on the outside with windows overlooking the spectacular landscape. This is another variant of Type 5 and may have some similarities to the tall forts of Ladakh.

The Type 5 style did not migrate westwards beyond Rondu, but Baltit fort has adopted some of its features – the courtyard effect of the *rani's* (queen's) summer room and a nineteenth-century modification comprising an internal courtyard and surrounding guest rooms at roof level. However, this seems an obvious arrangement for summer use and does not need to be interpreted as a transfer of architectural style.

During the 'colonial' times, further types of forts were introduced and designed by British military engineers, reflecting the needs of a modern-day garrison and its regional functions (the forts of Gilgit, Chitral, Chilas, and so on). Some other forts show features introduced by the maharajas of Kashmir via their Dogra troops (Kharpucho fort and the now disappeared Shigar village fort). Interesting as they are in terms of continuing local building techniques, these structures no longer fully reflect the traditional fort and palace styles and functions and are therefore not considered in this article.

STRUCTURAL CONCEPTS AND MATERIALS USED IN TRADITIONAL BUILDINGS

All traditional buildings in the Karakoram – whether houses, forts or religious buildings – illustrate a vernacular structural system, using the same basic set of components. The principle is one of simple construction so there is less to go wrong. Because all features are visible, repair is sustainable with minimal finances. Failed materials are easily discarded, with the exception of the often great and ornamented columns that are family heirlooms recycled over the centuries.

There is an inherent understanding of the three local building materials (stone, soil and wood). They are used on a daily basis and their strengths and weaknesses are well appreciated. Throughout the Karakoram there is a plentiful supply of building stone. The granodiorites and gneisses are preferred and the often very high mica content means that hammer blows easily fracture off the required lumps. However, slate, marble and basalt are utilised when found outcropping – whatever is used always has a strength and durability far better than is structurally necessary.

Soils are found throughout the region, deriving from a natural breakdown of the local rock and as a transported product of glaciers and rivers. There are endless variations, but consistent is the lack of clay minerals and the high silt and fine sand content. Generally, the soils are rich in quartz and biotite mica and it is the latter that makes them cohesive – the mineral particles stick together by having strong electrical charges and large pore suctions. The soil is commonly used as adobe blocks and its use in historic monuments suggests an introduction in the late nineteenth century. In Baltistan, rammed earth and wattle and daub are traditional soil building methods. The trick in using soil is to minimise shrinkage cracks and this is done by control of soil particle grading, the water used in its manipulation and

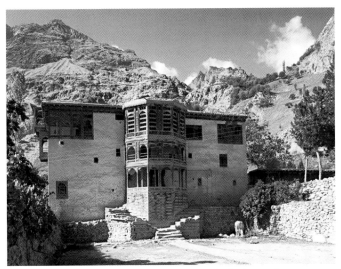

Fig. 92. Khaplu fort, the most impressive example of a 'Type 5' fortified palace in Baltistan (see also pls. 45, 46, 96).

by heavy compaction. Occasionally, chopped straw and oils are added to help stabilise it and achieve better durability. Most problems stem from weak and friable mortars, formed of a sloppy mud mix that results in major shrinking and fabric cracking. In Hunza, soil renowned for its strength is 'Damul', a fine grained lacustrine soil of a pseudo clay character, making it highly suitable for waterproofing flat roofs and compacted floors. At Kiris, the fine-grained calcareous soil, slowly formed in the bottom of a lake has superb strength and this is reflected in the beautiful tradition domestic architecture found there.

In the past, hardwoods such as mature Himalayan pine, walnut, mulberry and apricot were the common structural elements. In Hunza and Baltistan, juniper was the highly favoured wood for its strength and resistance to decay – thus being used for the cator beams and cribbage columns. Today, the main building woods are poplar and willow, fast-growing softwoods. But they are weak, very bendy and not durable. Pine of various sorts, a better structural timber, is now imported from south of Gilgit, but generally in short unsuitable lengths. In Baltistan, if special timbers are required, there are still some fine mountain forests.

Whilst considerable effort went into channelling water for agricultural purposes, there is very limited evidence of water management in historic buildings. We find poor siting with regard to springs and streams, no storage cisterns and no satisfactory lavatory systems and drains. Rainwater was not collected, either dripping off roofs or thrown off with simple spouts. Wall bases were not saved from water erosion and not protected with damp-proof courses and plinths.

The typical structure has external load-bearing walls founded on strip foundations. Internal walls supporting roof members are on similar foundations but columns are founded on local shallow pad stones. Partition walls are usually set on the internal ground. Wall foundations are always shallow – hand dug to an easily dug depth between 0.3 and 0.75 of a metre deep. Where the foundation trenches encounter boulders these hard spots are left in place and not extracted and where soft spots are found these are not replaced with compacted fill. Nearly always the foundations are stone footings set at the same width as the above ground walls. Such foundations are formed of dry-stone masonry, there never having been a cementation method allowing them to work as a rigid ground-beam This means there has been no understanding of spreading and reducing bearing stresses in places where the foundation soils are weak. Thus foundations are conceived independent from soils with variable strength which often results in differential wall settlement.

Typical walls of simple houses are built in stone but where buildings are sited on broad flood planes or terraces with suitable silty soils, earth wall construction was preferred. The walls are built directly off the foundation. Damp-proof courses, such as sheets of slate, are not used. In the simple buildings the walls are narrow (one stone or an adobe block thick), which means they are rapid to build, but have a high slender ratio making them susceptible to distortion. House walls are generally low, two metres or less, since room height responds best to harsh winter conditions. Because of the small size of stone and blocks the walls are generally irregular and traditionally had sub-rounded corners. (Sharp corners having no interlocking load-spreading long quoins would have been weak.) The stone to stone contact means that they are volume stable, with the mortar render thrown on to the faces to complete them. Soil walls are slower to construct as the material has to progressively dry out to achieve its working strength.

As previously described, the more sophisticated buildings have better formed walls, with double skins or formed in solid dressed masonry. This means the wall faces are more regular and can have well-built corners. The best quality walls as seen in the forts, mosques and expensive houses, incorporate timber members – usually cators and occasionally cribbage. The timber provides a degree of ductility, helping to strap the wall fabric together and able to accept large deformation strains (see below).

Windows and doors have timber lintels that are relatively short, allowing forces to tightly arch around the openings. These are kept deliberately small, in order to avoid structural weakening. The frames also provide additional stiffening to the wall structure but can easily fall out in an earthquake as the lintels are not so well tied into the wall.

Most domestic buildings have flat roofs, thus recognising their functional uses. Roofs are universally supported on timber beams – in simple buildings the beams are left as semi-round tree trunks which bare into the walls. In better-built structures, roof timbers sit on and are pegged to timber wall plates. This means the roof structure can work 'monolithically', gaining strength from a shear plate configuration.

A harsh climate can be modified internally by suitable design, materials and construction. In the traditional architecture of the region, thermal efficiency involved building thick walls, but there is no tradition of insulated wall cavities. Buildings are therefore set low, trapping air within an open fabric confined between rendered surfaces. Clustering of individual houses helps achieve better group performance. Exposed openings are sealed up in winter. Keeping animal byres and hay storage next to the house (or even below or above it) helped improve the insulation. It is clearly appreciated that the soil had a good thermal performance, now proved by our own scientific investigations. This efficiency is due to the high mica content – also a modern heat insulator in the electrical industry.

Render is usually seen as a finish to otherwise rough stone and soil walls. It may or may not be lime-washed and helps to retain mortar and earth blocks in place. Thus it has no structural function, but is a sacrificial

Fig. 93. The restored Shigar fort/palace as it is seen today, from the riverside (see also pls. 59, 88).

wearing material easily replaced. In rough walls it also helps to stop draughts and heat loss. Importantly, as it is weak it provides the first sign of structural movement. In conservation crack patterns act like instrumentation in providing evidence about the cause, severity and rate of structural movement.

Portland cements and concrete have got a bad reputation as forcing change in traditional building practices and are poorly manufactured here, causing rapid decay. Concrete has been responsible for horrendous earthquake death tolls. It is avoided in conservation, as it is often too strong and brittle and used for a 'quick-fix'. Transportation costs, until recent times, inhibited cement import and building lime was locally made. Thus we see lime renders and mortars being used on prestigious buildings from the 1920s onwards. Lime mortars are still functional at Chilas and Kharpucho forts and remnants of lime renders have been found in Baltit and Shigar forts.

ENGINEERING CONSIDERATIONS

The long vernacular tradition raises the question as to what extent construction of new buildings can and should follow past practice, without requiring more formal engineering design. Today, our designs are shown on drawings supported by engineering calculation and satisfying local authority regulations and codes of engineering practice. Some major factors contributing to a good engineering structure are discussed below, as an attempt to review traditional technologies and guide conservation approaches.

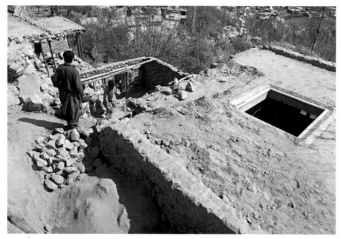

Fig. 94. Roof maintenance and repair is essential to avoid damage to traditional houses.

Wall slender ratio

In earth walls or single-thickness rubble stone walls a ratio of thickness to height of less than 1:10 would be appropriate, but often it is stretched to more than 1:15. Thus many old houses show tilting, bowing and twisting walls. In double-storey walls, these effects can be counteracted by the restraints provided by floor beams and wall plates. In monuments, the slender ratio is as much as 1:20. The façade of Baltit fort is about forty centimetres thick and ten metres high and it is for this reason that the walls of Baltit, Altit and Shigar forts are reinforced with a framework of cators and cribbage (see below).

The slender ratio is essential to keep the wall's centre of gravity within the middle one third of the wall's cross-section at foundation level. Clearly, once the centre of gravity lies outside the line of the foundation the wall can fall over unless restrained by floors and reinforcement. At Baltit, the grand façade is out of plumb by nearly 1.5 metres and, but for the timber elements, would have fallen a long time ago. Another trick that is seen in traditional cluster housing, such as Ganish, is to share loads on zigzagging party walls and have staggered wall junctions that provide buttressing effects, these stiffening up the thin walls.

Compressive, shear and tension stresses

It is well appreciated by everyone in the region that stone is strong and best for walls – far better than concrete blocks. But surprisingly it is expensive now. Soil is weak but adequate for providing mud bricks, mortar and render. Both stone and dried soil are not self-compacting when built up. This is why stone walls are often dry built, like a rubble field terrace wall with the mortar thrown on afterwards. In local terms, it is also well appreciated that the small modular units of stone or mud brick do not have a high resistance to tensional forces, they can easily be pulled or shaken apart by natural movements or human actions. Also, such walls can shear in case of stress concentrations and these only need to be small in the case of dried soil. Throughout the Karakoram, most old structures show complex strain-cracking patterns illustrating tensile and shear failure, such as diagonal cracks at wall corners, below the ends of beams bearing directly into walls or down through the core of a wall. Buildings are particularly prone to these failure modes when involved in earthquakes. Traditional timber cators and cribbage walls are the local solution to these problems.

Dead loads

Dead loads are the permanent loads resulting from a wall's own weight, along with roof loads and those of very permanent fixtures such as roof water tanks. Such loads do not significantly change during the life of the building. In the Karakoram, dead loads tend to be the only design consideration used when sizing the foundations, wall thickness and roof connections. Given the materials being used, a typical load for a single storey structure ranges from 10 to 25kN/m. The dead loads only increase when rooms are added on top of the building. The foundations are generally not designed with spare dead load capacity for this. Fortu-

35.

Previous page
34. View of the restored Baltit fort towering above the village, from the veranda of the restored Ghulwating mosque (fig. 105).

36.

35. Baltit fort sitting on a steep terraced hill, and surrounded by mountain peaks.

36. The royal dais on the second floor terrace of Baltit fort (see also fig. 300).

37. View from the dais into the Hunza valley.

38.

39.

40.

38. The small corner tower of Altit fort, above the village, with delicate woodcarvings on the window frame.

39. The main tower of Altit fort, as accessed from the west.

40. The vertical cliff of Altit fort seen from the riverside, with the village on the high plateau (see also pls. 10, 15).

41.

42.

41-43. The restored Amburiq mosque near Shigar (see also fig. 293), with its small prayer hall and the Tibetan-type lantern and spire.

44-46. The representative front side of Khaplu fort (see also pl. 96) in its present unrestored condition. Below, one of the elaborately carved lateral balconies (left), and the interior of the projecting room in the centre of the top floor, with typical ornamental ceiling.

43.

44.

45.

46.

47.

47, 48. Exterior and interior view
of Chakchan mosque in Khaplu
(see also fig. 148).

49. Tomb and shrine of Mir Aref in Tagas
(Baltistan), close to the *khanqah*
of the same saint (fig. 133).
In the background, the tomb and shrine
of Mir Ishaq (fig. 132).

48.

50.

51.

52.

50-52. Courtyard of the *khanqah* in Sefarkhur, Churga (near Shigar),
with its large maple tree. Below, the ornamented entrance door and the front side.

53. Interior of the Sayyed Mohammad *astana* in Khaplu.

54. Interior of the *khanqah* in Kiris (Baltisan).

53.

54.

55. The restored entrance to the Shigar fort/palace
with an ornamental frieze along the projecting beam
of the upper floor.

56. The restored Shigar fort/palace and the Old House
as seen from the river.

57, 58. Details of the ornamental frieze
on the projecting beam in pl. 55.

Following pages
59. View from the cliff of the restored Shigar fort/palace
complex and the surrounding settlement.
The restored fort/palace and the Old House are to the right
(site plan fig. 252), the new residence of the *raja* in the centre,
and Khilingrong mosque (pl. 60) can be seen on the left.
The Amacha garden is located between
the foot of the cliff and the fort.

56.

55.

57.   58.

60.

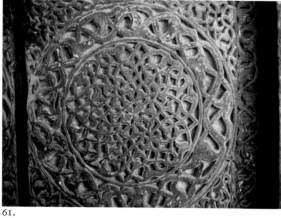

61.

60. The restored double-storey
Khilingrong mosque
near Shigar fort.

61. Woodcarving detail
from a door in Khaplu palace.

62. The carved door frame
of Khilingrong mosque.

62.

nately, in many places the additions consist of light-weight summer structures. Examples of thin wattle and daub panels are to be seen in the Shigar valley and along the road from Skardu to Khaplu.

Live and dynamic loads

'Active' loads result from forces imposed by the weight of people and movable furniture, for example, and from exceptional or infrequent events. 'Dynamic' stresses may result from people occasionally dancing on roofs and animals charging into walls. Or, they occur at times of very strong winds, avalanches, mudflows and earthquakes. These events cause additional, sudden stresses that spread down the walls to the foundation, often resulting in an additional ten to forty per cent of the dead-load, and much more in case of an earthquake. More significantly, such events cause large lateral forces through the walls that are not designed for this. The additional loads produce cyclical swaying, tilting and even torsional twisting and differential roof uplift. Once the movements have occurred, the elements rarely return to the original positions, which results in progressive and permanent distortion. As the load paths tend to follow places of weakness, the structural system tends to progressively degrade until sudden failure occurs. Excessive one-off dynamic loads cause catastrophic damage to domestic structures and account for the high levels of collapse observed in the earthquakes at Patan 1976 and Darel 1982.

Through their survival, historic buildings prove that they have absorbed (and recovered from) the impact of considerable dynamic loads. Usually they were better built and had a higher resistance capacity due to special engineering devices (see below). For the modern eye, some resulting structural distortion helps to create character and give a sense of age and survival against the ravages of nature.

Factors of safety

In the area, tradition dictates what works and what does not – a Darwinistic approach that has generally succeeded. If a building fails, then it is rebuilt with modifications, and if these work, then they are copied. In this sense, buildings are always 'fit-for-purpose'. Generally, they have an appropriate level of safety against everyday incidents, can be maintained to the original quality and can adapt to simple new uses – therefore they have good functional qualities. It is interesting to note that the Royal Geographical Society's 1980 Karakoram/Yasin studies found that priority for good housing was lower than other concerns, such as better living conditions, richer crops and improved education. This picture is now changing, as houses are upgraded, are built for fashion and have an investment value. More attention thus has to be given to the factors making it safe in the long run. Factors of safety are a measure of reserve capacity and usually apply to engineering parameters. For example, if a foundation soil has an 'ultimate capacity' of $100 kN/m$ but only $50 kN/m$ is applied, the factor of safety against failure is 2. While this factor of safety may be considered acceptable in terms of foundation failure, it may lead to foundation settlements that are unacceptable. The term 'allowable bearing capacity' considers the performance of the foundation. For example, if $30 kN/m$ is applied to the above foundation soil, a factor of safety of 3 against failure would be achieved. For soil, this would typically result in settlements of less than 25 mm. For a domestic structure using soil and stone rubble walls, one would generally be looking for an overall factor of safety for the building of 3 to 5, compared with a house in Islamabad that would be 5 to 10. Safety factors can also apply to resisting natural hazards such as strong winds, landslides, floods and earthquakes.

Determining safety factors for historic buildings undergoing conservation is important but very difficult.

Fig. 95. A small elevated mosque in Ganish, sitting on a tower base and exemplifying the 'cribbage' structure in the corners and the timber lacing in the walls.

The adopted safety factors must result in a building being safe for hundreds of years and this involves predicting and taking into account future unknowns. In the early days of a conservation project, a risk assessment is carried out as a result of condition surveys, design processes and likely reuse. The overall safety factor being derived from partial ones, comprehensively higher safety has an additional cost. However, it is difficult to obtain an appropriate level of future safety, as this implies thinking forward many hundreds of years and assuming one or more unique disasters. Conservation ethics require minimal and one-off intervention, yet there may be unpredictable global climatic changes, or extra security measures to be taken against new uses – some of which cannot be known at the time. Thus there is a delicate balance to be achieved between authenticity and retention of a scientific database on the one hand and functional design and economic viability on the other hand.

Risks

Part of a modern engineering process is the identification of development risks, which are then taken into account when prescribing building safety factors. In the past, hazards and vulnerability were clearly taken into account, confirmed by the fact that most older settlements were well sited. Modern development has a tendency, as previously noted, to occupy hazard-prone land. This is not always a success and there are examples where houses on denuding cliff edges have been abandoned, where whole villages have been swept away by mudflows and where whole chunks of landscape now lie submerged in new lakes. Risk assessment commonly examines: the quality of building materials; the location of suitable agricultural land; the potential for landslides, avalanches, cliff collapses, rolling stones and mudflows; floods, mudflows, local locations of torrential rainfall; local soft and hard soils difficult for foundation construction; earthquakes; supply of drinking water; and defence capabilities. It is evident from the above discussion that most risks result from sudden impact natural hazards and vulnerability to them.

Earthquake resistance

There are four construction techniques that would suggest regional familiarity with earthquake hazards. The simplest improvement method was to build a structure against a large well-embedded boulder, this serving as a stable anchor, free of vibrations that would induce damage in walls. Another earthquake resistant feature is the simple traditional house structure seen throughout the Karakoram and down the Indus to Besham. In the 1976 Patan earthquake, when over 1500 people were killed, there was substantial building damage. One observation suggested that the toll would have been greater but for the fact that many roofs performed independently of the walls. While walls fell down, the roofs stood up because the roofs beams, supported by posts and with structural pinned capitals and foundations, were built first and the walls afterwards. The next type of structure is found in the region spanning Skardu to Khaplu. Here walls contain large numbers of major-sized internal timber posts jointed to wall plate beams, altogether providing a hidden, hinged structural frame. Interestingly, the posts take loads separately from the first and second floors down to the foundations. It is said that such walls are tested by ramming with a farm animal, ensuring the structure can sway. The walls are effectively infill panels, somewhat independently working at each floor level, able to deform in an earthquake and to be replaced if damaged.

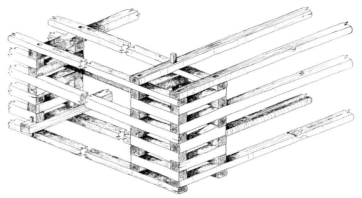

Fig. 96. Schematic drawing of the 'cribbage' cage in the wall corners, as well as the horizontal 'cators' to be filled with rubble stone and mud, and plastered on the elevations.

AN OUTSTANDING VERNACULAR ENGINEERING DEVICE

'Timber lacing', or the combination of cator and cribbage is a most sophisticated earthquake resisting construction technique, finely demonstrated in the great monuments of Hunza and Baltistan. Here, the walls of a structure are horizontally strapped with beams, locally known as cators. The timber is generally prepared to a five to twelve centimetre square section and kept as long as possible. The horizontal beams are placed into the inside and outside wall faces at vertical intervals of 0.6 to 1.3 metres. In walls of lower quality, the timber use is less frequent and may only reinforce the corners. Often the timber lengths are not jointed or nailed together. In better constructed walls, the face timbers are tied together through the wall thickness with joined/nailed cross pieces at one to three metre intervals. Where the beam is of insufficient length for the whole length of the wall, two or more pieces are connected with tension-resisting scarf and pegged joints. The beams at the corners are also cross jointed and pegged so that the whole building is strapped or laced together. Breaks in the integrity of the cator 'ring beams' may occur at doors and windows. Altogether, the beams form a lacing that straps the stone (or soil) elements together like the metal rings found around barrels. Thus the timber provides wall reinforcement and strong resistance against tension and bending, thereby complementing the qualities of stone or soil blocks that work well in compression. Reinforced concrete is but a modern version of this.

The advantages of constructing with horizontal timbers are manifold: this technique makes it easy to build straight-sided walls and dispenses with over-designed foundations. It creates strong corner joints due to long timbers providing tensile/bending resistance to out-of-plane wall movements. Finally, it also provides a system which allows the frame and roof to be built first and the walls to be filled in later. The disadvantages of timber lacing are its vulnerability to fire and to rapid decay, especially in the core of a wall and away from places where structural damage is easily observed. Also, timber can distort due to seasonal changes in moisture content and defects can cause the wall fabric above to be dislodged for repairs below.

As the forts in Hunza suggest, many structures that use timber lacing are of a military character, with the technique going back to pre-Christian times. It appears to have an origin in the eastern Mediterranean and Alexander the Great is known to have made use of the technology in his Asian campaigns. It is part of the classic *murus gallicus* described by Julius Caesar and it is later shown on Trajan's Column in Rome. From a general appreciation of warfare up to the twentieth century, the military advantages of timber lacing are obvious: walls could be built very quickly, with random rubble and without slow-setting lime mortars, the timber being the structural tie along and through the wall. Construction can be expedient reaching maximum height with a minimal volume of material and can occur in rugged terrain – where ordinary stone walls would need to be tied with foundations in to slopes and cliff. Timber-laced walls could not be easily breached by ballistics – from catapults and cannon – and could not be toppled by mining the foundations – the timber allowing for walls to span cavities and for corners to cantilever. Localised destruction could be rapidly repaired as the timber reduces the chances of collapse. Finally, the timbers can be dismantled and reused following a modular 'Lego' approach.

With respect to earthquakes, timber lacing can to a large extent absorb and resist wall cracking and distortion mechanisms. This effectiveness has been seen in recent major earthquakes, for example, in Turkey 1976, Pakistan 1981 and Yemen 1982. During conservation of Baltit fort in 1995 we personally felt the structure swaying around as a response to an earthquake that occurred in far-off Nuristan. Seismic testing of buildings on a 'shaking table' has also proved the value of timber lacing and in Turkey there is an engineering code of practice for the incorporation of timber 'hatils' into masonry walls.

Timber cribbage appears to be a wall building technique that is commonly found in the area from Nuristan to Baltistan, including Hunza, where it is strongly represented in Altit and Baltit forts. Whether its use in buildings originated in one place and spread into other areas, or whether it evolved independently in many areas is still unknown. The technique consists of short pieces of squared timber staked up two at a time and then in alternative directions to form an open box. Progressively they rise to become an open-frame column. The timbers are pegged together and the whole column can move around much like a human vertebrae. Cribbage columns are mainly built at wall junctions, to substitute for stone quoins and to supplement the jointing of timber lacing. They are commonly used along walls to provide tie walls and floors together and a mechanism to efficiently transfer loads down the floor to the foundations. Obviously, cribbage is a very useful construction technique in an earthquake-prone area.

While it was currently used in religious buildings and palaces, wall cribbage was most valuable for fort structures, since it has many military advantages over an ordinary rampart. Vulnerable corners are much stronger; the rampart can be made taller and narrower for the same quantity of rubble infill; the system can flex and recover much like a tree in strong wind; the pegging is engineered so that more load applied on the column makes it stronger and less susceptible to impact-induced lateral distortions; the column-beam connections absorb large dynamic stresses created by the defenders' cannon fire. Finally, it is very difficult to pull the system apart; rather it has to be slowly undone by a well-orchestrated attack. Thus, even from a modern engineering point of view, the traditional construction techniques provide ingenious and most efficient solutions to the problems encountered.

6. Traditional Art and Architecture in Hunza and Nager

JÜRGEN WASIM FREMBGEN

To study the tradition of woodcarving in the remote high mountain regions of Hunza and Nager means dealing with indigenous folk art at the periphery of the Muslim world. In this regard, we can expect artistic tradition to show less Islamic specificity and to be more rooted in local contexts, including exposure to cultural impulses from the nearby areas of Baltistan and Kashmir.

Within northern Pakistan, the former kingdoms of Hunza and Nager constitute important politico-geographical units situated in the mountain range of north-west Karakoram. They are inhabited by Burusho and Shina speaking Dards as well as by Wakhi, who immigrated from the nineteenth century onwards from north-eastern Afghanistan into the northern territory of Hunza, close to the border with China. The mountain peoples of Hunza and Nager are settled in oases along the main Hunza valley, with the Hunzukuts living on the right bank and the Nagerkuts on the left bank of the river. Furthermore, Nager also includes the side valley branching off at the village of Sumaiyar, as well as the area of Chalt-Chaprot and the Bar valley extending from the lower Hunza valley. The main river represents a clear-cut religious boundary with Twelver Shias in Nager and Ismaili Shias in Hunza. There is only a tiny minority of Twelvers (or Imami Shias) in the Hunza village of Ganish and its surrounding hamlets.

The population of these former centralised states share a well-defined and differentiated historical identity which must have been particularly developed since Islamisation in the period between the sixteenth and seventeenth centuries. History and religion found their manifestation in representative architectural monuments in which woodcarving traditions – the main subject of this article – feature prominently.

In both Hunza and Nager, architectural constructions of royal palaces, private houses, mosques (*masjids*), Shia places of assembly (*imambarhas, matam-sarais*), and shrines of saints are usually decorated by ornate woodcarvings. The main types of timber used for construction and carving are plane, pine, apricot, mulberry, and finally a high quality walnut wood particularly favoured for the *mimbar* (pulpit) in *imambarhas*. As an introduction to this folk art of woodcarving, an overview of the different types of secular and religious monuments will be given, before focussing in detail on the local

Fig. 97. Elaborately carved post in Altit fort (see also figs. 205, 206).

133

vocabulary of patterns and motifs. Mention will be made of a selected number of buildings considered to be representative examples of vernacular architecture. Notes and photographs of these structures and their woodcarvings were collected during field trips in 1981, 1982, 1991, 1992, 1999 and 2004. In the meantime, some of them have been renovated beyond recognition or even totally demolished; in other cases buildings and their specimens of artistic woodwork have been carefully preserved (such as the royal forts of Hunza). In some cases, loose single artefacts from dilapidated or destroyed buildings have been reintegrated into newly erected structures.

ROYAL FORTS

In their inner structure, the forts of Hunza very much reflect the age-old building traditions of the archaic house of the Central Asian mountain regions. In fact, they consist of a densely clustered and fortified agglomeration of such archaic, single-room housing units, each one centred on its *ha*, the core of the house, surrounded by four posts and a small roof opening to the sky.

The most ancient castle belonging to the royal dynasty of Hunza is situated on the edge of the village of Altit, in a commanding position on a cliff high above the Hunza river (pl. 40). Altit fort is probably around nine hundred years old, showing traces of several phases of construction. The oldest part of the building is to be found in a lantern-roofed room apparently used for official receptions. Laid out in the usual, roughly square form widespread in the Pamir, Hindukush, Karakoram and Western Himalaya, with the roof resting on four central wooden posts, it contains the most ancient surviving woodcarvings (fig. 97). The massive, elaborately carved post at the rear, relating to the platform on the right side of the room (which in private houses is still reserved for men), is of special significance, as it refers to the cosmological concept of the 'pillar of the world'.[1] Its profile tapers towards the triple voluted capital and it is intricately carved on all four sides within three delimited zones. Stepping outside the dark labyrinthine interior chambers, similar floral and geometric patterns on several broad decorative door frames attract the visitor's eye, for instance

Fig. 98. Carved door frame in a private home in Baltit-Diramishal (Hunza).

the portals of the tall central watchtower (sixteenth century) and of the adjacent small one-room building (fig. 13). Remarkably, door panels are never carved.

Likewise, in the over seven-hundred-years-old Baltit fort (restored 1992-1996 by the Aga Khan Trust for Culture) with its more than seventy identified phases of construction, central posts and door frames feature particularly rich carving. The stylised patterns are finely executed in different grades of high and low relief, often grooved, but also deeply cut through as can be seen, for example, in the ruler's bedroom on the second floor (pl. 78). Here, as well as in private houses, the door frames of the small cubicles, constructed in the corners of a room and used as storage space, show several narrow ornamental bands. Another element of interior architecture, typical for the private chambers of local palaces, are the decorative wooden niches inspired by the *chini-khanas* found between Ottoman Turkey and Iran in the west and Mughal India in the east. In Baltit fort, a beautiful older example can be seen in the queen's room on the second floor. A more recent one, dating from the first half of the twentieth century, made in open latticework is found in the sunny living room on the second floor and was used to exhibit precious objects. Lattice windows serving ventilation are a traditional feature of local mosques, but in the royal palaces of Hunza and Nager and in some private homes they assume a dominant role as architectural components of attached verandas, creating dramatic effects of light and shade.

This sort of 'open timberwork' with geometric patterns set into rectangular panels is widely known in the subcontinent as *jali*. In the Karakoram it is known as *Kashmiri panjira* and has apparently been borrowed from Kashmir quite late, during the nineteenth century. Characteristic specimens can be seen on the veranda shading the royal dais and in the adjacent balcony of Baltit fort, both made by Ustad Surato, from Tsil-Ganish, in the early twentieth century, and in a more elaborate form in the distinguished house of the late Raja Muzafar ud-Din Shah in the village of Ghulmeth in Nager. Throughout the twentieth century and up to today, latticework has been extensively used for the decoration of Twelver Shia and Ismaili assembly halls in Hunza and Nager.

Fig. 99. Ornamental woodcarving on a balcony in Baltit fort (Hunza).

Jali-screens also constitute prominent architectural features of the last remaining edifice formerly connected to the royal palace of Nager, situated on the glacier moraine in the main village of Uyum Nager. Judging by old drawings and oral descriptions, the former Nager fort was similar in construction to Baltit fort, but collapsed at the end of the nineteenth century.[2] According to oral tradition, it was built by craftsmen and workers from Baltistan. Another palace, dismantled in the middle of the twentieth century, was then built further up the moraine, with an adjacent and still existing royal assembly hall. The latter is an almost quadrangular, flat-roofed pavilion (measuring 8.5 x 8 m) with pillars, round arches, and a multi-cusped arch for the entrance (fig. 101).

During court sessions, the ruler used to sit on a dais along the back wall of this reception hall (called *marka thaang* in the local Burushaski language) facing the *qibla* (prayer direction towards Mecca). The structure of the reception hall with its latticework on the front side and its three multi-cusped arches in the centre shows strong influences of provincial Mughal architecture mediated by craftsmen from Kashmir.[3] According to oral traditions preserved in the families of carpenters (*tarkhan*) in Nager, it was

Fig. 100. Latticework in the house of the late Raja Muzafar ud-Din Shah in Ghulmeth (Nager).

Ustad Kudu from Srinagar who was invited by Mir Sikandar Khan at the end of the 1890s to construct this reception hall in Uyum Nager. He stayed for a year and collaborated with local craftsmen. The painted ceiling of the pavilion with its sun discs in different shapes also dates from that period. It is further narrated that a famous Kashmiri carpenter named Ustad Sono, who settled in Gilgit, had already come to

Fig. 101. Royal reception hall
in Uyum Nager (late 19th century).

Fig. 102. *Jali*-work in the home
of Ustad Mozahir in Chalt-Bala (Nager).

Nager in the time of Tham Zafar Khan (who ruled *de facto* 1839-1892) to embellish the old fort and adjacent wooden porticoes.

PRIVATE HOUSES

Until the abolition of both kingdoms in 1974 and 1972 respectively, the traditional societies of Hunza and Nager were distinctly stratified, with a tiny minority of privileged noble families occupying the top of the social pyramid. The homes of the well-to-do (and to a lesser degree those of commoners) were decorated with woodcarvings. In an affluent household, verandas, door frames, pillars and capitals, storage containers, cabinets, wall shelves, and furniture (such as cradles and boxes) were richly carved, whereas the small living room of a poor family probably only had the door frame of the box-like storage room adorned with chiselled patterns. Likewise, the house of a *wazir* or a powerful village headman could be two-storeyed. In this way, the layout of a private home and the quality and quantity of its artistic embellishment represented the rank, wealth, and sophistication of its owner. As an exception to this status-based use of woodcarvings, the houses of a carpenter could sometimes be richly decorated, thereby demonstrating his mastership – and this holds true up to the present.

Generally speaking, these craftsmen (locally known as *chake ustad*) do any kind of woodwork from the construction of buildings and the decorative carving of architecture to the manufacture of vessels of different shapes, water-pipes, cradles, boxes, musical instruments, household utensils, agricultural tools, and in olden times bows and arrows. As far as Nager is concerned, and for all the second half of the twentieth century, Ustad Yusuf Ali (Uyum Nager-Nikokhan) is considered the best carpenter. He was a disciple of the famous Ustad Shaban Mashqula from Uyum Nager-Gashakushal. The late *tarkhan* Ustad Mozahir's house in Chalt-Bala (dating from the late nineteenth century with later additions made in the first third of the twentieth century) is a good example of a number of architectural details (fig. 102). The showpiece veranda with octagonal columns, multi-cusped arches, and rectangular panels with elaborate latticework is clearly influenced by Kashmiri woodwork. Similarly, inside the main room, the fluted middle part of the central columns with their leaf-shaped endings point to provincial Mughal models. The capitals, however, show rosettes and horn-shaped volutes in indigenous style. Finally, the built-in cupboards are covered with carved floral motifs.

Fig. 103. Fluted pillar with voluted capital showing ram's horn design (Chalt-Bala/Nager).

Fig. 104. Carved floral ornaments on a cabinet in Ustad Mozahir's house (Chalt-Bala/Nager).

Within the domestic setting, many houses in Hunza have retained (or reproduced) the traditional scheme with four posts defining the square inner space (*ha*) of the dwelling. A number of old houses in Hunza and Nager still preserve the more ancient form of posts with two step-like transitions to the capital (as also observed in Baltit fort). Variations occur in the form and decoration of the base and of the adjoining bulbous, often fluted part. The different levels of working-, sitting-, and sleeping-platforms around the common *ha* of a traditional house are sometimes bordered by low balustrades decorated with floral patterns (fig. 120).

The central roof opening above the *ha*, composed of an overlay of decreasing, diagonally superimposed squares of small beams, constitutes an essential carpentry task and marks, structurally and symbolically, the navel of the house and the location of the fireplace (figs. 85, 97, pl. 25).

RELIGIOUS BUILDINGS

Turning our attention to the Islamic architecture of mosques, it must be remembered that Islam in Hunza has a relatively recent track record. Missionaries spreading the Twelver Shia faith (Ithna Ashari Shi'ism) reached the Karakoram from Kashmir via Baltistan in about the sixteenth century, but this by no means implies that the population converted at that time, nor that mosques were constructed in that early period. A more thorough conversion to the orthodox Twelver Shia creed apparently took place during the course of the eighteenth century and continued progressively through the nineteenth century.

The local type of mosque has no courtyard and no minaret. In principle it consists of a rather small cube-shaped and flat-roofed prayer chamber, used particularly in the winter season (figs. 95, 105; pls. 117, 118). It is generally surrounded by two arcades forming an angle (especially in Hunza) or preceded by just one front arcade (often in Nager). This corresponds to the so-called mountain type of mosque also found in other parts of northern Pakistan.[4] There are striking similarities, for instance, with the mosque architecture of the Shigar valley, a

Fig. 105. Ghulwating mosque in Baltit (Hunza) with two arcades.

137

Fig. 106. Shah Ghazanfar mosque in Baltit (Hunza).

Fig. 107. Aqhon Fazil mosque in Aliabad-Gulkhan (Hunza).

region of Baltistan culturally linked with Nager. In single cases one also finds three arcades, or even a circumambulatory hall on all four sides of the building. Early mosques, such as the tiny room adjacent to the watchtower in Altit fort and the Kamal *masjid* in Uyum Nager, are simple cube-shaped structures in the traditional half-timbered cator and cribbage construction technique (see chapter 5 in this book).

Woodcarvings are found on the door frame (consisting of up to six narrow bands each filled with stylised patterns), on open-work windows, and on the *mihrab* (prayer niche). The old community mosque of Baltit, built in the time of Tham Shah Ghazanfar Khan (in advanced state of dilapidation in 1981 and dismantled shortly after), had a rather spacious angled veranda hall in comparison to other smaller mosques (fig. 106). Dating from the middle of the nineteenth century,[5] its grille-like open timber work still bears a distinctive local character, independent from the Kashmiri *jalis* that emerged towards the end of the nineteenth century. The same holds true for two mosques situated right in the centre of the old fortified village (*khan*) of Ganish, the Rupikuts *masjid* and Mamurokuts *masjid* (fig. 126; pl. 118). Their arch-like fillings placed between the four posts on the front side are dominated by rosettes and multi-lobed niches – characteristic motifs to be discussed later in greater detail. This particular sort of niche is also found on two adjacent mosques (both allegedly built in the eighteenth century under the rule of Tham Silum Khan) at the assembly place of Dorkhan as well as on the small private 'hanging' mosque belonging to Wazir Qudratullah Beg's house in Baltit (fig. 277). In comparison, other mosques (such as the Budinkuts *masjid* in Ganish) show multi-cusped arches and a low railing between the veranda posts, filled with Kashmiri latticework. As confirmed by statements from local greybeards, such mosques are of later origin and have to be dated to the first half of the twentieth century. Apart from the woodwork on arcades – which can be used as a tentative method for dating the buildings – the peculiarity of the ancient Hunza mosques in Ganish, Dorkhan, Baltit-Diramishal (Ghulwating *masjid*) and Aliabad-Gulkhan (Aqhon Fazil *masjid*, fig. 107, dismantled in the 1990s) is the fact that each prayer chamber is entirely constructed of wood and almost completely covered with elaborate carvings.

This sweeping surface carving is not found in the neighbouring area of Nager where all the buildings are constructed in half-timbering. The cube-shaped, unpretentious Kamal *masjid* in Uyum Nager, three metres high with a base measuring 6.5 x 6.5 metres, somewhat resembles a truncated tower. Supposedly it is the oldest mosque in Nager, with a date of 1715 inscribed on a window lintel.[6] In addition to the date, there are Arabic inscriptions of the *kalima* and *basmala* formulas as well as the name of God and those of the *panjtan pak* (Muhammad, Ali, Fatima, Hasan, Husain). As usual in the Karakoram, the *mihrab* is small and low and in this case simply marked by a multi-cusped arch.

There were a further three old, already dilapidated mosques on the polo ground in Uyum Nager, each with a single veranda partly built in stonework, apparently following architectural models of Baltistan. They were constructed in the time of Tham Zafar Khan in the nineteenth century, commissioned by the noble clans of the Musharkuts, Potikuts and Qhutayating. The mosques of the latter two could still be seen in the early 1980s, but were then demolished. In comparison to the above-mentioned mosques of Hunza with their intricate woodcarvings, the aesthetics of Nager mosques surviving from the first half of the twentieth century are determined by Kashmiri *jalis*, multi-cusped arches and low veranda balustrades with carved panels. An exception are, however, the carved doors of religious monuments, such as those of the courtyard mosque in Askurdas or of the old Shia assembly hall of Sumaiyar-Jatorkhan.

Fig. 108. *Imambarha* of Uyum Nager-Nikokhan (Nager).

Fig. 109. Richly decorated lantern roof in the *imambarha* of Pheker-Khan.

While mosques in Nager are rather simple and less decorated structures in comparison to those of Hunza, Twelver Shia assembly halls are often lavishly carved, and have also been painted since the middle of the twentieth century. The old *imambarha* at Sumaiyar, for instance, built in the time of Tham Zafar Khan towards the end of the nineteenth century, had excellently carved posts and ribbed columns as well as fine open work on the *mimbar*. These carvings were reused in 1982 in a newly constructed communal hall. The main building components of contemporary *imambarhas* from the twentieth century are a spacious quadrangular hall usually surrounded by two arcades forming an angle and a flat roof with a central octagonal lantern. In addition to several windows, the lantern provides light and air to the building. The different exterior and interior elements of this architecture are carved and painted in the local style of popular decorative folk art (figs. 108-112).

Building upon the earlier door-carving tradition, special emphasis is laid on the luxuriant decoration of the portal-like door. Whereas earlier, unpainted specimens mostly had relief work of rosettes in different shapes set in panels or cartouches, the colourful modern doors show greater variety, as they are made by craftsmen competing in embellishing the *imambarhas*. Ustad Yusuf Ali, for instance, has created a particularly charming composition showing two arches set on top of each other through subdividing the rectangular door in-

Fig. 110. Carved and painted door of the *imambarha* of Hopar-Goshoshal (Nager).

Fig. 111. Portal of the *imambarha* of Sumaiyar-Raisman (Nager).

Fig. 112. *Mimbar* and ornamented rear wall in the *imambarha* of Bar (Nager).

to ten panels (fig. 110). The panels are symmetrically filled with flower vases and geometrical patterns. Several ornate frames further enhance the portal. This design can be found in many of the more than fourteen *imambarhas* constructed in Nager by this master craftsman. Other examples, such as the door of the assembly hall in Sumaiyar-Raisman (fig. 111), are typical expressions of folk art reflecting a sense of naivety — a phenomenon also encountered in the European Alps or in Scandinavia. Of distinctly modern taste are colourful doors with geometric mosaic work of stars or abstract kilim motifs, flanked by cassettes, and a round arch above the door filled with glass mosaic work. These techniques of decoration were borrowed in the late 1970s from Gilgit. Likewise, the contemporary Ismaili *jamatkhanas* of Hunza reflect modern taste in decoration and hardly show traditional woodcarvings.

The interior architecture of *imambarhas* is focused on the two-stepped *mimbar* and its ornamented rear wall (fig. 112), on the spandrels of the round arches, on the wooden partition wall between the men's and the women's section as well as on the ceiling. Craftsmen usually combine different techniques, such as relief work of more or less stylised floral patterns, geometric Kashmiri *panjiras*, mosaic work using small pieces of wood in the Balti style, glass mosaic work (windows and lantern roof), and painting. The colour spectrum is predominantly composed of black (symbol of ritual mourning), red (symbol for the martyrdom of Imam Husain) and green (symbol for Imam Hasan), plus shining white, yellow and different shades of blue. The richly coloured panelling of the *qibla* wall in the Doshkuts *imambarha* of Hopar-Hakalshal is a good example of such popular aesthetics. Recently, craftsmen also used plastic sheets with ornamental all-over patterning in combination with wooden mosaic work to create a vivid impression of sun discs and stars in the octagonal lantern roof (for example the *imambarha* of Pheker-Khan; fig. 109). Remarkable examples of local religious folk art are the depictions of Karbala scenes and ibex hunting painted on spandrels in the *imambarha* of Bar and the Arabic inscriptions and the depiction of a bird (both cut out from wood) on the rear wall of the *mimbar* in Sumaiyar-Jatorkhan.

Another common type of religious building is the shrine. In Nager and Hunza, a number of holy men are venerated – some of them Muslim saints who are thought to have been missionaries of Islam, others belonging to the pre-Islamic past. Their shrines were frequently renovated or newly built, sometimes changing the sites beyond recognition, such as in the case of Sayyed Shah Wali in the Nager village of Ghulmeth.[7] This is the reason why artistic woodwork has rarely survived up till now. On the other hand, holy places are often very simple structures because, according to an indigenous religious world-view, numinous power is often experienced in stones and rocks. Woodcarving therefore only appears at times on doors of stone enclosures, for instance in the *astanas* (nineteenth/twentieth century) of Sayyed Shah Wali in the Hunza villages of Maiyun and Khanabad. The only remarkable exception is a shrine in in the Fatima garden of Askurdas (Nager) – a half-timbered, flat-roofed *astana* supposed to contain the tomb of a small child belonging to a Sayyed family (fig. 114). The multi-cusped arches and the *jali* panels of the veranda section clearly show Kashmiri influence and could be dated to the late nineteenth/early twentieth century. However, inside the building, there are voluted capitals and carved patterns reflecting the local taste already seen in domestic architecture. Similarly, the insertion of small rectangular panels of open work into massive posts can be seen as a feature of local aesthetics sometimes found in religious buildings.

Fig. 113. Carved door frame in the *astana* of Sayyed Shah Wali in Khanabad (Hunza).

VOCABULARY OF PATTERNS AND MOTIFS

Having identified the architectural elements likely to be embellished with woodcarvings, a survey of the patterns and motifs (based on a documentation of more than 180 photographs) will confirm that there is no fundamental distinction in the decoration programme between domestic and religious architecture. The range of motifs includes a variety of stylised floral ornaments and a more limited number of geometric forms, but generally excludes figural representation, as found in local embroidery and jewellery. Since the focus of this chapter will be on the repertoire of traditional design before the middle of the twentieth century, I will not consider here the painted decoration of contemporary Shia assembly halls in Nager and Hunza with their more naturalistic depictions of flowers and even figural representations, but concentrate on the traditional ornamental patterns.

Fig. 114. Sayyed shrine in Askurdas (Nager) with multi-cusped arches and latticework.

Floral ornaments

The predominance of floral patterns and motifs becomes clear from the study of cardboard stencils (figs. 116, 117), which are a key for the understanding of the local decorative vocabulary (at least as far as nineteenth-century Kashmiri influence is concerned). These stencils used by

Fig. 115. Voluted capitals in the Sayyed shrine of Askurdas.

Fig. 116. Cardboard stencil with interlaced circles (Chalt-Bala/Nager).

Fig. 117. Cardboard stencils with floral ornaments (Chalt-Bala/Nager).

the carpenters and often inherited from their forefathers are very similar to those of the silversmiths. The latter preserve the tradition of cutting out motifs from a folded sheet of paper in order to apply them to the metalwork. As the silversmiths of Nager originally came from Kashmir in the eighteenth century, their forefathers most probably brought this technique from the east.[8] The cardboard stencils belonging to the family of the late Ustad Mozahir, a master carpenter from Chalt-Bala, show different symmetrical compositions of leaves (mainly five-petalled flowers, but also trefoils and transitions to buds) inscribed in squared frames or standing alone. Within the Shia universe, the preference for five-petalled flowers could be interpreted as a reference to the *panjtan pak*. In addition, there are quatrefoils, leafy scrolls and rosettes.

A look at the more ancient woodcarvings of royal palaces, mosques and assembly halls shows that floral ornaments are almost always set in square frames and repeated extensively to fill bands and to cover larger surfaces wherever possible – for instance in door panels or in open timber work. Arabesque-like scroll-work used for decorative bands is called *mudakhil*, a Persian term for 'border', which also denotes similar floral compositions on the rims of cross-stitched women's caps.[9] Likewise, bud-like shapes and entwined floral shapes standing in opposition form continuous scrolls. Rows of palmettes are sometimes used to decorate the long carved boards bordering the roofs of mosques in Nager. The ancient paisley (*boteh*) motif widespread in West and Central Asia and commonly associated with the flame or with fertility is also found on local woodcarved bands. Altit fort features a particular shape with the scrolled end of the leaf reaching out far to the right or left (fig. 118). Rosettes, usually six- or seven-petalled (*askuring, phitimuts*), are motifs with a great continuity, well-known from Gandhara culture, and they now dominate contemporary women's embroidery (fig. 121). In woodcarvings they are either placed as single accentuating motifs or arranged in groups, for instance on spandrels, wall panels and on the ceiling. Sometimes they appear in the form of discs divided into sections resembling solar emblems. Furthermore, woodcarvers found original solutions to combine a rosette or quatrefoil with a leafy part ending in a trefoil, thereby flexibly adapting to the narrow panel of a low balustrade (fig. 120). A rare motif consisting of an X-shaped stylised flower with horn-like leaves and set into a sort of sun disc appears at the Rupikuts *masjid* in Ganish (fig. 122). The same design called *turiangkishe phiti* is found in local cross-stitched embroidery.[10]

Fig. 118. Paisley-motifs in Altit fort.
Fig. 119. Voluted capitals in Baltit fort.
Fig. 120. Balustrade with floral ornamentation
in a private home in Baltit.

Fig. 121. Seven-petalled rosettes
in a mosque in Ganish.
Fig. 122. Woodcarvings showing the *turiangkishe*
phiti motif (lower right panel) and niches
in Rupikuts mosque in Ganish.

143

Fig. 123. Geometric patterns on the façade of Ghulwating mosque in Baltit (fig. 105).

The volute capitals may take multiple forms: usually they have two or three volutes on each side (fig. 119), sometimes even seven; they may also appear in the shape of stylised ram's horns. The latter are also found on door frames.

Geometric patterns

Within the traditional design repertoire of Hunza and Nager, geometric patterns play a less dominant role in comparison to more natural floral ornaments. On larger surfaces, we find compositions of intersecting octagons and circles (fig. 123), crosses in deep undercutting, tiny stars, and mesh-like configurations consisting of squares and triangles (fig. 124). The latter resemble those of the woodcarvings in Indus Kohistan.[11] In Hunza and Nager, square and triangle symmetries are shared designs also used on small wooden boxes and in embroidery on the flat, plate-like upper part of women's caps. More often one observes narrow bands created by rhombus (filled with floral designs), squares standing on top with inscribed crosses, rectangular shapes with inscribed crosses of the straight type and of the Andrew-type, zigzag and waves. A tracery of intersecting ogival units (that is to say a classic ornament of Islamic art known throughout the Iranian world and in Mughal India), appears on pillars of the old *imambarha* in Sumaiyar. Likewise, the variety of repetitive *jali*-work, particularly found in the Shia assembly halls of Nager but also in other buildings, is a truly Islamic pattern characteristic of Muslim architecture between Andalusia and India.

Symbolic motifs

A typical motif of local design is the swastika, an ancient symbol of the sun or fire already known from the Indus valley civilisation and widespread in northern Pakistan from the rock carvings of antiquity to contemporary folk art. In Hunza and Nager it appears in various geometric configurations in royal palaces, private houses, mosques, and as small infill in minute cross-stitched embroideries (fig. 125). Derived from the cross and imbued with the idea of movement, this motif is always carved in high relief and mostly turning to the right.

Another remarkable motif, to my knowledge almost exclusively found in the old mosques of Hunza, is a small symmetrically composed multi-lobed niche with a sort of peak on the top (fig. 126). This niche also marks the lintel of the entrance to Baltit fort. It is either fully cut out from wood, forming decorative open work on verandas and window-like openings of the prayer chamber, or it is deeply cut out from a board. There are single niches set into quadrangular frames, vertical rows of single niches, two niches side by side or ensembles of three niches showing a kind of larger triangle. Considering the particular form of this niche (with a basis and multi-storeyed structure) and its multiple use in local mosque design, it is tempting to refer to the form of the Buddhist *stupa*. Buddhism flourished for a certain period in the Hunza valley as can be deducted from the inscriptions and *stupa*-drawings on the 'sacred rocks' of Haldeikish near Ganish and

Fig. 124. Triangles and squares
on a post in the *darbar* hall of Altit fort.

Fig. 125. Board carved with floral ornaments
and swastika motifs in Altit fort.

from the former *stupa* of Thol (Nager) described by Sir Aurel Stein.[12] *Stupas*, as the main Buddhist monuments, were venerated and countlessly depicted in the upper Indus valley since the turn of the millennia at least until the eighth century AD. It has to be mentioned that, in addition to woodcarving, the same motif of the *stupa*-like niche is also found in the shape of large silver pendants in Nager jewellery (fig. 127) as well as in the shape of wall niches in local homes used for burning oil-lamps.

A unique, stylised figurative motif, which I only saw on a decorative board in Ghulwating *masjid* in Baltit-Diramishal, shows two fishes facing each other (fig. 128). The animal is depicted with a rosette in lieu of a head, scale-like dots on the body, a long tail fin, as well as a clearly indicated side fin. Both fishes are surrounded by snake- or dragon-like beings. The same motif often appears in the contemporary popular art of painted and decorated trucks and other vehicles in the lowland provinces of Pakistan. In the pre-Islamic past, many zoomorphic motifs of symbolic significance were in use, such as the depiction of a horse (symbol of status and wealth) on a capital in the *bazme thaang* (hall for entertainment) of Baltit fort and of pairs of stylised birds in Altit fort.[13] Another unusual motif appears on the Mamurokuts *masjid* in Ganish. It is

Fig. 126. Rupikuts mosque in Ganish with *stupa*-like niches (see also fig. 122).

Fig. 127. Silver pendant in the shape
of a *stupa*-like niche (Uyum Nager).

Fig. 128. Carved motif of affronted fishes with snakes in Ghulwating mosque in Baltit-Diramishal.

Fig. 129. Bow and arrow motif on Mamurokuts mosque in Ganish.

executed in open work and strongly resembles the form of a bow and arrow, the weapons of local warriors in ancient Hunza and Nager (fig. 129).

CONCLUSION

To summarise the discussion of the artistic woodcarving tradition in Hunza and Nager, first it has to be stressed that the number of artefacts, as well as the range of patterns and motifs, is more restricted and less elaborate in comparison to densely wooded regions such as Kashmir, Indus Kohistan or Swat with their lavish woodwork and greater richness of forms. Second, the overview of vernacular architecture and of the vocabulary of ornamentation has shown that we can distinguish different decorative styles: there is an ancient layer consisting of pillars with voluted capitals and of rather small-scale and simple floral and geometric patterns appearing on boards and door frames which constitute a distinct folk tradition pre-dating the introduction of Islam. It has been suggested earlier by Erika Schmitt (1971) that the decorative elements of this folk art of the Karakoram and Hindukush were borrowed from the art of Gandhara, representing a substratum of motifs within that historical region where Buddhism flourished in the Kushana period. Thus, similarly to Indus Kohistan[14] from where many kinship groups of Hunza and Nager trace their origin, there seems to be a continuous tradition of vernacular, stylistically rather homogenous decorative design on the level of folk culture. This might have been nurtured by early Iranian influences since late antiquity or by later ones absorbed via Badakhshan. Nevertheless, there must have been further external stimuli as well, encouraging the borrowing of visually meaningful symbols such as the swastika and probably the *stupa*-like niche.

The exposure to Muslim areas and the final conversion to Islam (with restrictions on the representation of living beings) paved the way to more prolific floral and geometric ornamentation. These influences of aniconic Islamic art with its emphasis on the principles of abstraction, symmetry, and repetition were, apart from Badakhshan, basically mediated via Kashmir with its characteristic wooden style of architecture. Trade and cultural transfer between Kashmir and especially Nager played an important role.[15] Columned verandas, *jali*-screens, decorative carving of door panels, arabesques and other curvilinear motifs known from the stencils of woodcarvers can be attributed to this late eastern influence. At least since about the middle of the nineteenth century Nager craftsmen were in contact with Kashmiri carpenters settled in Gilgit and in some cases Kashmiri experts were hired to supervise construction projects in Nager. Sometimes local carpenters, such as Ustad Surato, went to Kashmir to learn more about woodwork.

Nevertheless, Baltistan also might have earlier mediated traits of Kashmiri art. Whole kinship groups from Baltistan migrated to Upper Nager, others only stayed temporarily, and noble families of Nager intermarried with those of Shigar. Furthermore, it is reported that skilled Balti craftsmen came in the entourage of princesses to Hunza and Nager and worked on the construction of palaces. According to oral tradition, this happened in Hunza in the time of King Ayasho II and his son Prince Sultan. Thus, the impact of Baltistan on architecture and woodwork (and generally on material culture) must be seriously taken into consideration. A particular feature of religious buildings in Baltistan, originally borrowed from the architecture of Kashmir (mosque of Shah Hamadan and the *jami masjid*, both in Srinagar), is the form of pyramidal spires.[16] In Hunza they are found in Baltit fort and in several Shia assembly halls. Furthermore, D. L. R. Lorimer already mentioned a "pattern of door known as *Baloski hing*",[17] that is to say a 'Balti door' which has deepenings for the fingers to open the door. Another external stimulus for local folk art came through textiles imported from the Pamir region and from Eastern Turkestan.

In addition to the indigenous pre-Islamic style of woodcarving and to what could be called the Kashmiri style, local craftsmen from Nager recently created an exuberant style of decorating *imambarhas*. This innovative, albeit eclectic

Fig. 130. Pyramidal spire on the roof of Baltit fort showing eastern influence (see also figs. 185, 201).

style with its richly coloured and delicately carved architectural elements has been developing since about the middle of the twentieth century. Furthermore, inspiration brought back from pilgrimages to Iran also have to be taken into account. As a true expression of popular taste it shows the creativity, vividness and dynamics typically found in folk art. Apparently this folk art has already reached its zenith, since the most recent specimens of *imambarhas* in Nager are following the example of modern concrete mosques frequently seen all over Pakistan reflecting a more austere brand of Islam devoid of any aesthetic charms.

[1] Johannes Kalter (ed.), *The Arts and Crafts of the Swat Valley. Living Traditions in the Hindu Kush*, Thames and Hudson, London 1989, p. 146.
[2] Jürgen Wasim Frembgen, *Zentrale Gewalt in Nager (Karakorum). Politische Organisationsformen, ideologische Begründungen des Königtums und Veränderungen in der Moderne*, F. Steiner, Stuttgart 1985, pp. 91-94.
[3] See note 2, p. 90.
[4] Umberto Scerrato, "Survey of Wooden Mosques and Related Wood-Carvings in the Swat Valley", in *East and West* 1981, 31/1-4, p.181; Umberto Scerrato, "The Wooden Architecture of Swat and the Northern Areas of Pakistan: a Report on the Research Carried Out in 1984", in *East and West* 1984, 34/4, p. 501.
[5] Ahmad Hasan Dani, *Islamic Architecture. The Wooden Style of Northern Pakistan*, National Hijra Council, Islamabad 1989, p. 162.
[6] Jürgen Wasim Frembgen, "Aspekte der Oralität und Literalität: Ihre Implikationen für das Geschichtsbewusstsein der muslimischen Nagerkuts in Nordpakistan", in *Anthropos* 1986, 81/4-6, pp. 574-575.

[7] Jürgen Wasim Frembgen, "Sayyid Shah Wali – Missionary and Miracle-Worker. Notes on the Hagiography and Cult of a Muslim Saint in Nager and Hunza (Northern Pakistan)", in *Zeitschrift der Deutschen Morgenländischen Gesellschaft* (in press).

[8] Jürgen Wasim Frembgen, "Königskronen aus Nager", in *Tribus* 1988, 37, pp. 75-76.

[9] Jürgen Wasim Frembgen, *Stickereien aus dem Karakorum*, Museum of Ethnology, Munich 1998.

[10] See note 9, p. 37.

[11] Karl Jettmar, "Schnitzwerke aus den Tälern Tangir und Darel", in *Archiv für Völkerkunde* 1959, 14, pp. 87-118.

[12] M. Aurel Stein, *Ancient Khotan. Detailed Report of Archaeological Explorations in Chinese Turkestan*, Oxford 1907, p. 20.

[13] See note 5, pp. 158, 160.

[14] Jürgen Wasim Frembgen, "Indus Kohistan. An Historical and Ethnographic Outline", in *Central Asiatic Journal* 1999, 43/1, pp. 88-90.

[15] See note 8, pp. 72, 75-76.

[16] J. R. Nichols, "Architecture of Kashmir: Muhammadan Architecture", in *Marg* 1955, 8/2, pp. 83-85, 88.

[17] D. L. R. Lorimer, *The Burushaski Language. Vol. I Introduction and Grammar*, Oslo 1935.

7. Traditional Art and Architecture in Baltistan

MAX KLIMBURG

This article, based on several visits to the region and a recent trip to Kashmir, will summarise current knowledge on the Islamic architectural heritage of Baltistan, recognising that much remains to be done to fill remaining gaps in the scientific research after Ahmad Hasan Dani's pioneering 1989 study of *The Wooden Style of Northern Pakistan*.

One would expect that Baltistan, as a secluded region locked in by high mountain ranges, should have developed an art and architecture of its own, with only few characteristics shared with any of its neighbours. This is not the case, unless one wants to claim the large local buildings of *khanqah*, a combination of mosque and Sufi retreat centre, to be a Balti creation. With regard to virtually all the religious buildings, including the typically Shia congregation centres, the *matam-sarai* (also called *imambarha*), and possibly also with regard to palace and fort architecture, Baltistan appears heavily dependent on influences mainly from Kashmir, its great and dominant neighbour. Some additional influences have probably come from Ladakh, cul-

turally a part of western Tibet, with which it shares its Tibetan language. Indeed, communication with Ladakh, mainly along the Indus, is easier than with any other adjoining cultural and political entity. There were also important influences from Iran with respect to certain crafts, as described further below. Moreover, the southern Tarim basin, that is, Khotan and Yarkand, may well have contributed much to the emergence of the large type of *khanqah*-cum-veranda in Baltistan, and possibly also to the rich vocabulary of carved motifs. Thus we can conjecture that there was a strong south-north cultural movement, complemented by some influence from the east, Ladakh, from Central Asia, and from the more distant Shia world in Persia.

It is no surprise that the Islamisation of Baltistan in the fifteenth and sixteenth centuries came from Kashmir soon after that regionally leading cultural Hindu centre had fallen to Islam. This is when the strong south-north movement of ideas and of actual cultural influences developed, eventually wiping out Buddhism and possibly also some Bon and Hindu beliefs in Baltistan. Yet, while Tibet thus lost its religious impact on its former province of Baltistan, it still left a visible imprint on Baltistan's Islamic architecture. The question has to remain

Fig. 131. The Shah Hamadan mosque (*khanqah*) in Srinagar (from Kak 1933, pl. VI).

149

open, whether this is due to a locally surviving influence or to new inputs from the cultural melting pot Kashmir, which could have reinvigorated past traditions.

A mystic Shia missionary from Hamadan, Sayyed Ali Shah Hamadani, a member of the Central Asian Sufi Kubrawiye order, is credited with the first important Islamic mission in Kashmir, which he visited three times between 1372 and 1383. He died in 1384, being buried in Kulab in southern Tajikistan. According to Kashmiri traditions, seven hundred Sayyed and other followers, among them highly skilled craftsmen (the Kubra order was particularly popular among craftsmen) had come with Shah Hamadani from Iran and Central Asia to settle in Kashmir – including specialists in *kar-i qalam* (papier mâché work), *khatamband* (ornamental wooden ceiling), *panjira* (latticework called *jali* in Urdu) and calligraphy. It appears that the saint passed through Baltistan at least once on his way between Central Asia, where his later life centred, and Kashmir. His great *khanqah*/mosque in Srinagar, the Masjid-e Hamadan or Shah Hamadan mosque (fig. 131), became the symbol of early Islam in Kashmir and most probably served as the prime model for all the centrally designed wooden mosques in both Kashmir and Baltistan.

Fig. 132. The shrine of Mir Ishaq in Tagas.

A further important cultural influence from Kashmir to Baltistan is due to the missionary activity by followers of the mystic Sayyed Mohammad Nurbaksh, who had founded the Kubra-related Nurbakhshiye Sufi order in Iran in the fifteenth century. Around 1500 that movement was introduced by Shams-ad Din Iraqi to Kashmir, where he resided for some thirty years and where he is buried. In the middle of the sixteenth century, at the time of his son Mir Danyal Shahid, a cruel persecution of the Shia and Sufi orders suddenly developed. It was instigated by the Sunni hardliner Mirza Haydar Dughlat, one of Emperor Humayun's generals and also one of his uncles, and was aimed at the extinction of Shi'ism and all Sufi orders – and especially the Nurbakhshiye sect – throughout Kashmir. In 1550, Mir Danyal was summoned from Skardu to Srinagar and then beheaded. He was buried in Zaribal near Srinagar and is venerated as a *shahid* (martyr). All this led to a mass exodus of Shia and Nurbakhshiye families, among them many craftsmen, to Baltistan where they were welcomed by the local rulers.

There was a revival of the Nurbakhshiye order in Kashmir under the short-lived rule of the Chak family, but with the conquest of Kashmir by the Mughal Emperor Akbar in 1586 persecution started again. In the early seventeenth century, the Nurbakhshiye was virtually uprooted in Kashmir, while it was thriving in neighbouring Baltistan. During the whole of the seventeenth century, many Nurbakhshiye missionaries preached and taught all over Baltistan. Leading among them were the thirty-fourth *pir* (spiritual leader) of the movement, Mir Abu Said Sada (died in 1684, buried in Srinagar), his brother Mir Aref (died in 1651 or 1655, buried in Tagas), and two descendants of Shams-ad Din Iraqi – Mir Yahya (died in 1614, buried in Shigar) and Mir Mukhtar (died in 1718, buried in Kiris).

Thus a mystic Shia movement gained ground in Baltistan, while the ruling class, supposedly of Central Asian Turkish origin and adhering to the mainstream beliefs of the Twelver Shia, created a number of largely autonomous small kingdoms or princely states. They were headed by men bearing different titles, who later became known as *raja*. The division into small kingdoms may well have proliferated after the occupation of Baltistan (and later Gilgit) by the army of Gulab Singh, the Dogra ruler of Jammu and Kashmir, in 1840/1841.

Fig. 133. The *khanqah* and two tombs of saints in Tagas (pl. 49).

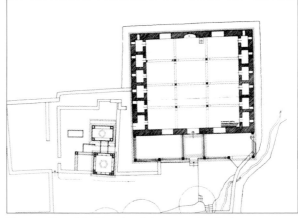

Fig. 134. Plan of the *khanqah* and the two tombs of saints in Tagas (from Dani 1989b, fig. 30).

Leading principalities were those of Skardu and Khaplu. The state of Skardu, which was ruled by the Makpon family, controlled the best lines of communication with Kashmir, leading across the up to 3900-metre-high Deosai plateau and the 4000-metre-high Burzil pass (fig. 2). Members of the same family also governed the state of Kharmang, situated on the path leading along the Indus to Ladakh, as well as those in Rondu and Astor, controlling the access to and from Gilgit and Chilas in the west. The other leading principality, that of Khaplu, located on the Shyok tributary of the Indus and ruled by the once powerful Yabghu family, controlled the paths into northern Ladakh, which in turn is linked with Khotan (Tarim basin) across the approximately 5500-metre-high Karakoram pass. The settlement pattern in Khaplu, located on a huge alluvial cone, is characterised by separate villages originally housing craftsmen of the same trade – a division according to professional skills found all over India.

There were, in addition, the princely states of Shigar and Kiris. Shigar, governed by the Amacha family, controlled the communications with Nagir and Hunza across the Baltoro glacier, and those with Yarkand and the Tarim basin across the forbidding, approximately 5600-metre-high Muztagh pass. The state of Kiris, once ruled by the Yabghu family, had a central location insofar as it was surrounded by other Balti principalities on three sides. Therefore, probably not by coincidence, one finds in Kiris the most important saintly tomb and thus the leading pilgrim centre of Baltistan.

THE BUILDING STYLE

The architecture of Baltistan is based on the use of a sort of log-house structure applied to practically all of the more prominent buildings, large or small, religious or secular. The monumental building repertory consists of the large structures of the *khanqah* dominating many of the settlements, the mosques (*masjids*), the tombs of saints (*astanas*), the congregation halls for the commemoration of the death of Husein (*matamsarais* or *imambarhas* or *huseiniyes*), and the forts/palaces (*khars*) of the different *rajas*. The style, locally called *thatar*, is strongly conditioned by the 'cator and cribbage' building technique (see fig. 96). Stone walls are

Fig. 135. The spire and *qubbah* of the shrine of Mir Ishaq in Tagas.

Fig. 136. The winged wooden 'bells' on the shrine of Mir Ishaq in Tagas.

reinforced with occasional vertical layers of parallel beams ('cators'), laid at some distance above each other. On the corners, the longitudinal beams are interlocked at a right angle. For further structural strengthening in the corners (and also inside the walls), one often finds vertical cages or boxes composed of pairs of short pieces of timber beams built up in alternating right angle directions (fig. 95), looking like ladders from the outside ('cribbage'). They are pinned to the longitudinal wall beams, connecting them and tying them together into a semi-rigid frame. The void between the beams (or within the cages) is filled with stones or mud bricks and earth, which makes the walls become rather heavy and sturdy. This building technique was once widespread in the western Himalayas, but rampant deforestation now makes it prohibitively expensive.

The same cribbage construction method was applied to the solid pillar-like frames constituting the corner columns of the tombs of saints (*astanas*). In the wide openings between the composite columns, ornamental timber panels or *jali* screens were inserted (pls. 53, 100).

Apart from this general construction method, another typical feature is the prominence of centralised cubic structures and the *stupa*- or *chorten*-like spires crowning the pyramidal roofs. They are the most important indications of strong influences from Kashmir (and probably also from Buddhist Ladakh), where these features are as widespread as in Baltistan. The top structures rise from a four-, six- or eight-sided lantern, called *masjid* (mosque), which carries the *cholo* (top), consisting of a slim pyramidal spire with four small crosswise projecting beams, which may feature two roof-like brackets. From the projecting beams were suspended wooden vase-like objects, some (or originally all?) of them featuring thin 'wings' as if meant to catch the wind, possibly imitating bells hanging from Hindu or Buddhist temples (figs. 135, 136). This *cholo* ensemble is topped by the *qubbah*, basically consisting of a small metal umbrella (also described as a dented canopy) with several suspended short chains. They hold a metal, often three-pronged *alam* (referring to the Shiah 'trinity' of Mohammad, Ali and Husein), which is also used for the finial on standards paraded during the annual periods mourning the death of Husein.

However, Baltistan has developed its own style of *khanqah*, different from Kashmiri models, consisting of large or even huge roughly square and occasionally multi-pillared halls with wide and high verandas attached to their front side.

KHANQAHS

The *khanqah* in Baltistan and Kashmir was developed as a multi-purpose structure for the formerly more numerous Nurbakhshiye followers in Baltistan and the Sufis of the Naqshbandiye, Qaderiye and other or-

Fig. 137. Interior hall of the *khanqah* in Khaplu.

ders in Kashmir. It serves as a congregational mosque, *jami masjid*, and as a retreat centre for mystics, Sufi, observing the *chila*, the annual forty-day retreat of the Sufi order. It is also used as a meeting hall for the *matam*, the performance of the memorial service recalling the passion of Husein in the month of Muharram (the Twelver Shia population performs the *matam* service in separate congregational buildings called *matam-saras* or *imambarhas*).

While it appears that the large *khanqahs* encountered in the region were first built in Kashmir and then in Baltistan, physically speaking the building types used in both regions have little in common except for the appearance of square or nearly square halls and the provision of seclusion cells for Sufi retreats. The famous precursor of all later *khanqahs* is the wooden Khanqah-i Moualla or Shah Hamadan mosque in Srinagar (fig. 131). Beautifully located on the right bank of the Jhelum river, it shows a large centralised structure with two storeys – the lower one supported by four large columns – and with seven seclusion rooms topped by a gallery (reserved for women) on each side. Built around 1400, after Shah Hamadani's death, it may have changed much of its appearance due to two destructions by fire and subsequent rebuildings, the latest one in 1731. The interior was badly restored recently. With its portico-like entrance structure, lateral verandas and balconies the building looks very different from the simple four- or multi-pillared halls and frontal verandas of the many *khanqahs* in Baltistan.

Only few *khanqahs* seem to exist (or to have survived) in Kashmir, and little is known about their style. The only other published *khanqah*, the one in Pampur, vividly recalls the structure in Srinagar, but is much smaller and single storeyed. The somewhat different *khanqah* in Chrar-i Sharif, which burnt down in 1995 (see

Fig. 138. The *khanqah* of Shigar.

below), and the structures reportedly still standing in Tral and Wachi could not be seen during my recent visit to the area.

In Baltistan there are at least ten *khanqahs*, and with their often enormous size they constitute landmarks dominating the skyline of many settlements – particularly in the eastern area, the centre of the Nurbakhshiye followers. Generally, they measure up to twenty-three/twenty-five metres on both sides, and up to some six metres in height; they count four, six or more columns supporting the roof, and often feature six to eight rooms or cells (*hujras*) on each side, used for retreats and overnight accommodations. All of them carry a large frontal veranda, *baramdah* or *wacha*, of the same height as that of the roof and they often feature balconies and large windows with complicated *panjira* latticework. Their roofs are either flat or tent shaped with a shallow slope, and probably all of them have (or had) a *qubbah* on top.

The largest of the surviving original *khanqahs* in Baltistan are located in Khaplu (fig. 137) and Kiris (pl. 54). The structure in Khaplu has six huge columns with square bases and large bracket capitals, more than twenty additional smaller columns in support of the weakened roof beams, eight *hujras* and a four-metre-wide veranda, which counts ten richly decorated arches topped by varying *panjira* latticework.

Generally founded by great Nurbakhshiye teachers and missionaries, certainly none of the existing *khanqahs* date back to the time of the great missionaries Sayyed Ali Shah Hamadani and Mir Shams-ad Din Iraqi. However, the exceptional wooden *khanqah* in Serfakhur (district of Churga, Shigar valley) is believed to be a creation by Shah Hamadani himself. The saint is also credited with planting the tree, around which a two-storeyed structure enclosing a court was built. The *khanqah* is reached after crossing that court, now dominated by a maple tree grown to monumental proportions (pls. 50, 52).

Each of the most important *khanqahs* is associated by a dated inscription with one of the great teachers/saints who lies buried behind or next to it. The oldest is probably that of Mir Yahya in Shigar, which was founded in 1647. The largest structure, the *khanqah* of Sayyed Mohammad in Khaplu, is dated to the year 1712. The most reputed building, due to the saintly prominence of its founder, Mir Mukhtar, is the Khanqah-i Maulla in Kiris, founded in 1706. Some structures may date from the nineteenth century, a few are even very new, such as those in Machilu and Kande in the Hushe valley, to the north of Khaplu.

MOSQUES

The mosques visited by the *rajas*, court dignitaries, and the Twelver Shia population (but also the Nurbakhshiye followers) differ from the *khanqah* not only in their much smaller size, but in most cases also in their more strictly centralised ground plan and their generally arcaded verandas, which are either located on the front of the prayer room or all around it. In addition, they feature steeper pyramidal roofs and rich carved decoration. With one exception, all the mosques are small, some even tiny, measuring only three by three metres, with one central column in the prayer room. Their entrance doors and small grilled windows are decorated with often exquisite carvings. Most probably all of them had, and many still have, on their roof a four- or six-sided 'lantern' crowned by a *qubbah*.

Two mosques, the one in Skardu fort and the other in Paroa near Tagas (figs. 139, 140), stand out for their particularly high, heavy corbelled roof cornices, thereby emphasising even more the 'towering' character of the roof and its crowning ensemble. This type of roof design appears to relate to tower-like Buddhist *stupas*, pagodas and *chorten*.

The Chakchan mosque in Khaplu (pl. 47), the largest and most impressive among the old Balti mosques, is special insofar as it should be understood as a Nurbakhshiye building with the function but without the appearance of a *khanqah*. It is said to be located on the site of a Buddhist temple, and allegedly it was founded by Shah Hamadani. It has two storeys, the upper one used as a summer mosque, the lower one serving as a winter mosque and as lodging for visitors and Sufi. A richly decorated, arched veranda surrounds the building on four sides, a pyramidal spire with a *qubbah* crowns the hexagonal lantern on top of the tent-shaped roof. A broad ornamental frieze decorates the lower storey facing north. The prayer room houses four slim, facetted pillars with cross-bracket capitals and bases with cusped arched panels in high relief. Several superimposed, richly carved corbelled cornices form the transition to the ceiling. The *mihrab* and the nine segments of the ceiling, five of them with a 'lantern roof', are decorated with exquisite *khatamband*. During recent restoration of the building, which was actually in a good condition, much of it was painted and the roof was covered with metal sheets.

Fig. 139. The mosque in Skardu fort in 1914 (from De Filippi 1924, p. 54).

Fig. 140. The mosque in Paroa in 1914 (from Dainelli 1924, pl. LIV).

Fig. 141. The Chaburonjo mosque in Shigar in 1914 (from De Filippi 1924, p. 75).

Another outstanding mosque of the type featuring a veranda surrounding the prayer room is the small, two-storeyed Khilingrong mosque in Shigar (pls. 60, 106), recently restored by the Aga Khan Cultural Service-Pakistan (AKCS-P). It also has a veranda at the entrance on the lower floor. As a mosque which once may have served as a 'court mosque' (in addition to a much smaller structure next to the *raja's* palace), it is a showpiece of refined and richly decorated wooden architecture. The prayer room on each floor has a central pillar topped by a carefully decorated cross-bracketed semivoluted capital. There are richly carved spandrels of the arcades of the lower veranda and refined ornamental carvings inside on the entrance, windows, and on the *mihrab*.

Other examples of mosques completely surrounded by a veranda are the ruined, double-storeyed mosque in the fort of Skardu (fig. 139), still standing in 1914, the one-storeyed Chahburunjo mosque in Shigar, which in 1914 still had some sections of its elaborate arcaded veranda and original roof (fig. 141), and the recently restored and painted Brakshan mosque, also a one-storeyed structure, below the Chakchan mosque in Khaplu. The other wooden mosques have a veranda only at the front and, occasionally, on one or two other sides as well. The best structures known to me are again in Skardu, Shigar and Khaplu: most noteworthy among them are the Tayur mosque in Skardu, with a modern mosque recently attached to it, the Ambariq mosque in Shigar (fig. 292; pl. 104), which was recently restored by the AKCSP, and the mosque in Khangsar Mohalla in Khaplu, featuring a veranda on two sides.

In Kashmir – at least in those areas I was able to travel to – no such mosques remain to be found. All the structures which look somehow similar to the described wooden mosques of Baltistan, thus featuring a centralised ground plan, a frontal, sometimes also surrounding veranda, and a pyramidal roof with a *qubbah* on top, are tombs of saints. There was, however, the beautifully carved wooden mosque of Ata Mohammad Khan in Chrar-i Sharif from the late eighteenth century, which must have been similar to the Baltistan mosques. Unfortunately, it was destroyed by fire during the war events of 1995, together with the shrine of Sheikh Nur-ad Din (fig. 142), the most exquisite wooden building in Kashmir, and the adjacent *khanqah*.

Fig. 142. The shrine of Sheikh Nur-ad Din in Chrar-i Sharif, Kashmir, before its reconstruction in the 1960s (from Wakhlu 1998, pl. 6).

TOMBS OF SAINTS

The same type of centralised structure surrounded by a veranda is seen in virtually all the tombs of saints (*astanas*) in Baltistan. They show the wooden construction method already described, but restricted here to the building of cribbage pillars at the four corners. The four open sides of the inner building constituting the tomb chambers are screened with often exquisite latticework. Originally, most of the surrounding poled or arcaded verandas may also have been partially or totally enclosed by decorative carved timber panels. The structures are held together by the dead weight of the four corner pillars, the surrounding veranda and the pyramidal roof with its characteristic superstructure.

A characteristic Baltistan feature is the design of the tomb chamber's interior, as there is no ceiling, but a heavy corbelled cornice leading into a hexagonal or octagonal chimney-like drum, the *chaman*, which rises some five to seven metres to the lantern, called *masjid*, on top. In the tomb of Mir Aref in Tagas (pl. 49) and in structures under repair or in ruins, the *chaman* can be seen from the outside. It may have been designed to enhance the spiritual links of the saint with heaven.

The *qubbah* consists of the same ensemble as seen on the mosques and *khanqahs* — a small pyramidal spire with crosswise projecting sticks hung with wooden 'bells' and crowned by a metal umbrella holding a metal *alam*. As seen in Tagas, the wooden 'bells' were originally equipped with wings possibly imitating winged metal bells suspended from Hindu temples or possibly also Buddhist temples or *stupas* in Ladakh.

The leading six *astanas* are: that of Sayyed Mir Yahya (died 1632) in Shigar (fig. 143); those of Mir Aref (died 1651 or 1655; pl. 49) and of Mir Ishaq (fig. 132), a son of Sayyed Mir Mukhtar, standing side by side next to Mir Aref's *khanqah* in Tagas (fig. 133); the tomb of Hazrat Mir Mukhtar (died in 1718) behind his Khanqah-i Moualla in Kiris (fig. 144); the *astana* of Sayyed Mohammad (fig. 145; pl. 53), a son of Sayyed Mir Yahya, behind his huge *khanqah* in Khaplu; and that of Mir Sayyed Ali Tusi (died 1670) at Kuwardo near Skardu. The two tombs in Kiris and Kuwardo were restored by the locals some time ago, resulting in a sad deformation of the structures. More recently the AKCS-P put the *astana* in Khaplu back into its original shape, and lately the restoration of the tomb of Sayyed Mir Yahya in Shigar (fig. 143) got under way, with the locals given advice by the AKCS-P. A number of other tombs are smaller and copy any of the models of the four described structures in a more modest way. Good examples are seen in Kiris, where next to the restored *astana* of Sayyed Mir Mukhtar one finds the tombs of three other saints in different states of dilapidation.

Fig. 143. The *astana* of Sayyed Mir Yahya in Shigar (before restoration in December 2004).

Fig. 144. The dilapidated *astana* of Mir Mukhtar in Kiris before its restoration (from Dani 1989b, pl. XXIX a).

Fig. 145. The dilapidated *astana* in Khaplu before restoration.

The two tombs in Tagas stand out not only for their comparatively good state of preservation, but also for their greater height and their two-storeyed structure achieved by placing an intermediate layer of hori-

Fig. 146. A window of Ambariq mosque.

Fig. 147. The frieze on the front of Chakchan mosque in Khaplu.

Fig. 148. The frieze inside Chakchan mosque (pl. 48).

zontal logs at half height. This method was certainly meant to increase the stability of the unusually high structures. The two 'storeys' of the two tombs show different latticework.

The saintly tombs in Kashmir (according to observations made during my recent visit covering only a small part of Kashmir), show a similar centralised design, but are generally built of bricks and stones. Featuring a ceiling above the tomb, they are without the wide chimney-like *chaman*, characteristic of the Baltistan *astana*. They are nearly devoid of woodcarvings and also painted decoration, except for the little decoration generally found on the lintels and jambs of the entrance doors.

RAJA PALACES

Each of these princely states had a rather modest 'palace', *khar*, and a court life complete with a number of dignitaries, secretaries, guards and servants, including grooms who cared for highly prized horses used in polo games, the rulers' favourite form of entertainment. It is likely that all the palaces and the connected court life date from a recent time, that is, not before the eighteenth or even the middle of the nineteenth century, when a somewhat stable political situation under the dominance of the Maharaja of Jammu may have induced the *rajas* to move from proper forts into unfortified palaces, thereby becoming an easier prey to invaders. Dani learnt that the palace in Khaplu was "built in the middle of the nineteenth century after the older mud fort on the top of the hill was deserted". I was told that the then *raja* had thrown a large stone from the fort, located on the hilltop behind the present palace, to let the stone decide where to build his palace.

Similar dates can be assumed for the palaces in Skardu and Shigar, though Dani suggests an earlier date for the structure in Skardu: This building presents "some late Mughal architectural features" and may thus be dated in the eighteenth century. However, the noted features may just as well date from the middle of the nineteenth century, after Skardu had fallen to the Jammu ruler and after the important local ruler had lost much of his power. He must then have realised that it would be useless to hold on to his strong castle on the Khardong hill, which dominates the wide Indus valley at Skardu. At about that time, the other rulers in

Baltistan may well have developed a similar new interest in improving their living conditions – a trend induced in part by new exposure to the much more developed culture in Kashmir.

Probably the palaces were built and decorated with competition between the ruling families in mind. It is related, for instance, that Hatem Khan, a powerful ruler of Khaplu at the end of the nineteenth century, had conquered most of Baltistan, including Skardu, and then brought – among other looted objects – an exquisitely carved door frame from the palace in Skardu to be built into the entrance to the court leading to his palace.

Among the five palaces to be mentioned, that is, those in Khaplu (fig. 92; pl. 46), Kharmang (fig. 90), Kiris, Shigar (fig. 93) and Skardu, that in Kharmang could not be visited. The palace in Kiris, the smallest and most modest building in the group, is still lived in. The most impressive palaces, namely those in Khaplu, (probably) Kharmang and Skardu (partially lived in), are in bad repair, while the (somewhat) fort-like palace in Shigar, known as *Fong Khar*, 'the palace on the rock', was in a ruinous shape in 1999 when the Aga Khan Trust for Culture started to restore it (see chapter 10). In the meantime, the building has been not only carefully restored, but also transformed into a very special guesthouse and a small museum holding a collection of carved wooden items, most notably fronts of large chests, as well as historic objects of daily use.

Fig. 149. The old frame of the entrance door (now moved back to its original position on the ground floor), and the corbelled cornice on the upper east elevation of Shigar palace (see also figs. 150-152, 219).

The palaces are flat roofed, as are all the secular buildings in Baltistan. The building technique is that of *thatar*, but with signs of haste or thrift regarding the adequate insertion of stabilising beams which had to be brought from far away. The apparently scarce use of timber reinforcements led to sagging of the walls, thereby reducing the strength of the structure.

The two palaces in Skardu and Khaplu have three storeys, a large three-storeyed timber portico (*jaroka*) at the front, a loggia (*angun*), and a balcony on one or more sides, partially with excellent wooden latticework, some ceilings ornamented with *khatamband* work, and exquisitely carved doors. The portico, which features cusped arcades and cusped arched windows, appears to distinguish more than anything else the two buildings as 'palatial'. The palace in Khaplu, known as the Tokhsikhar, 'the high(er) palace', appears even more imposing, as it stands on a raised terrace.

The outside of the palace in Shigar is decorated with a corbelled cornice showing a series of medallions (figs. 149-152), and inside both the palaces in Khaplu and Shigar one finds exquisite woodcarvings and *khatamband* work which reflect the courtly life style of the then rulers (see below).

Figs.150-152. Various motifs from the cornice on the façade of Shigar palace.

THE ARCHITECTURAL DECORATION

The monuments of Baltistan – whether *astanas*, mosques or palaces – show a wealth of characteristic woodcarvings generously applied to adorn structural and non-structural elements alike. These decorations appear on the horizontal squared beams used in the construction of the walls, on arcaded verandas, the often corbelled cornices both outside and inside, the cases of doors and windows, the door wings, the columns or pillars with their bases and capitals, on the *mihrab* and so on. In addition, windows and large openings are generally filled with *panjira* latticework, and on the ceilings one often finds *khatamband* work (pl. 46). Consisting of small rectangular wooden pieces joined together according to varied geometric patterns, these art works constitute important decorative and architectural features in their own right. Strongly influenced from Iran, from where the crafts of *panjira* and *khatamband* were originally brought to Kashmir and Baltistan by Shah Hamadani, their different geometrical patterns carry mostly Persian names.

In general, the carved decoration consists of several continuous ornamental bands side by side. One finds stylised arabesque- and acanthus-like scrolls, entwined floral, often lily-like configurations standing opposite each other, guilloches, denticulations and rows of four-petalled rosettes, circular motifs, swastikas or bud-like configurations. The combination of several such bands created broad friezes which appear as wall decorations and ornamental linings of doors and windows, thereby de-materialising the structural elements and creating evocations of paradise-like beauty certainly much appreciated by the faithful.

The carvings on the Ambariq mosque (figs. 146, 291), thought by Dani to be the oldest in Baltistan, look less inspired and rather flat and 'dry'. They cover the space with a dense network of single or intertwined, mostly geometrical motifs lacking plasticity. Another stylistically related example is provided by the broad frieze below the windows of the lower floor of the Chakchan mosque in Khaplu and on the corbelled cornice inside its prayer room (figs. 147, 148). The frieze on the outside is composed of a broad central band filled with a complicated design of three rows of swastikas alternating with circles, which are continuously interconnected. The two borders are formed by denticulations and a narrow flower scroll on the somewhat projecting and thus cornice-like top section. The broad frieze in the prayer room has in its centre a similar interconnected combination of three rows of circles and – in this case – diagonally placed three-lobed, lily-like flowers, both inscribed into a square motif. Among the bordering bands of ornaments there is one above which stands out by its wave-like appearance of small inclined spirals. All these carvings and the very broad decorations framing the windows of the mosque are strongly reminiscent of the network-like, mainly geometrical configurations composed of complicated guilloches, simple scrolls with a floral motif alternating in position, continuous angular swastika-meander bands, a kind of Vitruvian scroll and so on, noticed in the Ambariq mosque.

Designs of a different kind are seen on the corbelled cornice on the façade of Shigar palace, showing a series of large carved medallions topped by a band of rhombuses (or squares placed on their corners) filled with knot-like designs (figs. 150-152). Two of the medallions have a figurative design, each depicting a pair of birds – the one pair shown with intertwining necks, the other drinking water from a lotus-like flower (pl. 58).

In the former reception room (now the museum) of Shigar palace (fig. 232), a pillar with a square base and large half-convoluted bracket capitals, standing in the centre, shows such an exquisite carved decoration that it may be classified as a superb representative of the court style in Baltistan (fig. 157). It testifies to a specific interest in plasticity and in depicting three-lobed lily-like flowers and centralised configurations of highly ornamental appearance. The top of the column depicts one of the most characteristic motifs found in Baltistan, also seen on the lintel of the richly carved door frame leading into Shigar palace: it is a vase-like configuration seen all over Baltistan in the centre of door lintels, once possibly constituting an apotropaic motif (figs. 155, 156).

As would seem, such ornamental carvings represent a higher and more complex developmental stage corresponding to a 'court style' which may have evolved some time in the late eighteenth or in the course of the early nineteenth century. Good examples of this style with its interest in plasticity and floral motifs are seen on and in the Khilingrong mosque in Shigar (figs. 153, 154). The cornices on top of the windows of the upper floor are deeply carved with bands of palmette-like plants, and laterally one finds two rows of leafy scrolls in combination with bands of meanders. Similar cornices carved with a 'palmette-frieze' are above the door into the lower prayer room and on the *mihrab*. There is also a 'classic' looking broad cornice-like frieze which runs underneath the windows around the whole prayer room. It is composed of a band showing somewhat deformed swastikas inside circles, accompanied by two rows of continuous meanders and topped by a floral scroll in alternating opposites. The mainly geometrical carvings around the windows of Chahburonjo mosque also show an interest in providing more relief to the ornaments by combining them with embossed sections.

Fig. 153. A window of Khilingrong mosque in Shigar.

Fig. 154. Upper part of the *mihrab* in Khilingrong mosque.

Fig. 155. Door in the loggia of Khaplu palace.

Fig. 156. Door in the court of Khaplu palace.

Top quality carvings of the 'court style' can be seen on two doors inside the palace in Khaplu (figs. 155, 156). The decoration of the leaves of the double door in the loggia is dominated by five pairs of large disks of varied design, showing multi-lobed flowers inside broad rims filled with a network of densely interlaced strings or wavy guilloches. The single leaf of the other door, located in the open court inside the palace, shows a late Moghul-inspired design of two arched, multi-lobed niches, with a flowering tree inside the upper niche and a large circular motif, with a star in its centre, filling the lower niche. The borders of the door leaves as well as the lintels and jambs of both doors are carved with several ornamental bands of guilloches, scrolls with flowers in alternating opposite positions and so on. The V-formed, vase-like floral motif depicted in high relief in the middle of the second door's lintel appears as an outstanding sample of a design motif seen very frequently, often reduced to a simple configuration, on door lintels everywhere in Baltistan. This motif may have developed originally from a design related to an apotropaic horned animal head such as a bovine head suspended from the entrance door's lintel.

The two doors may be classified as very important art works representing two different styles. The double door (fig. 155) differs from the single door because of its finer, more intricate and less floral, apparently more locally-grounded ornamentation. The Moghul-inspired door may well be the newer of the two doors. It appears stylistically related to the richly carved frontal boards of large storage chests which were acquired for the Palace Museum in Shigar. Appearing closely related to the 'court style', the rather unstructured filling of surfaces with a network of mainly floral, often deeply undercut motifs betrays a probably late developmental stage.

All the described features – such as the *thatar* building style based on inserted wooden pegs rather than on any kind of joinery, the 'invention' of the *khanqah*, the strong preference for a centralised square ground plan, the pyramidal roofs crowned with the *qubbah* – point to strong influences from Kashmir and Ladakh. The layout of the Kashmiri buildings may have been inspired by Hindu architecture built in stone, since centralised square structures are widespread in both Kashmir and Ladakh. The slim spires with umbrellas, crowning the countless *stupas* and *chorten* in Ladakh, cannot but constitute the models for the *cholo* and *qubbah* ensemble seen in Kashmir, from where this architectural feature probably travelled to Baltistan. Thus it seems clear that the prime models for the Baltistan architectural style were the Khanqah-i Moualla (Shah Hamadan mosque) in Srinagar, related structures elsewhere in Kashmir, and wooden buildings similar to the more recent mosque of Ata Mohammad Khan in Chrar-i Sharif. Nevertheless, some specific Baltistan features such as the huge *khanqahs* with their wide and high frontal verandas and the *chaman*, the wide chimney-like drum of the saintly tombs, are without equivalents in Kashmir.

Given the fact that in Baltistan (where timber is a rare and precious commodity), wooden architecture had emerged to such a dominant position, while in well-wooded Kashmir the important religious structures are mostly built of bricks and stones, one wonders to what extent Kashmir's long-lasting Hindu tradition in building with stone is the explanation for this discrepancy. The exceptional character of wooden buildings, namely the *khanqahs*, *khanqah*-like mosques and some structures like those burnt in Chrar-i Sharif, especially the famous, beautifully decorated shrine of Nur-ad Din Nurani and the mosque of Ata Mohammad Khan, appear related to the more transitory concepts presented by Sufi culture. The shrine of Sheikh Nur-ad Din Nurani had been extensively decorated with excellent, but more recent

Fig. 157. Central column in the audience hall of Shigar palace. For more details of the restored audience hall, see the series of illustrations on pp. 228, 229.

Fig. 158. Front board of a carved chest in the Shigar fort museum.

woodcarvings, probably dating from the nineteenth century. (Apparently there are no published illustrations showing the building before its most recent modern reconstruction. During my recent stay in Srinagar I was able to purchase a few photos showing the old building and its carvings, which are unrelated to those in Baltistan).

The question remains how much of the architectural decoration owes its appearance to influences from Kashmir. Certainly, Kashmir with its highly developed crafts may well have contributed considerably to the development of the carved decoration in Baltistan, but there is little remaining evidence available with the sole exception of corbelled cornices, a favourite feature in both regions, and possibly closely related to similar looking cornices of Hindu temples in Kashmir. With regard to carved decoration, all the buildings visited during my recent stay in Kashmir show none or little, with the 'ancestor' – the Shah Hamadan mosque in Srinagar – being no exception. There is a richly painted decoration on its entrance door (the inside has been changed by the recent restoration), but carvings exist only outside on a heavy corbelled cornice running along the base of the building. They recall the 'court style of Baltistan'. Other examples of rare carvings, such as the recently painted ones on the door frame of the shrine of Batamaloo Sahib in Srinagar, relate to the 'average' carvings in Baltistan, but do not present any telling features.

There is also the rich vocabulary of ornamental motifs seen on the stone carvings of Hindu temples in Kashmir, most noteworthy are those in Martand and Avantipur. Some of these motifs also appear in Baltistan. However, if one wants to admit possible influences from Hindu architecture, by the same reason one could argue in favour of influences from the Buddhist monasteries which once existed in Baltistan without leaving any traces, except for rock carvings.

8. Towards an Inventory of Historic Buildings and Cultural Landscapes

YASMIN CHEEMA

In a region such as the Northern Areas of Pakistan, any attempt to compile an inventory of cultural heritage must be undertaken on the basis of the natural landscape and within the constraints of given geographical boundaries. As an administrative entity, the Northern Areas of Pakistan with its capital Gilgit are currently divided into five districts: Skardu, Gilgit, Diamir, Ghanche and Ghizer. All settlements are located in the transition from the Eastern Hindukush to the Karakoram and Western Himalayas. The three mountain ranges meet at Jaglot, an exceptional natural site at the confluence between the Hunza and Gilgit rivers. All in all, the mountain ranges between Central Asia and South Asia contain over a hundred peaks from 6000 to 8611 metres and thirty peaks above 8000 metres (including K2, the second highest mountain in the world), as well as some of the largest (up to sixty-two kilometres long) glaciers, such as Biafo, Hispar, Bualtar, Gasherbrum, Lungma and Batura – not to mention many rivers, lakes and the Deosai plateau, an outstanding 3464-square-kilometre high-altitude plain located between Skardu road and Indian Kashmir.

Information on the general landscape and the climatic, ethnic and linguistic characteristics of the Northern Areas have already been provided in chapter 2 of this book. Suffice it to add, that the flora and fauna of the regions show great diversity with several globally unique species represented. The rare fauna of the Northern Areas includes the snow leopard, red fox, wolf, golden marmot, Ladakh urial, Himalayan brown bear, markhor, Himalayan ibex, blue sheep and musk deer. Six species of pheasant: the Blue Peafowl, Khalij, Koklass, Cheer, Western Tragopan and Monal, out of the forty-nine in the world are found in the Himalayas. The agro-biodiversity distribution is very rich, with a variety of species such as the morel mushroom, alpha-alpha, wild thyme, cumin, wild rose, apricot, peach, pear, walnut, mulberry, pine nut and costus root. Ethno-botanical records show that over two hundred species of plants are used as 'folk' medicines.

The equally unique and complex cultural heritage of the Northern Areas is the result of diverse cultural influences and traditions which left their mark on the area from the fifth millennium BC onwards (see chapter 1 in this book). The respective heritage items include a variety of remnants, such as ancient petroglyphs and rock carvings, ruins of Buddhist *stupas* and monasteries, forts and ancient palaces reaching into the Islamic period, as well as historic mosques, tombs of saints, villages, dwellings and ceremonial open spaces used by local communities up to the present day.

From the early petroglyphs and rock inscriptions, it can be learnt that several travellers visited the area and left marks of a number of languages. The majority are in Kharashti, Brahmi, Sogdian; rarely in Bactrian, Tibetan, Chinese or Hebrew. Petroglyphs and rock carvings also testify to the regional and seasonal migration of nomadic forest hunters, herders and pastoralists from Central Asia, India, Persia, South Siberia, Sichuan, Tibet, Iran, Central Asian and Inner Asia.[1] They represent animals, hunting scenes and demon-like creatures in different styles. Hunting tools discovered in forests located above various villages confirm early human activity in the area.[2] Other archaeological remnants consist of faint traces of semi-sedentary settlements, man-made cultivation terraces and fields, ingeniously built irrigation channels and their unique distribution and storage systems. There are also ancient paths and several elements located along the routes to provide necessary relief to travellers during their strenuous journeys.

The sociocultural traditions of individual valleys have evolved over centuries, due to fusion with other ethnic groups, influx of different languages and religions, trade of material goods and mobility of ideas.[3] Hinduism, shamanism, Buddhism, and various sects of Islam succeeded or coexisted with each other. Cultural exchange materialised either through the interaction of peoples of different villages and travelling traders and religious missionaries, or through dynastic changes and shifts of political alliances between various chiefdoms. Such coalitions ranged from intermarriages between the ruling families to exchanges of gifts. The conversion and acceptance of new religions remained an important part of the processes of cultural transformation.

Independent of ethnic groups, languages and religions, people's major concern, however, was how to survive under extremely harsh high-mountain conditions; how to succeed in the daily struggle for basic subsistence. Animal husbandry and agriculture were prime preoccupations, as was the performance of rituals to harness divine powers and the forces of nature. The technology for agricultural production was introduced from the eleventh to the fifteenth centuries. Melting snow was brought down from the glaciers through large and small channels constructed to feed agricultural fields and provide water for human consumption. The steep stony mountain slopes were terraced to create stepped flat areas for cultivation of fields and permanent settlements.[4] For strategic protection, villages were normally located at the arid edge of river gorges or alluvial deposit areas located between rivers and mountains. The forts and palaces of the rulers of major settlements on the crossroads of trade routes such as Gilgit and Skardu, and those of the Hunza and Nager valleys, were normally erected in dominant positions overlooking the settlement – as in the case of Altit and Baltit forts. On the other hand, some forts of Baltistan are nestled within the fabric of historic villages. The best and largest available land was reserved for agricultural cultivation, leaving a minimum for human and animal habitat. Summer dwellings-cum-cattle sheds for summer pastoralism remained in semi-arid to semi-humid ecological zones at higher altitudes.

As could be expected in such secluded areas, many traditional customs from earlier periods have continued until recently in the form of established social structures. Various clans and sub-clans claim lineage from one or two or, at times, three ancestors. The villagers or clans jointly own the meadows, pasturelands and water sources, and splitting shared water rights remains a major issue. Most rituals and festivals celebrated in the Northern Areas are associated with nature, the seasons, agro-pastoral activities and particular religious practices (see Insert 1). The main spiritual legacy of the past is a deep-rooted belief in shamanism.[5] Its beliefs and ritual practices transpire in many traditional customs and represent a sort of syncretism underlying all the contemporary, more formal sectarian beliefs of various Islamic communities. Today, the entire population is Muslim and they belong to various sects: Sunni or Ithnashari Shia, Shia, Nurbakshi Shia and Ismaili Shia.

(This list does not include the well-known official Islamic festivals, such as *Eid-ul-Fitr*, *Eid-ul-Ahzar*, the birthdays of the Prophet and of various *imams*, and the month of mourning of *moharram* followed by the Twelver Shia)

Nowroz is the Zoroastrian New Year and is celebrated with great fervour in the Northern Areas.

Gaaruki celebrates the beginning of spring. *Bath*, a special dish, is prepared and distributed amongst the families of a village. *Sulathum* is practiced to celebrate the end of winter and move the animals to the meadows. Animals are fed and decorated with flowers to ensure that they breed during the summer.

Chaasa is celebrated at the start of winter in the second week of November. Normally the older animals are slaughtered and their meat is distributed through children between the families of each settlement. Seven- to eight-year-old boys take wooden swords, while girls carry bows and arrows to houses of pregnant women, a symbol to wish good luck and health for the unborn baby. Teenagers from the age of twelve to sixteen perform stage shows, for which they are rewarded with meals, flour, chicken, meat and dry fruit.

Thumusheling (fire festival) was celebrated on 21 December, to celebrate Siri-Badat, the cannibal king's death. Every household carried fired logs, stacking them in the middle of a communal area, the polo ground or the communal open space within the fortified settlements. The villagers danced all night around the fire while the *mir* of Hunza was the chief guest. This festival stopped when the Government of Pakistan abolished the *mir* system.

Bofao is celebrated at the start of the sowing season with a handful of seeds flung into a field by the most respected village elder. During the day milk with bread and *diramphitti* (a traditional sweet dish) is cooked and distributed.

Ginani is the celebration of the first day of harvesting. All village members assemble near one field. A stalk of wheat is covered with butter and sprinkled with flour. Ripe wheat or barley are cooked in milk and served.

New festivals have emerged with the change in agricultural products. The children and women cut the potatoes up and the men sow them and cover them with earth. The whole community lunches together near the field.

Shamanistic rituals have survived in Hunza to the present day. A *bitan* is supposed to have supra-natural powers of divination, through his bond with fairies who reside at high altitude. By putting himself into a trance, he prophesises the future. The *bitan* receives money from all families once a year. In turn he/she is employed to cure ailing humans and cattle, to release the community members from worry and interpret their nightmares.

A melange of shamanistic, Hindu and Muslim customs are practised in the Chaprot community. A bush (*sugu*) located below the settlement is believed to house a spirit which brings good luck. The Chaprot polo players tie a woollen string on a branch when leaving for a polo match, to bring good luck.

The Chaprot community prays facing certain stones they consider holy.

In some areas, women are separated from the family after giving birth. Together with women during their menses, they reside in a building, *Ashu-to-dori*, specially constructed for this purpose. Pregnant women are not allowed to enter cattle sheds for fear that the cattle may die.

Rasm-e-Ghulab is a day devoted to the memory of the dead. Wild flowers are picked and placed on the graves of those who are no longer in this world.

Haaku is the day when all the Hunzakutz / Nagerkutz officially start to collect fodder and store it for the winter months. The same day animals are slaughtered and consumed. This is done in the hope that no one in the communities will suffer from bad luck during the winter months.

The people of Baltistan hang yaks' heads or full dry pumpkins outside their houses to keep away the bad spirits. Ibex heads are used for the same purpose in Hunza and Nager.

One of the important collective activities to be mentioned is the cleaning and repair of the water channels before the melting of glacial ice and snow. An experienced senior community member leads a team of young men who implement his orders. This event lasts from two to seven days.

Figs. 159-161. Landscape character, as varying with different altitudes, from the glaciers to the high pastures and down to the settled areas of the valleys at around 2000-2500 metres (confluence of Hunza and Nager rivers).

A major impact on living patterns occurred with the opening of the Karakoram Highway (KKH) in 1978. Suddenly, new types of civilisation and economic exchange emerged, and traditional and modern living styles started coexisting side by side. While imported modern household tools became available, traditional stone and timber utensils remain in general use in the area. Similarly, traditional timber agricultural tools are still being used. Most of the men and women are educated today, and many men dress in Western style; yet the agro-pastoral social traditions have been maintained to a considerable extent. The majority of the communities still live in modest agro-pastoral dwellings, many of which are single-storey houses. Meanwhile, new construction modes based on reinforced concrete frames and cement brick infill, with large windows, spread along the main valleys.

The heterogeneous cultural trends within the area, based on the strong topographic sub-divisions and reflected in various sectarian religious groups, as well as in the variety of local languages (see chapter 2), continue to date. Communication between the valleys is still difficult, despite new road networks. In fact the KKH and the Skardu road have galvanised modern development in their immediate surroundings while leaving behind more remote areas, thus inducing a new type of cultural disparity. The Pakistani government (through its Public Works Department), and the Aga Khan Development Network (mainly through its Rural Support Programme), have been the major catalysts of progress and change over the past twenty to thirty years. Meanwhile, the Aga Khan Cultural Service-Pakistan (AKCS-P), by developing community-based planning strategies and implementing conservation projects for major monuments, have raised awareness about the value of the architectural heritage and the assets of nature (see chapter 12).

SCOPE AND METHODOLOGY OF THE HERITAGE INVENTORY

In 1999, when its activities started reaching out beyond Karimabad and Hunza, the AKCS-P decided to initiate the Northern Areas Heritage Inventory, with the aim of recording the surviving cultural and architectural heritage in conjunction with the natural settings they belong to. The fieldwork demonstrated that the Northern Areas cultural and natural heritage is a legacy that transcends individual buildings and settlement, in forming complete cultural landscapes which may include historic landmark buildings, such

Natural heritage includes:	Tangible cultural heritage includes:	Intangible cultural heritage includes:
mountain peaks glaciers forests meadows and pasturelands	cultural landscapes archaeological sites historic settlements with necessary components of water infrastructure storage with distribution systems and surrounding human created cultivation fields places where past events took place monumental historic buildings: palaces and mosques cultural open spaces historic individual dwellings	climate religion traditions and festivals rituals professional skills memory of leaders and elders languages games

as forts, historic settlements, religious buildings, remains of earlier settlements, archaeological relics, traces of silk routes, valleys, meadows and pasturelands, agricultural terracing, man-built channels and water storage systems. The inextricable association of the works of nature and those of man makes these cultural landscapes a unique, tangible heritage of universal significance.

If left to inconsiderate development, the nature-dominated environment of the Northern Areas may soon convert into a human-dominated environment with all the corresponding risks for the area's major assets. Data-based inventories are therefore essential for all government organisations as the custodians and managers of the nation's environmental and cultural heritage. Started in 2000 in collaboration with the International Union for the Conservation of Nature, the Inventory has been established to provide basic information and set priorities with regard to environmental protection plans, constitution of nature reserves and future conservation programmes. The mapping and analysis of heritage assets should be used as an important tool for regional planning and area development. It can also be seen as a detector of potential economic resources and as a guide for appropriate intervention, rather than as an obstacle to development. The government, the private development agencies and the tourism industry need to become aware of the Inventory, which should also be fed into the curriculum of various educational institutions. Most importantly, local communities, as the 'owners' of places to be protected, need to realise the value of the irreplaceable assets entrusted to them. Whether issued online or as a publication, the Inventory will provide valuable data for scholars of history, anthropology, architecture and social studies. Its completion is expected for 2006 or 2007.

Established as they are to analyse the history, nature and variety of respective cultural heritages, inventories imply scholarly research on settlement patterns and their evolution, on architectural history, and on the structural, functional and decorative characteristics of buildings of various periods. Ideally, they must be based on a thorough documentation, including surveys on cultural landscapes and regional maps, plans of various stages of settlements, and measured drawings of monuments and buildings. Much, if not most of the corresponding groundwork still remains to be done, and this is the reason why the Inventory can only proceed at a relatively slow pace.

Figs. 162-165. The cultivated landscape and the built environment. Top left, rubble stone enclosures defining the individual fields and leaving a narrow space for irrigation channels and footpaths between them. Top right, the open square in front of Altit village. Bottom left, a covered resting space (*baldi*) along a major pathway. Bottom right, the *himaltar*, or public meeting space, at the entrance to Baltit village. All pictures by D. Lorimer, 1935.

A certain amount of literature on the Northern Areas history and heritage assets has been published since the opening of the KKH in 1978, particularly by the multi-disciplinary German missions to the Karakoram. In the field of architecture, A. H. Dani's book on wooden architecture in the Northern Areas[6] is still a major resource. However, its focus is on mosques, *khanqahs* and forts, and even there, detailed documentation is obviously limited. As far as historic villages and traditional houses are concerned, detailed surveys are almost inexistent – except for the recent work of the AKCS-P – and comprehensive historic studies are sorely missing. Consistent mapping of cultural landscapes and particular focal areas within them is another outstanding and time-consuming task.

In designing the methodology developed for the Northern Areas it was therefore kept in mind that most of this basic information is still lacking. Based on the 2000 Pilot Inventory, it seemed logical to consider three main categories:

- identification of important, comprehensive cultural landscapes;
- comprehensive surveys of significant villages;
- concise, one-page information on individual buildings, monuments and cultural open spaces, followed by more detailed information on selected individual structures and monuments, which, after comparative analysis, are evaluated as the buildings of greatest cultural significance.

The Inventory is to become an evolving database of the important heritage resources in the Northern Areas of Pakistan. It will include anything of a physical, cultural or social nature that is of unique value and should be passed from generation to generation. A major selection criterion is the significance of a structure to the respective communities because of its association with their ancestors and past culture, or because it bears witness to the presence of one or several particular civilisations. There are also cultural landscapes that illustrate the history of several periods and are of universal value, or villages that belong to a certain historic era and have a unique historic tissue or some other valuable features (see also Insert 2). Moreover, sites can be significant because they are associated with an important person, event or historic trend. Their inclusion can also be decided simply because of their outstanding beauty or rarity.

It may not be possible to salvage all the cultural resources included in the Inventory due to the quantity of material resources and the nature of material used for their construction, as well as the rapid transformation of people's lifestyle and their financial limitations. However, in the future, the Inventory will provide a tool for comparative assessment of cultural and historic assets and for setting conservation priorities. Agencies intervening in the development of the Northern Areas will need to become aware of its contents in order to make informed choices and trade-offs.

The Gilgit region has been the testing ground for the comprehensive inventory. Selected areas include Gulmit in Upper Hunza, Central Hunza, Chalt/Chaprot of Lower Nager and three villages in Upper Nager: Hopar, Broshal, Holshal and Ghushoshal. These were first surveyed in 2002, in terms of a rapid preliminary assessment. In 2003, the villages were mapped, a more detailed survey carried out and the software upgraded. In Baltistan, initial surveys have covered Chinpapa and Halpapa in the Shigar valley, Sermik in the Skardu area and Khanga in Khaplu. The remaining work is scheduled to be completed in 2005/2006. Further work will require more detailed mapping with the help of high-resolution satellite images.

EMERGING CULTURAL LANDSCAPES

So far, four significant cultural landscapes have been identified, the Hopar valley, Central Hunza, Lower Nager and Shigar valley. Due to the constraints of this article, the discussion will be restricted to only two of them, Hopar and Central Hunza. Important heritage elements in the rich Shigar valley are discussed in chapters 10 and 12 of this book. Chalt, Chaprot, Budalas and Soni Kot, though different in sociocultural terms, form another cultural landscape that reflects the development in the area from the third millennium to the present time, but it cannot be discussed in this context.

Figs. 166-168. Three typical settlements in their natural and agricultural setting: top, Sumaiyar; middle, Thol; bottom, Altit.

Hopar valley

The Hopar valley has two main glaciers, Hopar and Barpu. The Hopar glacier has three different names: Hopar related to the valley, Bualter related to the meadow, and Kepal related to the peak. This glacier is nineteen kilometres long, 2.5 kilometres wide, and 129 metres deep. The second main glacier is the Barpu glacier, which is a culmination of Sumaiyar Bar and Miar glaciers, and is thirty-two kilometres long, 3.5 kilometres wide, and 132 metres deep. The smaller glaciers include Diranchi, Ghaynthur and Koar, which face the Hamdar valley. Nearby is Rush lake which has a large forest of juniper and pine trees.

Traces of a forest/hunter society still exist in Kepal Dongus. This tradition still continues as Kepal Dongus is a hunting ground for ibex and pheasants. Graves, crude shelters, petroglyphs and rock carvings are located at Hamdar, Hapakun and Shiskin. There are ruins of three semisedimentary villages in the area. The remains of Mainkun have been found in the Hononu meadows, located 150 metres above the present settlements. Ruins of two others are located on a plateau, both sides of which display faint traces of the receding Bualtar glacier. The Rush lake forest, ten historic meadows (located on average at 3550 m) and twelve pasturelands continue to be used as summer grazing lands for the domesticated animals of Holshal, Broshal and Ghashoshal. The agriculture fields and orchards of the three villages are mainly fed by a common channel, which originates and falls back into the natural Diranchi water stream.

The traditional route to the villages follows the bottom of the valley, linking Holshal and Broshal. A half-a-metre-wide footpath cutting through the fields connects Broshal to the Ghashoshal *bayak* (communal open space). The houses are attached and built in linear rows on man-made terraces, which gives the village its typical cascading profile. The roofs of the houses are normally at about the same level as the by-lane of the upper terrace, allowing sunlight to penetrate the houses. During the 1970s, the old pathway was broadened and diverted at places to create a jeep track.

The valley has not undergone any major transformation, though a few houses have started to be built in the fields by people who left the village. The Broshal settlement consists of one hundred and seventy properties, out of which sixty-five are in residential use. The rest have been converted to cattle sheds and animal fodder stores. All the houses are dwellings with only one *mun*, or 'platform'. (See the description of traditional houses below.) In Ghashoshal, of a total of thirty-six houses, thirty have single platforms and six have two platforms. In Holshal there are forty-two houses, of which forty-one are single-platform dwellings. Most Ghashoshal and Broshal traditional dwellings have been converted into cattle sheds and grass storage sheds. The Holshal villagers are economically underprivileged and continue to live in their traditional houses. The two or three rare old houses and a mosque have historic architectural and traditional craftsmanship value. The other buildings are of group value, and harmonise well with the surrounding natural environment and the man-made agriculture fields.

The main disturbing intervention is the new road constructed by the Aga Khan Rural Support Programme with aid from the Government of Pakistan. The road not only cuts through the heart of the valley but is also encouraging the growth of linear strips of low-quality buildings on either side. This intervention is perhaps not reversible, but needs the goodwill of all the involved to contain and minimise negative consequences.

Central Hunza
The Central Hunza cultural landscape consists of Karimabad, Altit, Baltit, Ganish, Sumaiyar, the Sacred Hunza rock and the Duiker archaeological site. The natural heritage consists of the mountains of Ultar (I and II), Lady Finger, Shisper peak, Ahmadabad peak, Diran peak and Sumaiyar peak (I, II, III). The glaciers include Ultar, Tsillkeyeng and Ahmadabad. The area has undergone heavy deforestation. Gantsupar, Buria Haria, Donadus, Multansa and Hanchinder meadows are the property of the Ganishkutz. Thamu Harai, Khowhat and Theeyeshar were forests owned by the *mirs* which are now reduced to meadows. The Yastaa meadows also belonged to the *mirs* and even today are frequented by them. The only meadow of Karimabad is at Ultar. The Sumaiyar meadow gives access to a substantial reservoir of semi-precious stones. Traces of a semi-sedimentary settlement and some graves have been found above Sumaiyar village.

Portions of the connecting Silk Route leading to the polo grounds of the settlements have survived the onslaught of modern development. The same is true of their polo grounds, water reservoirs, water storage tanks and the fortified walls or their foot prints. The original tissue of the Baltit *khan* (traditional settlement) is more or less intact, but the surroundings have undergone major transformation and are today engulfed by new development.

The construction of the Karakoram Highway caused major losses to Ganish *khan*, by cutting through its polo ground, separating it from the Hamchi Ghamun pasture land and demolishing a major part of it in the north (pl. 20). The new metal road joining Ganish with Karimabad and a jeep track connecting Karimabad with Altit has created a new layer of landscape. Under this lie glimpses of the historic stratum, consisting of foot prints of several physical elements of the past. If neglected, they will completely vanish, disappearing with the generation who – through their collective memory – can unravel the spatial organisation of the individual villages and historic cultural landscape maps of Central Hunza.

This area is endowed with a wealth of cultural resources, including the famous Altit and Baltit forts, scores of historic houses, many richly embellished mosques, Ganish (one of the few villages which still

Fig. 169. Survey plan of Broshal village in the Nager valley.

retains its fortified walls), and three *shikaris* (watchtowers). The four timber mosques located in the Ganish *jataq* (communal open space) are excellent examples of family mosques in the Northern Areas. The *wazir* family's 'hanging mosque' in old Karimabad, which forms a gateway on the way up to Baltit fort, is unique in its kind.

OBSERVATIONS ON SETTLEMENT STRUCTURE
In most scholars' descriptions, the settlements in the Northern Areas appear to be fortified by a wall with one or two entrances, giving access to winding narrow lanes, surrounded by closely clustered houses. The main lane leads to a central communal space. A water reservoir is usually located two to three metres away from the settlement's outer walls, with one or two communal water storages located at the beginning of a path which leads to a *shabaran* (polo ground). During the Inventory survey, a number of different settlement typologies have been identified, with variations according to size and density of settlements and to their topographic configuration:

Villages on man-made or natural plateaus, with three sides secured by a river gorge. Only the exposed side is fortified, with one to two openings protected by watchtowers. The dwellings usually occupy the entire ground, leaving constricted, normally two-metre-wide lanes between them. The interior lanes are partly covered by first-floor structures of adjacent dwellings. A communal space with one or two religious buildings is usually located within the fortification. All villages have a large water reservoir, water storage wells, and a polo ground outside the walls. Altit, Ganish, Thole, Holshal and Chaprot villages fall into this category.

Stepped villages constructed on man-made terraces cut out of mountain slopes. Single rows of connected, tightly packed houses are located along a lane that runs between two terraces of different heights. The roofs of some houses on a lower terrace are at times part of the lane, contributing to extending its width. The roofs of others are a little over one metre high if the house entrance is from the lane. The door frame of such houses rises to one metre above the lane, while the floor of the entrance vestibule is half to one metre below the lane. The main lanes of this type of village connect the outside public area with the inside *jataq*. The mosques and a village guest house (*sawab-ha*) are normally attached to the *jataq* but can also be located at the entrance of the *khan*. Broshal, Ghashoshal, Chaprot and parts of Thole are examples of this settlement type.

Several villages protected by hills and mountains have a common entrance (*himalter*), flanked by watchtowers (*shikaris*). At times the villages have an indivual protected entrance (*himalter*) as well. Hoshal, Broshal and Ghashoshal are of this settlement plan type.

Clustered houses built on a flat plateau with walled tunnel-like lanes totally covered by the extensions of the upper floors. Most settlements of the Skardu region are built in this manner for protection from severe winter winds.

Two rows of connected houses leaving between them a narrow curved lane, located on a man-made terrace. The access to the first row of houses is from the upper-level lane, while the other row of houses is entered from the lower-level lane. Baltit village is the only example of this type the inventory team has visited to date.

Rectangularly-shaped villages on flat areas, with streets of roughly equal length and two-storey houses. The Sumaiyar *khan* is planned in this manner. These villages normally feature a *jataq*, *imambarha* or *matam-sarai* (religious meeting places) and a water storage, as well as a polo ground near the entrance, similar to the settlements of Hunza and Nager lo-

Figs. 170-173. Various views of the Broshal settlement, with close-ups of houses and interior lanes.

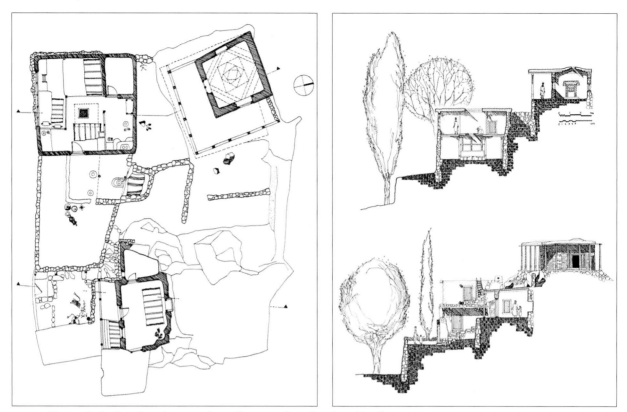

Fig. 174. Left, plan of two houses and a small mosque above them in Baltit village;
right, two sections across the little settlement cluster.

cated above a river gorge. However, in the case of Sumaiyar, the settlement has access to the river water from within the fortified village via a steep path.

Loose settlements formed by a group of houses interspersed with orchards and agricultural fields. Chalt is the only orchard house village included in the inventory.

Clustered houses on flat land, strung along a stream. The villages in Shigar are the only examples of such settlement patterns.

Most villages in Nager and Hunza consist of an outside communal area and a once fortified, very dense residential area, either located on a plateau approximately 214 metres above the river gorges or on man-made terraces absorbing the mountain slope. The communal area outside the *khan* is often vast, around a hundred times the surface of the very dense residential area. Historically, the entry to the settlements was through a half to one metre narrow lane, with poplar trees on either side, passing by the polo ground. Mosques often have a *gulk* (underground water storage tanks). Mosques, *gulks*, flour mills and *jamatkhanas* (religious assembly places) are often shaded by walnut, maple or mulberry trees. The width of the alleyways between the buildings is reduced to a few metres. The lane leading to a *pharee* (open water storage tank) winds between the fortified village and is embellished with willow, mulberry and walnut trees. In some villages, a small cabinet with shelves is placed on a stream, outside the fortifications: the locals call it their natural fridge. Milk products are stored and cooled in it during the summer months.

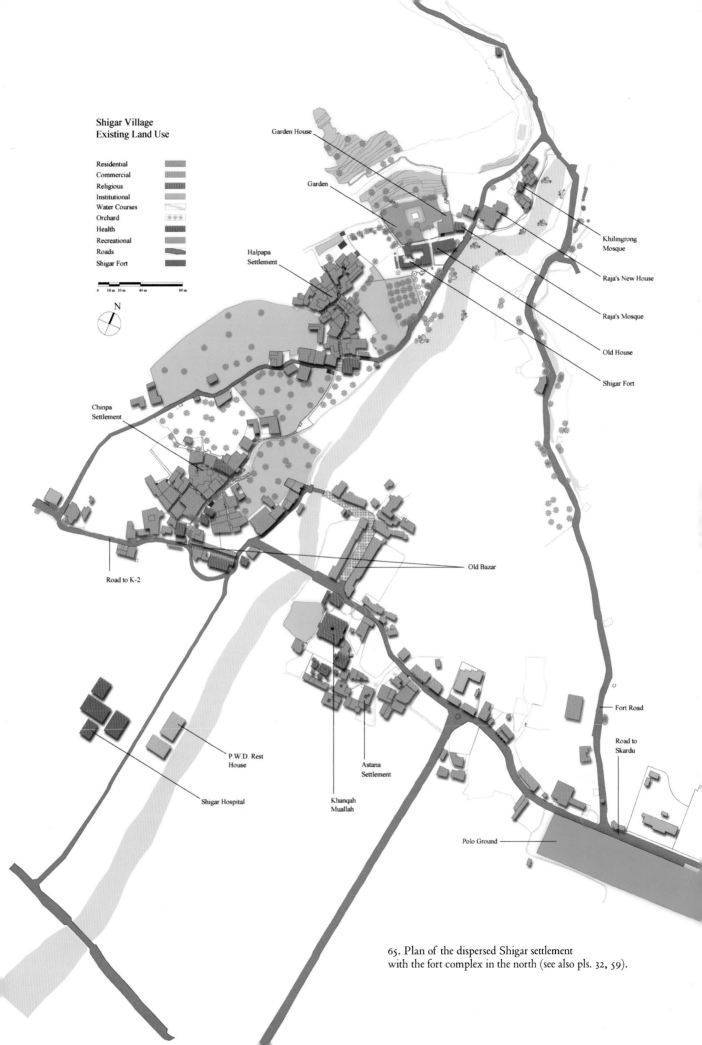

**Shigar Village
Existing Land Use**

Residential
Commercial
Religious
Institutional
Water Courses
Orchard
Health
Recreational
Roads
Shigar Fort

0   10 m 20 m   40 m   80 m

N

Garden House

Garden

Khilingrong
Mosque

Raja's New House

Raja's Mosque

Old House

Shigar Fort

Halpapa
Settlement

Chinpa
Settlement

Road to K-2

Old Bazar

Fort Road

Road to
Skardu

P.W.D. Rest
House

Astana
Settlement

Shigar Hospital

Khanqah
Muallah

Polo Ground

65. Plan of the dispersed Shigar settlement
with the fort complex in the north (see also pls. 32, 59).

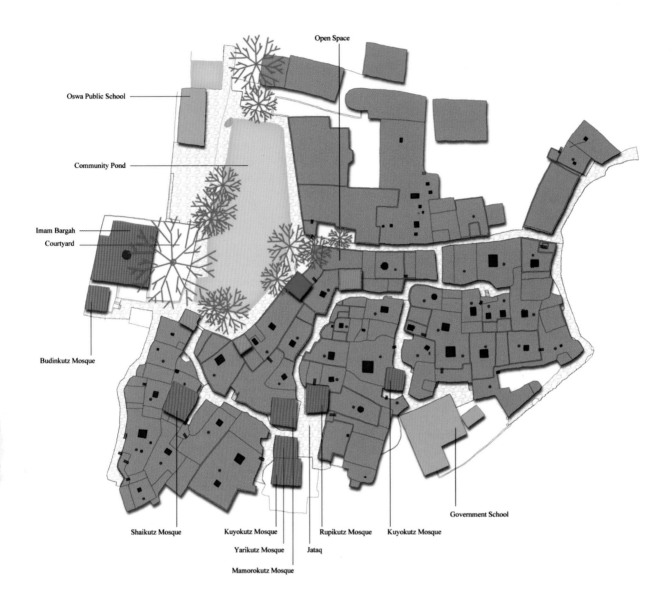

Open Space

Oswa Public School

Community Pond

Imam Bargah

Courtyard

Budinkutz Mosque

Shaikutz Mosque   Kuyokutz Mosque   Rupikutz Mosque   Kuyokutz Mosque

Yarikutz Mosque   Jataq

Mamorokutz Mosque

Government School

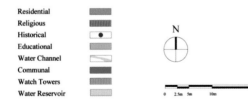

Ganish Village
Existing Land Use

Residential
Religious
Historical
Educational
Water Channel
Communal
Watch Towers
Water Reservoir

N

0   2.5m 5m   10m   20m

64. Plan of the historic nucleus of the fortified village of Ganish
around the communal pond (see also pls. 116-124). The small building marked in green
is the communal guest house (*sawab-ha*), accessible from *extra muros*.

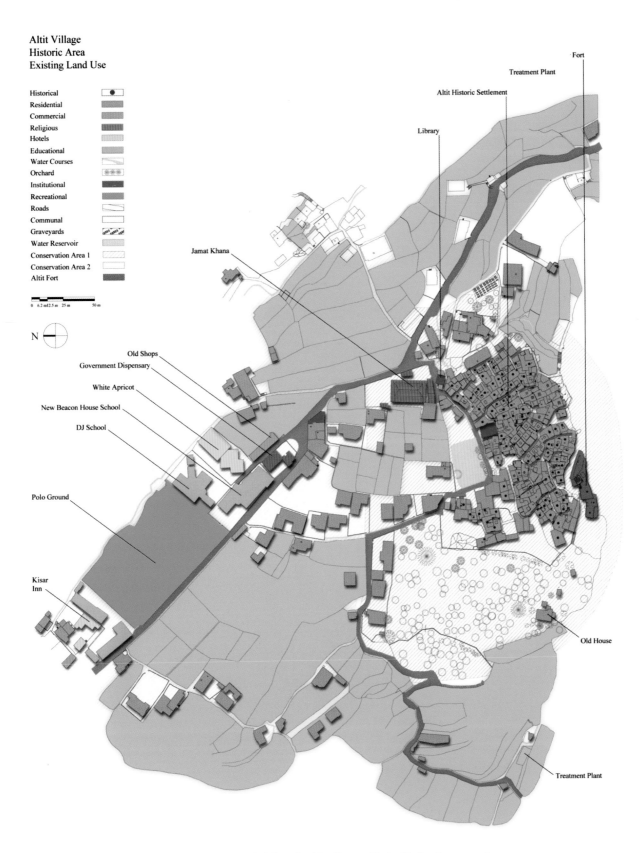

**Altit Village
Historic Area
Existing Land Use**

Historical
Residential
Commercial
Religious
Hotels
Educational
Water Courses
Orchard
Institutional
Recreational
Roads
Communal
Graveyards
Water Reservoir
Conservation Area 1
Conservation Area 2
Altit Fort

0   6.2 m12.5 m   25 m   50 m

N

Jamat Khana

Old Shops
Government Dispensary
White Apricot
New Beacon House School
DJ School

Polo Ground

Kisar
Inn

Library

Altit Historic Settlement

Treatment Plant

Fort

Old House

Treatment Plant

63. Plan showing the rehabilitated Altit village, with the *himalter* (entry space)
close to the water pond (see also pls. 10, 107). On the right, on the edge of the cliff, Altit fort.
Below the village and the fort the vast fruit tree orchard belonging to Altit fort (fig. 267).
Most of the old polo ground (fig. 319) has been occupied by new educational facilities.

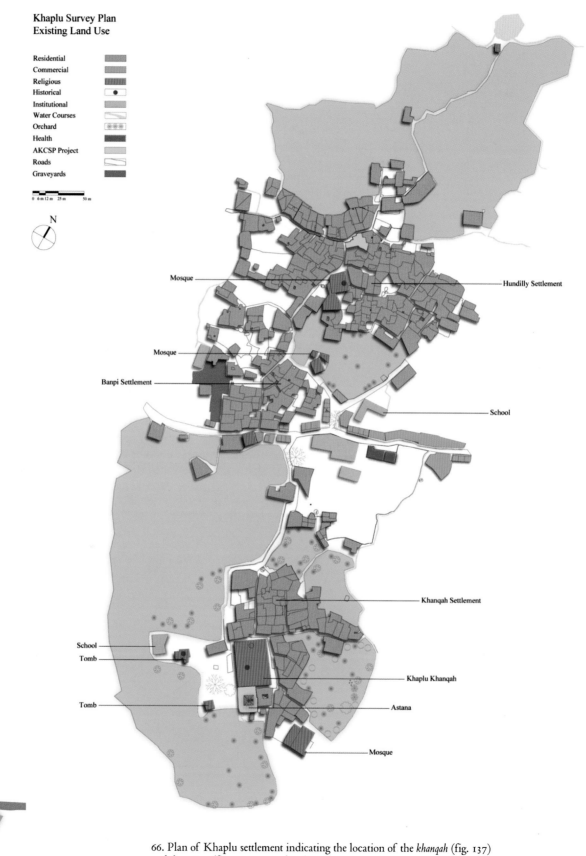

Khaplu Survey Plan
Existing Land Use

Residential
Commercial
Religious
Historical
Institutional
Water Courses
Orchard
Health
AKCSP Project
Roads
Graveyards

0 6 m 12 m 25 m   50 m

N

Mosque

Hundilly Settlement

Mosque

Banpi Settlement

School

Khanqah Settlement

School

Tomb

Khaplu Khanqah

Tomb

Astana

Mosque

66. Plan of Khaplu settlement indicating the location of the *khanqah* (fig. 137)
and the *astana* (figs. 294, 304; pl. 53).
Khaplu palace is located outside the perimeter of the plan.

A lane running between the *pharee* and the fortified walls, would have several *shikaris* rising along it at regular intervals. One or two *himalters,* flanked by *shikaris*, were the only openings into the village. Each settlement had a common communal space or square (the *jataq*) within its fortifications. *Jataqs* are located near the *himalters* or in the centre of the village. In Shia settlements the *matam-sarai* and at times a *sawab-ha* (guest house) are located in or next to the *jataq.*

OBSERVATIONS ON TRADITIONAL HOUSES

The Central Hunza dwellings have generally been described as three-storey structures, with a *ha* (winter house), an *agon* (summer house) and a *baldi* (covered loggia). The winter house consists of a vestibule and a *ha* which has three platforms, a *shite* (area around fireplace), a large store, a chest for grains,

Figs. 175-177. Above, two close-ups showing the use of the *muns* (by D. Lorimer, 1935). Below, a rendering of a typical *ha,* the focus of the traditional house, with a central opening in the roof (see also fig. 85) and the raised platforms (*muns*) around the central space.

flour, and so on. During the first cycle of the Inventory, the team discovered this to be factually incorrect. The dwellings are now normally two storeyed. Houses with a *baldi* are rare, while the typical winter house (*ha* in Burushaski, *got* in Shina) can have one, two or three *muns* (platforms) raised about twenty centimetres from the ground. In the case of single *mun* houses, the platform is not always raised. Half the house is used as an eating and sitting space and is called *nikeerad*, while the other half is used as the family's sleeping area. The two areas are physically divided by a low timber beam fixed on the ground. In the case of two *muns*, one of them (*uyum mun*) is the men's sleeping area, and the other (*jot mun*) serves for women and children. In three-*mun* houses the longest *uyum mun* is the bed of the elders and children, pregnant women and dying elders. The medium-sized *jot mun* is set aside as a sleeping area for young unmarried members of the family. The smallest *berichu mun* is reserved for newly-married couples. Musicians sit on it during marriage functions and it is also used as a work area for the men during the day while the other two *muns* are used for sitting on. According to the locals, all dwellings in Central Hunza were one-*mun* houses. The two- and three-platform houses started to be built after the Wakhi settled in the northern Hunza valley and introduced their three-platform houses.[7]

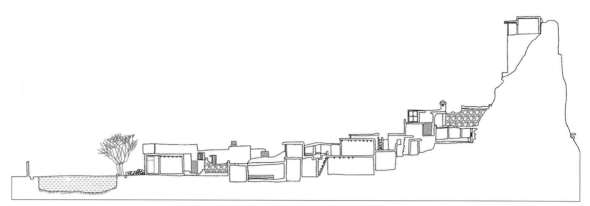

Fig. 178. Cross-section through the village at the foot of Altit fort.

According to earlier researchers, the embellishment of the timber elements was considered to confirm the age of the dwellings. The survey team found that most carved timber elements are incorporated into more recent dwellings by the house owners. At times they have been shifted two or three times in the lifetime of the current owner. Therefore it was imperative to undertake a door to door inventory of all dwellings in order to have a factual record of the different types of houses that exist within one village and to note important decorative elements.

All the dwellings surveyed in Hunza and Nager are constructed of stone masonry; the older structures feature double layer walls, more recent ones are built with simple walls. Timber 'cribbage' systems are only used on houses which are part of the fortified wall.

There are six types of ceiling: *Gandeleksi, Pangtani, Gasiraski, Uzwariski, Uzwariski* modified, and *Takhta*. The locals claim the *Gandeleksi* to be the oldest type of roof, as it can be constructed without timber cutting and shaping tools. The craftsmen of the area refer to *Pangtani* as the most ancient type. A *Pangtani* ceiling was supported by five columns, this number having a symbolic value for the Shia community and being

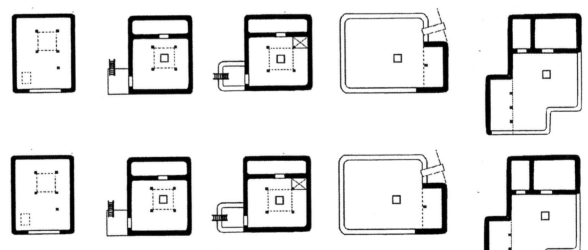

Fig. 179. Typical variations of the basic traditional Hunza house, with the *ha* in the centre, often accompanied by lateral sitting platforms and by attached rooms or storage spaces. Ground floor plans on the lower row and upper floor plans on the upper row (see note 7).

used for various purposes. (A hand with five fingers open is a popular pattern in Shia communities.) *Gasiraski* seems to have replaced *Gandeleksi* after the timber crafting tools had developed. *Uzwariski* is an Upper Hunza ceiling type, adopted by the Nagerkutz and the Hunzakutz.

The roofs are supported by (often decorated) timber columns and were traditionally water proofed by layers of birch-bark, covered with soil and *shinzak* (fine clay). At times thin strips of grass were integrated for thermal purposes. *Dambu* (local cane) can be used instead of birch bark, which at times is not available. The final waterproofing of the top layer was done with apricot paste. Today, the traditional roof materials have often been replaced by corrugated iron sheets, and polythene is normally used for water proofing.

CONCLUSION

The most striking aspect of the heritage of the Northern Areas consists in its rich and varied cultural landscapes that represent its history, its culture and its unique natural resources. To be properly conserved, the natural and cultural heritage has to be understood in its totality and in its complex interaction. In its present condition, it is a repository of early human attempts to harness nature and retains traces of important cultural exchanges, such as the Silk Route and other trade and missionary connections that passed through the region, creating a fusion of many civilisations over centuries of human history.

ID No: H-4-8

Resource Name:	**Akbar Hussain's House**
Address:	Broshal / Uyum Nagar
Village:	Nagar
Period/ Age/Date:	Around 100 years
Designation:	Not Protected
Ownership:	Private
Significance:	Age, Architecture, Rarity Value and Location
Description:	Akbar Hussain's house is a typical 40 *Khas* one *mun* (platform) plan type *ha* (traditional room) with a *Khunaj* (Vestibule). *Khunaj* (entrance lobby) leads to *kunjigash*, an area near the door of the *ha*. *Khunaj* serves the dual function of a vestibule and storage. The *mun* is 2'-3" in width, 14' long and 8" high. It is located on the east of the *ha*. The remaining area is the *shiti*, place for cooking and sitting in winter. *Shi* (fire place) is located in the centre of the *ha*, and is used for cooking and heating. The ceiling is a *gasiraski sagham* type, formed of five layers of thick planks. The upper planks are circumscribed by the lower and turned at 45, terminating at the *shagum* (opening in ceiling). Seven columns define the linear spaces running along all four walls, used for storage along with the *mun*.
Construction Materials, Method & Technique;	The house is constructed of stone slate set in mud mortar. Juniper is used for all timber. Timber dowel is used for fixing ceiling planks and joining storage chest planks. Juniper twigs placed on juniper logs surround the centre rotated square, both supported by timber beams.
Integrity:	Only one wall of the *Agon* remains, the rest has disintegrated, and collapsed.
	(Details)

Fig. 180. A typical example of an inventory sheet, in this case for a house in Broshal, Nager valley.

The cultural landscapes identified in the survey need to be protected against inappropriate development by conservation plans defining natural reserves and by legislation controlling modern building activities. Efficient application of land-use plans and building regulations, as well as permanent monitoring and proactive channelling of investments, are required. The one area which has already been heavily transformed to the extent beyond recognition is Central Hunza. Even here, important elements can be retrieved by highlighting remaining sections of the Silk Route, creating bridges and extending historic paths. Easy approaches to the semi-sedimentary settlements and the archaeological sites should be planned. The area should be presented adequately, as it has all the ingredients for becoming a World Heritage Site.

The Northern Areas have so far attracted adventure tourism – but if presented as a region where 'history can be experienced live', they can also attract culturally interested visitors, as well as school, college and university students. Scholars of different universities (both in Pakistan and abroad) have already done extensive research in the area. Coordinating and synthesising such research will be important so that it can be reflected in the Inventory as a vehicle for wider dissemination.

Hopefully, the Inventory will provide a management tool for government institutions and private organisations (such as the Aga Khan Development Network) for creating coherent frameworks of conservation and regional planning and for defining appropriate modes of intervention in the fragile cultural landscape of the Northern Areas. The Village Rehabilitation projects in Hunza and Baltistan, together with a variety of implemented conservation projects for landmark buildings (see the following chapters in this book), represent important pilot projects in this direction. Most importantly, they have helped to raise the cultural awareness of local communities and to revive traditional building techniques.

[1] H. Hauptmann, *The Indus-Cradle and Crossroads of Civilisations*, Embassy of the Federal Republic of Germany, Islamabad 1997, pp. 32-33.

[2] Discovered by Fazal Karim, at Kepal Dongus next to and above the Hopar valley.

[3] Jettmar suggests that the earliest influences were from Central Asia by Scythian nomads, later Tibetans. (K. Jettmar, *Beyond the Gorges of the Indus*, Oxford Unverstiy Press, Karachi 2002, p. 12.)

[4] See H. Kreutzmann and E. Ehlers (eds.), *High Mountain Pastoralism in Northern Pakistan*, Franzsteiner Verlag, Stuttgart 2000.

[5] Jettmar suggests that shamanism in the area was of Siberian origin. (See Jettmar in note 3 here.)

[6] A. H. Dani, *Islamic Architecture: The Wooden Style of Northern Pakistan*, National Hijra Council, Islamabad 1989.

[7] For Hunza houses, see also the article "Catching a Passing Moment: The Redeployment of Tradition", by Masood Khan in *Traditional Dwellings and Settlements Review*, vol. VII, spring 1996.

9. *The Restoration of Baltit Fort*

RICHARD HUGHES

For centuries, the construction, maintenance and repair of buildings in the Northern Areas was a purely local undertaking. People of the Karakoram are 'natural' builders, and they were only supported by itinerant craftsmen when available or for special jobs. Dark and cold winter months provided the ideal time for carving elements such as columns and panels, thus making each building a personalised structure. This has resulted in a great variety of buildings types and a fascinating wealth of ornamental features.

While the local approach to building tasks (as described in chapter 5) was often adequate, it also explains occasional structural and material problems we find when analysing historic buildings from a modern structural conservation point of view. To begin with, the later changes and repairs of originally well constructed historic buildings were commonly inadequate. Usually, the maintenance was conceived as a 'quick fix' – a short-term and temporary patch-up, cheaply done by unskilled workers, with a focus on materials and

Fig. 181. Enveloped in scaffolding: Baltit fort under restoration, seen from Ghulwating mosque (fig. 105).

not on structure, no recognition of heritage value and using poor quality locally made tools. Often the maintenance of religious buildings was neglected, perhaps because community motivation to carry out repairs was not sufficiently strong until a dangerous situation or an important religious occasion arose.

The principal cause for the loss of historic buildings is lack of proper maintenance related to progressive decay of structural timber components beyond a point when effective repair is still possible. Sometimes, their location and constricted spaces made them unsuitable for modern living styles. In stages of advanced decay, structural failures can no longer be handled in such a way as to recreate long-term stability. Further steps in this scenario of decay are the loss of the roof's integrity and walls being undermined at ground level, allowing water to seep in and accelerate the destructive process at critical structural connections, eventually resulting in the collapse of the whole building. The owner would not normally provide the right investment for new materials, for quality design and for large-scale structural intervention at the right time. Decayed buildings therefore are the 'norm' and once they have become ruins they serve as quarries of easily won materials for recycling.

A NEW CONSERVATION APPROACH

The creation of the Historic Cities Support Programme within the Aga Khan Trust for Culture in 1992 and the establishment of its Cultural Services company in Pakistan (AKCS-P), opened a new chapter with regard to conservation activities in the Northern Areas. For the first time, a consistent international conservation approach was applied to an increasing number of landmark monuments in the region. And, what is more, conservation became part of an all-embracing planning and socio-economic development strategy based on strong community involvement, training of local skills and building local institutional capacity (see chapters 12 and 13 in this book).

The conservation approach as such implied a few basic goals. The first goal was to stop further loss of historic buildings, since these now come under 'endangered species' in the region and constitute a finite and unique cultural resource. There are but a few monuments left, as compared with fifty years ago, and most of them have become untenable, unfashionable and too decayed for the modern living standards of their owners. Traditional houses are under considerable threat for replacement, with larger ones built from modern materials, especially reinforced concrete. The second goal, therefore, was to use conservation as a catalyst for upgrading traditional housing, ensuring a healthier environment with added modern facilities. The third goal was to utilise and extend the building skills of the local inhabitants and professionals, considering that restoration of historic buildings requires the use of the best conservation techniques – whether local and traditional or modern and imported.

The AKCS-P is committed to following conservation charters proposed by well-known international organisations such as UNESCO and ICOMOS (International Council of Monuments and Sites), which recommend retaining the authenticity, character and charm of monuments and traditional housing and retaining the historic context. Within this context, the AKCS-P develops acceptable local solutions and promotes technical, management and maintenance skills that are implementable in the long term by the local inhabitants. The implemented projects are to provide a vehicle for the promotion of the physical heritage of the Northern Areas in the rest of Pakistan and overseas – as an educational asset, for cultural exchange, for tourism and for scientific research.

The aim of the conservation methods developed for the region has been to ensure high-quality work, as required to give the monuments and important traditional buildings a new life for the next hundred and more years. This means there should be no need for new major interventions that would tend to degrade authenticity. The practical measures to achieve this objective have been based on the following processes. Before intervening there is a project design period often resulting in a master plan for the whole intervention. This is accompanied by a programme of staff training in Pakistan (and sometimes abroad), as well as by practical training workshops on site. For each project, specific conservation techniques are experimented and tested in advance, in order to ensure that quality procedures are in place before applying them to the monument. Simultaneously, there is a period of thorough survey and monument documentation followed by engineering and architectural analysis. The documentation and conservation design is then reviewed by peers to ensure the highest standards of conservation work.

Key elements of conservation interventions include temporary work to ensure the safety of people and prevent the monuments from being damaged. The interventions are designed to be as simple and as minimal as possible, with the aim of providing structural continuity, that is, to let the building work and move about in the same way as the structural system already in place. This principle recognises that the building has usually been operating successfully for a long time, but also anticipates weaknesses that may cause future distress. The interventions leave as much original fabric in place as possible. As far as timber is concerned, the methods involve chemical treatment of active decay, local replacement in cases where timber splicing can result in restoring the respective elements' structural capacities, and replacement where timbers are highly decayed and are no longer working. With stone, the main interventions are fixing them in position and applying proper (but not excessive) cleaning, as stone is a strong and robust material. However, a stone wall may need stabilisation and selective stone substitution. Where a stone wall requires full replacement, the technique is to record and catalogue each stone so it is replaced in the same location and position.

Figs. 182, 183. Repairing the terraces below the fort by placing 'cators' and anchors to consolidate the steep slope.

Fig. 184. The old central staircase leading up from the lower floor entrance gate to the intermediate level and from there up to the main upper floor.

Mud mortar can hardly ever be retained where structural work occurs and cannot be reused, for it would lose some of its cementing characteristics. Often this also applies to the conservation of mud bricks. Most problematic is the conservation of renders when they are hiding structural and material defects. In such cases, the renders cannot be taken off and then reattached. However, in case renders are loose and there are no structural problems involved, special techniques are available for their reattachment, including the dribbling in of cementitious grouts in the hollow interstices. This is a most delicate task, as the grout can cause the soil renders to soften and dramatically slump off the wall. Wherever possible on the most important monuments, conservation aims to retain the dirt and smoke residue crusts attached to beams and walls, and in so doing retain smells, for example of fire tar residues.

A particular challenge is the replacement of many highly ornate window traceries and roof edge mouldings. It has taken many experimental trials to achieve the right level of consolidation and replacement, that is, to retain authenticity and consistency with regard to pattern regularity, accuracy of geometry, and the precision of chisel-cut textures. This is always achieved via the archaeological evidence of the original carved and turned elements. Each pattern has a story relating to its style, derivation and cultural meaning. Generally, timber floors have been found to have no great heritage value, as they are replaced every few years. However, some, when archaeologically investigated, prove to be multi-layered with older surfaces buried below new ones. The aim here is to retain these by protecting them and adding new wearing surfaces above.

The final stage of the conservation programme is the production of drawings and other documents tracking the intervention, setting suitable programmes for managing and maintaining the building and providing reference information for possible future interventions. The project is then shared with the public through access and publications.

BALTIT FORT: THE SITE AND THE BUILDING
Baltit fort is dramatically located at the top of a natural amphitheatre formed by terraced slopes, and the site was carefully chosen to control water extraction routes from the Ultar (nullah) behind (fig. 272). Water discharge from this catchment is distributed throughout the district, sustaining agriculture and habitation. Today, as always, water is carefully controlled and monitored by appointed village committees. Hereditary rights on water are complex, and have become more so as systems of secondary and tertiary channels have been added to the primary routes and as inheritances have repeatedly divided the surrounding fields into a jigsaw puzzle of ownership.

Baltit village, now named Karimabad, is a very old settlement, and the size of the fort which dominates the village grew in response to the expansion and importance of the settlement. The villages of Ganish and Altit, the other two historic settlements of Hunza, are said to share a common ancestry with Baltit, resulting from migration into Hunza from Gor, an extremely old village located south of Gilgit, high up in the hills facing Chilas. Ganish village is situated on a plateau on the edge of the main river gorge, surrounded by large, fertile fields, and still today retains much of its original form. Altit village also developed around a fort and stands in a commanding position on a white marble bluff six hundred to seven hundred metres above the main river. Yet the focal point of the valley has always been the fort at Baltit.

Baltit fort is a remarkably complex building resulting from more than seven hundred years of 'organic' growth. When first inspected in 1980, the fort had been empty and not maintained for decades – hence the leaning walls, roof holes and graffiti all over the mud-stained, white-washed renders. Most possessions of monetary value had long ago been transferred to the *mir's* present palace, given away or stolen. Only a number of faded photographs and a range of local items, all in battered condition, remained within the desert-

Fig. 185. View of the restored roof, with a Tibetan-type lantern above the old reception room (see fig. 201).

Fig. 186. The restored projecting bay window and veranda. The bay window is a 'colonial' addition from the 1920s.

ed shell of the fort, providing some charm for the occasional visitors. It took more than ten years to unravel how the labyrinth of spaces and passageways evolved, with the restoration team becoming archaeological investigators and examining the finer details of how each wall was related to adjoining elements, both horizontally and vertically. More than sixty structural phases have been unravelled by forensic archaeology.

The fort is entered through a highly defendable small door, set in the main west façade. The route to it changed many times, originally being a footpath up loose scree slopes and then passing up between two grand flanking towers and bastioned curtain-wall. The outer wall seen today is a composite of two-storey rooms and spaces created in several phases less than two hundred years ago outside the older defences. Some added rooms created extra space but on the whole their main justification was to buttress older rooms inside the fort that were under threat of sliding down the hillside. The suspended and highly ornate verandas (figs. 186, 195) are more recent elements and add to the imposing image of a fort turned into a palace. As they cantilever considerably off the façade they had later to be supported by a series of tall posts.

Within the entrance of the fort, an older defensive wall can be seen, as well as the distance between it and the subsequent latest enclosure (fig. 189). This gap was the fort's weakest area, to be watched over by the garrison. The stairs then lead up to the main reception area (fig. 184). Turning to the right, the arrangement of spaces illustrates the strategy adopted for defence against attackers. Turning to the left, one can see the oldest part of the fort, a base room of a once three- or four-storey *shikari* tower – but then chopped off, as at some point it had dramatically tilted to the south (fig. 87). A later tower used for storing armaments is located just beyond the top of the stairs, and next to this is a suite of rooms used by guests in the summer (now the library) (fig. 199). Off the reception area is the fort's kitchen and one of the oldest winter rooms, surviving with all its highly ornate columns and capitals.

The south end of the fort is linked to the *rani's* (queen's) winter rooms (fig. 200) on the north end by a tunnel-like passage way. This illustrates how two, then three, original building complexes became joined (see plan fig. 193). The northern suite of rooms also illustrates the structures of a 'Type I fort' (see chapter 5), inasmuch as it was originally a *shikari* tower with dark and low single-storey rooms. (It now accommodates the emergency exit route.) Along the west side, the phased additional rooms became a series of guardrooms each with small shooting windows.

The second storey rooms were added to the older rooms below, often not on the same wall alignments, sometimes requiring the lower walls to be repositioned. Often walls also had to be suspended on beams in order to allow for bigger and nicer spaces above, mainly for summer use. Some of these rooms were then modified to create the *mir's* private rooms, reflecting influences of colonial architecture and furnishings (figs. 195, 197). The old bedrooms (fig. 196), however, were left in the traditional *ha* arrangement. The semi-round royal dais (fig. 202), the scene of so many royal receptions of internationally important guests and local festivities (fig. 300), was added after 1895. Attached to the *mir's* rooms, around an internal courtyard, additional quarters were arranged, used for servants (for example for the milk mothers) or as summer guest rooms. On the roof, the *mir* had his private mosque and stores. One can assume that here there was much summer activity, very similar to what still occurs down in the village.

THE CONSERVATION PROCESS

In 1992, when the physical restoration work started, Baltit fort was a in a state of advanced decay, the roof resembling a patchwork of holes. Rainwater was able to flow freely into all parts of the building and even down to the foundations. Not surprisingly, the timberwork had absorbed humidity like a sponge and the renders were reduced to piles of soil mounded on the floors. Many walls were tilting to the point where collapse was imminent. Others had settled by half a metre, because they did not have foundations or sat on loose soil slopes.

Based on the principles stated in the introduction of this chapter, the AKCS-P was able to set up a comprehensive work plan, as initiated in 1989 with the appointment of the site architect and engineer. The building was divided up into a series of 'work stations', these reflecting the construction phases and how subunits of the building worked as independent engineering entities. This was important, because if a cator-

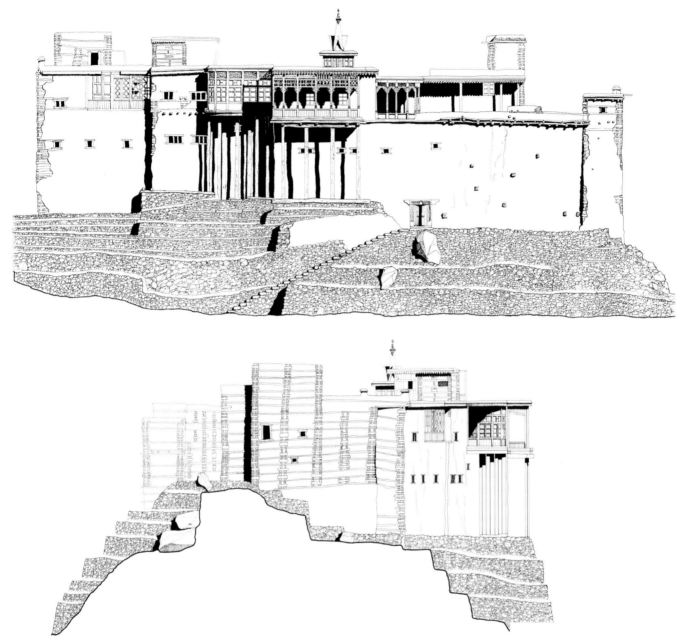

Figs. 187, 188. Above, the western elevation facing the village and the valley. Below, the northern elevation showing the tip of the precarious hill on which Baltit fort is sitting.

and-cribbage-framed building deforms at one location this can easily transfer damage elsewhere. The conservation work was planned in stages. First, it was necessary to determine and then remedy the structural problems around the foundations and load bearing walls. This reinstatement then allowed for conservation of the architectural fabric and finishes, followed by the insertion of new elements required for the new uses and safety of the existing structure. In practice, however, the reinstatement phase was often amalgamated with the engineering repairs.

The major engineering works were along the front façade, especially around the south end. Here, the stabilisation of the foundations (fig. 191) and structural frame took nearly three years, requiring sophisticated engineering designs and construction techniques. During this work, older archaeological remains were found and successfully incorporated into the conservation project. This had to be done first, as it was essential to guarantee foundation stability before repairing the walls and then the roof. At each work station, the structural unit was thus repaired from the bottom upwards, with the overall roof and wall finishes completing the conservation sequence.

As the work at the south end took longer than anticipated, planned interventions at the north end were brought forward – so effectively conservation was occurring simultaneously all over the fort, requiring considerable orchestration. Fortunately, at the north end most surfaces of the structural units, the foundations and the timber framing were found to be in a much better condition. Thus more of the original features could be retained. In the kitchen it was even possible to preserve the sooty fire residue crusts on the roof beams. In the north part of the fort, great attention was given to the character of the new render, the old one having generally fallen off. Here it became necessary to skilfully create new surfaces that reflected on the underlying structure and construction fabric – which meant many days were given to experimentation and testing.

Whenever possible, traditional building techniques were used to conserve the fort. However, on certain occasions modern interventions were needed and appropriate. For the first time anywhere, synthetic polyethaline reinforcement meshes ('geotextiles') and ('kelvar') polymer anchor cables (fig. 189) were used for giving extra structural support. Boron-based wood preservatives were also applied. In many places, following exhaustive experimentation and field testing, stabilised soils were used – for example, to produce hard wearing floor surfaces where visitors would be tracking through the museum display rooms. Attention to detail is also evidenced in the case of coloured glass windows, where the materials were matched to the original French source and replacement panes were imported.

A major achievement of the fort restoration lies in the high quality carpentry work and especially in the skilfully restored carved wood features (as seen today in the veranda canopies along the top of the main façade looking over Karimabad), all executed by local master craftsmen. The project's carpentry workshop gave a big boost to the revival of local building techniques which triggered a 'snow-ball effect' with regard to the renovation and upgrading of houses in the historic settlements of Hunza (see chapter 12). Finally, the way in which engineering and restoration techniques have been implemented and left visible – whether traditional or modern – is of great interest as a testament to a successful conservation campaign.

GIVING NEW LIFE TO THE BUILDING

Apart from its importance as a historic monument, Baltit fort has great cultural and symbolic value for the local community and constitutes a major economic resource for tourism. The adaptive reuse project for the fort thus had to respond to a variety of concerns: it needed to meet the constraints imposed by architectural conservation; it needed to illustrate the long history of the fort in the context of evolving local traditions; it needed to contribute to the economic opportunities for the residents of the village; and it needed to generate sufficient income to sustain its operation and maintenance costs. Accordingly, the main function selected for the restored fort was those of a museum of local history, combined with an active cultural centre

Figs. 189, 190. Left, the original 'cage' construction of two subsequent layers of outer walls being stripped of defective stone and mud infill to be restored in the traditional manner. In the background a tensile cable tying the leaning walls together can be seen. Right, workers monitoring structural movements during the restoration process.

with associated facilities. The fort is expected to act as a focal point for renewed civic pride, as well as a centre for exchange between international institutions interested in the Northern Areas.

Converting a former private residence into a public facility always entails functional and architectural problems. This is particularly true in the case of a historic building, and even more so with a structure that has grown as an accretion of narrow fortified houses, with constricted interior passages and low doorways. Installing a museum and cultural centre at Baltit fort therefore required a certain number of difficult decisions (and occasional compromises), in order to adapt the traditional structure to contemporary needs. For the purpose of creating viable circuits for visitors, it was necessary to open a few new connecting doors, to add an emergency stair, and to introduce plumbing and lighting for basic facilities. A small kitchen was also created in a side room of the former women's quarters to enable special functions to be held in the *rani's*

summer courtyard, which can accommodate up to twenty-five people for concerts of traditional music and similar events. Such functions have been introduced without causing harm to the original structure.

The reuse project – conceived in cooperation with the architect and designer Didier Lefort – was facilitated by the fact that five old houses adjacent to the fort had been acquired by the Aga Khan Foundation to provide space for ancillary facilities. One of the houses close to the street leading up to the fort has been transformed into a ticket office, another into a small coffee house

Fig. 191. Repairing the foundations after emptying the basement of rubble from collapsed older structures.

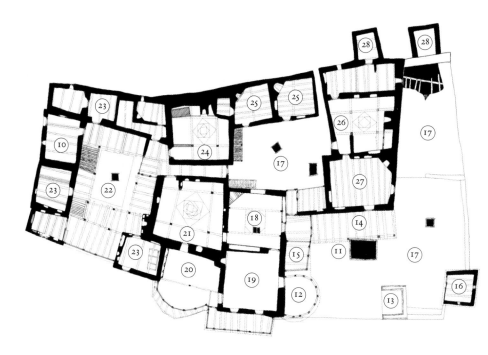

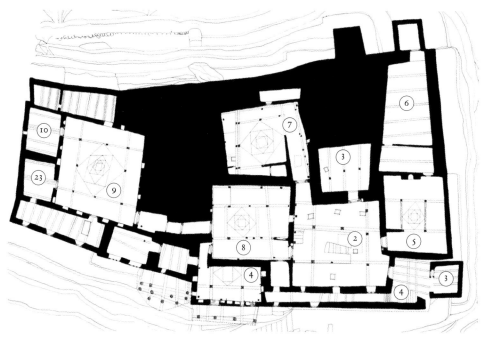

Legend:

1. Entrance staircase
2. First floor arrival lobby
   (fig. 184) and grain storage
3. Prison
4. Guard's rooms and guard's gallery
   (pl. 72)
5. Court room (now office)
6. Guest room (now library, fig. 199)
7. Kitchen
8. Living-room in former old tower,
   now audio-visual room
9. Queen's apartment (fig. 200)
10. Old tower, with new emergency
    staircase
11. Staircase landing
12. Royal dais (fig. 202)
13. *Wazir's* dais
14. Musicians' veranda
15. Armoury
16. Guard room
17. Open terraces
18. Waiting room with 'Tibetan'
    lantern (figs. 185, 201)
19. *Mir's* drawing and reception room
    (fig. 197)
20. *Mir's* living room and veranda
    (fig. 195)
21. *Mir's* bedroom (fig. 196)
22. Queen's summer apartment
    with courtyard (fig. 198)
23. Store rooms
24. Queen's summer bedroom
25. Guest rooms
26. Apartment
    for newly married couples
27. Living room
28. Toilet

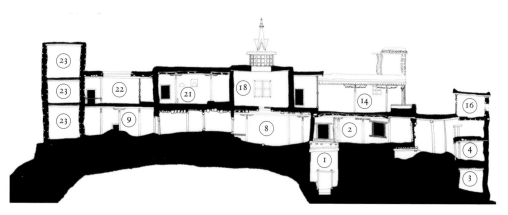

Figs. 192-194. Plans
of the second upper floor
(above) and the first floor
(below), as well as
the longitudinal
north-south section.

Figs. 195-200. Views of various interiors in the restored Baltit Fort.
Fig. 195: The *mir's* 'colonial' living room, with projecting veranda on the second floor.
Fig. 196: The adjacent traditional bedroom of the *mir*.
Fig. 197: The *mir's* drawing and reception room on the second floor
with embroidered ceremonial carpet on the wall.
Fig. 198: The *rani's* (queen's) summer room and courtyard on the second floor.
Fig. 199: The former guest room (now the library) on the first floor.
Fig. 200: The *rani's* bedroom on the first floor.

Fig. 201. The old reception room and the interior of the Tibetan-type lantern (see fig. 185).

with public toilet facilities, and the remaining ones into storerooms and additional showrooms and workshop facilities. As in the case of the fort itself, these functional changes have been carried out with a preference for 'minimum intervention' and utmost respect for the historic features of the buildings, which have not been altered in substantial ways.

The planning of the museum and the research facilities in the fort was undertaken with the intention of enhancing, rather than overshadowing, the architectural features, which constitute the main focus of attention. In most cases they can be removed with no effects to the conserved structure. Thus, the traditional rooms on the lower floor, with their attractive carved timber columns and beams, have been kept as they were and highlighted by integrated light fixtures (fig. 200). No modern showcases or modern exhibition items were foreseen except artefacts which relate to the traditional functions of the fort, such as wooden trunks and various utensils. Meanwhile, the more neutral and less decorated rooms, such as those along the defensive gallery between the two subsequent front walls of the fort, are used to exhibit documents relating to the history of the area and the building, including the conservation of the fort. The gentrified, more palatial rooms on the second floor provide the ideal setting to exhibit what was left of the *mir's* private collections (figs. 195, 197). Special features are some of the old carpets used in the fort (partly of Kashgar origin), furniture, ceremonial robes, and weapons. Wherever possible, existing niches and shelves have been adapted for exhibition purposes, complemented by a number of newly designed showcases providing security and good lighting. The massive timber frames of the new showcases respond to the predominance of wooden elements in the structure of the fort.

Figs. 202, 203. The restored dais on the main upper floor, and a local craftsman completing the missing ornamental timber features.

68.

Previous page
67. Interior of Altit fort before restoration,
with temporary shoring.

68. View of Baltit fort, before restoration.

69, 70. The first floor entry hall with the stair
leading to the upper terrace (figs. 192, 193)
before and after restoration.

71. Baltit fort under restoration, including the terraces,
retaining walls and houses below.

72. The restored first-floor former guard rooms
along the western front elevation,
now part of the museum exhibition.

73. The *mir's* drawing/reception room, restored,
with ceremonial embroidery on the wall.

74. The waiting room, with a showcase
containing the *mir's* ceremonial robe.

69.

70.

71.

72.

73.

74.

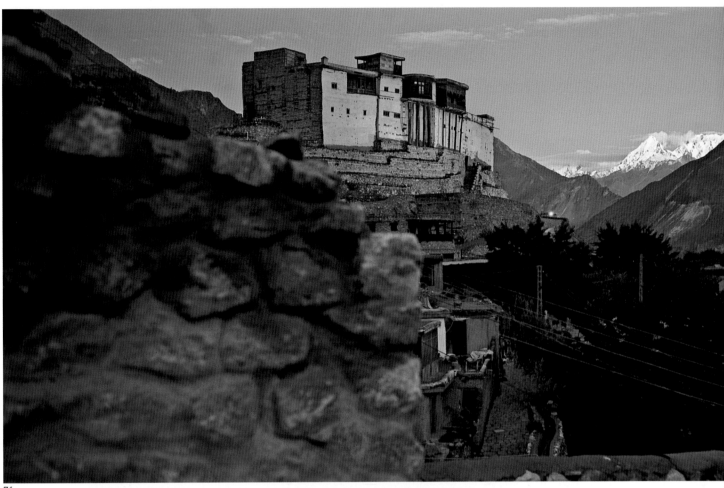

75.

76.

75. The restored and illuminated Baltit fort.

76. The *rani's* (queen's) summer quarters
on the second floor, a part of the museum
which can also be used for visitors' entertainment.

77. Old master carpenter repairing timber decoration
of the dais of Baltit fort.

78. The former *mir's* bedroom, restored, with historic utensils.

77.

78.

79.

80.

81.

79. Shigar fort/palace as found in 1999.
Left, the Old House; right, the steps
leading up to the Garden House.

80. Traces of the old audience hall of the fort,
buried in more recent construction (see figs. 228-233).

81. The *raja's* room on the second floor,
as found (see also figs. 246, 254).

82.

83.

84.

82. The courtyard of the fort on the raised platform
during works, after stripping all dilapidated structures
and before restoring missing elements (compare with pl. 88).
On the left side, the remains of Module I,
with the fragmented audience hall on the ground floor.

83. Rendering interior walls with stabilised soil plaster.

84. Mounting new *jali* screens on the restored bay window
of the *raja's* room on the second floor.

85. The on-site carpentry and joinery workshop
of the Shigar fort project.

85.

86.

87.

88.

86. The first floor vestibule of Module II giving access to the guest rooms of the new Shigar Fort Residence.

87. The ground level entrance to the 'fort on the rock' giving access to a new staircase built into the old watchtower.

88. The courtyard of the restored Shigar fort/palace, now Shigar Fort Residence, at night.

89, 90. Two typical guest rooms in Module II maintaining the essential architectural features of the old fort/palace and complementing them with light and unobtrusive contemporary furniture, as well as historic objects.

89.

90.

91.

92.

91. The restored audience hall of Shigar fort, now a museum of Balti woodcarving, with the reinstated central column and the reclaimed original room size (see also fig. 232).

92. Night view of the restaurant in the ground floor of the Old House adjacent to the fort (see plans in figs. 234-237) with 'cyclopean' stone masonry on the left wall.

93, 94. The lounge on the first floor of the Old House
and the adjacent veranda overlooking the river.

95. View of the restored Old House
and the entry courtyard to Shigar Fort Residence.

93.

94.

96.

96. View of the back side of Khaplu palace (for front side see pl. 44) in its present condition. This building is another candidate for restoration and adaptive reuse.

97. The former reception area inside the courtyard of Khaplu palace.

98. A room of Khaplu palace in its typical present condition.

97.

98.

99.

100.

101.

99. The Sayyed Mohammad shrine and tomb (*astana*) in Khaplu
before restoration. It had to be completely dismantled
and rebuilt by using as much as possible
of the old timber components (see also fig. 294).

100. The restored enclosure of the shrine, inside the veranda
(for interior see pl. 53).

101. The reconstructed roof spire.

102.

102, 103. Works on site during the restoration
of Amburiq mosque near Shigar (see figs. 291-293).

104. View of the restored Amburiq mosque.

103.

105.

105. The simple prayer room
in Shigar fort/palace, after restoration.

106. The restored Khilingrong mosque
near Shigar fort/palace.

106.

An important part of the collection, particularly the vernacular artefacts of daily use such as stone vessels, wooden utensils, metalwork, furniture items, and clothing, was donated by the residents of Karimabad, following an appeal launched in autumn 1994. Other items have been purchased from the local bazaar or from individual owners. When not on display, these artefacts have become part of a major stored collection available for research purposes. However, the cultural centre will not only preserve and exhibit items of the traditional crafts, but will also endeavour to create new development opportunities for local crafts people. A new initiative in this domain was begun in spring 1995 by the AKCS-P with the new Karakoram Handicraft Development Centre. The first products of this craft promotion project were the *sharma* weavings used to cover the floors of the museum and cultural centre.

The main rooms of the cultural centre have been accommodated on the first floor, around the small courtyard which is reached by the stairway leading up from the main entrance. A traditional living-room (*ha*) with a covered roof opening serves for audio-visual presentations, while on the other side of the courtyard, on the southern end of the building, a library and study centre have been accommodated, with their floors suspended above the excavated archaeological areas of the fort. The library will contain a basic stock of publications relevant to Hunza and the fort, and is expected to become a study centre and field base for national and international research missions.

The conservation and adaptive reuse of Baltit fort was completed in the spring of 1996. The restored building was officially opened by His Highness and the then President of Pakistan and handed over to the Baltit Heritage Trust (see chapter 13). The quality of the conservation can be judged by the fact that today, almost ten years after completion, the amount of maintenance has been minimal. In 2004, the fort was honoured with the highest conservation award of UNESCO.

THE FUTURE RESTORATION OF ALTIT FORT

Altit fort is another of the great monuments of the Northern Areas. Indeed, the *shikari* tower is some three hundred years older than the first phase of Baltit fort, making it the oldest surviving standing structure in the western Himalayas (see also chapter 5). Arguably, it is also the most spectacularly sited fort, built on the very edge of the main Hunza gorge and with 200-metre-high sheer cliffs before precipitous slopes cascade down towards the river (pl. 40). Its importance stems from the control it exercised on the local farming community and especially on the whole valley and the upstream communication routes. It participated in creating a safe environment, allowing agriculture to flourish in the natural Karimabad amphitheatre.

Fig. 204. On the gallery of unrestored Altit fort, close to the entrance to the *shikari* tower.

Figs. 205, 206. D. Lorimer's 1935 photographs of the main room in Altit fort, with elaborate woodcarving.

Like all other forts, Altit is abandoned and decaying. Some stabilisation measures on the roof were applied by the AKCS-P team a few years ago to keep out rain, and some walls were supported by temporary structural devices, as they were teetering on the edge of the cliff. Such failing is the result of wood decay, related to poorly formed stone and adobe walls, and is also due to the high level of exposure of the fort to strong drying winds and occasional storms.

The conservation strategy for Altit fort developed in 2004 is to preserve it 'as found', that is, basically as an empty shell. Most conservation works therefore will relate to mending structural defects, stabilising existing walls, reattaching render to the wall substrate, replacing some roofs, treating wood decay and providing a nominal amount of lighting. However, there are some walls that current investigation shows as being too unstable. Here the infill will be removed to allow the walls to be jacked back to more vertical positions. The stone and/or adobe soil blocks will be replaced in their original positions – making use of survey drawings and photographs. There will be virtually no works related to new functions, as any adaptive reuse has been discarded. This rather purist concept, an exciting objective in its own right, will significantly differ from solutions applied to Baltit fort, Ganish village and Shigar palace. Together, these buildings and the respective interventions exemplify the wide range of conservation approaches which can be pursued according to different circumstances.

10. Restoring and Adapting Shigar Fort / Palace

MASOOD KHAN

Shigar fort or *Fong Khar* (in Balti, the 'palace on the rock') is located on the northern bank of a mountain stream (*nullah*) that emerges from the mountains on the east separating Shigar from Thalle valley. The stream roars past the neighbouring settlements of Khlingrong, Shilpa and Halpapa, through the area of the bazaar and further west until it empties into the Shigar river, which irrigates the larger Shigar valley. The Shigar river flows south a bare fifteen kilometres before it meets the Indus at Skardu.

The old fortified palace and its annexes are situated at the foot of almost vertical rocky cliffs rising several hundred metres. Some two hundred metres above the present location the ruined *Khar-e-Dong* still stands – the ancestral fort of the Amacha rulers, said to be dating from a time before the Amachas first established their political control over the valley of Shigar, possibly during the eleventh century AD. Situated among orchards and fields, and at least one formal garden (the *Amacha Tsar*), the fort complex comprises several pieces of land measuring about 1.25 hectares (fig. 252).

Just to the east of the complex, nearer the *nullah*, only a few houses now remain of the village of Khlingrong besides its graceful, two-storeyed mosque – one of the key monuments of Baltistan. To the north and north-west lies the large village of Shilpa, and further down the slope all the way to the bazaar lies the settlement of Halpapa, both containing historic mosques and *imambarhas* (places of assembly). The three settlements cluster around the old palace fort and have been the source of servants and retinue for the *raja* and his court. Across the *nullah*, to the south, lie the settlements of Dozukhpa, Agepa and Bontopa. The unpaved approach road leading to the fort compound starts near the polo

Fig. 207. Aerial view of Shigar fort in the Shigar oasis, with a sweeping view towards the Indus valley.

Fig. 208. View of the fort (centre) from the cliff above the fort (see also pls. 56, 59). Shigar village is in the background.

215

Fig. 209. View from the river of Shigar fort complex enveloped in scaffolding, seen from the south-east.

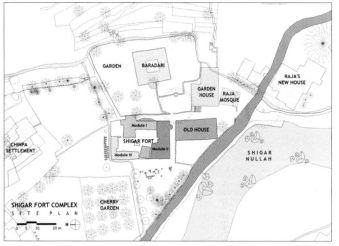

Fig. 210. Site plan of Shigar fort/palace complex, which clearly identifies the three 'modules'. For site details see plan fig. 252, which is turned by 90°. A larger plan of Shigar is in pl. 65.

ground, off the Skardu-Ashkole road, and passes through these settlements before it crosses the *nullah* on a timber bridge.

THE BUILDING COMPLEX

The defensive base of the fort itself is formed by a massive rectangular motte built of cyclopean masonry and rising some five metres from the ground (fig. 217). This platform partly surrounds a gigantic cone-shaped rock, which may once have fallen off the spectacular cliffs just east of the fort. It became occupied over three centuries ago by several structures representing three successive and distinct phases of horizontal expansion, to be called Modules I, II and III during the conservation process (fig. 210).

The Old Palace

Of these three phases, two constitute the main building mass in the form of two partly contiguous buildings. The first of these buildings (Module I) can easily be interpreted as a single, clearly conceived and executed structure, with a distinct and noble architectural expression. This is the original *Fong Khar* (probably dating from the seventeenth century AD), founded on top of the conical rock. On the eastern side, the building uses a structural system with weighted wooden beams radiating out from the centre, allowing the eastern stone and cribbage wall of the fort to cantilever some seventy-five centimetres over the rock.[1] Roughly rectangular in plan and with walls forming a modular grid, Module I had earlier occupied a considerable area of the platform, in such a way as to leave open terraces on the northern, western and southern sides.

Substantial portions of the architectural features of this earliest structure still remain visible. Apart from the typical cribbage-and-cator construction system, the structure shows massive carved beams along its perimeter that define the cornice on the exterior, and a fine random rubble masonry (using naturally cleft stone laid in lime mortar) that fills the timber framework integral to the wall structure. (See also chapter 5 in this book.) Foundations uncovered during structural consolidation provided evidence of earlier walls that had disappeared – evidence that would later support a partial reconstruction of missing elements. As the overlying debris in the extant open spaces and within the extant structures was cleared, the remains of a grand audience hall were revealed. Further examination of this sequence of rooms indicated its courtly

216

character and use (entrance, audience, retiring rooms for the ruler), even though one of them may have later served as a kitchen for a prolonged duration of time.

A tower in the north-east corner of the platform, as well as the rooms to the south that constitute the lower two floors of Module II, were added a little later. The added portions are structurally independent from the original main structure and are separated from it by vertical gaps that range in width from six to ten centimetres. As a result of these additions, significant lengths of the carved timber beams that were a part of the outer wall of the original structure later became enclosed as important features of the interior.

The rooms at the western and northern edge of the platform, comprising Module III, constitute a structure that appears to be of lesser importance and architectural quality. During the works, it was discovered from early twentieth century photographs that the rooms of Module III had been low-value ancillary structures, already subject to periodic changes. Module III also includes a small mosque for the private use of the family – much simpler and plainer in appearance than the *raja's* public mosque near the entrance to the complex. Both Module II and III comprise rooms that fulfilled a residential function. The residential spaces are mainly sleeping rooms, some more elaborate than others (such as the *raja's* sleeping chambers on the south-eastern corner). The residential part of the complex contains subterranean chambers (built into the body of the platform) that, together with the rooms above, served as the traditional Balti composting latrines (*chaqsa*).

Figs. 211, 212. Entry-way to the fort from the south, past the Old House on the left and the Garden House on the right (before restoration).

Upper floors were subsequently added to these base structures. At one point in the early twentieth century (when they were photographed by a visiting European party), these floors appear to have covered the platform of the fort in its entirety, with at least one extra floor above the topmost rooms that were found at the beginning of the project (fig. 213), except for its north-western corner. The disappearance of these uppermost rooms over the course of a few decades points to the utter neglect that the building had fallen into, its ruin possibly hastened by the removal of structural timbers to be used in the construction of new premises (see below) when the fort was abandoned.

Fig. 213. An old photograph of Shigar fort from around 1900
showing upper floors on the north-east corner, which since collapsed.

At the inception of the project, most of the western flank of Module I did not exist any longer, creating a courtyard-like hollow in the middle of the platform (fig. 216, pl. 82). Other than its evocative quality of a historic ruin, this space did not have any architectural or historical significance, coming into existence as it did as a result of the progressive collapse of the multiple floors that covered the platform. Crude and tentative rubble walls had been constructed enclosing the gaping open sides of what remained of the original *Fong Khar*. Some of the original features, such as carved central columns, had been used as props and stays to secure the weakness of these construction elements.

The 'Old House'

The building to the south of the fort is known as the Old House. Its lower floor had accommodated a horse stable, a pen for keeping cattle and storage spaces for animal feed. It appears to have existed as the royal stable for as long as the fort itself. The upper floor of this structure was built by the *raja* as new residential accommodation when the old fort was abandoned in the middle of the twentieth century (fig. 211).

The 'Garden House'

This modern building (now called the Garden House) was constructed by the *raja's* family in the 1960s on the eastern edge of the enclosed traditional garden (*Amacha Tsar*), to replace the quarters in the Old House which by then had become inadequate (fig. 212). These new premises served most needs of the household until 2004 (when the *raja* built his new residence outside the fort complex), and included a large room that served as a *baithak*. The Old House and the Garden House face each other, framing the roughly fifty metre long access way from the modern gate to the entrance of the historic fort/palace.

The pool and pavilion in the Amacha Tsar

It is not known when this decorative square pool – the central feature of the garden – was built or what its initial appearance was like (fig. 258). Two photographs from the first half of the twentieth century show a pavilion-like structure on the central platform of the pool, and a bridge that connected it to the main garden. This pavilion was built by Raja Muhammad Azam Khan, the father of the present Raja Muhammad Ali Saba, in the first quarter of the twentieth century.[2] At the time of the takeover of the site by the conservation team, exquisitely carved marble bases that would have supported free-standing and attached columns could still be found on the central platform. Although these marble bases appear in the photographs, their artistic quality, approaching the perfection of Kashmiri buildings of the high Mughal style, appears strangely mismatched to the pavilion building. Knowing that nothing of a quality approaching that of these column bases was built anywhere else in Shigar at the time the pavilion in the photographs was built, one can safely deduce that the column bases have a provenance in an earlier building.

The raja's mosque

The *raja's* public mosque is a handsome and ornate building adjacent to the entrance to the complex and is of significant antiquity and artistic value. It is similar in form and ornament to other mosques in the Shigar area: a single four-bayed room with a central column support and a veranda on the eastern side.

SHIGAR FORT AS A HERITAGE SITE

The Amacha family claims to have ruled Shigar for thirty-three generations. According to sources quoted by A. H. Dani, the Amachas begin with Cha Tham, a political figure from Hunza, who established the dynasty after upstaging his master with the help of the local people.[3] Other sources describe the Amachas as having their origins in the 'Hamacha' tribe of Ganish, Hunza. When the Hamacha tribe was massacred in Hunza, a few of its members managed to flee to Shigar where they gained power and became known as the Amacha dynasty. In either case, the passage from Hunza would appear to have been taken across the Hispar glacier, the Nunshik pass and the Arundo valley. The present *raja* believes that the Amacha originally belonged to China.

Place and setting

Buddhist ruins in the vicinity of Shigar fort testify to the

Fig. 214. The restored south front showing the massive stonework and reinforcing 'cators' forming the raised platform.

lengthy human occupation of the site. Local people assert that the old *Khar-e-Dong* on the cliffs is as old as the Buddhist monastery to its south, both these sites being part of the same settlement system. Shards discovered at depths of between one and two metres near the base wall of the present Shigar fort, and terracotta pipe sections excavated in the *Amacha Tsar*, bear witness to a rich pottery culture that appears to have become extinct.[4] In recent excavations in the *Amacha Tsar*, remains of a masonry wall with a lime render were discovered at a depth of two metres.

Fong Khar is the last remaining structure associated with the ruling Amacha family. The oldest of them was *Khar-e-Dong*, the fortification whose remains can still be seen high up on the cliffs overlooking the present site. In all probability *Khar-e-Dong* was captured and destroyed by Mughal forces sent by Shah Jehan,[5] in aid of Hasan Khan Amacha, the twentieth of the line, who consequently became ruler in 1634.[6] The destruction of *Khar-e-Dong* probably necessitated the construction of the present *Fong Khar*, which is said to have been built by Hasan Khan as the building where the business of the court was conducted. The present members of the Amacha family refer to a third building, *Razi Tham Khar*, of which no trace remains.

The fort/palace is situated in a powerful natural setting, full of dramatic contrasts (figs. 208, 257). The raw natural quality of this scenery, softened by human settlement that began at least two millennia ago, offers strong contrasts between rocky cliffs and cultivated terraces, as well as between the continuous thunder of the *nullah* and the quiet spaces within the garden-site and the buildings themselves. The buildings are sited in an orchard-like environment, with traditional and imported trees, some of them of considerable age (see chapter 11). The steep rocky escarpment forming the background of the palace, the stream passing in front of the complex and the many irrigation channels meandering through a well-preserved and authentic settlement, all account for the unique charm of the site.

Architectural significance

The architectural value of Shigar fort/palace in its earliest stages is focused on Module I, where the exposed surfaces of the main framing timbers, on the exterior as well as the interior of the audience hall and its adjacent spaces, are heavily and exquisitely carved (pl. 91). The ornamental motifs of these elements bear evidence of the first influences from metropolitan Kashmiri culture, while still retaining the flavour of a strong local idiom (see chapter 7 in this book). In certain instances, as in the ornate beams and the engaged columns of the audience hall, the Mughal/Kashmiri motifs are relatively pure. In the free-standing column in the same space, or in the pair of carved stanchions that were inserted to frame the door

Fig. 215. The projecting balcony of the top room (with missing *jali* windows).

opening introduced in the eastern wall of the audience hall, they occur in combination with earlier ornamental types (figs. 229, 231). It cannot be said with any certainty whether these latter elements were not brought from older buildings that had already evolved in the previous centuries. However elements like the engaged columns, the spanning beams in the interior or the cornice beam on the exterior were certainly created for this specific building.

That the earliest architecture at Shigar fort is more akin to local and Tibetan archetypes is attested more strongly in its architectural typology. Most other residential forts in Baltistan, exemplified by the forts at Khaplu, Skardu and Kharmang,[7] appear to be strongly influenced by the Kashmiri manor-house prototype such as the extant mansion in the Zadibal neighbourhood of Srinagar. This essentially domestic/palatial architectural type has a ground floor court-

Fig. 216. Plan of the ground floor (as found), on the top of the raised platform (north is to the left).

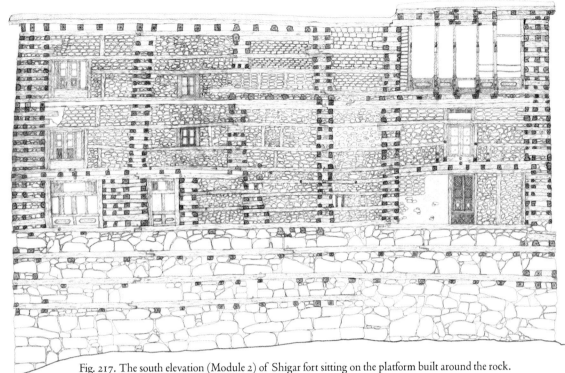

Fig. 217. The south elevation (Module 2) of Shigar fort sitting on the platform built around the rock.

yard associated with the entrance; the rooms are arranged in a regular grid on the four sides of the courtyard, served by circumambulatory corridors or balconies on each upper floor. In contrast to this, the fort at Shigar, as first built, was a complex of state rooms forming a tight rectangular assembly on the first level at the top of the platform. The courtyard typical of Kashmiri influence had not yet arrived, nor could the original configuration of buildings ever have made it possible for a formal courtyard to exist.

Until the late sixteenth century (when Kashmir became part of the Mughal Empire), Kashmiri influences in Baltistan had been balanced by Central Asian overlordship and by remaining religious and cultural ties with Tibet and Ladakh that had lasted for centuries before the advent of Islam. *Fong Khar* at Shigar is perhaps the only *secular* building in Baltistan which displays this intersection, and exemplifies the influence of cultural interaction with Kashmir at a very early stage.

In addition to these pivotal characteristics, Shigar fort contains a rich repository of traditional architectural details which materialise typical living patterns and local culture. Examples of these are to be found in the ubiquitous *shahnashins* (the traditional sleeping niches which are enclosed on three sides and partially enclosed on the fourth side by multi-arched, wooden space dividers), in lamp niches and storage *taqchis* hollowed out in the thickness of walls. To add immensely to its age-significance and sensory charm, carved and plain timbers from prior times and from earlier buildings have been reused in many places all over the building.

The building fabric of Shigar fort comprises variations of the traditional Baltistani construction technique, as presented in chapter 5. The elements of the earliest phases, which tend to occur in the lower floors, use heavier construction material and are thicker in section, with the walls tending to exceed sixty centimetres

in width. These differ markedly from the lighter construction of the uppermost floors, undoubtedly of later construction, where in some instances the window openings are filled with wooden lattice *jali* screens, or windows styled after British colonial exemplars, or both. Similarly, certain strong formal elements of the Kashmiri palace type, such as the half-octagonal *jharoq* balcony (fig. 215) on the upper floor pavilion in Module II appear, like the numerous instances of *jali* work, to be emulating buildings of the eighteenth century or thereafter.

In structural terms, the traditional cator and cribbage cage system is consistently used in all parts of the building (figs. 220, 221), including the outer walls of more recent components. The wall infill in the oldest parts of the building is rubble stone masonry, exposed on the exterior, and attractively laid in mud mortar. The infill material changes from stone to adobe blocks as one moves from the oldest to the more recent buildings. Wattle and daub, with the wattle constructed of wet branches of *shaq* (weeping willow) is another technique used as non-structural lightweight partitions. It is found in many rooms of the fort, at times suggesting connections to building components that do not exist any longer. The lightness of this form of walls is used effectively to create small cellular spaces.

PLANNING FOR THE SHIGAR FORT RESIDENCE
At the time when the Aga Khan Trust for Culture (AKTC) / Aga Khan Cultural Service-Pakistan (AKCS-P) took over the site, the main fort building was an almost complete ruin. A large part of Module I had collapsed. The roofs of its first floor rooms were non existent. Some of the rooms of Module II were being used by servants as living spaces and as cattle pens, even though much of the structure had failed and the building was bulging out precariously on the south side. The second floor rooms were missing their roofs.

The main entrance door (fig. 218), cut into the east wall of the former audience hall of Module I on top of the platform, was accessed by an earthen ramp that had been built by filling up earth over the formerly exposed rock. This earth fill appears to

Figs. 218, 219. Above, the entrance door cut at a later stage into the eastern wall of the audience hall, at the level of the raised platform. Below, the boulder around which the platform was built, as well as the reinstated original entrance on the ground level (the later entrance is still visible as a framed window on the upper floor wall in fig. 220).

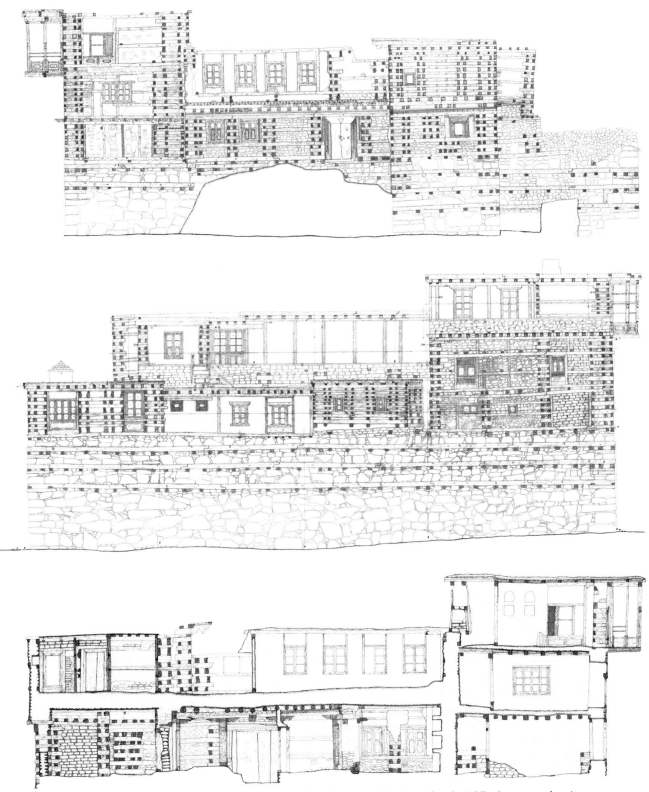

Figs. 220-222. Elevations and sections of Shigar fort/palace. Above, the eastern elevation as found; middle, the western elevation in restored condition; below, the north-south section through Modules I and II as found.

223

Figs. 223, 224. Two phases of restoration work around the courtyard on the upper platform. Above, Module I (left) and Module II (background) practically as found. Below, the upper floor reconstruction of Module I well under way, the extension of the ground-floor audience hall to its original size almost completed, and the upper floor of Module II fully completed.

have happened at an early time in the life of the fort and had resulted in the old ground-floor entrance through the north-eastern defensive tower being closed up. This original location of the entrance (fig. 219) at the foot of the giant boulder underpinning the fort was rediscovered during restoration work and the tower was cleared of debris in order to reinstate the original vertical connection.

The walls in the north-eastern corner of the audience hall were obscured behind a crude winding staircase (fig. 218) formed of a massive fill of earth and stone boulders. The mass of this overburden played a useful role in keeping the cantilevered radial floor beams tied down by sheer gravitational force. It was only when this earth and rock overburden was removed that the full artistic value of the interior of the audience hall was revealed.

Shigar fort in its 'received' state was an old, abandoned and neglected building that had undergone many changes. But it also came to us as a wonderfully preserved statement of its age and historicity. Centuries of oil lamps and coal fires had left layers of caked soot on the stones and timbers of the walls, covered over by decades of dust on the ceiling timbers. As the dirt was cleared from some of these old surfaces, they revealed the rich layering of human use.

Conserving and restoring this ruined building without any particular reuse in mind would have raised many questions difficult to resolve. Which earlier state to take as the reference? How to restore missing pieces and what uses to allocate to the many rooms? How to ensure income and proper maintenance for the restored building? To some extent, these issues also applied to Baltit fort. But Baltit fort did not offer the same adaptive reuse potential, its state of conservation was superior and its economic viability as a museum was higher because of the greater numbers of tourists visiting Hunza. To establish the future use of the Shigar palace – which had to inform all subsequent planning and design procedures – a range of choices had to be investigated and confronted with given conservation constraints. The emerging opportunities were strongly conditioned as much by social and economic factors as by architectural and artistic considerations, and, not least, by the requirements of international norms in conservation.

Social and economic factors
The project provided a perfect opportunity to act as a catalyst for comprehensive improvement of the local economy, by generating direct and indirect employment opportunities. Situated in the immediate proximity of a poor and unskilled village population, it was thought the Shigar Fort Residence project could raise the quality of life in the villages surrounding it, and boost economic enterprises in the bazaar area. This

Fig. 225. Completed restoration of Modules I and II, with the new external wall of the audience hall (left) rebuilt on the old foundations (see also fig. 233), and a new external stairway leading to the upper floor.

process was to be accompanied by a proactive village upgrading and rehabilitation programme in which micro-finance played an important role (see chapter 12).

The idea of promoting a new type of environmentally conscious cultural tourism (see chapter 14) was decisive for the reuse design of Shigar fort, both in terms of providing new opportunities to local residents and of ensuring financial self-sustainability for the restored building. In contrast to Hunza, Baltistan has so far been much less exposed to the tourism industry. The somewhat specialised international tourism here has been focussed on trekking and mountaineering. It has affected Shigar only indirectly, even though Shigar happens to lie on the main route from Skardu to the Baltoro glacier, K2 and other Karakoram peaks. With little commerce related to tourism, and the resulting lack of pressures on land, the Shigar context was relatively untouched by any major conflict between heritage and development. It was consequently possible to put in place mechanisms linked to social and economic development for appropriate management of cultural, scenic and environmental resources prior to the onset of the pressures of tourism. The establishment of a wide-ranging local institutional base before the commencement of tourism promotion programmes in the region was part of this strategy (see chapter 13 in this book).

Architectural and artistic evaluation
At an early stage of the project, the building's architectural values were carefully assessed, so that functions adapted to each of its components and its original use could be selected and fine-tuned in accordance with each room's specific character. The spaces of Module I, as revealed during the clean-up and structural con-

solidation process, were formal and relatively spacious, reflecting some of the importance attached to their former courtly function. Considering their exquisite carved wooden elements and the cultural and historic significance of these details, it became clear that this artistic treasure needed to be appropriately displayed and celebrated. The rooms in Module II and Module III presented another situation. They were much more numerous, closely packed and accessible through vertical connections (both for circulation and for servicing), reflecting their use as family living spaces and sleeping chambers and pointing to a similar potential reuse. In almost all parts of the fort buildings, the charm of the old rooms and the surviving architectural detail and other historic elements had to be preserved, displayed and enhanced in conjunction with an acceptable level of present-day use.

International conservation principles
Basic conservation norms as enunciated in international conservation charters such as the Venice Charter (1964), the Burra Charter (1979, 1999), the Nara Document on Authenticity (1994), the International Cultural Tourism Charter (1999) and the Charter on the Built Vernacular Heritage (1999) were used as the reference for arriving at the decisions that led to the final conservation project. Care was taken to identify original use, to adhere to that use or adopt a new use compatible with the original use so that there was minimal impact on the cultural significance of the building. In most cases, the proposed use tends to represent past use. In cases where the new use precludes a more direct illustration, then the appointment and decor of the heritage element was designed to adumbrate an earlier use.

The adaptive reuse concept
The conclusions defining the conservation and reuse modalities of Shigar fort/palace were reached after analysing the above-mentioned opportunities and constraints and considering a productive interaction between them. Thus the reuse concept for Shigar Fort Residence strikes a balance between, on the one hand, a museal site and, on the other, a very special resort-type guest house offering the unique experience of authentic guest rooms in a historic palace. The combined function of this residential retreat and museum was achieved by a well articulated concept, allocating specific uses to specific areas of the fort complex (figs. 242-244). The museum character of the palace is concentrated in the reception area and the partly reconstructed audience hall in Module I of the historic fort/palace (figs. 232, 250), where a permanent exhibit of Baltistan's wooden and architectural ornament is located; most of the residential functions have been located in Modules II and III, considering their specific architectural and spatial characteristics (figs. 246-249).

However, a certain overlap of functions exists. The large rooms located on the south-eastern corner on all three floors of Module II feature significant architectural elements and artefacts and can become part of a museum tour when they are not rented out. These rooms were the *raja's* personal residential space and were used seasonally, the uppermost room (fig. 246) serving as an airy summer pavilion. The so-called *rani's* (queen's) room in the south-west corner shares this dual role. Other guest rooms in Module II vary in size and accommodation and although somewhat plainer in appearance, carry considerable historic charm (figs. 247, 248). Meanwhile, in Module III, which was the part of least architectural and historic importance, the conservation interventions have tended to reinforce the value of characteristic architectural elements such as the triple-arched separating screens used to frame *shahnashins* (fig. 249).

The Old House (figs. 234-241; pl. 95), located at the entrance to the compound, was redesigned and converted to cater for service functions. A small room in the south-eastern corner of the building, directly facing the entrance to the site, serves as the first reception. Inside, the building accommodates a ground-floor restaurant with outdoor sitting space, an upper-floor lounge with a deep veranda overlooking the stream, a kitchen, a meeting room and administration facilities.

Opposite the Old House, the Garden House (a modern building with indifferent architectural qualities) has been refurbished and extended to offer seven additional guest rooms. Most of the rooms sit on a raised plinth and overlook the Amacha garden which adds to their attractiveness. The rooms in the Garden House are generally larger, and are offered as a more conventional alternative to the historic rooms in the fort building proper.

The various types and qualities of accommodation offered will enable the complex to cater for different tastes and types of clients. Within the fort/palace, there is a differentiation between rooms carrying higher architectural and historical value and a nobler history of occupation, and simpler rooms. Higher prices for the best historic rooms in the fort will reduce wear on the most precious parts of the building; lower rents for smaller and simpler rooms will achieve the intensity of occupation necessary to ensure a sustainable operation and maintenance of the building.

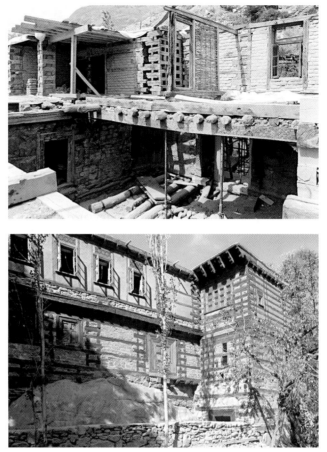

Figs. 226, 227. The eastern wing (Module I) before restoration, seen from the inner courtyard, and after restoration, seen from outside. In the upper photograph, the later wall which had cut the old audience room into half has been removed (see also figs. 228-232).

IMPLEMENTING THE PROJECT

The adaptive reuse concept for the fort was conceptually refined in the documentation phase of the project, during which a series of detailed surveys was initiated – the necessary prerequisite for the analysis of the structural and architectural issues faced by the monument. These surveys involved careful investigation and recording of the buildings, supported by photographic documentation, and included a complete survey of the site as a whole. Scaffolding was erected to enable access to the higher reaches of the external walls during the construction period, and to enable immediate and emergency structural stabilisation.

Although the foundation base of the fort building was still adequate, no doubt on account of the massive masonry structure of which the platform was constructed, the buildings that had been built above it exhibited various degree of structural failure. The roof structures of the uppermost storeys of the buildings

Figs. 228-231. Above, the old central pillar 'buried' in the more recent, poorly constructed infill wall, and highlighted in its original position in the restored audience hall. Below, the audience hall before restoration and expansion back to its original size.
In the rear, the opening of the later entrance cut into the eastern wall (fig. 218) is visible. To the right, the capital on a corner pillar indicates that the hall continued to the right into the present courtyard.

had collapsed and the timbers had either been removed or were still lying in the collapsed earth of the roof structure. Water had washed away much of the masonry (either mud blocks or stone masonry laid in an earthen mortar); the timber cribbage and cators and other framing elements had become loose in these upper storeys, and a substantial part of the wooden structural elements and wooden pegs that secured these in place had either rotted away or had been victims of boring insects. Plaster renders and mortars had detached and fallen away.

The structural consolidation and conservation of the building (carried out under the leadership of Richard Hughes) comprised several kinds of interventions. These were largely concentrated in the building super-

Figs. 232, 233. Left, the restored audience hall with the old central pillar once more serving as the focal point of the room. Right, the new outer wall of the audience hall in its old position, rebuilt on the old foundations made visible by a lighting slot.

structure where almost all deteriorated walls were opened up, and in certain instances realigned, both vertically and horizontally. Timbers that had rotted away or had been attacked by boring insects were identified and replaced. Anti-rot and insect repellent treatment was provided for the entire exposed timber structure. Timbers were pegged down again, particularly where the original pegs had rotted. Infill material (stone or earth block masonry) and wall renders were reconstituted where required, to accord with the original material.

Except the northern tower, where the structure had nearly failed, the extant structure of Module I was found in relatively sound condition. A small amount of masonry work was reconstituted taking care that unrendered good condition surviving stone masonry on the outer face of the historic walls was left undisturbed. Any portions of this kind of masonry that were added were made to differ from the old masonry by using subtle differences in stone sizes and the rhythm of the random stone pieces. The earth and stone overburden in the floor of the main audience hall was removed. This opened up the full space of the audience hall, and enabled the heavy timber cantilevers that formed the base of the Module I structure to be tied down into the stone fill behind the cyclopean masonry by means of stainless steel ropes and clamps anchored into concrete abutments.

Some of the old roof structures on the main (ground) floor of Module I were in relatively sound condition, but most floor and roof structures had to be taken apart and rebuilt so that they behaved again as stiff plates. In certain instances, fire damaged timbers were replaced. Inferior quality spanning joists installed in recent times in what remained of the main audience hall in Module I were replaced with beams and rafters made to accord with originals that remained in place or with evidence of original elements. Roofs were built up in the traditional layered manner above the spanning beams and rafters, with the ceiling made from the round willow branches that served in the original as the spanning elements between the rafters; water-proofing membranes of the traditional *hali* (birch-bark) were used.

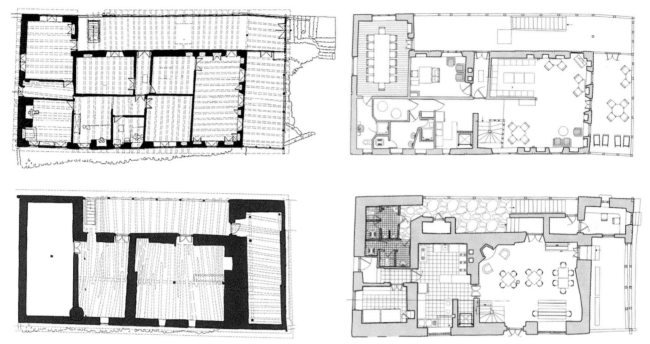

Figs. 234-237. Ground floor (below) and upper floor (above) of the Old House, showing, left, conditions as found, and right, the adaptive reuse plans after conversion into a restaurant facility. The Old House now features a kitchen and a restaurant (opening on to a garden terrace) on the ground floor, and a lounge, conference room, the manager's office and an outdoor sitting veranda on the upper floor.

ARCHITECTURAL DESIGN

In deference to the fort as a unique historic structure, important choices had to be made regarding the extent to which the received state of the building should be modified in terms of conservation and presentation. Some of these choices were based on the needs to extend the life of the building and to enable the projected reuse to take place. The most significant decisions, however, related to the search for authenticity, that is, basing the restoration on evidence of original location and the original shape of significant elements. This sort of evidence revealed itself in several stages – initially during the documentation phase, and then during the structural consolidation process of the building, when the floors of the open space on the defensive platform were dug up to reveal the pattern of the original foundation walls, or when in the audience hall a later roof structure was opened up and the marks of original structural elements were found. With the removal of fallen debris from the collapsed structure, a focussed examination of the building and its various components shed light on key elements of its former structure that had remained hidden under the debris. Apart from lending strength to the analysis of the structure of the building and its behaviour, these progressive discoveries also led to a more solid assessment of individual architectural and ornamental components, their history, their aesthetic and affective qualities, and how these were to be interpreted.

Although the utmost care was exercised in not compromising the characteristics representing the stages through which the building had passed, in certain cases choices had to be made on the basis of architectural and artistic worth between higher order (and older) elements on the one hand, and on other lower-value, temporary or more recent elements that were found to have covered up or partially replaced the earlier elements. An example is the relocation of the main entrance door (see above) which was moved to its original location in the north-eastern defensive tower. This recreated the authentic early entrance system, paving the way for the reinstatement of the audience hall.

Interventions in Module I, which is at the core of the heritage value of the complex, were limited to relieving or replacing weak structural members, to completing as found elements, such as the framing of the rooms, and to replacing a missing exterior wall above the uncovered original foundation structures, in order to restore the spatial impact of what must have been the old audience hall. New additions completing or reconstructing a broken off or adjacent piece were always kept distinct from the authentic original elements.

More extensive interpretive interventions have tended to be concentrated in those parts of the building that had lower authenticity and artistic merit. In the case of those portions of the building that suffered extensive loss, such as roofs or major sections of walls (as in the uppermost storey of Module II), reconstruction was limited to the parts that were only partially incomplete. In such cases the authenticity of the reconstruction was achieved based on the existing examples within the fort, or by referring to the traditional building practices in the area. Portions that were completely lost were not reconstructed, even though photographic evidence of their earlier presence existed – for example in the case of the western section of the upper floor of Module II, which has not been rebuilt, but is indicated by the contours of a sit-out terrace.

Figs. 238-241. Exterior and interior views of the Old House after its conversion. Above, outside view of the building from the entrance of the Shigar fort complex (with reception counter in the corner) and view of the lounge on the upper floor.
Below, a view from the upper veranda of the lounge on to the river (left) and a view of the ground-floor restaurant at night.

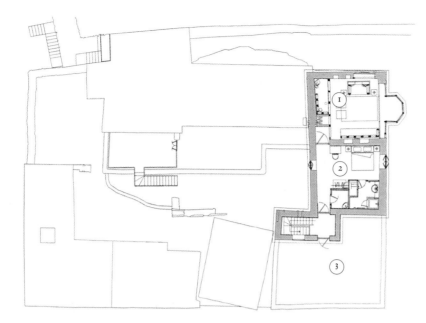

SECOND UPPER FLOOR:

The *raja's* most representative and most ornate living rooms, all in Module II, occupy the south-eastern corner of the building, one on top of the other. They overlook the entrance to the complex (fig. 251) and face both the river and the Amacha garden. The highest of them, on the second floor, contains a bay window (fig. 215) characterising the palaces of Baltistan. The south-western corner of Module II was too dilapidated to attempt a reconstruction and is now used as an open terrace.

1. The *raja's* room (fig. 246) now part of a suite, to be equipped with traditional furniture
2. Bedroom
3. Terrace

FIRST UPPER FLOOR:

This floor is composed of an eastern wing above the entry tower and part of the extended audience hall (all part of Module I) and of a southern wing forming part of Module II. The eastern wing has a new access via an open staircase from the courtyard (fig. 225). The southern wing is accessed via an old internal staircase at the southern end of the courtyard.

1. Bedroom facing Amacha garden (fig. 245)
2. Suite in entrance tower
3. Terrace above main entrance hall, linked to courtyard by outer stairs
4. The *raja's* first-floor suite (fig. 248) with *shahnashin*
5. Vestibule with three individual rooms

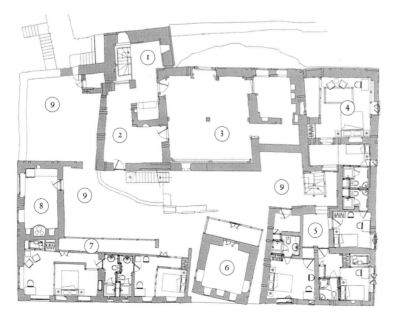

UPPER GROUND FLOOR:

The fort/palace is entered through a new staircase inside the north-eastern watchtower, starting from the lower ground level at the foot of the projecting rock (fig. 219). The bent vestibule gives access to the audience hall and to the courtyard, from where the other rooms can be reached.

1. Landing of entry staircase
2. Vestibule
3. Audience hall, now museum, enlarged to its original size (fig. 250)
4. The *raja's* ground-floor suite with *shahnashin*
5. Vestibule with three individual rooms, including the *rani's* room in the south-eastern corner
6. Palace mosque
7. Module III with two guest rooms (fig. 249)
8. Old kitchen
9. Courtyard/terrace

Figs. 242-244. Plans of the three upper levels of Shigar palace (above the platform) after restoration and conversion into a guest residence. (North is to the left.)

Figs. 245-250. Six interior views of restored and reused rooms in the fort/palace. For reference, refer to legends on p. 232.

The design of the residential facility is based on the potential offered by the cellular typology of the architecture, particularly as found in the residential sections in Modules II and III, which lend themselves admirably to individual guest room units. The emphasis on authenticity has helped maintain the historic character and enhance the rarity value of the rooms. Functional characteristics of some of the old rooms have been used to facilitate the introduction of modern amenities, so that the burden of intervention is minimised. The bathrooms, which involved considerable plumbing and mechanical engineering, have been sited in locations with identical, albeit primitive historic functions, using the same vertical connections which had

Fig. 251. General view of the fort/palace complex from the entrance
(after restoration), with the Old House to the left
and the Garden House to the right (compare fig. 212).

earlier functioned as a system of composting chambers. The interconnected and accessible underground spaces contain the modern water supply and waste water disposal systems. As such, all the piped network and the ventilation system of the bathrooms are capable of being reversed/removed without altering the historic core of the structure. The finishings in the bathrooms are the only allowance made to the demands of present-day life, but care has been taken that these finishings and fixtures stand clear of the historic fabric.

All new staircases have been executed in an idiom representing present-day architectural values and technology. Yet they were designed in sympathy with the articulated earthquake resisting characteristics of the old fabric; steel components manufactured in Skardu and Shigar also bring the not-very-refined quality of local steel fabrication.

Wherever possible, old surfaces in walls, ceilings and floors were conserved in the as-received materials, which often meant consolidating loose or detached elements *in situ*, in their as-found state. Where the surfaces were redone again, they were finished in their original treatment. In the case of ceilings which had not remained, and for which there was no evidence, new ceilings are carefully interpreted versions of ceilings in similar situations found elsewhere in the buildings. The wooden floors in the guest rooms are the only exception to this rule, necessitated in view of the special needs of the reuse function. In all other spaces, including the audience hall, the main reception area, in the open spaces and in verandas, the floor treatment has followed the authentic earthen floors.

Services
The projected needs of clean water had to be seen in relationship to the overall need of clean water for the neighbouring villages as well as the fort premises. Accordingly, a water filtration plant was designed and built at a discrete location at the bottom of the cliffs to the east. Water from here is gravity fed to two under ground reservoirs in the north garden. The water supply system is kept under pressure by means of automatic relay-started pumps, which keep an overhead reservoir filled with about five thousand gallons of water for emergency purposes.

Although electric power is available from the local hydro-electric station, located some half a kilometre upstream in the *nullah* gorge, standby generators will provide the Shigar fort complex with the excess electricity needed for running the facility. This arrangement makes the Shigar fort complex completely independent of the public electricity supply for fairly long durations of time.

The Shigar fort complex has been provided with a high standard of electrification and lighting, and care has been taken to make its electrical services environmentally friendly. The lighting is subdued and func-

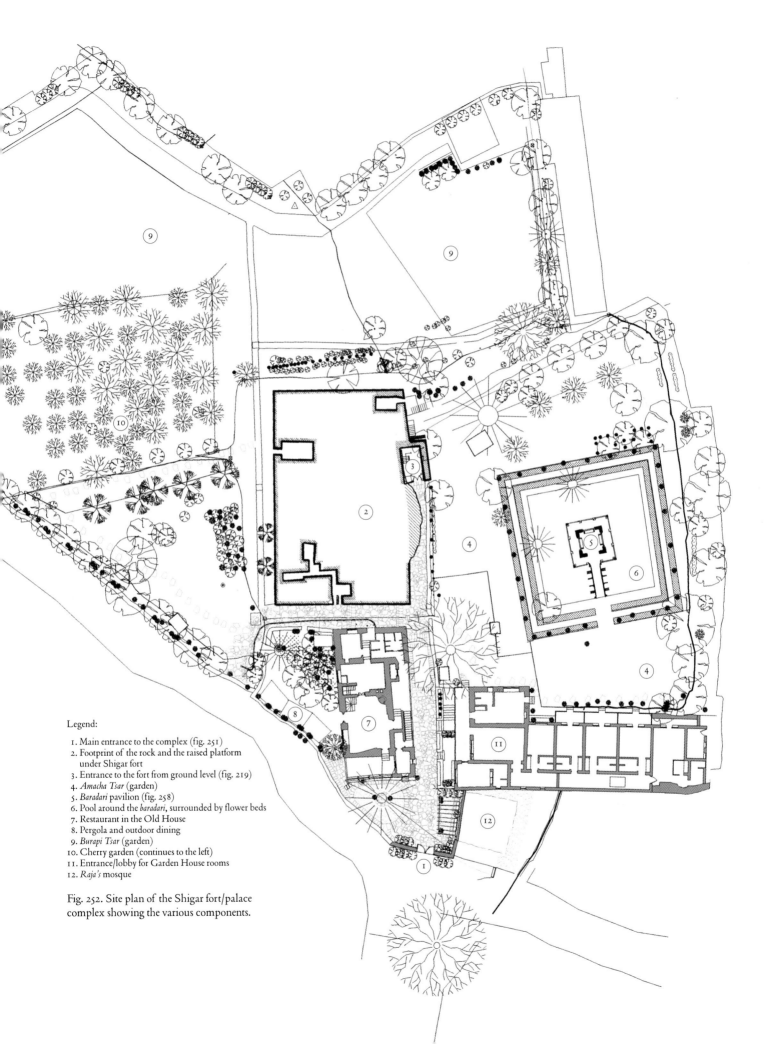

Legend:

1. Main entrance to the complex (fig. 251)
2. Footprint of the rock and the raised platform
   under Shigar fort
3. Entrance to the fort from ground level (fig. 219)
4. *Amacha Tsar* (garden)
5. *Baradari* pavilion (fig. 258)
6. Pool around the *baradari*, surrounded by flower beds
7. Restaurant in the Old House
8. Pergola and outdoor dining
9. *Burapi Tsar* (garden)
10. Cherry garden (continues to the left)
11. Entrance/lobby for Garden House rooms
12. *Raja's* mosque

Fig. 252. Site plan of the Shigar fort/palace
complex showing the various components.

Figs. 253, 254. The *raja's* top-floor living room (with projecting balcony) during restoration and restored *jali* frames in one of its windows.

tional, yet dramatically effective when the function so requires. Low lighting levels tend not only to be suitable for a historic setting, but reduce energy consumption. Lighting fixtures are simple and efficient, a significant number of them using energy-saving fluorescent lamps. A small circuit based on solar cells will illuminate the garden paths at night.

A disaggregated system of mechanical ventilation has been introduced, comprising in the main up-draft centrifugal exhaust fans located on roof tops. The system ventilates the kitchens and the bathrooms, and indirectly the occupied spaces (fig. 255). The two bathrooms in Module III, however, use an in-line blower type fan system, which discharges through the main wall on the western side.

INTERIOR DESIGN, EQUIPMENT AND FURNISHING OF THE BUILDING
The challenge for the interior design and furnishing of Shigar fort Residence (handled in cooperation

with Shenaz Ismail) was to reconcile the spirit and ambience of a historic building with a sympathetic, yet demanding, reuse function. The rooms of the restored Shigar fort, in their function as displayed conserved heritage and as a residence for guests, reflect this dual task. Original features such as bed niches, woodcarvings, screens, and so on, have been conserved and displayed as an integral component of the decor. The several *shahnashins* in the

Fig. 255. Bathroom (left) and ventilation shaft being built as light infill construction (to be plastered over) in one of the rooms.

bedrooms, for example, are available as extra sleeping spaces and can also be used as traditional sit-in spaces. Earthen plaster renders on the walls have been lightened up by a muted lime wash. The timber floors in the guest room have a utilitarian function, even though they bring the warmth and richness of fine local walnut and apricot woods. Interior lighting is adequate for most modern needs, with accent lighting dramatically displaying specific features of the rooms, such as old niches, wooden carvings, exposed stone masonry work, ancient ceilings, and so on. In the inserted modern bathrooms, walls have been finished in plain polished marble tiles, glassed-in shower stalls and high quality ceramic ware and fittings.

Furniture is sparse, restrained and carefully chosen to defer to the historic qualities of the interior spaces. As far as possible, timber furniture was designed and manufactured by AKCS-P architects and craftsmen on the Shigar fort site (fig. 302). Additional light rattan furniture, particularly for the lounge and dining room in the Old House, was custom-produced in Karachi to the team's specifications. Soft furnishings have played an important part in achieving the intended visual coherence inside Shigar Fort Residence. Hand-woven items featured in the guest rooms include the local *chharra* rugs for floors, felt *namdas* (a traditional type of rustic car-

Fig. 256. Staircase and corridor on the first floor of Module 2, with locally woven carpets on the floor.

pet almost died out) used as wall hangings, as well as blankets made from local wool and using natural dies from local vegetable sources. The *chharras* and *namda* rugs were made in Shigar, while the blankets were woven in Karachi by Shigar craftsmen on very basic four-frame handlooms. Their production was linked to the current revival of Shigar's traditional crafts promoted by the AKCS-P and local partner institutions. Professional and technical inputs for design and manufacturing, as well as the training of local craftsmen, were provided by the Department of Textile Design of the Indus valley School of Art and Architecture in Karachi, under the direction of Shehnaz Ismail.

Other textile items have also been produced by craftsmen from other parts of Pakistan. Quilted bed covers were specially produced by Sindhi craftswomen. Cotton bed covers and the cotton upholstery items used all over Shigar Fort Residence were woven in the Indus valley studios, with custom-designed fabric construction. Some of these have traditional running stitch embroidery also executed by Sindhi women. The windows are furnished with specially designed woven cotton and bamboo blinds.

All in all, the careful reuse of important historic interiors and the contribution of authentic local crafts, combined with a 'didactic' conservative approach and very selective restoration of missing features, will provide the future guest/visitor with a unique experience, to be found nowhere else in Pakistan. It is hoped that the Shigar Fort Residence, after its opening to the public in spring 2005, will find enthusiastic customers who can appreciate the exceptional quality of the site and the building.

[1] The marked similarity between this structure and the remains of *Khar-e-Dong* on the top of the cliffs to the east suggests a sharing of semantic and historic content.

[2] The photographs were provided by Raja Mohammad Ali Saba, who is the source for a significant amount of the information presented here. Raja Saba, now in his eighties, has also stated that his father died when he was a small child and that he could not say with any certainty whether there was anything else that existed here before the pool or the pavilion were built, or whether the building of the pavilion could have been a major reconstruction. Among his other recollections are a building that housed sericulture activities, known as the *sikkimkhang*, which existed in the part of the Amacha Tsar to the north of the present water tank.

[3] A. H. Dani, *History of Northern Areas of Pakistan,* Islamabad, National Institute of Historical and Cultural Research, 1991: p. 229 ff. *Amacha* is thought to have been derived from the Sanskrit *amatya*, meaning a wazir.

[4] Available cultural artefacts include a rich tradition of stone cooking and serving vessels. But pottery appears to have been dead beyond memory.

[5] Mohammad Saleh Kamboh, *Shahjahannama, Amal-e-Saleh*, copy of Persian manuscript in the Punjab Public Library, Lahore; cf. Dani, ibid. in note 3 here, p. 222 and note p. 240.

[6] Hasan Khan had sought asylum in Delhi from the persecution of Abdal Khan, the ruler of Skardu, who had had all eleven of Hasan Khan's siblings assassinated. Dani, ibid. in note 3 here, p. 231.

[7] This refers to New Kharmang fort. Old Kharmang fort (fig. 90) has now been disassembled and its carved wooden elements, containing archaic stylised ornament, have been on sale in the Skardu bazaar. It existed on an elevated site and may be distinguished from the newer building, which was built to the Kashmiri prototype on the floor of the valley in Kharmang probably sometime in the second half of the nineteenth century.

11. Gardens and Horticulture in Baltistan

BENEDICT BULL

Shigar, like other regions of the Northern Areas of Pakistan, has a specialised and strong horticultural tradition. Its cultivated land lies in a most sophisticated and extensive irrigation network. The Shigar Fort Residence project conducted by the Aga Khan Cultural Service-Pakistan (AKCS-P) has had to find imaginative solutions to the perennial problems surrounding gardens and their neighbourhoods by addressing issues of public access and private use, cultural identity, environmental health and improvement, and developing conservation norms and practices. An original blend of traditional and modern elements has been called on to safeguard parts of the landscape at Shigar, specifically the cyclopean masonry in the historic walls and the matrix of shade and fruit trees. Without any deliberate interpretation, or glossing, the various parts and epochs in its evolution from a simple traditional vegetable plot and orchard, to a ruler's private precinct and a modern heritage hotel are held in place cheek by jowl. It is at once a utilitarian landscape, an economic landscape, a social landscape and also a poetic landscape.

THE SITE AROUND SHIGAR FORT RESIDENCE

The Shigar fort garden, situated neatly at the junction of the Shigar *nullah* (stream) and the very wide Shigar river valley, dominates its environs. The fort gardens are comfortably nestled below the saddle of the

Fig. 257. The *Burapi Tsar* with Shigar fort and the rocky cliffs in the background.

239

Figs. 258, 259. The rehabilitated Amacha garden at Shigar fort/palace. On the left, the pool and the reconstructed *baradari* (pavilion). On the right, an old marble basin reintegrated into the irrigation system.

ridge running between the *nullah* mouth and the main valley. The fort sits between the river and the terraces of the ridge end, directly beneath the older rock fortress perched on the cliff high above (pls. 59, 65). This parcel of land was selected for its strategic military position, around which social and economic functions could be organised without interruption. 'Control' of the territory from this stronghold was the primary historical function of the landscape at Shigar fort. The complex community rights to land, grazing and water pertaining in Shigar and its upland hinterland, with the *rajas* of Shigar maintaining a dominant position, were determined by the mutual development of military and agricultural territories.

Considered individually, the garden of Shigar fort reveals in microcosm the development of the territories of Shigar. Development from the raw physical entity of 'land' to the yield-bearing cultivated landscape of the entire community is inextricably associated with good rule and, as such, legitimacy of tenure is identified by the successful cultivation of the land. Not surprisingly, each valley in the Northern Areas has some fruit or crop of which it boasts: at Shigar and Altit forts, it is the apricot which excels. This bounty proves a garden good, and it is defined in contrast to the unproductive lands, and those who inhabit them, in times of strong development.[1]

With the successful appropriation of a critical area of cultivated land, the elite developed the time and places to celebrate certain festivals; specific gardens with privileged prospects, pools, shady pergolas, or polo pitches within the matrix of irrigated plots will have intensified their experience of their landscape.[2] Some landscapes became associated with specific socio-political functions such as prayer, slaughter, rallying and merchandising, as well as with certain times in the calendar, by season and day.

Gardens developed as places to appreciate nature's bounty, places to seek refuge and privacy and to pause, places to compete and gather. In winter, a festival around 17 or 18 December was celebrated with music and dancing on the *Burapi Tsar* (fig. 257; an open space in the north-western corner of the site). This space is a 'pitch', a place for events, and there remains the possibility that some traditions may be resumed there, local hockey, cricket or football for youths or festivals for the community. The question is how subtly these traditions can be stimulated without being staged, and this 'pitch' is a live example for the management of Shigar Fort Residence.

There is limited literary description of the garden at Shigar,[3] although there is no lack of finesse in the quality of the gardens themselves, or in native ability to name their parts and to use them, whether by collecting fruit, knowing where to sit, or diverting water flow. This is significant for the conservationist as the inclusion of the wild and the productive within the aesthetic order of value resides in the use of traditional materials and skills, and the avoidance of alienating 'exotic' elements like barbed wire, moulded plastics and modern masonry pointing.[4]

LOCAL LANDSCAPING TRADITIONS

A cursory look at the settlement of Shigar and the landscape around it reveals a variety of open plots and enclosures: orchards, courtyards, graveyards, avenues, springs, woods, enclaves, open clearings, public meeting spaces, terraces, gardens, channels, bridges, pools, seats, balconies and pavilions. Irrigation and enclosure are the primary means of recognising a plot's place on the continuum between the wild, the productive and the delightful.[5]

Pleasure gardens are characterised by pergolas, ornamental pools, seats in the shade, views over the river and flower beds. Productive ground is known by the vegetable patches, orchards planted *a la ligne*, the community's wash rooms, laundries and silt collection pools. While wild ground is known by its

Figs. 260-262. Elements in the Shigar village landscape. Top, *shaq* fence enclosure; middle, paths, stone walls and irrigation channels in semi-wooded landscape; bottom, silt collection tank for the summer spate.

scrub for grazing, the paths made by animals along its ridges and the absence of enclosure and water. Significantly the orchard and the scrub are commonly included in the 'prospect'.

"The term 'garden' (*bagh*) denotes sites ranging in size from small vegetated plots to large imperial complexes. Some gardens have symmetrical layouts, repeating decorative elements and high enclosure walls; others were loosely arranged around natural springs, meandering streams, informal plantings and open prospects."[6] Such agrarian landscapes are inclusive and hierarchical, their garden metaphors and layouts concern familial privacy, good vistas and natural prospects, cool spots in summer and warm in winter, running water and abundant fruit. In the vernacular tradition, a good garden is known by its secure enclosure, good irrigation and diversity of plants, such as at Shigar fort.

Who are the stewards of the dynamic technologies of irrigation and propagation? Who has the knowledge of the ecologies of the main valley, the side valleys and passes? The farmer-gardeners and herders, the landscape which is the historical repository of their work, and the gardens in which they practice, are strategic assets. It is predicted that the value of well-established traditional 'gardens' and their commodities will increase in value as future urbanisation processes will transform the Northern Areas.[7]

A deep historical understanding improves the likelihood of intelligent strategic development. Nowhere is this more obvious than in a landscape and its buildings. The change of materials and construction skills differentiates all modern landscapes, and will probably increase the value of authentic autochthonous landscapes and the proven adaptability of its solutions to the harsh environment.[8] This premise lies behind the historical and imaginative restoration of the landscape. Interviews with local dignitaries and labourers led to the planting of roses and vines. In one instant, a plum tree that was sold some years ago, during the lowest slump of the garden's land use from productive orchard to stock grazing, was bought back and has been reinstated in the fort's garden.

THE IMPACT OF DEVELOPMENT

Periods of strong or weak centralised control affect the development of the landscape differently, with strong control resulting invariably in larger-scale projects and greater change, sometimes good, sometimes bad. The power exercised by the Government of Pakistan and other organisations such as the Aga Khan Rural Support Programme (AKRSP) and the World Bank in this period has led to the introduction of metalled roads, piped water, channelled water, hydro-electric power and electric lights in the Shigar valley.

In Shigar there is real scope to relate the different scales of landscape conservation into the wider projects of infrastructure development. Landscape planning can improve the results of engineering works, whether roads, lighting, or communal water channel repair. The survey skills, and the knowledge of local materials and plants gained at historic sites, can be fed into the process of wider community development to good effect. This can happen in parallel with other physical and social rehabilitation projects, such as those undertaken in Baltistan by the AKCS-P.

The extent to which the territory of Shigar is a viable cultural landscape remains to be defined. Who is responsible for safeguarding the landscape of the Shigar valley? The creation of this landscape over centuries, by many generations, has resulted in a versatile environmental solution to human existence in these areas that holds many answers. This tapestry of garden creations represents a series of personal and community solutions to questions about time, man and nature that pertain at all scales[9] and constitute a precious tradition. At the larger scale of infrastructure interventions, engineers can access little local information feedback and local communities and historic landscapes have little control on the engineering projects. Both project managers and villagers can benefit from an informed landscape consultation process, like that begun by the AKSC-P in Shigar, to navigate the complexities of modern development.

The 'social cost' of road building in remote areas or the 'value' of a traditional apricot orchard is very difficult to evaluate over different lengths of time and size of area. From the perspective of landscape impact, much construction degrades the amenity value of the landscape in ways that could be avoided by proper planning and land-use control systems. Likewise, how does one relate the taste of the 'Margulam' apricot to the yield of the 'Five Star' apple, when thinking of productivity? When the experience of a garden is directly related to its landscape, and the landscape or society relates to a particular type of garden, the likelihood of a garden prevailing are much higher. For example, the decline in popularity of polo at Altit fort, Hunza, and the subsequent urban encroachment on the Altit polo pitch is telling. Even if there are additional socio-political and economic motives, there are similar motives in Shigar, but it is hard to conceive this happening in this generation in Shigar because of the popularity of the game within Shigar society. Measuring and understanding the 'suitability' of modern landscape to its users is critical to steering the landscape development process successfully.

IN SEARCH OF THE BALTI GARDEN

In the glossary of *Il giardino islamico – architettura, natura, paesaggio*[10] there is an interesting but incomplete series of terms in Arabic, Kashmiri, Persian, Sanskrit (including Hindi and Urdu derivatives) and Turkish. The landscape features evident in Balti appear most closely allied with those described in Persian, but this reflects the linguistic status of Persian rather than the real material influence. For example the influence of Turanian elements is more poorly represented and understood, but like the Tibetan influence is a key part of the historical jigsaw. Apposite comparisons offer a way out of the widespread and flimsy brand of generic somnolent conservation that insinuates itself in all societies.

An example of a new and characteristic Balti garden is the one created by an elderly single man up the Shigar *luma* – the upland territory in the tributary valley above Shigar, irrigated by the *nullah* that runs by the fort. The garden is part productive and part ornamental, eked out of very marginal conditions. It represents an important part of the landscape of Shigar, like the herders' and croppers' camps or the small mosque and enclosed vegetable garden[11] still higher up the *nullah*. Mosques are traditional elements of the landscape like the fort itself; they represent nodes of organisation within the whole, as well as the house of prayer, while this maverick garden is almost another world, set up in defiance to both the traditional order of land holding and in opposition to the modernist visions of the government, half in the owned land of the lowland settlements, and half in

Fig. 263. The Shigar *luma* juniper forest with a specimen sorbus.

the shared lands of the upland settlements. The garden-maker does not usually allow visitors in, his is a recluse's garden – an imaginative landscape, relating to the historical tradition of upland dwelling by hermits (whether fierce or gentle) in Shigar and Thalle. Significantly in such marginal geographic conditions his plot is immediately recognisable anywhere across Asia as a 'garden', a poetic landscape.

The historical conservation and development of the landscape at Shigar under the auspices of the AKCS-P has been tempered at each juncture by complex environmental considerations. For example, the choice to use locally sourced plants was immediate and uncompromising, with only some considered exceptions for specific roles – for example sourcing some old damask, gallica and china roses known to have flourished here, but which have not survived. Research at Shigar revealed that the Baltis recognise thirty-two named grafted variety of apricot, each with different uses, some for storing, some for immediate eating. At a later stage it is hoped a complete plant list will be prepared from the data collected so far. Likewise, the choice to use the traditional gravity fed channels and sluices was immediate.

Figs. 264, 265. The Shigar *luma* mosque garden and mosque with its 'Hermit'.

The short- and long-term roles of paths and lights and the issue of materials has been a matter of long discussions in order to find a design language adapted to the place.

What is the relationship of the people of Shigar to their landscape then and now? Was the last social order, a feudal system that pertained in Shigar and every independent 'valley-principality' for the last five hundred years, a successful patron of 'sustainable development'? And if so, is that body of inherited horticultural knowledge still serviceable?[12] Are the many plant selections resulting from this time available and useful today? Will traditional horticulture be useful tomorrow? Has the goal of sustainable landscape development been clearly identified, both historically and in the future for the Shigar?[13] And if so, is it a viable or even desirable way forward for Shigar and other settlements like it? And if not, what are the alternatives for the farmer-gardeners and herders?[14]

MAINTAINING HORTICULTURAL TRADITIONS

Horticultural knowledge is passed on orally and by example, that is, practice in the field; it is not written down. Thus it is vulnerable to dilution and even loss with the advent of rapidly changing lifestyles, as often occurs when a metalled road appears.[15] So what is agricultural improvement here in Shigar, and what are the advantages of progressive technology to the gardeners of Shigar? Equipment like secateurs, bow saws and rollers are useful for gardeners, not because they do something that could not previously be done but because they increase precision and reduce the duration of horticultural activities. Better record keeping of plants, improved propagation facilities, grafting and budding workshops, education about root desiccation, learning Latin names, making trials using more or less organic matter, and so on, are some goals for training on the gardeners and ensuring a well-kept garden as befits a luxury heritage hotel.

At the same time, the traditional selections of grafted fruit trees offer the best agricultural opportunity for the social development for this community, rather than the generic selections of apple, universally available in the area. The role of specialised agricultural production, intimately tailored to this climate is most promising economically. Firstly, it is a hedge against fluctuations in tourism. Secondly, it is a means of producing high quality organic fruit for a niche market down country or abroad. Thirdly, it is a way of conserving the fabric of the landscape that made and still continues to make Baltistan and the Northern Areas beautiful to natives and non-natives alike.

The gardens and orchards maintain the status quo; they frame the settlements and hold things in place. There is a proverb which might have some currency here in Shigar and the Northern Areas: if a land owner loves and looks after his trees he can hold onto his estate; if he is blind to them he can lose his land. In the lowland valley plots the tree population is healthy with a good standard distribution of species and ages. But up the valleys near the passes and high pastures in the juniper forest there is a serious problem; the wood is not able to regenerate, and autumn by autumn the big trees are being taken and the wood resource depleted. This wood is the best fuel wood for heating in the very cold winters and there are no favoured alternatives. Unfortunately the depletion of juniper or equivalent coniferous (cedar/pine/fir) forests is not unique to Shigar, it is one the most serious sylvicultural problems noted by the author across the Northern Areas.[16] What is a viable alternative for this firewood and what implications do these alternatives have, on both the lifestyle of Shigar community and on the landscape? No other wood burns as well; what of coal or coke admixture to lower grade woods? What of piped or bottled gas? What of a detailed project proposal for a juniper reforestation programme in Shigar *luma* and Thalle *broq*,[17] where there is no longer any juniper at all? Oral accounts collected in 2004 say there used to be some at Thalle *broq* during the last hundred years.

Fig. 266. The *pharee*, or communal water reservoir; a ubiquitous landscape feature in the Northern Areas.

In the village of Kwardu near Skardu, an inherited skill in the cultivation of grapes has made this village known as the premier vine producing area between Skardu and Shigar. This village produced the vine 'Aligarh' to replace the one grow-

245

ing on the entrance pergola to the fort two generations ago. Further up the valley at Hashubee, the Government of Pakistan has a fruit nursery producing some good local grafts of apricots, as do many private nurseries in the village of Shigar itself. Both these sources have been used in order to secure more apricots and apples to plant in the traditional manner inside the boundary wall of the fort garden. These informed horticultural selections are priorities in landscape rehabilitation because of the agricultural basis of landscape design and maintaining the strong extant horticultural stock.

The role of water in the garden is critical, as is conformation to water rights and maintenance of the existing channels for downstream communities.[18] For example, at Shigar fort, some channels run permanently, others occasionally, and there must be return loops built into the irrigation system for water to return to the main channel in the relevant quarters. In Balti, like most languages in the Northern Areas, there are three different words for the three sizes of channel. This indicates precision and suggests the efficient use of water, which is the key index of sustainability in a landscape in semi-arid and arid conditions.

DESIGNING THE GARDEN OF SHIGAR FORT RESIDENCE

Because of the perceived change at Shigar, inherent in the adaptive reuse project, the conservation of established traditions in the garden, and especially its points of contact with the community, is vital from a sociological perspective. Traditional practices such as locals entering the fort garden at their discretion and changing sluices on channels to water their plots, become important. Likewise, activities such as consulting neighbouring houses and agreeing to plant trees to promote privacy on the fort boundaries with their houses, or the restoring of weakened party walls, or training in horticultural techniques (such as laying even turf, formative pruning and dead wooding trees above benches), are all conciliatory moves that take on greater significance as the new landscape identity emerges.

The integration of progressive horticultural elements within the traditional landscape is a necessary requirement for upgrading an uninhabitable fort into a luxurious residence. The most difficult areas to reconcile within a historical landscape are always the modern services such as piped water, storage tanks, electricity, sewage, lighting, sump drains, and laying out paths and circulation hierarchies on site. It is a question of how subtle is the engineering? How elegant is the palimpsest?[19]

How does one control the real and apparent use of modern materials in a traditional landscape? In one way the restored landscape of Shigar fort can never be more than a modern landscape because it has so much technology invested into it now, and it caters mostly to foreigners. It is differentiated. There have been compromises; for example, the garden has an uncomfortably large area of hard paving around the fort; it has a modern lighting system; it has a dedicated service block and access road. All these landscape elements contribute to the vital modern utilitarian identity of the Shigar landscape, yet one hopes the terraces, orchards, pools and channels and *baradari* will engage our sensibilities above all (fig. 252).

The elegant white marble basin in the Amacha garden between the large plane tree and the *baradari* pool (figs. 258, 259) are the dominant features noted by visitors, together with the shady ruined buttress on the historic wall connecting the old cliff fortress with the main fort, and the old Kashmiri mulberry staining the dust with its purple fruit. The interrelationship of the physical and the cultural realms that make up the garden remains rooted in the patronage of the *rajas* of Shigar and the landscape improvements dating

Fig. 267. The orchard below Altit fort in Hunza.

from their tenure, specifically the *baradari* pergolas, arbours and the pool and marble basin filled with Shigar's abundant clear water.

To protect vegetables, the people of Shigar traditionally used either round stone walls topped with mud and sea buckthorn[20] if between buildings, or a *shaq* fence made out of living willow sets in February if new. A traditional vegetable garden with *shaq* is being reinstated on its historic site in the north-east of the garden, because goats remain a perennial pest to gardens in Shigar. There are many small walled or fenced vegetable and flower plots in Shigar from where seed for vegetables and flowers have been collected for the fort via the labour force.

The skills of the stone-dykers building the round rubble walls and those of the traditional woodworkers, who contributed to the Shigar fort, the Amburiq mosque, the *raja's* mosque and the *khanqah* define the Balti identity in the landscape at Shigar. The tradition of high-quality carving and woodwork derives from a dynastic alliance with neighbouring Tibeto-Kashmiri nobility. On a horticultural level, red and black cherries are thought to have arrived at the same time from Kashmir. Likewise the plane tree, which denotes a feudal territory, probably also arrived in this period. In the Shigar fort landscape the plane trees dominate, one at the entrance in the historical meeting place outside the gate, one beneath the *rajah's* balcony and one up the top of the saddle of the *nullah* ridge beyond the entrance to the old high fortress, marking the appearance of the channel round the corner form the *nullah* proper. There are others too, associated with the *khanqah*. This horticultural language of 'ruling' plane trees (and the cultivation of vines) has currency all the way from Ferghana to Kashmir and Iran.

Figs. 268-271. Agriculture and harvesting in the Northern Areas: pressing *balagutoy*; the mulberry harvest; working the fields; terraced fields and irrigation channel (from the D. Lorimer collection).

THE CONTEXT OF THE KARAKORAM LANDSCAPE

Einar Eberhardt's dissertation "Plant life of the Karakoram" reveals in great detail the distribution of flora and their phytogeographical associations within the various geomorphologic and climatic scenarios of the Karakoram. The Karakoram has a complex flora linked with the cold mountain deserts of north-west Tibet and the south-west rim of Central Asia, and the north-west Himalayas.

"The (Karakoram) mountain range separates the Irano-Turanian steppe and the Saharo-Sindian desert flora to the south-west from the Central Asian and Mongolian desert flora to the north-east, and furthermore acts in a way as a filter between the species rich Sino-Himalayan mountain flora to the south-east and the other holarctic Eurasian high mountain floras to the west and north-west."[21]

The nature of plant life in Shigar can be related to Hermann Kreutzmann's larger orogeographic framework on the Northern Areas as a whole, and the phytogeographic distribution studies of Einar Eberhardt and others[22] in the Karakoram range, and the socio-economic framework and land use history and cultivation in specific parts of the valley and side valleys. Eberhardt cites the dendrochronological work of Bonher, demonstrating that in the Northern Karakoram and the Tien Shan a most favourable 'Medieval Warm Period' (AD 800 to 1000) and a least favourable 'Little Ice Age' (AD 1139 to 1770) prevailed. This proved the hypothesis that the growth of these upland plants is limited by temperature. At about twenty-eight per cent glaciation, the present temperature level is slightly more favourable than the measured average, with an estimated 190 day growing season in much of the Karakoram.

The short sharp season with only one crop relates directly to the abrupt seasonal changes common in April and September. On top of this the altitude, the aspect and the location within the south-west/north-east gradient of decreasing precipitation allow one to scientifically predict wild species distribution and change – even to the observation that conifers occur where the low level monsoons penetrate the mountains. However in the case of cultivated plants, in the main settlement and horticultural zone, say below 2700 metres, a different scenario pertains. Shigar has good strong water sources and there are great numbers of their five willows – the red, green, black, gold and old – while in drier moraines up the Indus and Shyok valleys at a similar altitude, there is often only the gold one. So, at a horticultural level, in the semi-arid (below 2700 metres) and the arid zone (below 1000 metres), the amount of channelled water is the decisive factor, with the influence of location within the Karakoram range, altitude and aspect less significant.[23]

The garden landscapes of the Northern Areas are an important cultural and natural resource, having social, economic, political and agricultural functions. Today, they begin to accommodate new opportunities, which require imaginative and informed landscape development planning. By soundly identifying the assets and liabilities embedded within the landscape, it is possible to inform the social development process as well as conserve the cultural traditions. The extensive orchards of fruit trees, the shady groves of poplar and willow, and the clear pools and fast flowing water channels remain the vital elements of this landscape within the zone of permanent human settlement, and it is in this context that the garden of Baltistan is made and kept.

[1] This reference refers to lowland plots and it is important to recall their associated summer upland pastures, where a choice natural bounty speaks of an 'order' in the landscape. In an upland community it might be a well-churned yoghurt or a special cut of mutton. The important point is that upper and lower landscapes are complimentary, with the upland grazing producing vital animal fodder and food stuffs for the winter.

[2] The way the 'agrarian landscape' of the Northern Areas is experienced is distinguished from that of the metropolitan settlements by its use of wood not stone, though both share the use of open spaces bordered by trees for equestrian exercise.

[3] The AKCS-P Shigar archive includes some important historic photographs, whereas all linguistic material appears to have come from oral sources.

[4] Suffice to say here that this point identifies something valuable and useful at Shigar, though less so at Skardu, Gilgit or

Karimabad, due to their more advanced stage of urbanisation and encroachment of their historic landscapes. This all-inclusive nature of the rural landscape is a key priority for the landscape conservation of historic landscapes, and Shigar is fortunate to have its context preserved because of its traditional remoteness.

[5] No plot's place is fixed forever and the goal of landscape conservation might be seen as the insightful balancing of these various elements in the interests of today and tomorrow with the benefit of yesterday.

[6] James Westcoat's definition of a garden in his essay "Mughal Gardens and the Geographic Sciences, Then and Now" holds good here, in Gardens in the Time of the Great Muslim Empires: Theory and Design, special issue of Muqarnas, A. Petruccioli (ed.), E. J. Brill, Leiden 1997.

[7] The urban process in the Hunza valley and the Indus near

Skardu is much more developed than that in the Shigar valley. Shigar and other more rural communities can benefit from these case studies.

[8] In architecture, the suitability of cribbage construction over concrete (see chapter 5) is well documented, while in horticulture the parallel examples in the materials and designs in fencing, seating, irrigation, storage and access systems are slightly less tangible.

[9] This idea is derived from Michel Conan's analysis of Bernard Lassus' studies of working-class French gardens in his essay "From Vernacular Gardens to a Social Anthropology of Gardening" (in *Perspectives on Garden Histories*, M. Conan (ed.), Dumbarton Oaks, Washington DC 1999) which makes this very point.

[10] Attilio Petruccioli (ed), Electa, Milan 1994.

[11] This mosque has the highest enclosure and vegetable plot seen by the author up the Shigar *luma* in 2004.

[12] The key relationship to define in the landscape development plan for Baltistan is that between modern infrastructural developments by the government and non-governmental organisations, like the AKRSP, and the local communities and their traditional management of water and other landscape resources.

[13] Terence Young, in his paper "Confronting Sustainability" (in *Sustainable Landscape Design in Arid Climates*, AKTC, a symposium for Dumbarton Oaks, Washington DC 1996), gives a powerful historiography of sustainable development and identifies its origins in utilitarian resource management.

[14] These questions are derived from Terence Young's essay "Confronting Sustainability" (see note 13).

[15] The paved road from Skardu to Shigar is a major landscape event. It is hoped that the socio-economic stimulation will be managed in a coherent development plan that safeguards the key features in the landscape, such as the mosques and their prospects and the polo pitch and traditional channels throughout the village, for example.

[16] Some other horticultural problems still to be addressed in Baltistan include the ill-advised use of *Ailanthus altissima*, the promotion of generic imported apples, the loss of indigenous cultivars of fruit trees, the concrete rendering and pointing of new surfaces willy-nilly, and the loss of traditional knowledge, skills and management systems.

[17] This is the upland territory of Thalle, like the *luma* of Shigar, except in Thalle it is also a more specific proper name for the upper section as well.

[18] Hermann Kreutzmann's essay "Water Management in Mountain Oases of the Karakoram" (in *Sharing Water - Irrigation and Water Management in the Hindu Kush-Karakoram-Himalaya*, Oxford University Press, Karachi-London 2000) details the status quo in Hunza, reveals the seriousness of this matter and the obstacles that must be overcome, and describes the intelligence implicit in the working of the channel irrigation systems of the Karakoram, Hunza and Shigar.

[19] Conservation is double edged – no action is often better than doing the wrong thing. In the author's experience, a landscape restoration process does not necessarily safeguard a historic landscape; indeed, it can sometimes hasten its demise.

[20] A multi-purpose plant, it is used for fencing and scree slope containment, while the berries are eaten medicinally for a host of complaints. Its conservation outside Skardu on the way to Shigar is an important horticultural conservation undertaking with wider implications for traditional landscape skills.

[21] Einar Eberhardt, "Plant Life of the Karakoram - The Vegetation of the Upper Hunza Catchment (Northern Areas, Pakistan) Diversity, Syntaxonomy, Distribution", *Dissertationes Botanicae*, Band 387, Berlin 2004.

[22] H. Hartmann, W. B. Dickore and G. Miehe are other significant primary researchers in this field.

[23] See Hermann Kreutzmann's essay, note 18, for a full discussion of the role of irrigation in these valleys.

12. Village Rehabilitation and Community Development

MASOOD KHAN

From the inception of their various conservation and upgrading activities in 1992, the Aga Khan Trust for Culture (AKTC) and its affiliate the Aga Khan Cultural Service-Pakistan (AKCS-P) have recognised that the new economic forces associated with development and tourism, if not properly steered, could spoil the impressive natural setting and the cultural heritage which are the Northern Area's major resource base. Whatever short-term benefits may be derived from them, in the long run economic progress and well-being will be largely dependent on preserving the outstanding cultural assets and environmental qualities of the valleys.

Unlike the conservation of individual historic monuments, which can be implemented under tightly controlled technical and administrative conditions, the rehabilitation of historic villages and their farming environments require a much more complex socio-economic and institutional approach, combined with physical planning and land-use decisions which may demand sacrifices with regard to traditional property rights. A strategy for the combined preservation and appropriate development of the built environment – including monuments, architectural ensembles, settlement structure and the man-made landscape – could not succeed without a prior change of people's attitude towards the legacy of the past and its importance for the present – and the future. In practice, this attitude must be translated into collective decision making and corresponding internal arbitration and compensation mechanisms, and it must eventually be sanctioned by an institutional apparatus capable of legitimising such changes and social mechanisms.

It is with this background in mind that AKCS-P projects in the area have initiated a broad community-based effort to save, revive and develop local heritage –acknowledging that sustainable use of natural and cultural assets hinges on the commitment and support of local residents. In Hunza, the AKCS-P's involvement began in Karimabad (in parallel with the restoration of Baltit fort), and was then followed up in Ganish, Altit and other, smaller villages. In Baltistan it started with the group of hamlets that constitute Shigar, and is being replicated in other valleys such as Khaplu. The resulting village rehabilitation and community development efforts aim at triggering a paradigmatic shift in the way communities relate to their physical environment – by enabling them to connect the fruits of economic development with a major revalorisation of the cultural heritage as seen in landscapes, human settlements, historic villages, and individual architectural monuments and more ordinary historic buildings. Improving the quality of life is thus to go hand in hand with enhancing the meaning of the physical environment and preserving cultural identity.

This strategy was implemented by acting simultaneously on a number of levels: first, nurturing – through the very project activities – the growth of new community-based municipal institutions and pressure groups for better management of civic functions; second, helping these institutional elements in regulating land use, preparing new infrastructure projects (roads, sanitation and refuse disposal and water supply) to alleviate the pressure of development on the historic and scenic assets of the physical environment; third, improving health and daily hygiene by introducing sanitary waste disposal systems (in certain cases without disturbing the ecological and social components of existing traditional systems), and improving environmental conditions in the collective spaces of the village by paving lanes and squares; and fourth, rehabilitating traditional homes and groups of houses and rendering them compatible with contemporary lifestyles.

The concept of integrated cultural development pursued by the AKCS-P was based on identifying elements of high cultural and historic value in the physical environment and initiating projects for their conservation, with the involvement and participation of concerned local communities. Such elements of the physical heritage have included individual buildings and monuments, architectural ensembles and other groups of buildings, vernacular settlements and villages of cultural and architectural significance, cultural ensembles and cultural landscapes (see chapter 8).

Together, these elements were considered as components of a more complex environmental and socio-economic system, into which they had to be reintegrated and to which in turn they could actively contribute. Implementing corresponding integrated project activities meant, by necessity, working closely with existing interest groups in order to address, through planning and development programmes, issues of land use, environmental management and heritage care. In response to their needs, the rehabilitation of the physical environment includes projects for clean water and sanitation, as well as physical interventions for the conservation of typical individual houses, whole streets and public spaces, and complete traditional neighbourhoods. This cooperation in turn offered the opportunity to use these projects as vehicles for establishing local institutional entities responsible for planning and environmental resource management. Restoration projects also provided employment and training for local craftsmen – an aspect then extended to wide-ranging craft revival programmes and institutions promoting enterprise development and sales of local products.

ENABLING COMMUNITIES TO MANAGE THEIR ENVIRONMENT – THE CASE OF KARIMABAD
Begun in 1992 with the intention of managing the physical and socio-economic ramifications of the conservation of Baltit fort (see chapter 9), the Karimabad project was the ground-breaking Historic Cities Support Programme (HCSP) initiative in community-based village planning and rehabilitation, and the forerunner of similar operations in the surrounding communities and, later, in Baltistan.

Until the late nineteenth century, Baltit was a tightly clustered fortified settlement surmounted by the fort. What remains today of the clusters of houses huddled together at the foot of the fort, are the ancient villages of Diramishal and Khurukshal, named after the Diramiting and the Khurukutz, two of the four ancient tribes of Baltit. In the early twentieth century, with the arrival of the British, the fortified group of villages had opened up, leading to several changes in village form and the establishment of newer villages in the farming terraces lower down in the valley. Despite these changes, the geography of the place still continued to retain a strong resonance with past ways of building habitat, making sure that agricultural land was not sacrificed to new development.

Fig. 272. Aerial view of Baltit fort on a steep hill, with the historic village below it and the gorges of the Ultar river behind it.

By the time the conservation project for Baltit fort was commenced in 1989, the traditional settlements at the foot of the fort were being abandoned, mostly because of the prevailing unsanitary living conditions and the inadequacy of the houses to support a desired standard of modern life. The consequence of this process was the building of new houses in the open farming terraces, where a family could create separate stables for their animals and supply itself with rudimentary sanitary waste disposal by digging cesspits. This often resulted in contaminated water percolating through the hillsides and affecting open fields and other houses. Moreover, the spectacular cultivated hillside surrounding the 'bowl' of Karimabad was being dotted with new construction, at the cost of the centuries-old farming terraces and orchards.

The patterns of change outlined here have accompanied Karimabad's transformation from a secluded rural system into a semi-urban agglomeration (figs. 273, 274). They are typical for most traditional villages in the Northern Areas and involve problems of infrastructure, traffic, commercial activities and new construction modes, all of which can have a considerable impact on the physical environment. With the aim of steering the future development of Karimabad away from the potentially negative aspects of such transformations, an analysis of the current situation was initiated in 1992. This activity, implemented with the help of a local technical cell and a social organiser from the AKCS-P, involved discussions with the citizens of Karimabad about the consequences of present trends and desirable corrections. Eventually, a consulta-

Fig. 273. The harmonious village landscape,
with its terraced fields, paths and irrigation channels,
is highly sensitive to the intrusion of vehicular traffic.

Fig. 274. The main bazaar street in Karimabad.

tive Conceptual Development Plan was worked out to provide a strategic framework for the orderly physical growth and development of Karimabad, and for the maintenance of its environmental and cultural assets. This multi-faceted planning process had a number of corollary objectives:

- the establishment of a local institutional base, the Karimabad Town Management Society (TMS),[1] sufficiently representative to harness community support, to resolve upcoming internal conflicts and to develop its own practices and priorities in response to local problems;
- the rehabilitation of the traditional settlements and their architectural heritage, together with the protection of the scenic environment;
- a more conscious management of land use, based on creating a balance between tourism-related economic activities and traditional occupational patterns and enabling the benefits gained from tourism to support the conservation of traditional, but less profitable activities;
- slowing down adverse trends in building construction by means of revalorising traditional settlements and planning for the growth of new settlements that were either adjacent to existing villages, or on new sites agreed within the planned land-use framework, and that were shaped by an environmentally and culturally conscious sensibility;
- establishment of an adequate road and service infrastructure base to support a well-functioning civic economy and a healthy community, and to provide the necessary incentives for appropriate land-use patterns.

While this attempt to put in place an operational TMS in parallel with a wide range of planning, conservation and physical upgrading activities is further described below, we will first dwell on the institutional and legal aspects of this complex effort. Although the zoning and building regulations embodied in the Plan for Karimabad, as first conceived in 1995, are still not enforceable by law, the Plan has increased the awareness of people about the issues at stake and helped forge a consensus on fundamental choices for ongoing and future development. This is manifest in the degree to which the people of Karimabad have adhered to it: deviations are few and far between and, despite certain key developmental components still lagging behind, the implementation of major urban sanitation projects has provided sanitary sewerage to the entire area of Karimabad, while at the same time channelling the future development into desirable directions. Through discussing and adapting land-use details with the directly concerned territorial and social

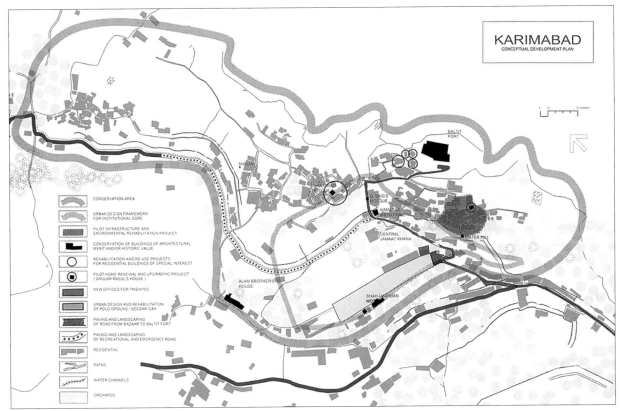

Fig. 275. Plan of the historic area of Baltit/Karimabad.

units (the tribal councils and Village Organisations – VOs[2]) the development of the Plan has given birth to a participatory process at grass-roots level. This approach was instrumental in mobilising a high degree of commitment to Karimabad's cultural and scenic resources, in facilitating the internal resolution of conflicts arising from strategic long-term development options, and in ensuring the continued access of all segments of the population to shared natural resources and their economic fall-outs, with a particular eye to the equitable distribution of economic benefits gained from the tourism industry.

The establishment of the TMS happened in a local government context which was unable to respond to the urbanisation trends discussed above. Under the Northern Areas Local Government Act, municipal councils have been created only in a few large towns, such as Gilgit, Skardu, Khaplu and Chilas, which are administered by a District Commissioner. Areas like Karimabad or Shigar have not been considered as meeting population size or urbanisation criteria that would classify them as urban communities. The Village Councils or Union Councils established under the local government law did not have any power to carry out land-use planning or prepare development projects. In Karimabad, the TMS has continued to strive for government recognition of the Conceptual Development Plan, in the expectation that the government will finally agree to create a municipal council, a Town Committee, and the TMS would move away from its civic governance functions to an oversight and monitoring role as a civil society organ. The Town Committee, created under the local government laws, would be able to enforce the land use components of the Conceptual Development Plan.[3]

Despite the limitations outlined above, the TMS model has been adopted by the inhabitants of other large villages and towns, such as Altit, Aliabad and Ganish in Hunza and in Shigar and Khaplu[4] in Baltistan, where there are active and aware town management societies today. In most cases, the AKCS-P is extending specialised technical assistance as needed, but does not interfere in constitutional matters.

PROTECTION OF CULTURAL AND SCENIC ASSETS

An important initial step taken as part of the planning process was the identification of those elements of Karimabad that are of special scenic and cultural value. A conservation area was delimited, to include the historic villages of Khurukshal and Diramishal, an extension of Diramishal called Domet, the old orchards in the immediate vicinity of the historic villages, and the polo ground. Outside this zone, individual spots were earmarked as places of special environmental, social, or cultural significance. The most important scenic viewpoints were also identified, as well as a list of architecturally or historically important buildings and open spaces within and outside the contiguous conservation area (fig. 275).

Acknowledging the limitations of legal constraints, a range of strategies and mechanisms, tied to certain collectively agreed land-use principles defining the future development of housing and infrastructure, were adopted to preserve the traditional character of the landscape and the environment of Karimabad. Apart from the current practice of dialogue and conflict resolution within the village organisation, recourse was taken to regulative tools (such as planning and design guidelines), supported by appropriate incentives. At the level of the historic zone, incentives for the conservation of individual houses were offered in the form of soft loans and small grants. The provision of sanitation infrastructure, the rehabilitation of streets and public open spaces, and the conservation of individual places, buildings, and building elements of special architectural and cultural value provided further impetus for the rehabilitation of the historic area as a whole and spurred collateral private efforts (see below)

Special consideration was given to the conservation of public open spaces, as they are not only characteristic for the environmental qualities of Karimabad, but also valuable in terms of places of social interaction and collective identity. Projects included the improvement of the polo ground, the stone paving of the access way to the fort (fig. 277) as the main pedestrian spine of Karimabad, as well as the enhancement of special nodes (fig. 280) and places of gathering, such as the central *jamatkhana* and the *himalter*, the site of the former main entrance gate to Baltit (fig. 323). A similar treatment was accorded to zones of special sensory and aesthetic character in the built environment outside the historic zone, such as other villages which are now over a hundred years old, the walk along the Samarkand water channel, and points which offer spectacular views of distant natural landscapes. These points and areas are to be upgraded through modest but sensitively designed interventions.

LAND-USE, ROAD AND INFRASTRUCTURE PLANNING

The land-use plan for Karimabad (fig. 278) has evolved in a series of cycles, moving from more aggregate ways of strategising at the level of the TMS to consensus-building among the directly concerned tribes, villages and land owners. The resolution of conflicts relating to land use and equitable trade-off of economic benefits arising from tourism is seen as an internal community matter, and while the AKCS-P offered technical advice, it did not interfere in the decision making.

Through the community-based negotiation process, several objectives have been achieved: first, certain decision-making competencies have moved from the TMS to the subsidiary level of the VOs, especially concerning the identification of buildable land and the future management of collective territories. Second, issues relating to contained residential development have been articulated and first schemes for new clustered compounds have been developed through an intense planning and design dialogue. Third, owners of agricultural land which contribute to the scenic landscapes in important ways now see themselves in a more positive engagement with land-use issues, as new compensation mechanisms for better distribution of the surpluses created in the tourist industry are discussed within the VOs and the tribal councils. In regard to the Land-Use Plan for Karimabad, this latest round of grass-roots discussions has also witnessed a few instances of individual violations, and there is a growing need for the Plan's validation as a planning instrument under the local government law. With the latter undergoing radical reformulation throughout Pakistan, the Land-Use Plan of Karimabad has acquired a pivotal importance as an exemplar of planning by consensus in rapidly transforming rural communities.

Anchoring the Plan in the social and territorial realities, as well as seeking endorsement from the concerned communities, is essential to ensuring its successful implementation. Further momentum for the materialisation of the Plan principles is expected from a co-ordinated set of incentives, such as exclusive provision of feeder roads and infrastructure connections to the areas demarcated in the Plan. Controlled road construction and infrastructure investments are thus essential tools to help implement the plan. Institutional back-up under the local government legislation, in the form of new procedures and building applications never before used in the Northern Areas, should provide additional support in due time.

Traffic planning
Vehicular access is critical to the viability of historic districts, but can also be detrimental for their environmental quality, if not sufficiently controlled. Karimabad is no exception to this rule. At the beginning of the planning process, a major issue faced by the community was the impending construction of a new road through one of the historic settlements near the fort, linking the newer villages on the western side of the valley directly with the Bazaar road. This project would have destroyed nearly half of Khurukshal village,

Figs. 276, 277. The main village spine leading up to Baltit fort, before and after installing sewerage collectors and flag stone pavements (see also figs. 9, 10).

257

and would have encouraged the bazaar to grow into the heart of the historic area, compromising its qualities as a quiet residential neighbourhood.

By proposing an alternate road alignment around the historic core, the planning team eventually succeeded in averting this threat. Further advantages were obtained by making the new road part of a larger planning framework, which will eventually provide a second access from the Karakoram Highway (KKH)at the bottom of the valley. The new road will also serve as a market access road for the farms and orchards in a part of the valley not yet accessible to vehicles. Through the link with the KKH, it will constitute an alternate access point to the village from the other side of Karimabad and thus help alleviate development pressures in the present bazaar district, where all the tourist hotels and most commercial facilities are currently located.

The new bypass around the historic core, completed in 1996 with the assistance of the Northern Areas Public Works Department, was the fruit of a participatory planning process and represents the first step of a comprehensive network of major roads that will condition the future physical structure of Karimabad. Small feeder access roads from the main road network will provide vehicle and infrastructure access to residential neighbourhoods, and access of agricultural machinery to the farming terraces. Provision of vehicular accessibility is closely tied to the land-use strategy for the valley, which encourages certain functions to be developed in specific locations and defines areas where no construction activity should take place in the foreseeable future.

Infrastructure
In Karimabad, traditional rural ways of disposing sanitary waste have become impractical in a context of creeping urbanisation. Sanitary sewerage has therefore been one of the most keenly felt needs of the community. Initially, as people saw water-borne disposal systems set up by the local hotels in operation, they tended to emulate these systems by setting up crude water-borne cesspits for scattered individual homes – not a sustainable solution in the long run. A comprehensive sanitation project for Karimabad, based on water-borne disposal and anaerobic treatment, was proposed in 1994. The first and second phases of this project (described below) were supported by the Norwegian development agency (NORAD) and completed in 1996, with priority given to the conservation zone, including the historical settlements and the Baltit fort area, several other villages, and the bazaar and hotel area. In 2003, the third phase of Karimabad's sanitary sewerage project was completed by the TMS, with financial assistance from the Government of Japan, and technical assistance from the AKCS-P. It provides sanitation to the remainder of the town, chiefly along its western flank, adjacent to the Hyderabad gorge. In these projects, large even by the standards of government-run projects, voluntary labour and management inputs were provided by the community. The TMS also negotiated a development/connection charge to be levied on each household, and a room charge levied on hotels.

THE REHABILITATION OF THE HISTORIC NUCLEUS OF KARIMABAD
In order to enhance the value of the historic settlements of old Baltit, it was imperative to first demonstrate that they can sustain life at contemporary standards. The approach adopted by the AKCS-P was to link increasing community awareness of the local architectural heritage with collective self-help habits, modelled on *rajaki* – the traditional form of voluntary labour used for the development of infrastructure such as the

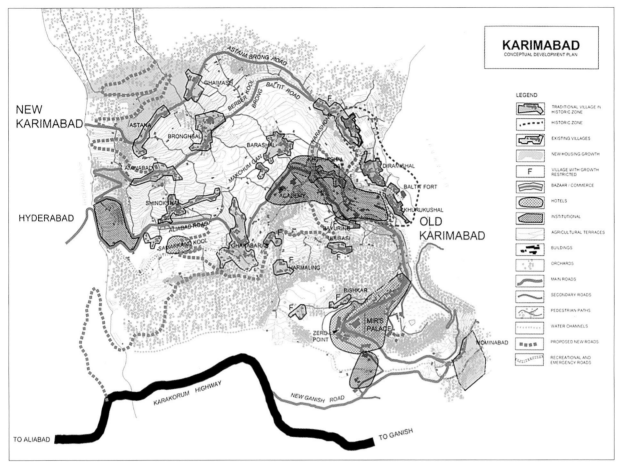

Fig. 278. Proposed land-use and development plan for wider Karimabad.

historic water channels. In Khurukshal, the rehabilitation and modernisation of amenities in a single trad-itional house in 1993-1994, was welcomed by the residents of the village and quickly grew into a Pilot Re-habilitation and Sanitation Project covering a portion of the Khurukshal village. The community of the Khurukutz participated actively by providing leadership and organisation, unskilled labour and local ma-terials. The Khurukshal pilot project eventually catered to a total of thirty-one houses, which rapidly un-derwent additions, alterations, or reconstruction as a result of the raised consciousness generated by the pro-ject. This project also foresaw the provision of sanitary sewerage in difficult mountain terrain, and the introduction of flushing toilets, connected to an anaerobic treatment tank and a soakage pit, pending the connection with a trunk sewer. In addition, it included the improvement of house exteriors, the stone paving of village lanes and cul-de-sacs, and the creation of public open spaces in the village (figs. 279, 280). In-terventions by the people were closely monitored by the AKCS-P with respect to appropriate materials and building techniques, and earthquake-resistant construction techniques were promoted.

The Khurukshal pilot project helped in turning the attitudes of the people of Karimabad around, and the old settlements, on the verge of being totally abandoned, began to be repopulated. This relatively small intervention in a part of one of the historic villages resulted in multiplier effects involving the entire popu-lation and spreading into other historic villages in Karimabad. As a development model it eventually expanded far beyond the limits of Karimabad. It created a new attitude towards the local environment, and dramatically slowed down the scattered random construction of new houses in the scenic farming terraces further down the valley. Together with new standards of health and hygiene, it has tended to revive sound building techniques based on tradition, such as those first introduced in the Baltit fort conservation project.

COMPACT RESIDENTIAL DEVELOPMENT OUTSIDE THE HISTORIC AREA OF BALTIT
The revalorisation of traditional settlement patterns made the community understand the need for clearly defined, self-contained built-up areas, and for protecting the orchards and agricultural terraces from the sprawl of haphazard residential development. The rationale for such development policies draws on three inter-related arguments: first, only a well planned and concise new development will allow for cost-efficient provision of infrastructure, such as roads, water supply, sanitation systems and electricity; second, securing the landscape and the environmental quality of Karimabad will help continue to attract tourism and protect the population's major economic assets; and third, conceiving the growth of Karimabad in the form of a number of villages will allow an old settlement tradition to be continued hand-in-hand with the introduction of modern amenities.

The proposed physical development will allow for careful extension of existing villages, as well as for planning and construction of new housing clusters. In the case of existing settlements, possible extensions have been identified with a ten-year perspective in mind. Where this process has been initiated, the limits of growth of each such village are being demarcated through negotiation with the affected land owners, and the demarcated areas are subjected to a physical development plan conforming to standards of density, building types and architectural guidelines. The pilot project in the village of Shinokshal was the first demonstration of this approach (figs. 281-283). It draws strongly upon a Design Manual for new houses prepared by the AKCS-P, and uses research on appropriate forms of cluster housing undertaken in cooperation with faculty and students from the Aga Khan Program for Islamic Architecture at the Massachusetts Institute for Technology. Apart from social and cultural factors, this research also considered earthquake resistance, passive solar heating and simple ways to improve thermal insulation.

In the case of new, separate housing clusters, suitable new development areas were selected through a dialogue involving the TMS, the AKCS-P and those VOs which wanted to create new opportunities for their members or preferred not to extend their existing village clusters. Assistance for preparing appropriate plans for layout, plot sub-divisions, alignment of access roads and allocation of public facilities, collective open spaces, and shops and guest houses, and so on, has been provided by the AKCS-P.

PROJECT REPLICATION IN GANISH AND ALTIT
The community-based village planning and rehabilitation efforts in Karimabad described above had an effect much beyond their immediate area of application. Other villages in the area realised the positive change achieved, and consequently the demand increased for similar assistance from the AKCS-P and its donors, in particular the Norwegian and Japanese bilateral aid organisations, NORAD and JICA. Replication was facilitated by a number of factors: first, the Karimabad projects had already clarified the partnership conditions between the AKCS-P and the local community; second, new demand arising from the convincing visual demonstration effect, created a 'competitive' situation, in which each village was bound

Previous page
107. The local community celebrates the completion of village rehabilitation works in Altit village square, inside the gateway *(himalter)*.
Outside the gate, the community pond.

109.

110.

111.

108.

108. One of the horizontal residential alleyways in Karimabad, before rehabilitation. Moving animal sheds outside the village was a precondition for introducing sanitation and upgrading.

109. Rehabilitating a house on the steep hillside below Baltit fort.

110. The first of many rehabilitated old houses in Karimabad.

111. One of the stepped 'vertical' alleyways in Karimabad after introduction of sewerage channels and proper flagstone paving. To the left, a restored old mill making use of a descending water channel.

112. Alleyway in a rehabilitated district of upper Karimabad below Baltit fort.

113.

114.

113. Residents participate in the village upgrading works in Karimabad by digging channels for the sanitation system under the narrow alleyways, later to be covered by stone steps and flagstone pavement.

114. The housing renewal project in Karimabad well under way. Residents built new bathrooms and kitchens in former stables after being connected to the new sewerage system.

115. A rehabilitated traditional house in Karimabad, with the cooking and heating stove in the centre of the living room.

116.

116, 117. The old *jataq*
(community square) of Ganish
during the community-driven
rehabilitation works (below)
and during one of the community
events following completion
of the project.

118. The rehabilitated *jataq*
with the restored small family
mosques surrounding it
(see also fig. 126). In the background,
one of the restored old watchtowers
of the fortified village.

117.

119.

119, 120. The community pond in front of the fortified village of Ganish during the rehabilitation works (below) and after completion (above).
At the far end of the pond, the newly constructed half-sunken public bathhouse. To the left the restored communal guest house (*sawab-ha*).

121. Reconstructing a dilapidated house to fill the gap in the enclosure wall of the village of Ganish, right of the *sawab-ha* (pl. 119).

120.

121.

122, 123. Good use of the reclaimed community space around the pond by the local youth: girls studying and boys jumping from the public bathhouse into the water.

124. The rehabilitated entry zone to the village of Ganish on the other side of the pond: a restored meeting space for the village elders (for a complete site plan of the village see pl. 64).

122.

123.

124.

125.

127.

126.

125-127. Community participation in the rehabilitation programme for Altit village:
repairing an individual house,
carrying bricks, and carrying sewerage pipes through the narrow alleyways.

128. Altit village square before rehabilitation (see also pl. 107).

129. Village elders during an informal Town Management Society meeting on the rock below Altit fort.

130. The roofs and narrow alleyways of the old Altit village as seen from the fort above, before rehabilitation (for a plan of the village see pl. 63).

128.

129.

130.

131.

132.

131, 132. Discussing village rehabilitation projects
with residents in Khaplu, and initiating
stone pavement of alleyways.

133. Reviewing the packaging
of local apricot kernel oil at the BEDAR office
in Skardu.

133.

134.

135.

134. View of a village section of Khaplu (for a complete plan see pl. 66).

135. Drying apricots for home consumption during the winter, and for sale.

136. A lady-weaver
at a promotional event
of the Karakoram Handicraft
Development Project
in Karimabad.

137. A local silversmith
with traditional jewellery.

138. Spinning the wharp
for local *sherma* production.

139. The carpet weaving
workshop of the Karakoram
Handicraft Development Project.

136.

137.

138.

139.

140.

140. Mountain trekking
– one of the major tourist
attractions of the Northern Areas.

141. Crossing the gorge
on a rope – once a necessity,
now part of an adventure trip?

141.

to increase its own stake and participation; third, the training effect achieved in Karimabad, both with respect to the local AKCS-P staff and to local labour, made new projects more efficient and less cost-intensive.

From 1996 onwards, several immediate neighbouring communities of Karimabad, including the historic villages of Ganish and Altit, engaged in combined planning, infrastructure upgrading and housing rehabilitation projects in cooperation with the AKCS-P. As in Karimabad, the projects in Ganish and Altit gave rise to a wide range of integrated activities, from single, small building conservation to entire historic villages and large scale planning and infrastructure projects.

In the small village of Ganish, the AKCS-P started with the conservation/restoration of an intimate but spectacular architectural ensemble composed of the four family mosques of Yarikutz, Rupikutz, Kuyokutz and Mamorukutz. This group of typical small wooden Hunza mosques is organised around a historic open space used by the community, the *jataq* – formerly the site of ritual, ceremonial and politically important happenings (figs. 286, 287). The conservation project included this historic community space, as well as other architectural and environmental features such as three other mosques, a couple of defensive watchtowers (*shikaris*), the historic village water reservoir (figs. 284, 285), and the village *sawab-ha* (guest quarters). Once full support from the community was ensured, activities were extended into a larger project, covering the conservation and rehabilitation of the remaining parts of the important historic village of Ganish, one of the oldest on the historic route of access to Western China along the Hunza river and a prized example of a traditional fortified settlement (see map in pl. 64).

Advocacy and awareness raising in the larger Ganish area resulted in a major sanitation and water supply scheme for Greater Ganish. A concealed electric supply system was installed hand in hand with new flagstone

Fig. 279. Rehabilitated village sector of Karimabad, with restored watchtower (*shikari*).

Fig. 280. New street pavement with buried sewerage and electricity lines – a major contribution to improvement of living conditions.

paving of the dusty old village lanes, to complete the environmental upgrading. Lastly, as a result of the intensive participation of the community of the old village in its conservation, a small social welfare society was registered which assumed responsibilities relating to the management of the conserved village, its heritage assets and the revenues the village is now gaining from the tourist influx to the restored village.

In Baltit/Karimabad, the AKCS-P's village upgrading initiatives had started simultaneously with the conservation of the fort, preceding community based planning and development. At that time, interventions by the government and of international tourism had already started to sharply impinge on the local context; the economic benefits were beginning to collide with the sustainability of the social order and the traditional built environment, with at least the latter a key resource in the tourism industry. The effects of investments made in the fort project had set off forces that were not easy to manage by the community in Karimabad.

In the twin community of Altit, the AKCS-P was in a position to proactively anticipate the socio-economic consequences to be expected from a tourism boom related to the conservation of the fort. In an inversion of the sequence, village rehabilitation preceded the intervention on the fort to ensure that the right community planning procedures were in place early on: fostering collective decision making through arbitrating mechanisms such as the TMS was given priority at the cost of delaying the conservation of the principal monument. This meant a longer preparatory period for community activism that would generate better adjustments to negative external pressures, while giving new heritage-related values the chance to take root more firmly.

As a result, in Altit all the interventions in the realm of village planning (figs. 288, 289) have taken place under a citizen managed land-use programme, prior to the monument conservation project, which is to gather pace in 2005 and the following years. A very interesting aspect of this work is the topographic surveys carried out by young women of Altit and its surrounding villages who were trained by the AKCS-P in plane table surveying and computer digitisation (fig. 308). The physical interventions implemented so far under this programme include the rehabilitation of historic Altit and its water pond, with sanitary sewerage and waste disposal, street paving, and building renewal and replacement (see map in pl. 63). The land use regulation process is still ongoing with several important decisions as to the location of the principal tourist-related commercial precinct still to be resolved. The conservation project of Altit fort will be the last step to materialise in this series of interventions.

MOVING INTO BALTISTAN

In late 1996, after the successful inauguration of Baltit fort and the Karimabad village improvement projects, a number of prominent citizens from Baltistan came to the office of the AKCS-P in Gilgit with resolutions from individual villages, requesting the AKCS-P to extend its activities to Baltistan. This was a tempting proposition, since the AKCS-P had been directed to become also involved in non-Ismaili areas in the Northern Region and because Baltistan has a wealth of architectural heritage no other region in Pakistan can equal (see chapter 7).

The extensive fieldwork carried out in Baltistan during a first feasibility study in 1997 provided the opportunity to establish dialogue with local communities with the local *rajas'* families and the religious leaders, in order to raise public awareness and to receive feedback and active support from them. The dialogue on heritage and environmental issues was facilitated by the Aga Khan Rural Support Programme which

Figs. 281, 282. The cluster housing project in Karimabad: building adapted new houses with traditional materials and improved technology and equipment.

had greater access to local VOs and Women's Organisations as grass-roots cells of social and economic progress (see chapter 3). Government institutions, including the two municipal bodies in Baltistan,[5] the Northern Areas Public Works Department, as well as several local non-governmental organisations (NGOs) were also highly supportive of the proposed programme direction. These discussions resulted in a broad-based consensus that cultural heritage, the environment and sustainable development are interconnected themes, and that a partnership was needed between the community institutions, the public and private sectors, donors and development intermediaries to respond to the risks being faced by the tangible and intangible heritage and livelihood systems of Baltistan. In early 1998 a more extensive framework of activity was formulated, defining strategies and aims of a broad-based programme and identifying specific objectives.

To demonstrate the merits of heritage conservation and to engage the local communities, the AKCS-P undertook pilot restoration projects for the Amburiq mosque in Shigar (1998-1999), and the *astana* (mausoleum) of Sayyed Mohammad in the village of Khanqah in Khaplu (1999-2000). The fourteenth-century Amburiq mosque (figs. 291-293) is a relatively small, but unique, monument, both in its historic significance and architectural quality. It is highly valued by the local community because of the historic association of its foundation with Amir Kabir Sayyid Ali Hamadani, the first Muslim preacher in Baltistan. A predominant timber structure with cribbage and delicate carvings, the small single-roomed mosque desperately needed emergency repairs – due to the collapse of the roof and infiltration of water to the foundations in its rear. The technical complexity of the project, including jacking up the entire structure by approximately sixty centimetres in one corner (which had settled due to weak foundations) provided a good test of the technical expertise available with the AKCS-P, as well as an opportunity to demonstrate appropriate conservation techniques. The positive response of

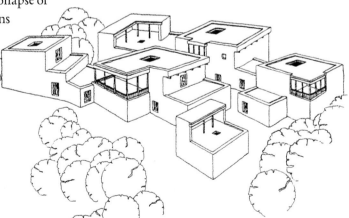

Fig. 283. An example of new cluster housing in Karimabad inspired by traditional settlement structures.

279

Fig. 284. The dredging and repair of the water reservoir (*pharee*) in Ganish, done in cooperation with the community.

Fig. 285. The repaired water reservoir with a small public bath house (in the centre) with the restored enclosure walls and towers.

Figs. 286, 287. The small community square (*jatak*) in the centre of the old Ganish village, surrounded by mosques, during and after restoration (see also pls. 116-124).

the community towards the restoration effort was manifested in free labour and the donation of land and timber. The mosque, its new ablution annexe and its widened yard are now in extensive use. The conservation and restoration of the *astana* was perhaps even more dramatic for its own community in Khaplu, since that building was on the edge of total collapse when the pilot project was undertaken (figs. 294, 304).

As a consequence of these activities, the Baltistan Culture Foundation (BCF) was launched and taken up enthusiastically by local circles. Still in its formative phase, the BCF is eventually expected to protect, manage and promote cultural heritage as an integral part of sustainable overall development. With the establishment of local chapters, it will enable effective and participatory community stewardship of heritage and environmental resources and create new income and enterprise opportunities for local communities based on proactive cultural heritage management.

VILLAGE REHABILITATION IN KHAPLU
Khaplu is the capital of Ghanche, one of the six administrative districts in the Northern Areas. It therefore has a strong government presence with the usual prominent judicial/magisterial and law enforcement

functions. The area of the limits of the town is defined by a great alluvial fan which has been transformed over the centuries of human occupation into expanses of lush agricultural land and orchards interspersed with numerous small villages, some of considerable age. At the bottom of the slope, near the bazaar area and close to the river Shyok is the recently built district headquarters zone. Development initiatives on the part of the government have been focussed at the level of education and health facilities and the roads and trunk infrastructure. As a result of this and the active presence of NGO's, the town itself is rapidly changing, and large new buildings added over the last five years compete for space among the poplar trees and apricot orchards (see map in pl. 66).

The villages and their fine-grain social and physical fabric have been affected by the impact of these sudden changes, which had achieved only marginal improvements in economic well-being, while negatively impacting the pre-existing ways of life in the traditional built environment. Without adequate guidance, the people had started building with new and unfamiliar building technology, and consequently suffered from the considerable thermal and structural inadequacies of the newer structures. The oldest historic villages were the most conspicuous examples of this disjuncture, and therefore the obvious choice for locating the first AKCS-P initiatives.

Hunduli is one of the eight old settlements in Khaplu town which are still inhabited. Originally settled by craftsmen and artisans who came to Baltistan from Kashmir and other parts of South Asia with the early preachers of Islam who built the early mosques and *khanqahs*, Hunduli is now home to eighty-eight families. The first step in the upgrading strategy was to select a typical house rehabilitation project, which the team did in consultation with the local VO members. The residents unanimously chose a traditional house,

Figs. 288, 289. Laying sewerage lines and repairing a house in the old village of Altit.

Fig. 290. Public celebration at the forecourt (*himalter*) to the historic village of Altit, after completion of the rehabilitation works.

belonging to the poorest family of the village. In acknowledgement of this help, the family decided to donate one third of the plot for the construction of two community halls for social and ritual gatherings and education of adult women and girls, needs identified by the community.

281

Figs. 291, 292. The restored Amburiq mosque in Shigar, now being used by local young people.

The work over the next five years is representative of typical replication effects and the expansion of the project from more focussed to more general and collective concerns. Accordingly, in Hunduli the upgrading and improvement of aged old homes (figs. 296, 297) has become an ongoing process and by 2003 a total of twenty houses had been improved by the owners themselves. The community was led to identify specific issues of hygiene and health, such as conflicts between traditional use of water channels and waste water generated by modern piping systems, the impact of inadequately located composting latrines on the drainage system, the effects of using detergents, the need for better drainage, for more public toilets and latrines, and for bathing houses for men. Addressing these issues in the context of a heightened respect for traditional village structures has resulted in the improvement of, or the construction of, bathhouses, pit-latrines and public washing areas. Together with paving of village streets, this led to a dramatic improvement of living conditions. Funding from NORAD and the Grass-Roots Assistance programme (GRA) of the Government of Japan were the main external resources applied to this programme, apart from HCSP/AKCS-P resources and the material and human contributions of the community of Hunduli themselves.

The AKCS-P work in Hunduli duly spilled over to the neighbouring historic settlement of Banpi – comprising forty-five households. Here a further fifteen homes were improved by the owners themselves, and new and upgraded public amenities were added with GRA funding. The community in Banpi has been able to prevent the demolition of their ancient bazaar and mosque as the result of a road widening and paving project, and the community has been able to redirect the road to prevent this from happening.

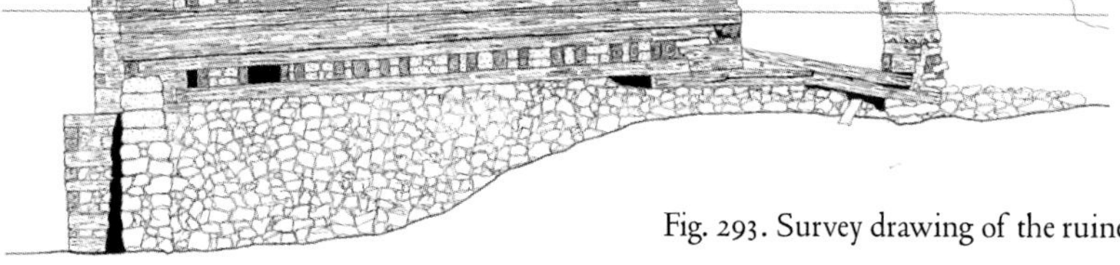

Fig. 293. Survey drawing of the ruined Amburiq mosque, before restoration.

Another 'multiplier' effect has been the participatory involvement of the Nurbakshi community in Khaplu in a major environmental upgrading programme combined with a heritage care and community facility improvement project – that in Khanqah Sayyed Mohammad, the village named after the saint, down the slope from Banpi. It is in this village that the *astana* of Sayyed Mohammad, mentioned above among the 'pilot demonstration projects', is located (figs. 294, 304). With guidance from the AKCS-P, the community is now pursuing a major addition to the *khanqah* with minimal change to the historic building and with appropriate and designed modifications to the village environment.

ACTIVITIES IN SHIGAR

The valley served by the Shigar river is dotted by numerous villages, the majority of them located on the east of the river (see map in pl. 65). In Shigar proper, there are twelve villages which send elected representatives to a Union Council. Of these, three villages – Khlingrong, Shilpa and Halpapa – form a linear continuity north of Shigar *nullah*, the rapid stream which flows out from a mountain pass in the east and disgorges into the Shigar river, beyond the main bazaar. At the easternmost extremity of this stretch of settlements is Shigar fort, to which the communities of Khlingrong and Shilpa were closely attached, providing servants, musicians, guards and other elements of a courtly retinue.

Between 1998 and 2002, the villages of Khlingrong, Shilpa and Halpapa were the subject of upgrading interventions similar to those pursued in the Khaplu region. The primary focus has been on health and hygiene issues. Community composting latrines were upgraded, relocated and new ones built, for both men and women, in Shilpa and Halpapa. Two public bathhouses each for men and women were built in Shilpa and Halpapa with facilities for hot water, and an adjoining communal cloth washing area in Shilpa.

Figs. 294, 295. Above, the restored Sayyed Mohammad *astana* in Khaplu (see also figs. 145, 304).
Below, the shrine of Sayyed Mir Yahya in Shigar during the community-driven restoration process (see also fig. 143).

283

Clean drinking water for these communities has been a major thrust of the upgrading operation. The new water filtration unit at Khlingrong provides water tested at World Health Organisation standards to the communities of the three villages as well as to two villages across the *nullah* and to the Shigar fort facility. Connections are provided upon payment of a connection charge. In addition a total of fourteen community taps have been provided to two of the villages, and connected to the supply mains. A total of twenty-two historic homes were rehabilitated, partly with Japanese funding, by the year 2002. And almost all the village lanes have been paved integrating surface storm-water drainage.

The AKCS-P-led upgrading of these villages (figs. 298, 299) is closely linked to the project for the conservation and reuse of Shigar fort (see chapter 10). Both activities were included in the dialogues that were held in the summer of 1998 with the members of the Shigar Union Council and with the *rajas* of Shigar as a prelude to the conservation project. During these dialogues the backdrop of extreme poverty faced by the residents of these villages loomed large. As compared with the people of Hunza with their runaway urbanisation and their social and econom-

Figs. 296, 297. Community-based village rehabilitation works in Khaplu.

ic mobility, the situation in Shigar appeared to be depressingly static. Subsistence farming, working as porters for the trekking and mountaineering groups, as domestic servants in far-off places and in low-level jobs in the government administration were the chief occupations of these people. It was still very much a barter economy, as was revealed during efforts to draw people into micro-credit mechanisms that would pay for the upgrading projects. Families could only afford to pay so-many eggs per week, rather than cash. Health conditions, specially among women and children were quite dismal. The chief needs of the people communicated by their representatives were bathing facilities for the women, and improvement of their traditional composting latrines.

Village upgrading in Shigar was undertaken by the AKCS-P with the realisation that it could be more closely associated with monument conservation than at Baltit, where the operational premises had been different. Although in Baltit, too, local residents found employment in the fort conservation project, they had been employed by the building contractor. In Shigar, monument conservation and village upgrading were the consequence of a combined set of initial negotiations between an external agency and the local stakeholders. The early establishment of the Shigar Town Management Society, with both a community de-

Figs. 298, 299. Paving streets with integrated water channels in Shigar village.

velopment and planning function, and the anticipated formation of a local chapter of the Baltistan Culture Foundation (the ultimate custodians of the fort facility) brought the village upgrading operations into a far stronger relationship with the monument conservation project than at Baltit. It was from the villages of Khlingrong, Shilpa and Halpapa, where the village upgrading had been initiated, that most of the workers in the fort project were recruited. With the opening of the Shigar Fort Residence in 2004, new opportunities and occupational skills were introduced among these workers. The communities now have trained carpenters, masons, plumbers, electricians and woodcarvers among their citizens, as well as promising young talents in the service sector.

[1] The TMS, established as a social welfare society under the Societies Act of 1891, equals a non-governmental municipality, as it were. It evolved from a group of nominees representing the pre-existing institutional 'building blocks' of Karimabad: leaders of the Shi'a Imami Ismaili religious institutions, the chairperson of the Union Council (the rural local government entity), the representative of Hunza in the Northern Area Council, delegates of the VOs, and local notables such as the former *mir* of Hunza. With the inclusion of the *numberdars*, the leaders of the five tribal constituencies of Karimabad, by a modification of its founding constitution, the TMS is now highly representative of the local community.

[2] After the dissolution of the old system of governance under the *mir*, the tribal councils and the VOs represented two important aspects of community structure, the former continuing the traditional forms of social and territorial order, and the latter representing the emerging social and economic forces.

[3] This effort has however not borne much fruit, and as a consequence the Karimabad TMS has continued to play its quasi-municipal role. Due to its lack of enforcement powers, the TMS has had to depend on advocacy and moral persuasion and has focussed its activities around fund-raising for and implementing development projects. The Karimabad TMS and the AKCS-P are expected to participate in the modal-

ities of the conversion of the Development Plan into a 'master plan' as ordained in the Local Government Act. However, a number of areas of TMS concerns not mandated under the local government laws would continue to engage its attention. Among these are its functions as a social welfare organisation, one which would continue to play a strategic building role in relation to the conservation of the cultural landscape and the built heritage, and in relation to the difficult balance between traditional economic activities, and those occasioned by external factors such as tourism.

[4] The town of Khaplu, Baltistan, has been a district headquarters of the Northern Areas administration for about two decades. As a consequence, a Town Committee exists in Khaplu, with the usual municipal powers and functions under the local government laws of Pakistan. In Khaplu a Master Plan exists, prepared under these laws by the district administration in 1997/1998. Despite this institutional precedent, the citizens have felt the need to establish a Town Management Society, which functions as a civic organisation with social welfare functions, and additionally as a pressure group for the protection and conservation of environmental and heritage assets, which are not provided for under the Local Government Act.

[5] The Town Committees at Skardu and Khaplu.

13. Building Institutions for the Management of Cultural Assets

SALMAN BEG

The conservation and village rehabilitation initiatives described in the previous chapters could not have happened without well orchestrated cooperation between the Aga Khan Trust for Culture (AKTC), as the agency responsible for conceptualisation and overall direction of projects, and the Aga Khan Cultural Services Company Pakistan (AKCS-P), as the local implementing agency on the ground. As could be expected, resolving managerial, technical and logistical issues was a basic precondition for successful project implementation. However, three additional components needed to be considered in order to underpin the physical improvement process and to achieve related objectives of a non-physical nature. These were, firstly, training and skills enhancement of local craftsmen and professionals (if possible recruited within the area); secondly, fostering the awareness and interest of the local beneficiaries directly concerned, in order to make them responsible 'owners' of the project; and, finally, building up local non-governmental institutions which, through their involvement in the project, could harness community participation, resolve arising internal conflicts, and eventually even replicate completed projects with a modicum of external technical and financial assistance. Paying due attention to these collateral implementation factors was an essential precondition for rooting the projects in local communities and steering them towards eventual self-sustainability.

In terms of training and skills enhancement, the various conservation and village rehabilitation projects provided ample opportunities for young local professionals, such as architects, engineers and social organizers to work under the overall supervision and direction of experienced international consultants. Systematic improvement of various capacities and on the job training enabled the AKCS-P to build a core body of talented professionals who took on increasing responsibilities in parallel with the expansion of AKCS-P's activities, thus allowing the AKCS-P to achieve an increasing scope of work with reduced inputs from international consultants – and eventually to become itself an important local institution which could provide technical, socio-economic and institutional development assistance to the societies of the Northern Areas. The manner in which local communities were involved in the AKCS-P's cultural development projects has already been discussed in chapter 12. In the following paragraphs, the emphasis will be on the institution-building process, which was essential to safeguard, sustain, manage and promote local cultural assets – whether these consisted of landmark buildings, historic villages, or non-physical skills and local traditions.

FORT OWNERSHIP ISSUES

The forts and palaces of the Northern Areas represented not only the most demanding physical conservation projects, but also posed the most complex institutional problems with regard to ownership, operation and future maintenance. On the one hand, the traditional owners – the old *raja* and *mir* families – no longer

Fig. 300. A local celebration with the *mir* and local dignitaries at the dais on the second floor of Baltit fort in the 1930s (D. Lorimer).

Fig. 301. The *mir* participating in a local marriage ceremony in the 1920s (D. Lorimer).

had the means, nor the willingness, to maintain these historic structures as lived-in buildings, and indeed they had already moved to more practical modern premises. On the other hand, the AKTC and other donors (such as the Norwegian development agency, NORAD) could not invest in the restoration of property belonging to private owners, but had to find ways to let local communities and the public domain at large become the beneficiaries of the restoration. A possible way out of this dilemma was first articulated in the tripartite arrangement which led to the restoration of Baltit fort in the early 1990s and was then repeated, with some modifications, in the cases of Shigar, Altit and Khaplu forts.

Baltit fort (see chapter 9) had been abandoned in the early 1950s, when the *mir* moved to his newly constructed residence in Karimabad. As a precondition for the restoration of the fort, the AKTC launched the idea of creating a semi-governmental Baltit Heritage Trust (BHT), with a Board bringing together official representatives from the Pakistani Government and from the Northern Areas, representatives from various non-governmental organisations that operated in the Northern Areas, eminent personalities connected with archaeology, culture and tourism, as well as Mir Ghazanfar Ali Khan as the 'patron'. The formation of this new body then enabled Mir Ghazanfar to generously donate the fort to the BHT as a public institution, upon which the Aga Khan Trust for Culture took up the commitment to restore the fort and to hand it back to the BHT in the form of a fully restored building with a well equipped museum and cultural centre. The BHT eventually assumed responsibility for the restored Baltit fort at its inauguration in 1996 and has since been in charge of operation and maintenance, keeping the building accessible to the public. A staff of twenty employees headed by a manager takes care of all daily activities, such as guided tours, setting up exhibitions and special events, exchange with foreign research groups, and so on.

As a protection against possible shortfalls, the BHT did some fund-raising and constituted an endowment fed by Pakistani sponsors. Its regular sources of income, from which it covers staff expenses and maintenance, are entrance fees (US $ 5.0 for foreign visitors and a nominal fee for local visitors) and special events. Ever since its formal inauguration in September 1996, a considerable flow of visitors has helped the BHT

Figs. 302, 303. Training at the carpenter workshop set up in conjunction with the restoration of Shigar fort.

to meet staff and maintenance costs. 2001 was a good year, with around nine thousand foreign tourists and eleven thousand domestic tourists visiting Baltit fort before the tragedy of 9/11. The year 2002 saw foreign tourist figures plummet to around eight per cent of 2001 figures, while domestic tourism increased by twenty per cent. The year 2003 brought a slight revival in visitor numbers, while in 2004 the figures climbed back to almost half those of 2001. Expectations for coming years are built around increasing domestic tourism, higher numbers of groups travelling down from China over the Karakoram Highway, and more adventure tourists passing though the area.

Judging from the experience of Baltit fort, there is no doubt that restoration and reuse of forts and palaces are by their very nature complex undertakings. The scale of investment in terms of human resources, time and finances calls for high standards of professionalism – and for inventiveness with regard to possible reuse functions. It is thus critical to develop a consensus with local communities and their representatives, ensuring that staff recruitment, capacity development and the acquisition of skills and expertise happen in keeping with the given opportunities of the project, and that the nature and the consequences of the reuse are agreed upon in advance. Adaptive reuse has to generate sufficient income over a period of time, enabling daily operations to become self-supporting, as well as a reserve for maintenance and repairs to be built up. Furthermore, it should also be viewed as a stimulus for collateral projects and activities, generating benefits in the form of outreach, employment, increased business opportunities, skills enhancement, and so on. This process provides an occasion to form responsible local institutions and to allow them to attain sufficient capacity, community support and credibility – eventually empowering them to become responsible partners in the running of a restored building. Given the differences in local context, site conditions and local capacities, each place is unique in its own way and calls for institutions adapted to the particular communities and circumstances.

Baltit fort was a relatively simple case, since its main reuse was to be a museum, and existing flows of tourists to Hunza were sufficient to ensure financial self-sustainability, while the available skill base in Hunza made it comparatively easy to recruit local staff. In other cases, such conditions did not always exist to the same extent, and therefore one had to take recourse to more commercial functions – such as attached guest house facilities – to inject new life to the historic structures and to make them self-sustainable. The situation was also complicated by the fact that most forts or palaces other than Baltit were part of a larger property, with gardens or commercially valuable land attached to them. (In Baltit, the *mir's* main land holdings were separate from the fort and enabled him to build a large hotel in a privileged location, that benefits from increasing tourism flows into Karimabad.)

For these reasons, the approach used by the AKCS-P in later, similar projects was to serve as an active custodian of the forts/palaces to be donated. This meant not only investing (together with other donors) in their restoration and adaptive reuse, but also operating the completed buildings on a non-profit basis in the interest of the respective communities, with the participation of newly created institutions representing local residents. These new institutions would be involved in all strategic decisions regarding operation of the restored building and promotion of cultural tourism in general. Moreover, they would financially benefit from the net revenues of the guest house operations linked to the restored forts/palaces, and they would be supported by the AKCS-P in parallel projects, such as craft revival, skills enhancement and enterprise development programmes to be carried out under their own responsibility. At a later stage, they could be given full operational responsibility for the guest houses, provided they proved capable of coping with that task efficiently. It is in such a context that other *mirs/rajas* have agreed to donate their palaces/forts for public use, while they were adequately compensated for the land around the building, acquired by the AKCS-P at current market rates.

This was the solution found for the transformation of the ruined Shigar fort into the Shigar Fort Residence, as described in chapter 10. There, the AKCS-P drew on its local partnerships with the new Baltistan Culture Foundation (BCF) and the Shigar Town Management and Development Society, which are now involved in much wider cultural development activities. Further synergies are expected from the cooperation with the Aga Khan Tourism Promotion Services with regard to the opening of a wider eco-tourism market and to continued training and quality control of the Shigar Residence staff.

Taking into account the earlier Hunza experience with the Town Management Societies (first described in chapter 12), the BCF was structured as a region-wide body that brings together the various interest groups around common objectives, and tries to inform the development of various levels of local institutions in a more systematic manner. In Baltistan, the Town Management Societies (TMSs) were made to form subchapters of the BCF at the local township level, while representatives of each TMS sit on the BCF Board. Proper election modes authorise the BCF to represent the whole of Baltistan and to be responsible for the overall range of cultural development and management of heritage assets in partnership with the AKCS-P.

The Baltistan Culture Foundation was formed and registered in November 1998 and is maturing by undertaking projects in various cultural development fields. More recently, it has played a significant role in getting the Baltistan Enterprise Development and Arts Revival (see below) approved and implemented for a first four year phase. The BCF has also taken on a ninety-nine year lease of the Manthal Buddha Rock at Satpara, instituted collaboration with the Tibet Foundation, including use of traditional Tibetan script for Balti, and revived the holding of a number of festivals in Skardu and Khaplu. The BCF Board includes selected representatives from the five valleys of Baltistan (Skardu, Charming, Khaplu, Shigar and Rondo), as well as the *rajas* that have donated forts/palaces for restoration and reuse.

A full transfer of responsibilities from the AKCS-P to the BCF regarding the Shigar Fort Residence is expected to happen when the BCF and its local Shigar chapter will have developed sufficient capacity, community support and financial self-sustainability for this to take place. At present the BCF already participates in operational and staffing decisions, while the initial start-up and training were handled by the AKCS-P with assistance from the Aga Khan Tourism Promotion Services. As soon as the Residence generates a net revenue, the BCF and the AKCS-P will each receive ten per cent of the surplus, while the Shigar Town Management Society will get twenty per cent. The remaining sixty per cent will be retained as a major maintenance and repair fund and as a reserve for periods when tourism is affected by local, regional and global conditions.

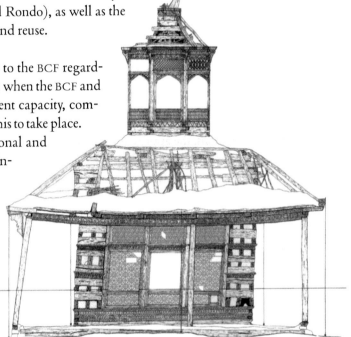

Fig. 304. Survey drawing of the nearly collapsed Sayyed Mohammad *astana* in Khaplu, saved by a community effort (see also figs. 145, 294).

In the case of Altit fort, various options are currently being explored. The most likely solution will probably be to extend the BHT to form a Hunza Heritage Trust or a Hunza Culture Foundation that will become responsible for both Baltit and Altit forts, rather than creating a new Altit Heritage Trust. This would also fall in line with the institution building principles adopted for Baltistan, where the BCF represents the whole region and its various sub-chapters.

Experiences so far indicate that there may even be a need for an all-embracing Northern Areas level body with sub-chapters in Baltistan, Hunza, Ghizer and other regions, for coordinating policy-making in the domains of cultural heritage development, environmental management and the promotion of eco-tourism. Future tasks for such a new institution at Northern Areas level may include: promoting new legislation to back up the protection of the built environment and the implementation of specific land-use plans; coordinating regional development strategies and facilitating revenue-generating mechanisms for heritage management; sponsoring cultural heritage activities, including festivals, promotion of arts and crafts and so on; and entering into contractual obligations with professional institutions (such as the AKCS-P) for management and reuse of forts/palaces.

TOWN MANAGEMENT SOCIETIES

The creation of Town Management Societies, an attempt to set up community-based development agencies, is an institutional consequence of the village rehabilitation projects – much in the same way as the

Cultural Foundation or Heritage Trusts are a necessary by-product of the restoration and adaptive reuse of landmark buildings. Building on the earlier Aga Khan Rural Support Programme tradition of social development through Village Organisations (VOs) and Women's Organisations (WOs) described in chapter 3, the Town Management Societies (TMSs) have now extended their scope of work to the management of the built environment as a whole. They were formed in areas where a historic village forms the nucleus of a larger settlement (or an agglomeration) which is gradually evolving into a township. In a period of rapid change from rural to urban modes of life, they have the mandate to review strategic planning and development issues, to settle emerging internal land use conflicts and to protect the environmental assets of local communities.

Hunza has been the starting point for the progressive establishment of a pilot TMS, as a community-based urban planning and management unit. When the physical work on Baltit fort initiated in 1991, it was also realised that this restoration project would transform Baltit into a focus of interest, thus unleashing forces of change which – if not understood by the local community and if not tackled proactively – could have an adverse impact on Karimabad's natural setting and its cultural heritage. This led to a planning process (see chapter 12) guided by experts in active consultation with the local community who suggested the setting up of a broad community-based institution, the Karimabad Town Management Society (Karimabad TMS). Other TMSs were later established in Altit and Ganish for Hunza, and in Shigar and Khaplu for Baltistan. All of them are bodies with elected members and, in the more recent cases of Altit and Khaplu, they include female representation too. Regular interaction with the AKCS-P is taking place, in order to develop capacity and, where necessary, receive technical support. Joint planning efforts at the village or small-town level are eventually expected to result in planning instruments validated by community consensus – such as land use and infrastructure development plans in addition to building guidelines and approval procedures.

Since its formation, the Karimabad TMS has had three elections, all of them giving rise to hotly pursued campaigns, thus indicating the awareness and interest of the community. Karimabad TMS has a number of successes to its credit. Coached by the AKCS-P, the Karimabad TMS was able to obtain direct funding from the Japanese Grass-Roots Assistance (GRA) Programme (US $ 600,000) to complete, in 2003, Phase II of the Karimabad Sanitation Project. This project was meant to provide sanitation to the remaining seventy-five per cent (almost eight hundred households) of Karimabad and Ganish who were without this facility. (Earlier, twenty-five per cent of households in the main historic areas of these locations had already been provided with sanitation by the AKCS-P in partnership with the Karimabad TMS and NORAD.) This is by far the largest such project in the region to have been initiated, led and implemented by a local community institution. A highly important side effect of the sanitation project was to pin down the community's commitment to choices in the land-use plan, by consolidating the agreed areas of planned future growth and by excluding new construction in protected zones, since these will not be serviced by the sanitation scheme. The community individually and collectively resolved all issues related to the alignment of infrastructures, the provision of free collective labour and the collection and use of user fees in order to sustain the project, which means that it acquired 'ownership' of the planning process.

After Karimabad (pls. 108-115), Ganish was the second historic settlement rehabilitated by the AKCS-P in cooperation with a local TMS and with Norwegian co-funding. Village upgrading included the provision of sanitation, improvement of common spaces and the traditional water reservoir, paving of pathways, laying of underground electricity lines, and restoration of various mosques, historic houses, watchtowers and the remaining part of the perimeter wall (pls. 116-124). After detailed deliberations, the community got together to take ownership of the planning process and maintenance of the various facilities. The most remarkable and positive change is the impact on gender. Women are taking greater responsibility in all affairs of the Society. This is of the utmost importance for the community itself as it clearly demonstrates pride in the rehabilitated historic environment and full involvement of the community in the restoration process. The Society was able to generate funds in 2001 and subsequently in 2004 through selling entry tickets to visitors of their historic settlement. This money has been used to set up a vocational training centre for women and a computer literacy centre for both boys and girls.

Figs. 305, 306. A meeting of the Shigar Town Management Society.

The Society also built consensus on the priorities for future development work, the most important issue being provision of clean drinking water. Since Ganish lies on the river edge at the bottom of the Hunza valley, its drinking water came from irrigation channels that ran down the slope of the whole Karimabad bowl before reaching Ganish. All kinds of run-off contaminated the water, leading to unsafe health conditions. The Society therefore prepared a proposal for clean drinking water with assistance from the AKCS-P and gained support from the Japanese embassy to cover the costs for the supply of materials (pipes, filters and a pump) while volunteering to provide community labour and to manage the future operation in a sustainable manner by collecting fees from the users. The project was made operational in spring 2004.

Realising the positive impact of rehabilitation in Karimabad and of the extension of this work to Ganish, the nearby community of Altit also requested support from the AKTC for its historic settlement. Whereas Karimabad (and to a lesser extent Ganish) was an example of a 'push' strategy, where incentives and subsidies had been used to get the programme started, in Altit the AKCS-P decided to use a 'pull' strategy – letting the community take the initiative and asking for increased community participation and contribution. Getting higher community participation was thus a result of the positive demonstration of effects achieved in Karimabad and Ganish and of the new 'competitive' situation established in that respect.

A number of village rehabilitation projects similar to those implemented in Karimabad have been completed in Altit, with rehabilitation projects funded by Japanese grants (pls. 107, 125-130). Altit TMS now has forty per cent women members on its executive committee, as well as a fee collection committee consisting of women only, who are very regular and efficient in collecting fees and keeping accounts. The achievements of the Altit TMS in terms of resolving pending issues, mobilising community efforts and free labour, and assisting in the planning process have been remarkable. Altit is also operating an income-generating project based on a 'stone-bank', which helps in providing cheaper stone (a local and environmentally suitable building material) to local residents. In 2004, a new Altit TMS building, located in the heart of the historic settlement was constructed. Besides housing the office, this building provides space for three shops and a big community hall meant to facilitate the approximately 150 households of the historic settlement and also earn income for the Altit TMS.

Baltistan, Shigar and Khaplu also saw the emergence of Town Management Societies modelled on the Karimabad experience. The Shigar TMDS (the community of Shigar preferred to add 'Development' as part of the name) was set up in 2000 with a broad-based representation. Rehabilitation projects, such as community latrines for men and women, bathing facilities with provision of hot water for women, shared washing places, where women can collect and wash clothes while socially interacting and exchanging news, were some of the projects initiated, completed and taken over by the communities. Subsequent projects included improvement of the bazaar, paving public pathways and rehabilitation of houses using traditional materials and techniques.

Shigar TMDS has now collectively voiced the need for a school in Shigar, which it would like to have designed and implemented in keeping with local cultural traditions and building materials. Lately, the community of Shigar, on the suggestion of the Shigar TMDS, requested the AKCS-P to help in the planning and designing of the Jamia Masjid in Shigar – a sign of great trust. The earlier plan was to construct a modern concrete mosque, similar to some of the religious buildings that had been built before, but with no understanding of the importance of the built heritage. Through the advocacy of the Shigar TMDS, the local community is now convinced that a traditional design using cribbage work, poplar columns and the local Tibetan-type roofing for the mosque is more appropriate.

Khaplu already has the status of a town with its own Municipal Committee. Therefore the role of the Khaplu TMDS (originally formed along the lines of its Shigar counterpart) is now being refined, allowing it to grow into a civil society agency that influences government policies. The Khaplu TMDS has already undertaken the Japanese-funded rehabilitation project for Hunduli and Banpy villages, including provision of community latrines, washing spaces, bathing facilities and drinking water outlets. In addition, it has undertaken to extend the historic *khanqah* and mosque at Khaplu, in keeping with traditional construction techniques.

Until recently, in both Hunza and Baltistan, land-use plans for individual villages and/or historic settlements have remained a priority. However, with the greater environmental awareness resulting from projects and activities implemented over the last ten years, there is now scope for strategic planning at the regional level. This is a natural step forward, as planning at the micro-level does not sufficiently take into account wider developments in the valley, which have a direct bearing and far-reaching implications on the vil-

Figs. 307, 308. Local girls being trained in the survey of historic buildings, at Altit fort garden.

lages/settlements. Central Hunza, with Hyderabad, Dorkhun, Aliabad, Garelt, Karimabad, Ganish and Altit, is being taken as the first pilot area where an all-embracing master plan concept is to be developed. Each village is being surveyed and mapped through plane-table surveys undertaken by community volunteers, both men and women, trained by the AKCS-P. These maps will then be digitalised and put together to form a valley map. The valley map will be presented to a forum bringing together the various TMSs, the government departments responsible for planning and public works, members of the Northern Areas Legislative Council, members of Union Councils and representatives of various institutions of the Aga Khan Development Network. A detailed workshop will then be held to define plans for infrastructure and future development. Various plans, to be approved and prioritised, will be developed together with respective cost-estimates and phases of implementation, as a basis for determining comprehensive and well-coordinated investment.

INSTITUTIONS FOR CRAFTS AND SMALL ENTERPRISE PROMOTION
After the Heritage Trusts and the Town Management Societies, a third major institutional building block created to support AKCS-P activities are the non-governmental organisations involved in the revival of traditional crafts and small enterprise development. In contrast to the TMSs, they are working on a regional level, focusing on Hunza or Baltistan. With the help of other donors, the AKCS-P has nurtured several such NGOs, providing technical and financial assistance, particularly during the critical early stage.

The first pilot initiative was the Swiss-funded Karakoram Handicraft Development Programme, with a focus on reviving the traditional art of embroidery work, which has since been subsumed by the Karakoram Area Development Organisation (KADO) in Hunza. The Handicraft Programme was initiated in 1996 as an action-research programme, when the community in Hunza, the Swiss development cooperation agency (SDC) and the AKCS-P decided to revive crafts and promote enterprise and economic development with a special focus on women. The success of the action-research phase in 1996 and the formation of a regional body – KADO as a local institutional body representing the Hunza valley – offered the AKCS-P the opportunity to transfer the operational responsibility for the Handicraft Programme to KADO in a staggered manner. Capacity building for KADO during the early phase of the project, especially in administrative and financial skills, facilitated this handover.

Figs. 309-312. Old handicrafts documented by D. Lorimer in the 1930s. Top left, a blacksmith at work; top right, turning wooden bowls; bottom left, weaving local textiles; bottom right, embroidery work.

The Handicraft Programme allows three thousand women, working from home, to enhance their incomes through production of embroidery work – a craft which Hunza women had prided themselves on over generations but which was dying out. The women are paid at piece rates according to various embroidered quality standards. The embroidery pieces are then applied and sewn together at central production units, after which they will adorn larger woollen or cotton fabrics, or textile objects such as jackets, handbags, caps, belts, and so on. Finally, they are marketed at a number of authorised and specially designed outlets in the Karimabad, Gilgit and Islamabad markets, as well as major hotels. In addition KADO runs the 're-habilitation centre', which allows disabled people suffering from various handicaps to be involved in the production of traditional woollen rugs, made of yak and goat hair. In recent times a women's rehabilitation centre has also been established (figs. 313-315; pls. 136-139).

Other KADO activities include the Hunza Environmental Committee which looks after the collection and disposal of garbage in central Hunza through provision of garbage bins at various spots, removal by tractors and stocking of garbage as landfill. All the activities are funded through user fees and managed by KADO as a municipal service. Another initiative is the Hunza Arts and Culture Forum, established to revive and promote music and other performing arts through apprenticeship of young students with masters in the old traditions and through reviewed production of local indigenous musical instruments. More recently, some young men from Chitral have also been trained here. KADO is now diversifying into other fields and other geographic areas. Of special mention is the entry of KADO as an Internet service provider in Hunza, with Internet access operational by the end of 2004.

In Baltistan, a similar organisation, the Baltistan Enterprise Development and Art Revival (BEDAR) was set up by the BCF and the AKCS-P with funding from the Swiss development cooperation agency (SDC). BEDAR is the Urdu word for 'awakening' and was chosen for its symbolic connotations with regard to the resurrection of traditional values. Initiated in July 2003, BEDAR selected four product lines for its first four-year term of operation. The first one deals with apricot kernel oil, a typical and potentially valuable product of the Northern Areas. A model enterprise for production and marketing of apricot kernel oil has been set up. Traditionally, apricot kernel oil was widely used in the Northern Areas for a variety of purposes ranging from lighting and cooking to skin care. Baltistan has the distinction of producing the richest harvest of apricots, with a large quantity no longer being collected and going to waste. The project encourages women to collect the kernels against cash remuneration. It then proceeds with proper pressing of the kernels and sophisticated bottling of apricot oil, in order to reach the high-end natural cosmetics market. The major hotel chains in Pakistan have expressed their willingness to sell bottled oil in their boutiques and to use it in their health clubs. The impact of the project is already evident as prices of kernels have seen a major increase in the last year.

The second product line deals with woodwork and in particular with woodcarving and the production of *jalis* (perforated screens) – a traditional skill that was recently on the verge of extinction. These crafts are being revived by apprenticing young trainees with *ustads* (masters) and the products are being sold in the market. A small workshop is already in place, and furniture and construction carpentry are being added to its product lines. This will allow for a substitution of imported goods, since presently furniture items are trucked in all the way from Islamabad, a road journey of two days. Producing local poplar wood furniture of a reasonable standard in Baltistan will help the local economy. The large numbers of poplars planted with the help of the Aga Khan Rural Support Programme will become an economic resource, and plenty of wood-related employment opportunities will emerge. Construction car-

Figs. 313-315. A choice of craft products promoted by the Karakoram Handicraft Development project.

297

pentry will be encouraged by selling traditional doors and windows (including frames), which will in turn improve the architectural quality of new buildings.

The third product line is based on the large quantities of local gemstones available in Baltistan, but hitherto sold in the Peshawar gem market. Aquamarine, tourmaline and a host of others are mined here using inefficient techniques. Establishing Skardu as the principal centre for gemstones from Baltistan – by holding exhibitions, and by training people in improved extraction techniques, as well as cutting and polishing – will allow for added value, increased income and better employment opportunities. Public-private partnership is being developed, since the Northern Areas Administration has welcomed the idea of working with the local Baltistan Gems Association and with BEDAR and the Aga Khan Rural Support Programme in this field. The Government is planning to provide finances, while BEDAR and the Gems Association provide technical input and will implement the programme.

The fourth and last product line is based on the revival and marketing of local weaving products. Given the long winters, woollen weaves in the form of rugs and shawls were popular in Baltistan. In recent years, however, shawls and carpets from down country have spoiled the market. With new opportunities emerging through tourism in the Northern Areas, an attempt is being made to occupy a new market niche based on high quality products made from the best raw material, improved weaving techniques and enhanced traditional designs. The first hand-woven woollen products have been used in furnishing the Shigar Fort Residence and similar items will also be marketed through the various outlets of the BCF, the AKCS-P and the local bazaars, as well as the Shigar Fort Residence and other hotel shops.

14. Prospects for Cultural Tourism in the Northern Areas

SAFIULLAH BAIG

The Northern Areas possess some of the most dramatic mountain sceneries on earth. Of the world's fourteen summits above eight thousand metres, five are located in the Northern Areas, including K2 (*Chogori*), the second highest mountain in the world. While the natural beauty of the area attracts a significant number of tourists every year (which also brings a substantial amount of foreign exchange to the country), the unique cultural heritage of the Northern Areas, as presented in previous chapters of this book, has not received so far the attention it deserves. Yet a better appreciation of the local heritage and the active promotion of responsible cultural tourism could have far-reaching implications – fostering a deeper understanding of cultural diversity in the conflict-ridden region and beyond, further improving economic growth, and helping in the rescue of many of the region's natural and cultural jewels that are threatened by overuse or by neglect. Moreover, cultural tourism could help find development alternatives that avoid the trend towards ubiquitous uniformity and help maintain a truly human and enriching environment.

TOURISM IN THE NORTHERN AREAS

Since the end of the nineteenth century, when the earliest Western explorers visited the region, the Northern Areas of Pakistan have been an attraction for alpinists, adventurers, backpackers, individuals, groups and cultural tourists from around the world. The opening of the Karakoram Highway (KKH) in 1978, as well as the establishment of scheduled flight services to Gilgit and Skardu, facilitated access to the area and enabled tourism to grow at a new scale. So far, the fledgling tourism industry of the Northern Areas is currently geared to meet four main categories of tourists: (i) group tourists (using the services of international tour operators); (ii) individual tourists (using occasional local tourist services), (iii) mountaineers and high-altitude trekking expeditions; and (iv) domestic tourists. While Silk Route Tours have gained in importance over the past few years, the category of cultural tourism is still underdeveloped.

Despite the Northern Areas rich mix of natural and cultural heritage, tourism activities in the region are still heavily based upon the areas' outstanding landscape and dramatic mountain scenery (see the insert below). In 2001, before 11 September, an estimated fifty thousand foreign tourists visited the region including a record breaking seventy expeditions with over 450 mountaineers and 1300 trekkers. But 2002 brought a disaster for Pakistan's tourism industry as a result of the September 11 events. However, according to the Ministry of Tourism and Culture, the situation began to improve in 2003. One year later, in 2004, around four thousand foreign mountaineers and trekkers visited the region on the eve of the K2 Golden Jubilee. These statistics clearly show that the Northern Areas are famous for a particular kind of tourism, while the vast potential for other kinds of tourist activities is not being fully realised.

S. No	Peak	Altitude (m)	Range	World Ranking
	THE HIGHEST PEAKS OF THE NORTHERN AREAS			
1	K2 (Chogori)	8,611	Karakoram	2
2	Nanga Parbat	8,125	Himalaya	9
3	Gasherbrum I	8,068	Karakoram	11
4	Broad Peak	8,047	Karakoram	12
5	Gasherbrum II	8,035	Karakoram	14
6	Gasherbrum III	7,952	Karakoram	15
7	Gasherbrum IV	7,925	Karakoram	17
8	Distaghil Sar	7,885	Karakoram	20
9	Kunyang Chish	7,852	Karakoram	22
10	Mashebrum NE	7,821	Karakoram	24
11	Rakaposhi	7,788	Karakoram	27
12	Batura	7,785	Karakoram	28

During the last couple of decades, a number of tour operators have made efforts to diversify tourism by encouraging group tourists interested in nature to visit Hunza or Baltistan during the blossom period and in autumn. This applies mainly to Far Eastern tourists (who also have a potential interest for Buddhist sites), and to some European tourists. Nonetheless, the major focus on the part of the government has been the promotion of mountaineering and high-altitude trekking, which generate precious foreign exchange. The existing trends suggest that most of the mountaineering expeditions and high-altitude trekking groups visit the Baltistan region, whereas normal tourist groups, backpackers, families and individuals prefer Gilgit and the Hunza region. The numbers of domestic tourists visiting Hunza and Baltistan (largely unorganised groups and families) have also increased, particularly during the summers. A largely untapped potential of visitors exists in the Gulf States, since Arabs in search of cooler vacation settings have tended to reduce their trips to Europe and the United States after the events of 9/11.

MAJOR CONSTRAINTS

Despite increasing government attention to tourism development, many restrictive factors have seriously undermined not only the above-mentioned, highly profitable sub-sectors of tourism but also the overall potential for tourism in the Northern Areas. The current policy formulation process for the region's tourism sector has tended to be highly centralised, with little consultation of stakeholders taking place. Important local issues were hardly accorded the priority they should deserve. This framework did not sufficiently enable the private sector to grow and play a positive role in tourism promotion. Rigid procedures, such as restriction on photography of certain sites and features (given the disputed status of the Northern Areas), deprive tourism of incentives and potential. Similarly, security for tourists in the Northern Areas, particularly along parts of the KKH, is a concern in some locations. Border skirmishes, tension with India and other international conflicts have all received large amounts of international media coverage and, unfortunately, created a negative perception of Pakistan and its security situation. Insufficient information, exposure and lack of reliable tourist market data hinder the identification of different tourist preferences and effective planning and policy formulation.

Natural factors restricting the growth of the tourism industry are the Northern Areas peculiar geography, which renders access difficult, and widely varying climatic conditions. Particularly harsh winters result in shorter tourist seasons, mainly from March to the end of November. Though the Northern Areas are well connected with the rest of the country via the KKH, road conditions are often poor, making journeys long and tiring. Landslides and rock falls frequently lead to road closure and at times present serious danger. The two airports in the Northern Areas, one at Gilgit and the other at Skardu, provide tourists with an alternative to the long journey by road, but the lack of modern navigation facilities at both airports does not allow predictable flight operations during bad weather conditions and results in frequent delays and flight cancellations.

Existing tourism infrastructure is limited to a relatively small number of hotels and motels, located primarily in a few urban centres which provide a relatively poor standard of services and where the quality of accommodation varies greatly. Lack of trained professionals, such as hoteliers and tour operators, also affects the quality of services. Moreover, very few archaeological sites and other attractions in the region dispose of interpretation centres or supporting facilities, such as resting areas, toilets and refreshment points. All major towns and villages are connected to the national telephone network, but its performance is far from satisfactory.

Figs. 316, 317. Above, Rush peak enveloped in clouds; below, Lady Finger peak above Karimbad.

THE NEED FOR SUSTAINABLE MANAGEMENT OF RESOURCES

While a largely unplanned and uncoordinated tourism development in the Northern Areas has spurred the region's economic growth, the narrow interest in mountaineering and trekking (with little concern for the social and cultural context) can have negative effects on the environment and on local communities. One major impact is the construction of roads and hotels in often inappropriate locations and with excessive volumes, to the detriment of the scenic value of the landscape – a problem dealt with at some length in chapter 12. Another typical impact is the large amount of solid and human waste left by expeditions along the trekking routes and at the base camps, which is not only an aesthetic concern, but also poses a threat to wildlife and human health and safety. In general, there is a lack of awareness about environmentally-sensitive mountaineering and trekking techniques, proper waste management and the use of alternative energies. On a less material plane, the negative impact can manifest itself in a loss of collective local memory. For instance, *Chogori* (K2) means king of mountains, and *Bubulino Tin* ('Lady Finger of the Ultar range in Hunza) refers to *Bubuli*, a sacred fairy in local mythology. These and many other traditional concepts, which have meaning and significance for the people of the area, are in danger of being lost. Linked as they are with the immediate human environment, they derive their life and meaning from it as an essential part of local attitudes and beliefs.

In isolation and uninformed by local values and customs, tourism can thus have serious repercussions that can put the natural resources under threat and can cause irretrievable losses in the traditional cultural heritage. This raises the issue of preserving basic cultural rights and emphasises the need for well-coordinated protective action, since traditional cultures are in need of integrated strategies for conservation and sustainable management of their heritage. A partnership with the tourism industry can help local societies, as the custodians of heritage assets, to derive material benefits from them by collecting dividends on an entrusted 'capital'. But in order to preserve that 'capital' for future generations, the tourism industry clearly needs to be framed and controlled by much more comprehensive human and cultural development concepts.

For various reasons, the Northern Areas in general – and tourism in particular – have long suffered from neglect. However, since the early 1990s, significant actions have been taken to promote broad-based sustainable development through conservation and revitalisation of cultural heritage. In 1992, the Aga Khan Cultural Service-Pakistan (AKCS-P), on behalf of the Aga Khan Trust for Culture (AKTC), initiated a programme of documentation, restoration and rehabilitation of cultural assets in the Northern Areas. The restoration of the historic Baltit fort was the first major step in this regard, followed by rehabilitation of the traditional settlements of Karimabad, Ganish and Altit in Hunza and Chinpa, Halpapa and Banpi in Baltistan (see chapters 9 and 12). The opening of the restored Baltit fort in 1996 as a museum/cultural centre was a landmark in the history of conservation in Pakistan and introduced the idea of opening local cultural heritage for tourism in the Northern Areas. Focusing on landmark monuments, the AKCS-P identified some of the architecturally significant landmark monuments – forts, palaces, sacred and mundane buildings – for restoration and rehabilitation. In certain cases, adaptive reuse schemes were designed to accommodate contemporary requirements and to ensure long-term viability of these conservation projects through realisation of their economic potential. At the same time, the conservation efforts are also aimed at creating opportunities for tourists to acquire a unique personal experience of the treasures of the local cultural and natural heritage.

In parallel with the physical rehabilitation of the traditional built environment, the non-material expressions of culture have also been considered. These are reflected in the region's languages, its traditional music, festivals, food, sports and handicrafts. Traditional dances and music have their own distinctive style linked to regions and different royal courts. Festivals are multidimensional and represent religion, culture and agricultural practices (see Insert 1 in chapter 8). These festivals are significant for the local people because they also highlight the importance of natural phenomena such as seasons, environment, water, wildlife and life at large. Polo is the most popular traditional sport in the region and was patronised by local *rajas* and *mirs* for generations. It is played throughout the Northern Areas and Chitral but is particularly popular in Baltistan. The famous Shandur Polo Tournament is held every year in early June at Shandur pass (over 3660 metres above sea level) and attracts a large number of national as well as international tourists. Drawing on these traditions, the AKCS-P has initiated the Silk Route Festival in various locations of the Northern Areas, to keep local customs alive and to promote cultural exchange with neighbouring regions and countries.

People from the Northern Areas, and particularly women, are skilful in handicrafts, carpet weaving and embroidery. Hunza, where more than three thousand women are engaged in embroidery and handicraft, is famous for such products. Women not only work with geometric patterns but also use traditional themes

Figs. 318, 319. The old polo grounds of Baltit (left) and Altit (right) in the 1930s, as taken by D. Lorimer.
In the meantime, these prime traditional community spaces have partly been eaten up by encroaching public buildings or by roads.

taken from history, religion and sacred animals (ibex). Similarly, fine woodcarving with Tibetan and Kashmiri influence, precious stones and herbal medicines from the Baltistan region are of interest to a large number of tourists. The region is also famous for various dry-fruit products and healthy apricot kernel oil, which can be used for cooking as well as for skin care. Recent initiatives aimed at reviving traditional arts and crafts with the financial assistance of international donors have enabled master artisans to transfer their traditional knowledge and skills to younger generations and complement other cultural development efforts launched by the AKCS-P.

THE SHIGAR FORT RESIDENCE AND ITS IMPLICATIONS

In this overall context, the opening of the Shigar fort as an exclusive heritage guest house (Shigar Fort Residence) in July 2004 heralds a new experience in Pakistan. This bold initiative will provide new prospects to the dying architectural heritage of the region. The reuse concept for the Shigar fort, as explained in chapter 10, attempts to strike a balance between, on the one hand, a museal site which impresses the visitor with its massive seventeenth-century stone construction, containing a number of preserved original or partly reconstructed rooms, and, on the other, a very special type of resort offering a unique experience through a number of authentic guest rooms in the historic palace. The conversion of the fort/palace into a guest house has been designed in such a way as to remain faithful to the original structure and minimise modern architectural interventions. The cultural attraction of the site is founded on the architectural merit of the fort and on the exquisite woodcarvings in the interior and on the exterior of the building. The presence of several historic buildings and old settlements in its vicinity constitutes another asset, further enhanced by the ongoing village rehabilitation projects (see chapter 12).

Drawing on the pilot character of this project, a series of related initiatives are now being studied which in due time should materialise in a much wider cultural development framework for the Northern Areas of Pakistan, based on the promotion of a new type of culturally and ecologically sensitive tourism. Experience from many other places around the world suggests that visitors from 'over-developed' countries are hungry for cultural diversity and highly receptive of vernacular environments. They have a keen interest in experiencing and understanding traditional living cultures of different origins – quite apart from the appreciation of virgin natural sites. Future projects, such as additional guest houses set inside the Altit and Khaplu compounds, the revival of festivals and promotion of traditional arts and crafts, as well as the rehabilitation of part of the first jeep road in the Hunza-Nager valleys, will be part of the emerging cultural development framework, the database of which will be provided by the Inventories (see chapter 8).

NEW VISITOR CIRCUITS

The future guest houses will become the qualitative highlights in a series of tourist Heritage Circuits that will allow tourists to absorb living mountainous cultures perfectly in harmony with their natural environment. The following circuits have been considered so far:

Shigar circuit

Shigar valley, the gateway to the mighty K2 and Concordia peaks, is the most fertile and flat valley in the whole of the Northern Areas. The Braldu river (also known as the Shigar river) runs through it. At the northern end of the valley is the Baltoro glacier from whose snout the Braldu emerges, one of the most memorable views of pristine nature. Treks both over glaciers and alongside various streams allow for all kinds of adventures, from one-day strolls to strenuous, challenging treks over five-thousand-metre-high passes. Three eight-thousand-metre peaks, K2, Broad Peak and Gasherbrum, greet those who can afford to trek for about ten days.

Similar to the Karimabad area, the built heritage around Shigar has the quality of a World Heritage Site. Key features are: the restored Shigar Fort Residence (*Fong Khar*, or 'palace on the rocks'); the old ruins of the old fort on the top of the steep rock overlooking Shigar fort; the Khanqah-e-Moallah (a religious retreat for prayer and meditation), the second largest in existence after the one in Srinagar; the delicate and exquisitely decorated wooden *astanas* (tombs) of a number of saints; the restored fourteenth-century Amburiq mosque, allegedly the oldest in Baltistan; the impressive Buddhist rock site with interesting engravings, about an hour's walk from Skardu town.

Visits can also extend to a number of historic settlements demonstrating the traditional harmony between built environment and the natural setting. In some villages, it is possible to watch craftsmen weaving shawls in the traditional manner, while others carve local serpentine stone or produce apricot kernel oil. New training workshops for woodcarving have also been set up by the AKCS-P.

Options for trekking up the Shigar stream (day trips and longer ones arriving at Hushe valley) or to the lake lying between Shigar and Skardu, Jarbasho Lake, add to the attractions of Shigar. Two hours from Shigar, there are hot springs in Chatron to be visited. In Shigar itself, polo matches are generally played in summer on the excellent polo ground.

Skardu circuit

Skardu combines sandy desert dunes with verdant irrigated plains set amid towering mountains. The Indus river, which by the time it reaches Skardu has travelled over a thousand kilometres, lazily spreads out in the valley and then gathers itself up and hurtles down the gorge as it takes leave of Skardu.

Figs. 320, 321. Public celebration with music and dance in the *himalter* of Aliabad, at the bottom of the valley below Baltit, in the 1930s (D. Lorimer). This community space no longer exists as the village has been heavily impacted by the Karakoram Highway.

The Kharpocho fort guards Skardu and is a good vantage point. Visits to the Manthal Buddha Rock just below Satpara lake are particularly fascinating for visitors. A stroll through the old bazaar can follow, where unique handicraft items of varying age are on sale alongside the best aquamarine and tourmaline gems, as well as trekking and mountaineering equipment.

A day trip by road can be planned to the 3900/4200-metre-high Deosai plateau, about two hours drive away and coloured by flowers in their millions in July and August. If one is fortunate the famous brown bear may be glimpsed.

Khaplu circuit
Khaplu is a steep narrow valley with irrigated terraces more in keeping with the appearance of the Hunza valley. Khaplu palace (to be restored), the polo ground, the famous Chaqchan mosque and the *khanqah* are the most attractive traditional buildings and spaces in Khaplu. A good part of the day is required to visit these.

Khaplu town is a bustling place with stone utensils, goat and sheep hair rugs and other traditional items available. Khaplu makes a good starting point for treks to Hushe valley or father afield over the Gondoghoro pass to the Baltoro.

Gilgit valley circuit
Gilgit is the teeming growth pole of the Northern Areas and has served as the administrative headquarters since the beginning of the British period. It is also the melting pot for various ethnic groups both from inside and outside the Northern Areas. Throughout history, Gilgit was invaded by the Chinese, Hindus, Buddhists, Tibetans, Kashmiris, Chitralis and, last in line, the British. These frequent raids resulted in destruction of the old heritage and reconstruction by the new invaders, consequently, there is not much in the shape of attractions for tourists left except the British colonial heritage – and the colourful markets full of local and Chinese products brought in via the Khunjerab pass.

Fig. 322. Trekking in the high mountains of the Karakoram.

The proposed circuit within and nearby Gilgit include the site of Taj Mughul Minar/Shikari, built on a prominent ridge overlooking Gilgit. It was probably a Buddhist *chorten* which was rebuilt when the legendry Badakhshani general, Taj Mughal, took Gilgit and brought Islam here. This visit can be followed by a day-long trek to Jutial Gah. A day could be spent visiting Chinar Bagh with its memorial dedicated to the liberation of Gilgit situated along the Gilgit river, shopping in the bazaar area, and then visiting the British cemetery, which contains Hayward's grave, and finally to the Buddha rock at Kargah *nullah*. Fishing in the Kargah stream could bring the day to a close.

Half a day could be spent visiting the educational facilities and institutions in Konodas, driving across the old Danyor suspension bridge (built in the early 1960s) and visiting Danyor Rock with its inscriptions and also the Chinese memorial to the KKH builders. In season, there will also be occasions to watch a polo match (played in the traditional style without umpires/referees) on any one of the three polo grounds. Other possibilities for a day trip are: a visit to the alpine resort of Naltar (about two hours jeep drive from Gilgit) or an equally exciting trip to Bagrot valley for views of Haramosh peak and for visiting traditional settlements.

Hunza-Nager valley circuit
This is possibly the most picturesque circuit of all in terms of nature, culture and, most importantly, local communities. The majestic Rakaposhi dominates the skyline with the triangular Diran standing next to it, followed by the Golden Peak, Dastaghil Sar, Ultar Peaks and Bubulino Tin forming a circle around Central Hunza and Nager that keeps the visitor spellbound.

Other attractions are the human complements to the works of nature, such as the irrigation channels along the bottom of surrounding mountains, terraced fields from the river bed up towards skilfully constructed traditional settlements and apricot gardens. Irrigation channels, such as the 'Samarqand *kohl*' which runs over fifteen kilometres and the whole network of other channels from the single source of the Ultar glacier are a true work of art, considering the very basic and rudimentary tools that the communities had to build them with.

Visiting the Hopar and Hispar glaciers – one dark brown and the other gleaming white – is about an hour's jeep drive from Karimabad in the Nager valley. It is also possible to drive to the Batura glacier en route to the Khunjerab pass, to see colonies of ibexes, marmot and yaks and possibly get a glimpse of a marco-polo sheep in the Khunjerab National Park. Other suggestions are to walk up the Gulkin glacier which overlooks the KKH; take a break at Borith lake and watch the migratory birds enjoying themselves; trek up to the Ultar for a day trip or drive up to Duker and have a sunset and sunrise view on the Rakaposhi. Walking down to Altit is an experience providing a cross-section of mountain geography. The highlight may then be a visit to the preserved historic settlements of Karimabad, Altit, Ganish and

Haldeikish Sacred Rock. Trekking up to the base camp of Rakaposhi (three days) or Rash lake in Hopar (seven days) are possibilities for experienced mountaineers.

CONCLUSIONS

Through the interactive aggregation of the AKCS-P's past, current and future initiatives, a new cultural tourism strategy is being implemented. The proposed guest houses will enable tourists to choose between relaxing vacations of a few days or adventure-type holidays, with each location providing a unique cultural and social ambiance. By linking them up, the various circuits can extend to form longer tours connecting more cultural sites and individual circuits such as Chitral, Kalash, Gilgit, Hunza, Shigar, Khaplu, Skardu and Islamabad. Some components of these circuits are already tourist attractions, despite the fact that very few of them provide opportunities for well-informed cultural tourism. Hunza-Nager, Gilgit valley, Karimabad, Skardu, Shigar and Khaplu are well-known destinations and have good potential to develop into hubs of future tourist circuits. The new conservation and rehabilitation initiatives will establish them as destinations for authentic cultural tourism, based on a heritage concept that gives value, meaning and context to the buildings and places to be visited.

Fig. 323. The main spine of the rehabilitated village of Karimabad leading up to the restored fort. New business opportunities emerge along the major tourist circuits which have to be properly managed.

The traditional cultural heritage of the Northern Areas has great potential to stimulate the local economy through the development of tourism, which, if handled properly and buttressed by national legislation, can also boost natural and cultural conservation. Promotion of sensitive cultural tourism in the area can foster a deeper understanding of regional (as well as international) issues linked to the protection of the environment, sustainable development, poverty reduction through cultural development and positive interpretation of cultural diversity. Meanwhile, a deeper involvement with the traditional cultural heritage of the Northern Areas can also provide incentives to reflect on the character and implications of a somewhat aggressive type of 'modernity' that often tends to judge and dismiss traditional cultures as being backward and having no future. In this fractured world, where ideological polarities have provoked so many avoidable conflicts, cultural pluralism and mutual understanding have become essential, since they can do away with prejudices and can help abolish implicit or explicit assumptions of cultural superiority, which have to be overcome to open the door for genuine and productive ways of cooperation.

Biographies

SAFIULLAH BAIG holds postgraduate degrees in Sociology and Development Studies from the University of Karachi, Pakistan, and the University of East Anglia, UK. He has been working with different AKDN agencies since 1996. His career in social development began with the Aga Khan Rural Support Programme and later moved to the Aga Khan Education Service-Pakistan, where he worked with local communities, particularly in non-Ismaili areas of Northern Pakistan. Before joining the Aga Khan Cultural Service-Pakistan (AKCS-P) he assisted Afghan refugees in the North West Frontier Province and Balochistan. He has conducted a number of field research projects, such as 'Girls' Access to Post-Primary Education' and 'The Role of Non-Formal Education in Closed Social System Societies of the Northern Areas'.

SALMAN BEG has been the chief executive officer of the Aga Khan Cultural Service-Pakistan (an affiliate of the Aga Khan Trust for Culture) since October 1998. He has a multifaceted background and a diverse education, which includes almost a quarter century in the army. He holds masters degrees from the United States Army Command and General Staff College Fort Leavenworth, and Lahore University of Management Sciences. He belongs to a well-known Hunza family and is committed to pursuing community-based development in the Northern Areas that allows for maintaining a fine balance between modernity and the environment. He is closely associated with AKCS-P's current efforts at using culture as a catalyst for development as well as integrating different development sectors with a view to stimulating the local economy.

STEFANO BIANCA, a Swiss architect and architectural historian, holds a master degree and Ph.D. from ETH in Zurich and has spent much of his professional life in the Muslim world. As of 1976, he has directed a number of major planning, urban design and conservation projects in cities such as Fez, Aleppo, Baghdad and Riyadh. Since 1992 he has been the director of the 'Historic Cities Support Programme' of the Aga Khan Trust for Culture in Geneva in charge of building up the current portfolio of area conservation and development projects in Cairo, Zanzibar, Kabul, Aleppo, Mostar and the Northern Areas of Pakistan. Stefano Bianca has widely published in the fields of Islamic architecture, cities, gardens and arts, his most recent books being *Hofhaus und Paradiesgarten* (Munich 1991 and 2001) and *Urban Form in the Arab World* (London/New York, 2000).

BENEDICT BULL holds a graduate degree from the Department of Architecture in the University of Edinburgh and a Horticultural diploma from Merrist Wood College. He has been studying and working as a landscape gardener for fifteen years, including a botanical scholarship to *Il Giardino Botanico Hanbury* of the University of Genoa in Italy. His career began in landscape planning, design and management in the UK and Ireland, specialising in racing stud farms and large private estates and pleasure gardens. He has consulted on a wide range of conservation projects in Afghanistan, Bulgaria, England, France, Ireland, Italy, Greece, Mongolia, Pakistan and Uzbekistan. He has made seven plant hunting treks in the Hindukush, Himalaya and Karakoram and he researched and presented two short films on plant hunting in Pakistan and the gardens of Uzbekistan.

YASMIN CHEEMA holds a diploma in Architecture from the National College of Arts, Lahore, Pakistan, a Master of Science in the Restoration of Monuments and Historic Sites, and a degree in the same subject from the Middle Eastern Technical University, Ankara. She graduated as the first female architect of Pakistan in the year 1966 and worked with several well-known architects of the country including Arif Hasan, before she set up her own practice. At the height of her professional career she left Pakistan in 1975 to enrol in the Urban and Regional Planning Department, University of Wisconsin at Madison. On her return she continued her practice and also started her teaching career at the National College of Arts in Lahore. Besides conducting design studios, she prepared and organised a multi-disciplinary fourth year urban planning course involving Lahore's most qualified lawyers, economists, anthropologists, sociologists and development experts.

JULIE FLOWERDAY holds a doctorate in Social Anthropology from the University of North Carolina-Chapel Hill (1998) where she began studying, visualising and writing about the relationship of changing landscape and shifting knowledge. She has exhibited photographs at Lok Versa (Islamabad), the University of London's School of Oriental and African Studies (London), the University of North Carolina (Chapel Hill, NC), and Georgetown University (Washington, DC). Upcoming publications include "Changes Over Time" in the book *Karakoram in Transition* (June 2005), "Framing Change" in the *Journal of Visual Communication* (October 2005) and a forthcoming book titled, *Power Informs Vision: Hunza in Treble Vision 1930s and 1990s*.

JÜRGEN WASIM FREMBGEN is chief curator of the Oriental Department at the Museum of Ethnology in Munich as well as lecturer in Islamic Studies at the University of Erlangen-Nuernberg. Since 1981 he has been teaching Anthropology and Islamic Studies at different universities in Germany. He has also been a visiting lecturer at the Quaid-i-Azam University in Islamabad (National Institute of Pakistan Studies), the National College of Arts in Lahore, as well as Ohio State University in Columbus, OH/USA. Since 1981 he has been conducting annual ethnographic field campaigns in Pakistan. His numerous exhibitions include "The Scent of Roses and the Sheen of Sabres. Islamic Art and Culture of the Mughal Period" (1996) and "Food for the Soul – Worlds of Islam" (2003). He has published over ninety articles and fifteen books and catalogues, many of which deal with material culture, Sufism, the veneration of Muslim saints, and popular culture, particularly in Pakistan.

HARALD HAUPTMANN is professor emeritus of Prehistoric and Near Eastern Archaeology at the University of Heidelberg and former director of the German Archaeological Institute at Istanbul. Between 1968 and 2003 he has conducted several excavations in eastern and south-eastern Turkey covering the periods from Early Neolithic to the Middle Ages. Since 1989, he is the head of the research project 'Rock Carvings and Inscriptions along the Karakoram Highway' at the Heidelberg Academy of Humanities and Science, and leads the annual field research of a Pak-German archaeological mission to the Northern Areas of Pakistan. He is the editor of several monographs on the archaeology of the Balkans, Greece and the Turkish Euphrates region. The results of the research in the Northern Areas have been published in two series: *Antiquities of Northern Pakistan*, vols. 1-5, 1989-2004, and *Materials for the Archaeology of the Northern Regions of Pakistan*, vols. 1-7, 1994-2005.

RICHARD HUGHES is a trained engineer and building conservator who has undertaken projects for many international and national organisations including the Aga Khan Trust for Culture, UNESCO/UNDP, ICOMOS, Ove Arup and Partners, and the Egypt Exploration Society. His specialities are structural evaluation and conservation of historic buildings and archaeological sites. He gives scientific advice to many firms of engineers and architects on engineering practices relating to historic sites, as well as correct use of traditional building materials, especially wood, soil and stone. He is internationally well known for his work on traditional structures in hazard prone areas (affected by earthquakes and floods) and on the new use of soil as a structural building material. Over the last two decades he has conserved many historical wooden buildings in the Northern Areas of Pakistan and is a senior consultant of the AKCS-P team that has won four UNESCO and British Airways conservation awards. He has been extensively involved with the science of *in situ* preservation of archaeological remains (including sites in Britain and Mohenjo Daro) and has widely published on this subject.

IZHAR ALI HUNZAI currently serves as the General Manager of the Aga Khan Rural Support Programme (AKRSP). After the start of his professional career with the AKRSP in 1984, he went on in Pakistan to become the CEO of the Aga Khan Culture Services in 1996 and returned to the AKRSP in 2003 after working with the International Water Management Institute (IWMI) in Colombo for five years. His academic qualifications include a degree in International Development from Cornell University and a masters degree in International Relations from Karachi University.

SHEHNAZ ISMAIL is a graduate of the National College of Arts in the faculty of Design. She is one of the founders of the Indus Valley School of Art and Architecture, Karachi, and heads the department of textile design. Her major focus is on education and the revival of the indigenous textile crafts of Pakistan. She has extensively researched on weaving and embroidery, covering the mountainous regions of Pakistan and the Potohar plateau. The results have been published in magazines, catalogues and a book on Asian embroidery published by the Crafts Council of India in 2004. She is committed to teaching and training craft persons in Baltistan (and in the adjoining valleys of Hunza and Manshera) in natural dyes, weaving and product diversification, and to make the craft revival economically sustainable. It is in this function that she was strongly involved in the interior decoration of the Shigar Fort Residence.

MASOOD KHAN is an architect trained in Pakistan and in the United States who has worked for nearly two decades in the conservation of cultural heritage. He was responsible in 1986-1988 for the World Bank sponsored study for the conservation of the Walled Study of Lahore, in Pakistan, and since 1993 has been a senior consultant for the Historic Cities Support Programme of the Aga Khan Trust for Culture. In this capacity, he has been responsible for technical support in community development and cultural support programmes, and for the conservation of a series of monuments, including Shigar fort and the Ganish village conservation project. Masood Khan has also been active in architectural education and has taught at the National College of Arts in Lahore, at the Aga Khan Program for Islamic Architecture at Harvard and MIT (Cambridge, Mass.), and, as a Fulbright professor, at the University of Engineering and Technology in Lahore.

MAX KLIMBURG holds graduate degrees in Art History and Ethnology from the University of Vienna and has been studying and writing for decades about Afghanistan, Central Asia and, especially, Nuristan and the Kafirs of the Hindukush (Afghanistan). He taught at the universities of Kabul, Los Angeles (UCLA) and Vienna, holding a lectureship on history and the ethnic arts of Central Asia. In 1972-1978 he was the director of the Kabul branch of the South Asia Institute of Heidelberg University. In the 1980s and early 1990s he co-directed the activities of the Austrian Relief Committee for Afghan Refugees. From 2000 to 2002 he was a research associate at the Munich Museum of Ethnography. Since 2002, he heads the newly founded Austrian-Afghan Society which has recently managed to carry out a restoration project in the National Museum of Afghanistan. His publications include *Afghanistan – Das Land im historischen Spannungsfeld Mittelasiens* (Vienna 1966) and *The Kafirs of the Hindu Kush. Art and Society of the Waigal and Ashkun Kafirs* (2 vols., Stuttgart 1999).

HERMANN KREUTZMANN holds the Chair of Cultural Geography and Development Studies and is director of the Institute of Geography at the Friedrich Alexander University in Erlangen-Nuernberg, Germany. His academic career includes studies of anthropology, geography and physics at Hannover and Freiburg University; his Ph.D. was awarded from the Free University in Berlin. Post-doctoral research was conducted within the framework of the interdisciplinary research programme 'Culture Area Karakoram' in which he functioned as the field director. Since 1977 he has participated in fieldwork and academic research in South and Central Asia with a special focus on northern Pakistan. His publications include over a hundred articles in academic journals and proceedings volumes as well as monographs and edited books such as *Sharing Water* (OUP Karachi 2000) and *High Mountain Pastoralism in Northern Pakistan* (Stuttgart 2000).

ABDUL MALIK is currently heading the Monitoring, Evaluation and Research Section of the Aga Khan Rural Support Programme in Pakistan (AKRSP). He did his first degree in Agriculture Economics from the University of Agriculture, Faisalabad (1996), and then went on to acquire a masters degree in Business Administration from Lahore University of Management Sciences (2001). During his seven-year-long association with the AKRSP, Abdul Malik has mainly worked on the issues of poverty and livelihoods in the Northern Areas and Chitral (NAC). He has also played a central role in supervising fieldwork and documenting the Participatory Poverty Assessment (PPA) for the Northern Areas.

Selected Bibliography on Northern Pakistan: Reference, Research and Documentation

1. GEOGRAPHICAL, HISTORICAL AND ANTHROPOLOGICAL SOURCES

(i) Classical Descriptions, Gazetteers and Reports

BIDDULPH, J., *Tribes of the Hindoo Koosh* (reprint: Graz 1971, Karachi 1977), Calcutta 1880.

BLACKER, L. V. S., *On Secret Patrol in High Asia*, London 1922.

BONVALOT, G., *Through the Heart of Asia. Over the Pamir to India*, 2 vols, London 1889.

CONWAY, W. M., *Climbing and Exploration in the Karakoram-Himalaya*, London 1894.

DAINELLI, G., *Spedizione Italiana de Filippi nell'Himalaja, Caracorùm e Turchestàn Cinese (1913-1914)*, serie II: Risultati Geologici e Geografici, vols. 1-12, Bologna 1924-1934.

DE FILIPPI, F., *Karakoram and Western Himalaya. An Account of the Expedition of H. R. H. Prince Luigi Amadeo of Savoy, Duke of Abruzzi*, London 1912.

DE FILIPPI, F., *The Italian Expedition to the Himalaya, Karakoram and Eastern Turkestan 1913-1914*, London 1932.

DREW, F., *The Jummoo and Kashmir Territories* (reprint: Graz 1976, Karachi 1980), London 1875.

DURAND, A., *The Making of a Frontier* (reprint: Graz 1974, Karachi 1977), London 1899.

FRANCKE, A. H., *A History of Western Tibet* (reprint: New Delhi 1980), London 1907.

GENERAL STAFF INDIA, *Military Report and Gazetteer of the Gilgit Agency and the Independent Territories of Tangir and Darel*, Simla 1928.

GENERAL STAFF INDIA, *Routes in Chitral, Gilgit & Kohistan*, Simla 1942.

GHULAM MUHAMMAD, "Festivals and Folklore of Gilgit", in *Memoirs of the Asiatic Society of Bengal*, 1/8, pp. 93-127 (reprint: Islamabad 1980), 1905-1907.

GODFREY, S. H., *Report on the Gilgit Agency and Wazarat and the Countries of Chilas, Hunza-Nagar, and Yasin, including Ashkuman, Ghizr, and Koh. 1896-97*, Calcutta 1898.

HASHMATULLAH KHAN, A.-H. M., *History of Baltistan* (translation of the 1939 Urdu version, published by Lok Virsa, Islamabad 1987), 1939.

KNIGHT, E. F., *Where Three Empires Meet* (reprint: Lahore 1986), London 1895.

LAWRENCE, W. (ed.), *The Imperial Gazetteer of India*, provincial series, vol. XIII, *Kashmir and Jammu* (reprint: Lahore 1983), Oxford 1908.

LEITNER, G. W., *The Hunza and Nagyr Handbook, Being an Introduction to a Knowledge of the Language, Race and Countries of Hunza, Nagyr, and a Part of Yassin, in Two Parts*, Calcutta 1893.

LEITNER, G. W., *Dardistan in 1866, 1886 and 1893* (reprint: New Delhi 1978, Karachi 1985), Woking 1894.

LOCKHART, W. S. A. and WOODTHORPE, R. G., *The Gilgit Mission 1885-86*, London 1889.

LORIMER, D. L. R., "The Supernatural in the Popular Belief of the Gilgit Region", in *Journal of the Royal Asiatic Society of Great Britain and Ireland*, pp. 507-536, 1929.

LORIMER, D. L. R., "An Oral Version of the Kesar Saga from Hunza", in *Folk-Lore*, 42, pp. 105-139, 1931.

LORIMER, D. L. R., *The Burushaski Language* (ser. B. XXIX 1-3. vol. 1: *Phonology and Morphology*, 1935; vol. 2: *Texts*, 1935; vol. 3: *Lexicons*, 1938), Instituttet for Sammenlignende Kulturforskning, Oslo 1935, 1935, 1938.

LORIMER, E. O., *Language Hunting in the Karakoram* (reprint: Karachi 1989), London 1938.

MASON, K., "Indus Floods and Shyok Glaciers", in *The Himalayan Journal*, I, pp. 10-29, 1929.

MASON, K., "Karakoram Nomenclature", in *The Geographical Journal*, 91, pp. 123-152, 1938.

MUNPHOOL MEER MOONSHEE, *Relations Between Gilgit, Chitral and Kashmir*, Calcutta 1867.

NEVE, A., *The Legacy of Kashmir, Ladakh & Skardu*, Lahore n.d.

PRELLER, C. du Riche, "The Racial and Economic Conditions of Transhimalaya (Upper Indus Basin: Ladàk and Baltistan)", in *Scottish Geographical Magazine*, XL, pp. 334-344, 1924.

SCHOMBERG, R. C. F., *Between the Oxus and the Indus* (reprint: Lahore 1976), London 1935.

SCHOMBERG, R. C. F., *Unknown Karakoram*, London 1936.

SINGH, T., *Assessment Report of Skardu Tahsil of the Ladakh District*, Lahore 1914.

SINGH, T., *Assessment Report of the Gilgit Tahsil*, Lahore 1917.

VIGNE, G. T., *Travels in Kashmir, Ladak, Iskardo, the Countries Adjoining the Mountain-Course of the Himalaya, North of the Panjab*, 2 vols. (reprint: 2nd edition 1844 in Karachi 1987), 1842.

VISSER, P. C., "Explorations in the Karakoram", in *The Geographical Journal*, 68, pp. 457-473, 1926.

VISSER-HOOFT, J. and VISSER, P. C., *Among the Karakoram Glaciers in 1925*, London 1926.

YOUNGHUSBAND, F. E., *The Heart of a Continent* (reprint: Hongkong 1984), London 1896.

(ii) Results of Recent Research and Documentation

AFRIDI, B. G., *Baltistan in History*, Peshawar 1988.

AGA KHAN RURAL SUPPORT PROGRAMME, *An Assessment of Socio-Economic Trends and Impact in Northern Pakistan (1991-1997)*, Gilgit 2000.

ALI, T., "Ceremonial and Social Structure Among the Burusho of Hunza", in FURER-HAIMENDORF, CHR. VON (ed.), *Asian Highland Societies in Anthropological Perspective*, pp. 231-49 (reprint: Delhi 1984), 1981.

ALDER, G. J., *British India's Northern Frontier 1865-95. A Study in Imperial Policy*, London 1963.

AZHAR-HEWITT, F., "Women of the High Pastures and the Global Economy: Reflections on the Impacts of Modernization in the Hushe Valley of the Karakorum, Northern Pakistan", in *Mountain Research and Development*, 19 (2), pp. 141-151, 1999.

BESIO, K., "Steppin' in it. Post-Coloniality in Northern Pakistan", in *Area*, 35 (1), pp. 24-33, 2003.

DANI, A. H. (ed.), *Shah Rais Khan's History of Gilgit*, Islamabad 1987.

DANI, A. H., "Gilgit and Baltistan in International Perspective", in *Pakistan Journal of History and Culture*, 9, pp. 5-14, 1988.

DANI, A. H., *History of Northern Areas of Pakistan up to 2000 AD* (ser. *Historical Studies (Pakistan)*, 5, updated 2nd edition), Lahore 2001.

DERBYSHIRE, E., FORT, M. and OWEN, L., "Geomorphological Hazards along the Karakoram Highway: Khunjerab Pass to the Gilgit River, Northernmost Pakistan", in *Erdkunde*, 55 (1), pp. 49-71, 2001.

DESIO, A., "Geologic Evolution of the Karakorum", in ABUL F. and DE JONG, K. A. (eds.), *Geodynamics of Pakistan*, pp. 111-124, Quetta 1979.

DICKORÉ, W. B. and NUESSER, M., *Flora of Nanga Parbat (NW Himalaya, Pakistan)*, (*Englera* 19), Berlin 2000.

EHLERS, E. and KREUTZMANN, H., (eds.) *High Mountain Pastoralism in Northern Pakistan (Erdkundliches Wissen* 132), Stuttgart 2000.

FELMY, S., "Division of Labour and Women's Work in a Mountain Society. Hunza Valley in Pakistan", in RAJU, S. and BAGCHI, D., (eds.), *Women and Work in South Asia. Regional Patterns and Perspectives*, pp. 196-208, London 1993.

FELMY, S., *The Voice of the Nightingale. A Personal Account of Wakhi Culture in Hunza*, Karachi 1996.

FINSTERWALDER, R., Accompanying text for the "Hunza-Karakorum 1:100 000" map, in *Erdkunde*, 50 (3), pp. 169-172, 1996.

FREMBGEN, J. W., "Die Nagerkuts im Licht der populären Reiseliteratur. Ein Beitrag zur Vorurteilsforschung in Nordpakistan", in SNOY, P. (ed.), *Ethnologie und Geschichte. Festschrift für Karl Jettmar*, pp. 147-162, Wiesbaden 1983a.

FREMBGEN, J. W., "Tourismus in Hunza: Beziehungen zwischen Gästen un Gastgebern", in *Sociologus*, new ser. 33/2, pp. 174-185, 1983b.

FREMBGEN, J. W., *Zentrale Gewalt in Nager (Karakorum). Politische Organisationsformen, ideologische Begründungen des Königtums und Veränderungen in der Moderne*, Stuttgart 1985.

FREMBGEN, J. W., "Hunza und Shagri-la. Ein Bergvolk in der Tourismuswerbung", in *Münchner Beiträge zur Völkerkunde*, 2, pp. 51-68, 1989.

FREMBGEN, J. W., "Local Dignitaries as Historians: Guardians of Traditional Culture from Gilgit, Hunza and Nager (Northern Pakistan)", in BASHIR, E. and ISRAR-UD-DIN (eds.), *Proceedings of the Second International Hindukush Cultural Conference*, pp. 97-104, Karachi 1996.

FUSSMAN, G., *Atlas linguistique des parlers Dardes et Kafirs*, Paris 1972.

HALVORSON, S., "A Geography of Children's Vulnerability: Gender, Household Resources, and Water-Related Disease Hazard in Northern Pakistan", in *Professional Geographer*, 55 (2), pp. 120-133, 2003.

HALVORSON, S., "Placing Health Risks in the Karakoram. Local Perception of Disease, Dependency, and Social Change in Northern Pakistan", in *Mountain Research and Development*, 23 (3), pp. 271-277, 2003.

HEWITT, K., "The Altitudinal Organisation of Karakoram Geomorphic Processes and Depositional Environments", in *Zeitschrift für Geomorphologie*, new ser. 76, pp. 9-32, 1989a.

HEWITT, K., "European Science in High Asia. Geomorphology in the Karakoram Himalaya to 1939", in TINKLER, K. J. (ed.), *History of Geomorphology: From Hutton to Hack*, pp. 165-203, London 1989b.

HEWITT, K. "Catastrophic Rockslides and the Geomorphology of the Hunza and Gilgit River Valleys, Karakoram Himalaya", in *Erdkunde*, 55 (1), pp. 72-93, 2001.

HUTTENBACK, R. A., "The 'Great Game' in the Pamirs and the Hindu-Kush: The British Conquest of Hunza and Nagar", in *Modern Asian Studies*, 9, pp. 1-29, 1975.

JANJUA, Z. J., "Tradition and Change in the Darel and Tangir Valleys", in STELLRECHT, I. (ed.), *Karakorum-Hindukush-Himalaya: Dynamics of Change* (ser. *Culture Area Karakorum, Scientific Studies*, 4/I), pp. 415-427, Cologne 1998.

JETTMAR, K., "Bolor - A Contribution to the Political and Ethnic Geography of North Pakistan", in *Zentralasiatische Studien*, 11, pp. 411-448, 1977.

JETTMAR, K., *The Religions of the Hindukush. Vol. 1: The Religion of the Kafirs*, Warminster 1986.

JETTMAR, K., *Beyond the Gorges of the Indus. Archaeology Before Excavation*, Karachi 2002.

KAMAL, N. A., "Karakoram Highway: A Nation-Building Effort", in *Strategic Studies*, II/3, pp. 18-31, 1979.

KEAY, J., *The Gilgit Game*, London 1979.

KHAN, M. H. and KHAN, S. S., *Rural Change in the Third World. Pakistan and the Aga Khan Rural Support Program* (ser. *Contributions in Economics and Economic History*, 129), New York, Westport, London 1992.

KITAMURA, S. (ed.), *Plants of West Pakistan and Afghanistan (Results of the Kyoto University Scientific Expedition to the Karakoram and Hindukush 1955, vol. III)* (reprint: Karachi 1977) Kyoto 1964.

KREUTZMANN, H., "The Karakoram Highway - Impact of Road Construction on Mountain Societies", in *Modern Asian Studies*, 25, (4), pp. 711-736, 1991.

KREUTZMANN, H. "Challenge and Response in the Karakoram. Socio-Economic Transformation in Hunza, Northern Areas, Pakistan", in *Mountain Research and Development*, 13 (1), pp. 19-39, 1993.

KREUTZMANN, H., "Habitat Conditions and Settlement Processes in the Hindukush-Karakoram", in *Petermanns Geographische Mitteilungen*, 138 (6), pp. 337-356, 1994.

KREUTZMANN, H., "Globalization, Spatial Integration and Sustainable Development in Northern Pakistan", in *Mountain Research and Development*, 15 (3), pp. 213-227, 1995.

KREUTZMANN, H., "Tourism in the Hindu Kush-Karakoram: A Case Study from Hunza", in BASHIR, E. and ISRAR-UD-DIN (eds.), *Proceedings of the Second International Hindukush Cultural Conference*, pp. 427-437, Karachi 1996.

KREUTZMANN, H., "Development Processes in the Hunza Valley: A Case Study from the Karakoram Mountains", in ISRAR-UD-DIN (ed.), *Studies in Pakistan Geography*, pp. 297-312, Peshawar 1998a.

KREUTZMANN, H., "The Chitral Triangle: Rise and Decline of Trans-Montane Central Asian Trade, 1895-1935", in *Asien-Afrika-Lateinamerika*, 26 (3), pp. 289-327, 1998b.

KREUTZMANN, H., "Ethnic Minorities and Marginality in the Pamirian Knot. Survival of Wakhi and Kirghiz in a Harsh Environment and Global Contexts", in *The Geographical Journal*, 169 (3), pp. 215-235, 2003.

KREUTZMANN, H., "Accessibility for High Asia. Comparative Perspectives on Northern Pakistan's Traffic Infrastructure and Linkages with Neighbours in the Hindukush-Karakoram-Himalaya", in *Journal of Mountain Science*, 1 (3), pp. 193-210, 2004a.

KREUTZMANN, H., "Development Problems in the Mountain Regions of Northern Pakistan", in MUFTI, S. A., HUSSAIN, S. S. and KHAN, A. M., (eds.), *Mountains of Pakistan: Protection, Potentials and Prospects*, Global Change Impact Studies Centre, pp. 164-179, Islamabad 2004b.

KREUTZMANN, H. (ed.), *Sharing Water - Irrigation and Water Management in the Hindukush-Karakoram-Himalaya*, Oxford, London, Karachi 2000.

KREUTZMANN, H. (ed.), *Karakoram in Transition. Culture, Development and Ecology in the Hunza Valley*, Karachi, Oxford, New York (in press).

MACDONALD, K., "Population Change in the Upper Braldu Valley, Baltistan, 1900-1990: All Is Not as It Seems", in *Mountain Research and Development*, 16 (4), pp. 351-366, 1996.

MACDONALD, K. and BUTZ, D., "Investigating Portering Relations as a Locus for Transcultural Interaction in the Karakorum Region, Northern Pakistan", in *Mountain Research and Development*, 18 (4), pp. 333-343, 1988.

MIEHE, S., CRAMER, T. and JACOBSEN, J., "Humidity Conditions in the Western Karakorum as Indicated by Climatic Data and Corresponding Distribution Patterns of the Montane and Alpine Vegetation", in *Erdkunde*, 50 (3), pp. 190-204, 1996.

MILLER, K. J., *Continents in Collision: The International Karakoram Project*, London 1982.

MILLER, K. J. (ed.), *The International Karakoram Project*, 2 vols., Cambridge 1984.

MOTT, P. G., "Karakoram Survey 1939: A New Map", in *The Geographical Journal*, 116, pp. 89-95, 1950.

MÜLLER-STELLRECHT, I., *Materialen zur Ethnographie von Dardistan (Pakistan): aus den nachgelassenen Aufzeichnungen v. D. L. R. Lorimer. Bergvölker im Hindukush und Karakorum*, vol. 3, Akademische Druck- u. Verlagsanstalt, Graz 1979.

N. N., "Ancient Routes Through the Pamirs", in *Central Asian Review*, 13 (1), pp. 44-54, 1965.

NUESSER, M., "Change and Persistence: Contemporary Landscape Transformation in the Nanga Parbat Region, Northern Pakistan", in *Mountain Research and Development*, 20 (4), pp. 348-355, 2000.

NUESSER, M. and CLEMENS, J., "Impacts on Mixed Mountain Agriculture in the Rupal Valley, Nanga Parbat, Northern Pakistan", in *Mountain Research and Development*, 16 (2), pp. 117-133, 1996.

NÜSSER, M. and DICKORÉ, W. B., "A Tangle in the Triangle. Vegetation Map of the Eastern Hindukush (Chitral, Northern Pakistan)", in *Erdkunde*, 56 (1), pp. 37-59, 2002.

PECCI, M. and SMIRAGLIA, C., "Advance and Retreat Phases of the Karakorum Glaciers During the 20th Century: Case Studies in Braldo Valley (Pakistan)", in *Geografia fisica e dinamica quaternaria*, 23 (1), pp. 73-86, 2000.

POLZER, C. and SCHMIDT, M., "The transformation of Political Structure in Shigar Valley/Baltistan", in DITTMANN, A. (ed.), *Mountain Societies in Transition* (ser. *Culture Area Karakorum Scientific Studies*, 6), pp. 179-210, Cologne 2000.

RAHIM, I. and MASELLI, D., "Improving Sustainable Grazing Management in Mountain Rangelands of the Hindu Kush-Himalaya: An Innovative Participatory Assessment Method in Northern Pakistan", in *Mountain Research and Development*, 24 (2), pp. 124-133, 2004.

RIECK, A., "Sectarianism as a Political Problem in Pakistan: The Case of the Northern Areas", in *Orient*, 36 (3), pp. 429-448, 1995.

SAGASTER, U. (ed.), *Die Baltis – Ein Bergvolk im Norden Pakistans*, Museum für Völkerkunde, Frankfurt 1989.

SAUNDERS, F., *Karakoram Villages*, Gilgit 1983.

SCHALLER, G. B., *Stones of Silence. Journeys in the Himalaya*, London 1980.

SCHICKHOFF, U., "Socio-Economic Background and Ecological Effects of Forest Destruction in Northern Pakistan", in STELLRECHT, I. (ed.), *Karakorum-Hindukush-Himalaya: Dynamics of Change* (ser. *Culture Area Karakorum Scientific Studies*, 4/I), pp. 287-302, Cologne 1998a.

SCHICKHOFF, U., "Interrelations Between Ecological and Socio-Economic Change: The Case of the High-Altitude Forests in the Northern Areas of Pakistan", in ISRAR-UD-DIN (ed.), *Studies in Pakistan Geography*, pp. 29-38, Peshawar 1998b.

SCHMIDT, M., "Interdependencies and Reciprocity of Private and Common Property Resources in the Central Karakorum", in *Erdkunde*, 58 (4), pp. 316-330, 2004.

SEARLE, M. P., *Geology and Tectonics of the Karakoram Mountains*, Chichester, New York 1991.

SHEIKH, A. G., "Ladakh and Baltostan Through the Ages", in STELLRECHT, I. (ed.), *Karakorum-Hindukush-Himalaya. Dynamics of Change*, vol. II (ser. *Culture Area Karakorum Scientific Studies*, 4/II), pp. 337-349, Cologne 1998.

SHEIKH, M. I., and ALEEM, A., "Forests and Forestry in Northern Areas", in *The Pakistan Journal of Forestry*, 25, 3-4, pp. 197-235, 296-324, 1975.

STALEY, E. *Arid Mountain Agriculture in Northern West Pakistan*, Lahore 1966.

STALEY, J., *Economy and Society in Dardistan: Traditional Systems and the Impact of Change*, Lahore 1966.

STALEY, J., "Economy and Society in the High Mountains of Northern Pakistan", in *Modern Asian Studies*, 3, pp. 225-243, 1969.

STALEY, J., *Words for My Brother. Travels Between the Hindu Kush and the Himalayas*, Karachi 1982.

STELLRECHT, I. (ed.), *Bibliography - Northern Pakistan* (ser. *Culture Area Karakorum Scientific Studies*, 1), Cologne 1998.

STELLRECHT, I. (ed.), *Culture Area Karakorum Scientific Studies*, 12 vols, Cologne 1998-2004.

STREEFLAND, P. H., KHAN, S. H. and LIESHOUT, O. VAN, *A Contextual Study of Northern Areas and Chitral*, Gilgit 1995.

WHITEMAN, P. T. S., *Mountain Oases*, Gilgit 1985.

WITCOMBE, J. R., "The Distribution of Cropping Systems in Northern Pakistan", in *Agro-Ecosystems*, 3, pp. 285-290, 1977.

WOODMAN, D., *Himalayan Frontiers: A Political Review of British, Chinese, Indian and Russian Rivalries*, London 1969.

WORLD BANK, *The Aga Khan Rural Support Program. A Third Evaluation*, Washington 1996.

WORLD BANK, *The Next Ascent. An Evaluation of the Aga Khan Rural Support Program, Pakistan*, Washington 2002.

2. PRE-ISLAMIC HISTORY AND CULTURE

BANDINI-KÖNIG, D., BEMMANN, M. and HAUPTMANN, H., "Rock Art in the Upper Indus Valley", in HAUPTMANN, H. (ed.), *The Indus. Cradle and Crossroads of Civilizations*, Pakistan-German Archaeological Research, Islamabad 1997.

BEAL, S., *Travels of Fah-Hian and Sung-Yun. Buddhist Pilgrims from China to India (418 A.D. and 518 A.D.)*, London 1881.

BEAL, S., *Si-yu-ki. Buddhist Records of the Western World: Translated from the Chinese of Hiuen Tsiang*, London 1884.

BEAL, S., *The Life of Hiuen-Tsiang, by Hwui Li*, London 1911.

BECKWITH, C. I., *The Tibetan Empire in Central Asia: A History of the Struggle for Great Power Among the Tibetans, Turks, Arabs, and Chinese During the Early Middle Ages*, Princeton 1987.

CUNNINGHAM, A., *The Ancient Geography of India*, London 1871.

DANI, A. H., *Chilas. The City of Nanga Parvat (Dyamar)*, Islamabad 1983.

DANI, A. H., "The Sacred Rock of Hunza", in *Journal of Central Asia*, 8 (2), pp. 5-124, 1985.

DANI, A. H., *Human Records on Karakorum Highway*, Lahore 1995.

DUNCAN, J. E., *A Summer Ride Through Western Tibet*, London 1906.

FRANCFORT, H.-P., KLODZINSKI, D. and MASCLE, G., "Pétroglyphes archaïques du Ladakh et du Zanskar", in *Arts Asiatiques*, 45, pp. 5-27, 1990.

FRANCKE, A. H., "Notes on Rock-Carvings from Lower Ladakh", in *Indian Antiquary*, 31, pp. 398-402, 1902.

FRANCKE, A. H., "Some More Rock-Carvings from Lower Ladakh", in *Indian Antiquary*, 32, pp. 361-363, 1903.

FUCHS, W., "Huei Ch'ao's Pilgerreise durch Nordwestindien und Zentralasien um 726", in *Sitzungsberichte der Preußischen Akademie der Wissenschaften, Philosophisch-historische Klasse*, 30, pp. 1-47, Berlin 1938.

FUSSMAN, G., "Les inscriptions Kharoṣṭhī de la plaine de Chilas", in *Antiquities of Northern Pakistan*, 1, pp. 1-39, 1989.

FUSSMAN, G., "Chilas, Hatun et les bronzes Bouddhiques du Cachemire", in *Antiquities of Northern Pakistan*, 2, pp. 1-60, 1993.

HAUPTMANN, H., "Religiöse Graffiti in Asien", in KONFERENZ DER AKADEMIE DER DEUTSCHEN WISSENSCHAFTEN (ed.), *Geld, Musik, Mythos, Macht. Geisteswissenschaften im Dialog*, pp. 63-81, Mainz 1996.

HEICHEL, W., *Chronik der Erschließung des Karakorum. Teil I - Western Karakorum. Wissenschaftliche Alpenvereinshefte, Heft 36*, Munich 2003.

HERRMANN, A., *Historical and Commercial Atlas of China*, Cambridge 1935.

HILL, J. E., *The Western Regions According to the Hou Hanshu. The Xiyu Juan* (chapter on the Western Regions from Hou Hanshu), 2nd edition, 2003.

HINÜBER, O. VON, "Die Erforschung der Gilgit-Handschriften", in *Nachrichten der Akademie der Wissenschaften in Göttingen*, I, *Philologisch-historische Klasse*, 12, pp. 329-360, 1979.

HINÜBER, O. VON, "Brāhmī Inscriptions on the History and Culture of the Upper Indus Valley", in *Antiquities of Northern Pakistan*, 1, pp. 41-71, 1989a.

HINÜBER, O. VON, "Buddhistische Inschriften aus dem Tal des Oberen Indus", in *Antiquities of Northern Pakistan*, 1, pp. 73-106, 1989b.

HINÜBER, O. VON, *Die Palola Ṣāhis. Ihre Steininschriften, Inschriften auf Bronzen, Handschriftenkolophone und Schutzzauber. Materialien zur Geschichte von Gilgit und Chilas*, (*Antiquities of Northern Pakistan*, 5), Mainz 2004.

HULSEWÉ, A. F. P., *China in Central Asia: The Early Stage*, Leiden 1979.

JETTMAR, K., *Bolor & Dardistan*, Islamabad 1980a.

JETTMAR, K., "Neuentdeckte Felsbilder und –inschriften in den Nordgebieten Pakistans", in *Allgemeine und Vergleichende Archäologie*, 2, pp. 151-199, 1980b.

JETTMAR, K., "The Art of the Northern Nomads in the Upper Indus Valley", in *South Asian Studies*, 7, pp. 1-20, 1991.

JETTMAR, K. and THEWALT, V., *Between Gandhara and the Silk Roads. Rock Carvings Along the Karakorum Highway*, Mainz 1987.

KLIMBURG-SALTER, D. E. (ed.), *The Silk Route and the Diamond Pass. Esoteric Buddhist Art on the Trans-Himalayan Trade Route*, Los Angeles 1982.

KUBAREV, V. D., *Drevnie Rospisi Karakola*, Novosibirsk 1988.

LEONT'EV, N. V. and KAPEL'KO, V. F., "Steinstelen der Okunev-Kultur", in *Archäologie in Eurasien*, 13, Mainz 2002.

LEVI, M. S. and CHAVANNES, É., "Voyages des pèlerins bouddhistes: l'itinéraire d'Ou-K'ong (751-790)", in *Journal Asiatique*, 9 (6), pp. 341-384, 1895.

MANP = *Materials for the Archaeology of the Northern Regions of Pakistan*.

MANP 1: BEMMANN, M. and KÖNIG, D., *Die Felsbildstation Oshibat*, Mainz 1994.

MANP 2: KÖNIG, D. and FUSSMAN, G., *Die Felsbildstation Shatial*, Mainz 1997.

MANP 3: BANDINI-KÖNIG, D., *Die Felsbildstation Hodar*, Mainz 1999.

MANP 4: BANDINI-KÖNIG, D. and HINÜBER, O. VON, *Die Felsbildstationen Shing-Nala und Gichi Nala*, Mainz 2001.

MANP 5: BEMMANN, M., *Die Felsbildstation Dadam Das*, Mainz 2005.

MANP 6: BANDINI-KÖNIG, D., *Die Felsbildstation Thalpan I: Kataloge Chilas-Brücke und Thalpan (Steine 1-30)*, Mainz 2003.

MANP 7: BANDINI-KÖNIG, D., *Die Felsbildstation Thalpan II: Katalog Thalpan (Steine 31-195)*, Mainz 2005.

NASIM KHAN, M., "Rock-Carvings at Kinro Kor: A Prehistoric Site of the Northern Areas of Pakistan", in *Lahore Museum Bulletin*, 13 (2), pp. 2-7, 2000a.

NASIM KHAN, M., *Buddhist Paintings in Gandhāra*, Peshawar 2000b.

NAZIR KHAN, M., "Chaghdo Rock Paintings, Baltistan, Northern Areas", in *Journal of Asian Civilisations*, 21 (1), pp. 100-104, 1998.

NOVOČENOV, V. A., *Petroglifi Sar'i Arki*, Almaty 2002.

RIZVI, J., *Trans-Himalayan Caravans. Merchant, Princes and Peasant Traders in Ladakh*, 1999.

SHASTRI, M. S. K., "Report on the Gilgit Excavations in 1938", in *The Quarterly Journal of Mythic Society*, 30/1, pp. 1-12, 1938.

SCHLAGINTWEIT, H. VON, "Die Pässe über die Kammlinien des Karakorum und des Künlün in Balti, in Ladak und im östlichen Turkistan", in *Das Ausland*, 48, pp. 413-437, 1875.

SIMS-WILLIAMS, N., *Sogdian and Other Iranian Inscriptions of the Upper Indus II. Corpus Inscriptionum Iranicarum: Part II, Inscriptions of the Seleucid and Parthian Periods and of Eastern Iran and Central Asia*, London 1992.

STEIN, M. A., *Ancient Khotan: Detailed Report of Archaeological Explorations in Chinese Turkestan*, London 1907.

STEIN, M. A., *Serindia. Detailed Report of Explorations in Central Asia and Westernmost China*, vol. 1, Oxford 1921.

STEIN, M. A., "Archaeological Notes from the Hindukush Region", in *Journal of the Royal Asiatic Society of Great Britain and Ireland*, pp. 5-24, 1944.

TSUCHIYA, H., "Field Research Along the Ancient Routes in the Northern Areas of Pakistan (1991-1995)", in STELLRECHT, I. (ed.), *Karakorum-Hindukush-Himalaya: Dynamics of Change*, vol. II (ser. *Culture Area Karakorum Scientific Studies*), 4, pp. 45-70, Cologne 1998.

TSUCHIYA, H., "Tracing Ancient Routes in Northern Pakistan. Field Research (1991-1996) (Preliminary Report)", in ALRAM, M. and KLIMBURG-SALTER, D. E. (eds.), *Coins, Art and Archaeology. Essays on the Pre-Islamic History of the Indo-Iranian Borderlands*, in *Österreichische Akademie der Wissenschaften, Philosophisch-Historische Klasse, Denkschriften*, 280, pp. 353-390, Vienna 1999.

UJFALVY, K. E. VON, *Aus dem westlichen Himalaya. Erlebnisse und Forschungen*, Leipzig 1884.

3. ISLAMIC HISTORY AND ARTS

ANSARI, N., "The Traditional Architecture of Kashmir", in AFZAL QADRI, S. M. (ed.), *The Cultural Heritage of Kashmir*, Srinagar 1997.

ARIF, M., "A Brief Note on Wooden Mosques in Baltistan", in *Journal of Central Asia*, 19/2, pp. 83-97, 1988.

DAINELLI, G., *Paesi e genti del Caracorùm*, Florence 1924.

DANI, A. H., *Islamic Architecture. The Wooden Style of Northern Pakistan*, Islamabad 1989.

DE FILIPPI, F., *Storia della spedizione scientifica italiana nel Himàlaia, Caracorùm e Turchestàn Cinese (1913-1914)*, Bologna 1924.

ENCYCLOPAEDIA OF ISLA, Articles on Baltistan, Kashmir, Nurbakhshiya.

FREMBGEN, J. W., "Aspekte der Oralität und Literalität: Ihre Implikationen für das Geschichtsbewusstsein der muslimischen Nagerkuts in Nordpakistan", in *Anthropos*, 81/4-6, pp. 567-581, 1986.

FREMBGEN, J. W., "Königskronen aus Nager", in *Tribus*, 37, pp. 69-82, 1988.

FREMBGEN, J. W, *Stickereien aus dem Karakorum*, Munich 1998.

FREMBGEN, J. W., "Indus Kohistan. An Historical and Ethnographic Outline", in *Central Asiatic Journal*, 43/1, pp. 70-98, 1999.

FREMBGEN, J. W., "Sayyid Shah Wali - Missionary and Miracle-Worker. Notes on the Hagiography and Cult of a Muslim Saint in Nager and Hunza (Northern Pakistan)", in *Zeitschrift der Deutschen Morgenländischen Gesellschaft*, in press.

HASSNAIN, F. M., *A Cultural History of Kashmir and Kishtawar*, New Delhi 1992.

JETTMAR, K., "Schnitzwerke aus den Tälern Tangir und Darel", in *Archiv für Völkerkunde*, 14, pp. 87-118, 1959.

KAK, R. C., *Ancient Monuments of Kashmir*, London 1933.

KALTER, J. (ed.), *The Arts and Crafts of the Swat Valley. Living Traditions in the Hindu Kush*, London 1989.

KAZMI, A. S. M., "Woodcrafts of Baltistan. Documentation", Skardu (unpublished manuscript) 2003.

KLIMBURG M., "The Wooden Mosques in the Northern Areas of Pakistan", in AUSTRIAN EMBASSY (ed.), *Austrian Scholarship in Pakistan - A Symposium Dedicated to the Memory of Aloys Sprenger*, pp. 148-174, Islamabad 1997.

LORIMER, D. L. R., *The Burushaski Language. Vol. I: Introduction and Grammar*, Oslo 1935.

NICHOLLS, W. H., "Muhammadan Architecture in Kashmir", in *Archaeological Survey of India. Annual Report 1906-7*, pp. 161-170, New Delhi 1907.

NICHOLS, J. R., "Architecture of Kashmir: Muhammadan Architecture", in *Marg*, 8/2, pp. 76-92, 1955.

SCERRATO, U., "Survey of Wooden Mosques and Related Wood-Carvings in the Swat Valley", in *East and West*, 31, pp. 178-181, 1981.

SCERRATO, U., "Survey of Wooden Mosques and Related Wood Carvings in North-West Frontier Province, 3rd Report - 1982", in *East and West*, 33, pp. 325-328, 1983.

SCERRATO, U., "The Wooden Architecture of Swat and the Northern Areas of Pakistan: A Report on the Research Carried Out in 1984", in *East and West*, 34, pp. 501-515, 1984.

WAHEED, M., "Documentation of Wood Carving Patterns" (unpublished manuscript, AKCS-P), Shigar 2003.

WAKHLU, S., *The Rich Heritage of Jammu and Kashmir*, New Delhi 1998.

Acknowledgments

OVERALL PROJECT DIRECTION

AGA KHAN TRUST FOR CULTURE, Geneva: Stefano Bianca, Director, Historic Cities Support Programme
Nicholas Bulloch, Financial Director

NORTHERN AREAS PROJECT ADMINISTRATION

AGA KHAN CULTURAL SERVICE-PAKISTAN: Salman Beg, CEO (1998 to date), Izhar Hunzai, CEO (1996-1998), Ghulam Mohammed, Executive Officer (1992-1996), Syed Sajid Ali Shah, Manager Finance and Administration (2002 to date), Khalid Nadeem, Manager Finance and Adminstration (1996-2002), Mohammed Arif, Chief Accountant, Shoukat Khimani, Karimuddin, Mohammed Ali, Nauroz Shah and Zilha Pari, Accountants, Ibadat Khan, Salman and Shahid, Secretaries, Kamil Jan, Assistant Secretary, Hidayat and Ibrahim, Assistants, Ibrahim Khan and Asadullah, Drivers

BALTIT FORT PROJECT

SENIOR CONSULTANTS: Didier Lefort, Richard Hughes

AKCS-P AND PROJECT STAFF: Andrew Cox, Project Engineer, Sohail A. Khan (late), Project Architect, Abbas Ali Shah, Architect, Hidayat Shah, Office Assistant, Imam Dad and Moula Madad, Watchmen, Bukht Ummer and Ahmed Gul, Carvers, Nahidullah Baig and Ali Ahmed Jan, Carpenters, Wazir Khan, Head Mason, Abdullah, Electrician, Muhammad Ishaq, Plumber

AKP&BS (AK Housing Board): Rehmat Ali, Site Manager, Qayum Ali Shah, Engineer, Elmuddin, Assistant Engineer, Israr Ali, Foreman, Gohar Hayat, Generator Operator

HUNZA REHABILITATION PROJECTS (KARIMABAD, GANISH, ALTIT, CHUMERKHUN)

SENIOR CONSULTANTS: Masood A. Khan, Richard Hughes

AKCS-P AND PROJECT STAFF: Essa Khan (late), Manager, Barkat Khan and Karimul Hayat, Social Organisers, Assadullah Jan and Abbas Ali Shah, Regional Architects, Sher Ghazi, Regional Engineer, Moazzam, Salman Muhammed, Wajahat Ali, Ali Ahmed Shah and Inam-ul-Haq, Architects, Jawaid Iqbal, Assistant Architect, Iqbal Rasul, Rubina Shahzadi and Ali Yad Khan, Engineers, Shukurullah Baig, Ehsanul Karim, Ayazullah Baig and Salman Ali, Project Engineers, Iqbal Karim, Shah Mansoor, Ali Madad, Khairullah, Muhammad Shah and Nad Ali, Foremen, Taj Gul, Izzat Ali, Farman Ali and Arman Ali, Carpenters, Ishaq, Syed Kaim, Karim Khan and Bulbul Jan, Plumbers, Ali Maqsat, Ghulam Hussain, Gari Khan, Ibadat, Gul Aman, Zaman Gul, Gul Bashir, Imtiaz, Jangi Khan, Ali Madad, Manzoor, Shulurullah, Alam Khan, Hayat Baig, Rasool Din, Ghulam Hussain, Sulaiman, Hajat Mir, Qanber and Doulat, Masons, Amir Hayat, Steel Worker, Shah Makeen, Ghulam Qadir, Talib Shah and Sakhi, Electricians, Bulbul Shah, Driver/Supervisor, Amin, Driver

PARTNERS:
WASEP: Wilfried Schlosser, Director, Mirza Murad, Project Supervisor

Karimabad Town Management Society: Wajidullah Baig, President (1999 to date), Moula Madad (1996-1999)

Altit Town Management Society: Sarfaraz Khan, President (2004 to date), Zakir Hussain, President (2001-2004)

Ganish Heritage Care and Social Welfare Society: Iftikhar Ali Khan, President (2000 to date), Ali Gohar (1998-1999)

ALTIT FORT PROJECT:

SENIOR CONSULTANTS: Richard Hughes, Masood Khan

AKCS-P AND PROJECT STAFF: Abbas Ali, Regional Architect, Ali Yad Khan, Project Engineer, Jawaid Iqbal, Assistant Architect. Documentation: Rizwana, Nasira, Ruqia, Adiba, Nasreen, Farida, Naima, Alia and Salima

HALDEIKISH SACRED ROCK PROJECT

PARTNERS:
NORWEGIAN CULTURAL HERITAGE DIRECTORATE: Lyder Marstrander
HEIDELBERG UNIVERSITY: Harald Hauptmann

AKCS-P AND PROJECT STAFF: Safiullah Baig, Deputy Manager, Fazal Karim, Site Leader, Hidayat Shah. Documentation: Masuma, Shamim, Nasreen, Jabin, Naik Bano, Yasmin, Gulzar, Habina and Zohra

LAND USE, MAPPING AND DIGITISATION PROJECT:

AKCS-P AND PROJECT STAFF: Safiullah Baig, Deputy Manager, Jawaid Ali, Assistant Architect. Documentation: Nasreen, Shahina, Nasim, Zadi, Sher Bano, Zinat, Ahsar, Nasreen, Gulzar, Gulshan, Dilshad, Meher Nigah, Noushad, Taj Nisa, Gul Sara, Ferzana, Shazia, Imtiaz and Naik Ali, Mapping Team

INVENTORY PROJECT

SENIOR CONSULTANT: Yasmin Cheema

AKCS-P AND PROJECT STAFF: Safiullah Baig, Deputy Manager, Ali Ahmed Shah, Architect, Darvesh Ali, Computer Resource Person, Waheed Murad, Artist, Fazal Karim, Graphic Designer. Inventory Team: Aqila, Shamaila, Meher Zadi, Zamrud, Fatima, Gulzar, Husn Bano

SOCIO-ECONOMIC SURVEY PROJECT

SENIOR CONSULTANT: Julie Flowerday

AKCS-P AND PROJECT STAFF: Safiullah Baig, Deputy Manager, Karimul Hayat, Social Organiser. Field Team: Ajeeba, Shamim, Noor Jehan, Yasmin and Farman

MUSIC AND FESTIVALS

Ali Gohar, Abdul Karim, Amir Hayat and Fazal Karim, Master Musicians

ENTERPRISE DEVELOPMENT: KARAKORAM HANDICRAFT DEVELOPMENT PROGRAMME

Karakoram Area Development Organization: Khawaja Khan, Chairman, Jawaid Iqbal, General Manager, Ghulam Amin Beg, former General Manager

SHIGAR FORT PROJECT

SENIOR CONSULTANTS: Masood A. Khan, Richard Hughes, Shehnaz Ismail, Ben Bull, Zahoor Qureshi, Ahmed Ali Tariq

AKCS-P AND PROJECT STAFF: Khalid Nadeem, Programme Manager Baltistan, Safiullah Baig, Deputy Manager, Abbas Ali Shah, Regional Architect, Sher Ghazi, Regional Engineer, Iqbal Rasul and Abid Hussain, Engineers, Shukurullah Baig, Project Engineer, Abdul Rahim, Ali Ahmed Shah, Salman Muhammad, Wajahat Ali and Mubashar, Architects, Farman Karim, Assistant Engineer, Mohammad Nazar, Site Leader, Karimuddin, Iqbal Karim, Ali Ahmed Jan and Mohammed Ali, Accountants, Imtiaz Hyder and Jaffer Ali, Social Organisers, Yaqub, Office Assistant, Ali, Driver, Shahkir Hasan, Akhon Razi, Mohammad Irfan and Muhammad Khan, Supervisors, Ghulam Mehdi, Generator Operator, Sangi Khan, Kacho Mehboob, Dinar Khan, Noor Khan, Asghar Khan, Mohammed Musa and Ghulam Rasool, Carpenters, Musa Ali, Younis and Mohammad Baqir, Masons, Muhammad Kabir, Electrician

AMBURIQ MOSQUE RESTORATION

SENIOR CONSULTANTS: Masood A. Khan, Richard Hughes

AKCS-P: Abbas Ali Shah, Regional Architect, Sher Ghazi, Regional Engineer

ASTANA SAYYED MOHAMMAD RESTORATION

SENIOR CONSULTANTS: Masood A. Khan, Richard Hughes

AKCS-P: Ehsanul Karim, Project Leader, Abbas Ali Shah, Regional Architect, Sher Ghazi, Regional Engineer

BALTISTAN REHABILITATION PROJECTS (SHIGAR AND KHAPLU)

SENIOR CONSULTANT: Masood A. Khan

AKCS-P AND PROJECT STAFF: Khalid Nadeem, Programme Manager Baltistan, Sher Ghazi, Regional Engineer, Ehsan ul Karim, Project Leader, Jan Alam, Noor Ali, Ali Ahmed, Amanullah and Ghulam Rasool, Site Supervisors

Shigar Town Management and Development Society: Fida Ali, President

Khaplu Town Management and Development Society: Mohammed Iqbal, President

SHIGAR FORT RESIDENCE

PARTNER: Tourism Promotion Services (TPS)

AKCS-P: Safiullah Baig, Deputy Manager AKCS-P, Karim Khan, Manager, Imtiaz Hyder and Ali Ahmed Jan, Assistant Managers

ENTERPRISE PROJECT BHDP/BEDAR

AKCS-P: Khalid Nadeem, Programme Manager Baltistan

PARTNER: Baltistan Culture Foundation (BCF): Mohammed Ali Azizi, Chairman (2002 to date), Raja Shah Sabah, Chairman (1998-2001), Ahmed Ali, Manager (2002 to date), Syed Abbas Kazmi, Manager (1998-2001)

BHDP (2002-2003): Ahmed Ali, Manager, Munawar Anjum, Cost Accountant, Ali Khan, Supervisor, Apo Rozali, Master Carver, Sher Ali, Carpenter, Jaffar Ali Driver

BEDAR (2003 to date): Ahmed Ali, Manager, Tahir Asghar Shah, Manager, Khan Bibi, Business Manager Apricot Oil, Wazir Ejaz, Development Officer Woodcrafts, Wazir Shabbir Akhtar, Deputy Manager, Imtiaz, Development Officer Gems, Hassan, Intern Finance Officer, Abbas, Computer Resource Person, Ahmed Ali Ancho, Office Assistant, Jaffar Ali, Driver, Mohammad Hussain, Watchman, Ghulam Mohammad, Office Boy, Apo Sher Ali and Haji Mohammad Allam, Master Carvers, Bilal, Master Carpenter

PUBLICATION CREDITS

The visual documentation for this book represents a collective effort of all the involved AKTC and AKCS-P staff and AKTC consultants, as well as external contributors of individual chapters and professional photographers commissioned by the AKTC

ARCHITECTURAL DRAWINGS: AKCS-P team Gilgit and Shigar directed by Masood Khan, Richard Hughes, Benedict Bull and Yasmin Cheema

PHOTOGRAPHY: Stefano Bianca, Benedict Bull, Julie Flowerday, Jürgen Wasim Frembgen (figs. 97-130), Harald Hauptmann, Katherine Hinckley, Richard Hughes, Fazal Karim, Masood Khan, Pervez Khan, Max Klimburg (figs. 132-158 and pls. 30, 47-49, 51-54), Hermann Kreutzmann, Marco Marelli, Jean Mohr, Waheed Murad, Mathew Paley, Pierre Neyret and Géraldine Benestar, Gary Otte, Jean-Luc Ray

Historic photographs from the David L. R. Lorimer collection are reprinted with kind permission from the School of Oriental and African Studies (SOAS), London

PROCESSING: Document research/processing by Robin Oldacre-Reed; text processing by Marie-Martine de Techtermann; processing of plans and drawings by Siméon Duchoud, the AKCS-P team and Masood Khan

*

COPY-EDITING HARRIET GRAHAM

LAYOUT ALESSANDRA BARRA

PHOTOLITHOGRAPHY FOTOMEC, TURIN, ITALY

PUBLISHED BY UMBERTO ALLEMANDI & C., TURIN, ITALY

SECOND EDITION REVISED
PRINTED IN ITALY, JUNE 2007
ISBN 978-88-422-1330-7